A BRIEF JOLLY CHANGE

A Brief Jolly Change

The Diaries of Henry Peerless, 1891–1920

Edited by
EDWARD FENTON

DAY BOOKS
OXFORDSHIRE

ISBN 0 953 2213 5 0

British Library Cataloguing in Publication Data

A catalogue record for this book is available from the British Library

This edition first published by Day Books, July 2003

Printed in England by MPG Books Ltd, Bodmin, Cornwall. This publication is printed on acid-free paper

Contents

Introduction

The nineteenth century was an age of inventions: and one of the greatest of these was the invention of the annual holiday. By Victorian times the upheaval of the Industrial Revolution had created a whole new class of people with an appreciable quantity of spare time and spare money to spend as they wished. It had also laid down the foundations of a massive communications network which, though originally intended for commerce, was soon being used by millions of people in the pursuit of pleasure. Indeed, especially after the introduction of the Bank Holiday Act of 1871, it must sometimes have seemed that the great monuments of industrialisation—the railway tunnels, the bridges and viaducts—had been designed for the sole purpose of hastening the masses from the towns and cities to the holiday resorts of Southend and Ramsgate, Blackpool and Brighton.

As if to ensure that the new cult of the holiday was undiminished by Protestant guilt, a philosophy developed which sought to justify it not merely as a frivolous indulgence but as a social good and even a moral duty. In a book published in 1891—the year that Henry Peerless began his travel diaries—the journalist W. Fraser Rae speculated that 'the excursions and tours which were unknown before 1841' might have led to the rise in the average life-expectancy in the United Kingdom during the intervening half-century. The book also quoted Gladstone's description of the package tour as 'among the humanising contrivances of the age'.[1] And three years later, an article in the *Fortnightly Review* declared: 'The high pressure of our keenly competitive modern life has made at least a yearly holiday not just a luxury of the wealthy, but a necessity of the workers.'[2]

Henry Peerless was typical of his age, therefore, in taking his holidays seriously. While he obviously enjoyed them to the full, he also believed that his holidays were intended to fortify him for the rest of the working year, and for the future. That was perhaps the main reason why he recorded everything with such care—especially those things that gave him pleasure. 'Here is one of the charms of a holiday,' he wrote at Malvern in 1894, when he was 27 years old: 'In the mind's eye you can revisit the

[1]*The Business of Travel*, pp.316–17. The book was published to commemorate the fiftieth anniversary of the first excursion organised by Thomas Cook, from Leicester to Loughborough by rail.

[2]John Verschoyle, *Fortnightly Review*, Aug. 1894, pp.305-14.

scenes . . . and thus enjoy again your youthful jaunts.' And one loses count of the number of times that he uses an expression such as 'I do not think a prettier ride could be found' (on the road to Shanklin) or 'Honestly I never enjoyed anything so much' (of a river trip at Tonbridge).

Yet the fact that he sustained his diary for so long, and so methodically, makes it far more than a private record of where he went and what he did. It amounts to one of the fullest pictures that we have of a whole class of people seeking diversion, at a time of unprecedented and—ultimately—cataclysmic change.

* * *

Henry Peerless was born in Brighton in December 1866, a few doors away from his future school, and within sight of the timber-yard where (from the age of fourteen) he was to spend his entire working life.[3] In another town, or another age, the narrowness of this world might have severely restricted his horizons: but Brighton was one of the great boom-towns of the Victorian era. The coming of the railway had led to an explosion in the town's population, which in turn brought great opportunities for anyone involved in the building trade: including the Peerlesses and also their close friends the Garretts, who feature so prominently in these diaries. The two family firms—Peerless & Son, and W. & T. Garrett—both prospered, and Henry Peerless slipped easily into the role of the successful middle-class businessman. Although his forebears had hardly been illustrious (his grandfather William had been a semi-literate wheelwright in the Sussex village of Wilmington), the diarist reveals no trace of irony when he refers to 'the ancient house of Peerless', or later when he criticises a self-made man for being 'a little purse-proud in his talk,' and observes that 'a man . . . who has handled money all his life would never dream of letting it dominate his utterances.' Henry Peerless's genial pomposity is one of the diary's great delights: especially when—as so often—it is punctured.

Brighton's prosperity not only gave Henry Peerless the means to take regular holidays; its character as a bustling holiday town must also have given him the appetite for travel. In his essay 'Sunny Brighton', the naturalist Richard Jefferies described the air of tangible excitement at Brighton's railway station on any day during the holiday season. 'The scene is as lively and interesting as the stage when a good play is proceeding,' he wrote. 'Can anything look jollier than a cab overgrown with luggage, like huge barnacles, just starting away with its freight? One can imagine such a fund of enjoyment on its way in that cab. . . . I often

[3]Respectively numbers 33, 21 and 47 Middle Street, Brighton.

used to walk to the station just to see it.'[4] Henry Peerless also loved watching the ebb and flow of people at stations and harbours—'We feel we are seeing life,' he wrote of the crowds at Paddington Station in June 1920—and one is constantly reminded that he is a part of these crowds, and that his experiences and attitudes were not exclusive to him, but would have been shared by countless numbers of his fellow travellers.

Britain's seaside towns were still the most popular destinations for day-trippers and holiday-makers at the turn of the twentieth century—although there were often clear distinctions between the middle-class resorts (such as Ilfracombe and Paignton) and the proletarian ones (such as Southend-on-Sea, which became notorious after a detachment of artillery had to quell a riot started by a group of excursionists from an East London timber-yard).[5] Henry Peerless gravitated naturally to the respectable surroundings of the so-called 'coastal spas'. But he also managed to describe a wide cross-section of the different sorts of holiday that his contemporaries enjoyed: for instance at the great spa towns of England and Wales, which had once attracted the cream of society, and which had learnt that there was an even more lucrative market among the new middle classes; and, further afield, at some of the holiday destinations first popularised by entrepreneurs such as Thomas Cook—Paris, Naples and the Swiss Alps.

At the beginning of Victoria's reign, the railway had been crucial in determining which holiday resorts would flourish and grow, and which would fall into decline. In the closing years of the century, however, another revolution was brought about by the popularisation of the safety bicycle. Henry Peerless became an instant convert, and his 1897 diary starts exuberantly. 'It is absolutely surprising what a prominent part the bicycle plays in modern life,' he wrote. 'Ridden by all, young and old, rich and poor, gentle and simple, it has come amongst us, conquering all, and bids to remain for all time.'

The railway had offered only a limited type of freedom, for it tended to concentrate people together and herd them all to the same place. The bicycle, on the other hand, dispersed them, leading directly to the mass discovery of the countryside. For Henry Peerless, it was the bicycle that first brought him to the New Forest, which quickly became his favourite destination, and which inspired him to seek out the wild places of Wales, the West Country and the English Lakes. 'These places get you in some mystical way in their power,' he wrote in 1907. 'I think it is the fact of being right away from the bricks and mortar that pen one in, in towns

[4]From *The Open Air*; London, Chatto & Windus, 1885, pp.68–9. Richard Jefferies had gone to Brighton to seek relief from the tuberculosis that was eventually to kill him.
[5]J.K. Walton, *The English Seaside Resort*, p.195.

and cities.' Five years later he returned to the theme, at Haytor Rock on Dartmoor, which he described as 'an ideal place to recuperate from nervous strain':

> One might tramp off day after day and return ready for such sleep as cannot be obtained by town people cribbed, cabined and confined by legions of houses. . . . There is something in the immense stretch of rough moorland, a rugged passive strength, as though time and the things of time had no significance here.

The irony is that Henry Peerless was passionately interested in 'time and the things of time'. It was not simply that, even in the midst of 'wild nature', he still managed to enjoy four hearty meals a day: he was also fascinated by new inventions, new social trends and innovations of every description, and usually he embraced them wholeheartedly. For example he applauded the decline in Sunday observance, and 'the advance that is being made . . . towards the opening of picture galleries, museums, etc.' He was equally enthusiastic about mixed bathing, which had only started to be introduced on English beaches in the 1890s. 'That any harm can come of it is absurd,' he wrote in 1901, the year that it was first introduced in Brighton. 'Mixed bathing is quite decent and moral, and much to be commended.'

He also showed a professional interest in the design of Britain's first garden city, Letchworth, which was 'clean, well laid-out . . . and undoubtedly a model village', and which provided a striking contrast to the way that Brighton had been allowed to expand virtually without restriction ('as a fungus,' according to the sculptor Eric Gill, who had grown up in Brighton in the 1880s and 1890s—'wherever the network of railways and sidings and railway sheds would allow').[6]

Despite having observed in 1897 that 'the motor-car seems to lag dreadfully' behind the bicycle, a decade later—on holiday in the New Forest—the diarist was marvelling at his brother-in-law Tom's new tourer. Indeed 1907 was not just the year that Tom Garrett bought his first car: it was also the last year that Henry Peerless went on holiday by bicycle. Once again, the entire social landscape was changing; and although Lyndhurst in 1907 was still full of 'horse traffic, . . . tradesmen's carts, farm wagons, . . . private traps, coaches and wagonettes', their demise was already inevitable. 'I have never seen in any district more motor-cars than there are in and around Lyndhurst,' he observed on the same June day that he took what may have been his first ride in a car. 'From morning till night they pass up and down our High Street, and we are never many minutes without them.'

It was in North Wales, some years later, that Tom Garrett eventually

[6]Eric Gill, *Autobiography*; London: Jonathan Cape, 1940, p.77.

gave his brother-in-law a lecture on the workings of the internal combustion engine, prompting him to observe that 'there seems no limit to human progress at present'—a remark which seems almost ironic today, since the year was 1915, and most of Europe was embroiled in the Great War.

In fact the full impact of the war was not felt immediately by most civilians, and although Henry Peerless gives a detailed account of the changes and restrictions on the Home Front, he continued to take his annual holiday as before. His sense of national pride ('I fancy we have surprised the world by our efforts,' he wrote in 1916) gave way only slowly to anger at the futility of it all. The death of his eldest son Cuthbert—whom he had once envisaged as a middle-aged man, with children of his own—must have affected him deeply, but he betrays no self-pity, only disgust at the extent of the losses and the suffering. 'Oh! how damnable are the effects of this wicked War,' he wrote in June 1918, four weeks after his son's death, on finding himself in the same railway carriage as a young ex-serviceman with an artificial arm. 'It makes my blood boil to see these wrecks, in the first flush of youth, maimed for life—and all for what?'

His refusal to dwell on his son's death may in part have been an attempt to buoy up his wife's spirits: but there are other indications, on a more trivial level, that his love affair with the modern world was over. Having previously embraced change, he now found it increasingly difficult to accept; and impositions such as jazz music and margarine could work him up into a quite disproportionate level of irritation.

To those who knew Henry Peerless after the Great War, he could appear to be a stern and remote figure. His nephew Robert Peerless (born in 1910) was later to describe him as distinctly pompous, while his niece Mrs Marjorie Fox (born Marjorie Garrett in 1908) has said that, as a little girl, she was unnerved by his constant desire for order. Yet this is not the impression created by the diaries, as Robert Peerless admitted in August 2001 after reading them for the first time. 'They have disclosed to me an aspect of my uncle,' he wrote, 'of which I was not aware.'

Pompous and over-fastidious he may have been; but in what Osbert Sitwell has described as 'the sweet and carefree atmosphere' before the Great War,[7] Henry Peerless was also a child of his time: genial, fond of practical jokes, patriotic to the point of jingoism, and little troubled by self-doubt. Above all, he was an excellent travel companion and guide: something which we can enjoy as much now, through his diaries, as his friends did a century ago. As his brother-in-law Tom wrote in August 1915, endorsing his Beddgelert diary as 'a faithful account' of their

[7] *Great Morning*; London: Macmillan, 1948; p.229.

motoring holiday together: 'It is so complete that I can find nothing to add, and so true that I can discover nothing to correct. . . . I do not wish for better company or for more amiable, helpful or considerate passengers.'

A note on the text

The diaries are contained in 27 pocket-sized notebooks, which grew thicker as Henry Peerless became more confident in his abilities as a diarist. The first notebook is one of the shortest, at just eighty pages; it is also the only one to contain the accounts of two holidays. The longest is the 460-page notebook which deals with the disastrous car-journey to Bude in 1916. There is none for 1913, when the Peerlesses did not manage to get away for a proper holiday; and the notebook for 1902, when Henry and Millie Peerless took their children to the New Forest, has unfortunately not been traced.

The surviving manuscript runs to almost 300,000 words: and it was felt that substantial cuts could be made without detracting from the picture which Henry Peerless gives us of himself, his travelling companions, or the times in which he lived. He expended many thousands of words on guidebook-style descriptions of the places that he visited, but most of these seem to have been copied straight out of published pamphlets. He also described all his travel arrangements in exhaustive detail, and these sections have been greatly abridged; elisions have also been made in order to avoid repetition and excessive verbosity. However, little if anything that relates directly to the diarist or his companions has been cut.

Sometimes, where the constant variation between tenses was considered distracting (Henry Peerless frequently switched from the past to the present within the same sentence), this has been standardised—together with spellings, the styling of the dates, and the use or otherwise of numerals, abbreviations and ampersands. Some adjustments have been made to the punctuation, for the sake of clarity. On occasion, also, Henry Peerless made minor slips of the pen, and these have been silently corrected where necessary. Anyone wishing to inspect a faithful transcript of the entire text for scholarly purposes should contact the publishers.

Selected reading

Atterbury, Paul, and Fagence Cooper, Suzanne (2002) *Victorians at Home and Abroad*. London: V. & A. Publications.

Bagwell, P., and Lyth, P. (2002) *Transport in Britain from Canal Lock to Gridlock*. London and Hambledon: London.

Benson, John (1994) *The Rise of Consumer Society in Britain, 1880–1980*. London: Longman.

Carder, Timothy (1990) *The Encyclopædia of Brighton*. Lewes: East Sussex County Libraries.

Colls, Robert, and Dodd, Philip (1986) *Englishness: Politics and Culture 1880–1920*. Beckenham, Kent: Croom Helm.

Ensor, R.C.K. (1975) *England 1870–1914*. Oxford: Oxford University Press.

Freeman, Michael J. (1999) *Railways in the Victorian Imagination*. New Haven: Yale University Press.

Gard, Robin (1989) *The Observant Traveller: Diaries of Travel in England, Wales and Scotland in the County Record Offices of England and Wales*. London: HMSO.

Gilbert, Edmund W. (1954) *Brighton: Old Ocean's Bauble*. London: Methuen.

Gloag, John (1979) *Victorian Comfort: A Social History of Design 1830–1900*. Newton Abbott: David & Charles.

Gregory, Alexis (1991) *The Golden Age of Travel, 1880–1939*. London: Cassell.

Hadrill, John (1999) *Rails to the Sea*. Penryn, Cornwall: Atlantic.

Halévy, Elie (1999) *Edwardian England*. London: Folio Society.

Harris, Jose (1993) *Private Lives, Public Spirit: Britain 1870–1914*. Oxford: Oxford University Press.

Hart-Davis, Adam (2001) *What the Victorians Did for Us*. London: Headline.

Hibbert, Christopher (1987) *The English: A Social History*. London: Grafton.

Horn, Pamela (1999) *Pleasures and Pastimes in Victorian Britain*. Stroud: Alan Sutton.

Horrall, Andrew (2001) *Popular Culture in London, 1891–1918: The Transformation of Entertainment*. Manchester: Manchester University Press.

Hughes, M.V. (1988) *A London Home in the 1890s*. Oxford: Oxford University Press.

Jackson, Alan A. (1991) *The Middle Classes 1900–1950*. Nairn, Scotland: David St John Thomas.

Lauder, Rosemary Anne (1993) *Exmoor Travellers*. Stroud: Alan Sutton.

Mackenzie, John M., ed. (2001) *The Victorian Vision: Inventing New Britain*. London: V. & A. Publications.

Masterman, C.F.G. (1909) *The Condition of England*. London: Macmillan.

Neville Havins, Peter J. (1979) *The Spas of England.* London: Robert Hale.

Newsome, David, ed. (1981) *Edwardian Excursions: From the Diaries of A.C. Benson, 1898–1904.* London: John Murray.

Nowell-Smith, Simon (1964) *Edwardian England 1901–1914.* London: Oxford University Press.

O'Connell, Sean (1998) *The Car and British Society: Class, Gender and Motoring 1896–1939.* Manchester: Manchester University Press.

Ousby, Ian (2002) *The Englishman's England: Taste, Travel and the Rise of Tourism.* London: Pimlico.

Pimlott, J.A.R. (1947) *The Englishman's Holiday: A Social History.* London: Faber.

Priestley, J.B. (2000) *The Edwardians.* London: Penguin.

Rae, W. Fraser (1891) *The Business of Travel.* London: Thomas Cook & Sons.

Ring, Jim (2001) *How the English Made the Alps.* London: John Murray.

Somervell, D.C. (1950) *100 Years in Pictures.* London: Odhams.

Swinglehurst, Edmund (1974) *The Romantic Journey. The Story of Thomas Cook and Victorian Travel.* London: Pica.

Thompson, F.M.L. (1988) *The Rise of Respectable Society.* London: Fontana.

Turner, E.S. (1967) *Taking the Cure.* London: Michael Joseph.

Tosh, John (1999) *A Man's Place: Masculinity and the Middle-Class Home in Victorian England.* New Haven: Yale University Press.

Walton, John K. (1983) *The English Seaside Resort: A Social History 1750–1914.* Leicester; Leicester University Press.

Walton, John K. (2000) *The British Seaside: Holidays and Resorts in the Twentieth Century.* Manchester: Manchester University Press.

Walvin, James (1978) *Beside the Seaside. A Social History of the Popular Seaside Holiday.* London: Allen Lane.

Walvin, James (1978) *Leisure and Society 1830–1950.* London: Longman.

Wigg, Julia (1996) *Bon Voyage! Travel Posters of the Edwardian Era.* London: HMSO.

Withey, Lynne (1998) *Grand Tours and Cook's Tours: A History of Leisure Travel 1750 to 1915.* London: Aurum.

Ziegler, Philip (2000) *Britain Then and Now.* London: Seven Dials.

Publication details for titles mentioned in the reading list are not repeated in full in the notes above or from p. 268.

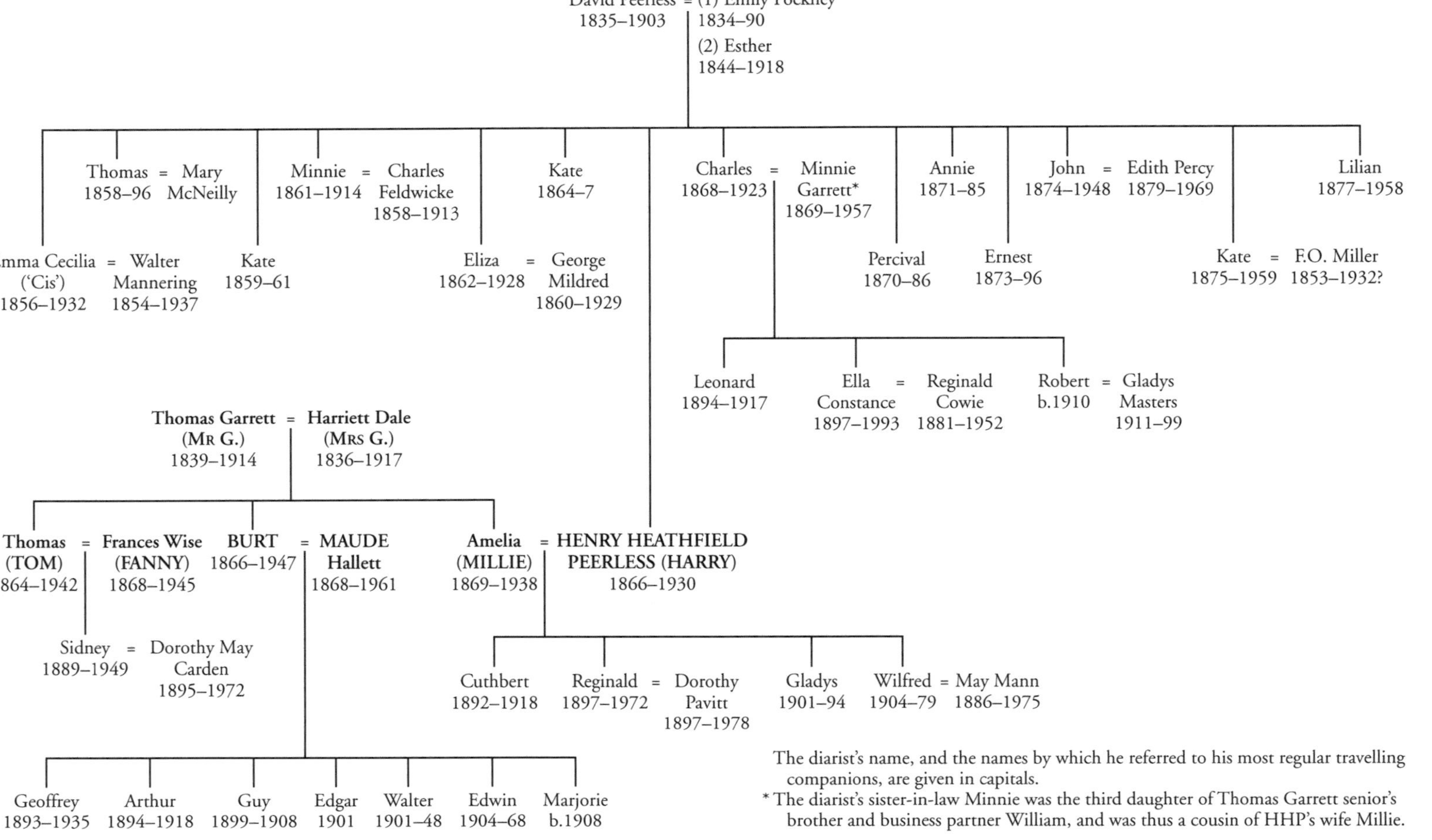

The diarist's name, and the names by which he referred to his most regular travelling companions, are given in capitals.

* The diarist's sister-in-law Minnie was the third daughter of Thomas Garrett senior's brother and business partner William, and was thus a cousin of HHP's wife Millie.

Southsea and Ryde

1891

Monday 20 July. Our honeymoon.

Under a fierce fusillade of old boots (one of which knocked my cigar out of my mouth) we jumped into a cab which drew up to 6 St Margaret's Place, Brighton, at about 3.35. At the station we took tickets for Southsea.

We went on the platform and tried to seduce the guard, who promised to see what he could do, and were soon whirling on our way. At Barnham the guard gave us a cheery 'Now then, sir,' and it was the work of a moment, and we were safely ensconced in a second-class carriage alone.

At Fratton we jumped out, and after remunerating our friendly guard, who was highly pleased, we got in another train and arrived at Southsea.

This is a terminus. We felt strangers in a strange land and, a slight drizzle coming on, for a minute we thought we should have taken rooms before coming down. However, we put up our portmanteau in the cloakroom and went in just opposite the station to tea. After settling up, we asked the woman if she could recommend us to an hotel; she suggested the Queen's at other end of town. Following the tram-lines we soon found it and engaged our bed for the night.

Tuesday 21 July. Took boat to Ryde and secured our lodgings at 9 High Street, Lord's Temperance Hotel. We caught a boat for Cowes, by some beautiful scenery and a number of handsome yachts and men-of-war, then retraced our steps. A nice run.

Wednesday 22 July. On the top of a coach-and-four, we rattled off in gallant style to Osborne, then to Whippingham Church. The Princess Beatrice was married here, and the Queen worships here. We saw the royal pew and books; then to Carisbrooke and up to the castle.

We gained admission by payment of fourpence each, and were soon on the walls, where Mill was obliged to fall down sprawling, which frightened me not a little, for had she rolled over she must have had a serious if not fatal fall.

When we got back the coach was gone, and the guard came running back for us. We mounted and off we went again, up hill and down dale. Then it rained heavily and the coachman shouted out: 'Churley, get out some rugs.' We were soon well covered, and arrived all right.

Thursday 23 July. Having fortified ourselves with a splendid breakfast, we took tickets *per* the *Heather Bell* for Alum Bay at the trivial cost of one shilling each return, a distance of 36 or 38 miles. The people on the steamer were not quite so good as we should have wished. I do not mean to say that they were not very respectable and all that, but there was an excursionist air about them that jarred upon our supersensitive feelings. I should think we had over three hundred on board.

At Alum Bay we disembarked and climbed up the steepest and roughest ascent you can imagine. The houses were conspicuous by their absence. There was only one hotel, and we had been warned that they would victimise us. They did not belie their reputation. For a poor dinner of cold mutton, a few potatoes, pickled walnuts and two lemon-and-dashes they had the audacity to charge us seven shillings. Attendance was charged at sixpence, and the waiter was deeply disappointed that I did not 'tip' him, but really I could not do it after being swindled in such a barefaced manner.

On board again, the steamer emitted some awful, hoarse, discordant screeches, intimations to the people that it was time to start. On they came flocking like bees—ding-a-ting went the communicator, round went the paddles—cast off the cables, and away we went.

Both going and returning, we were enlivened by music and songs. One was a very catchy thing: 'The girl that *I* know, that *you* know, that we *all* know.' When we passed a splendid ship of Her Majesty's Navy (we could not see her name), the band struck up 'God save the Queen', and the sailors who lined the deck saluted us.

Friday 24 July. Second-class return for Ventnor (I may mention there is no third class here), and then caught the 2.10 train for Shanklin. Outside the station were some little cob carriages to hold three. We bargained with the driver and set off at a terrific pace for Shanklin Chine. He deposited us safely at the Crab Inn, and on payment of threepence each we passed the gate and were confronted by a chalybeate fountain. We tasted the water, and found it stronger than that at Tunbridge Wells. Then we meandered down and sat on a seat. It was cut all over with names of visitors, and we noticed one inscription

FRED AND MAY MANNERING

which I said must be Fred.

Coming back to our hotel, we noticed a grocer's establishment named Garrett. Mill disowns these people, because the shop is small and dingy, but claims relationship with a confectioner on the front, of the same name. The first day she saw it she rushed away from me, darted in the shop and bought something, just for the sake of the name.

After tea, I wrote up this diary and Mill worked with her needle. Then we sallied forth and bought two eggcups as a souvenir of our visit.

Saturday 25 July. To the pier, and on to steamer. One of the men commenced hoisting a flag: it had 'Royal Mail' on it, and he told me whenever they had mails aboard they must fly it. I asked him how many times they took mails per day and he told me the different times, in all seven.

Entering Portsmouth Harbour we saw a steamer submerged to her gunwales; we made her out to be the *Dandie Dinmont*, a passenger steamer that makes trips round the island. She had sunk the day before, because some of her valves gave out.

We jumped on the pier, put up our luggage at the cloakroom, and were immediately pounced upon by a gang of watermen, each one ambitious of securing the honour of conveying our sacred persons to look over the *Victory*. One of them seemed to take us as his own private prey, and assured me Saturday was a bad day to look over the dockyard, which he said was shut now till a quarter past twelve o'clock, which would just give us time to go over the *Victory*, which was '*the one* thing to be done', much as the citizens of Venice say 'see Venice and die'. But although I look very green, I was not to be had, so we made our way to the dockyard, and in a minute had entered the gates and were two of about sixty persons who, under the guidance of the nicest policeman I ever saw, were being led round the wonders of our gigantic national shipbuilding-yard.

What a place it is. It would be impossible for me to describe all we saw. Amongst the most striking I may mention the *Calliope* man-of-war, which you will remember was exceedingly notorious some time ago on the occasion of her steaming out of a foreign harbour during a tremendous hurricane (the injuries she received necessitating her being put in dock for repair now), the *Malabar* troopship, the *Euphrates*, torpedoes, torpedo-boats, gunships, the Prince of Wales' yacht, etc.

Giving our friendly bobby a small *douceur*, we went for a walk and passed the baths. A notice-board informed the public that price of gentlemen's swimming-bath then was twopence; when we repassed in the evening it was a penny. This struck me as cheap.

A dessert of strawberries brought us to tea-time, when a band arrested our attention. A gathering of socialistic working men marched past: banners informed us they believed in eight hours' work, eight hours' recreation, etc.

We then wended our way to Portsmouth Harbour Station, ran the gauntlet of the boatmen, and on to the platform. The train was very late, and the officials very fussy and not at all obliging; however at last we were safely ensconced, and arrived home very pleased with our holiday, and ready to settle down in our new home.

Tunbridge Wells

1892

Saturday 6 August. Over a year has passed since I penned the lines on the preceding pages—an eventful year. I am older, wiser, stronger and more married. I have successfully passed through a month's dispensation of doctor and nurse who invaded the privacy of our domestic *ménage* on the tenth of June, and between them managed to produce me an heir—heir to all our wealth and possessions and heir to that good name which the ancient house of Peerless has upheld spotless through so many centuries and which I trust will never be tarnished by me or mine.

But to business. On Saturday afternoon at 5.15 Millie and I and Cuthbert Henry took leave of our dear old home (consisting of drawing-room, bedroom, kitchen, pigeon-house and meat-safe) and started for the station. I must confess to feeling a slight kind of shamefacedness (shared in a minor degree by my dear wife) when we appear in public carrying our little offspring. But I think it is to be understood: he is such an enormous bundle of clothes. I prefer short-coats myself.

We took two tickets for Tunbridge Wells, and after a most pleasant journey arrived safely at our destination. We hailed a cab and were successfully tooled to our diggings, 34 Dudley Road, where we were received with open arms by our new landlady Mrs Head and her *femme de chambre.*

After a comfortable repast of ham and tongue, washed down by a bottle of Guinness' stout, I put on my hat, and a short walk brought me to a lively scene of lighted shops, dense crowds of people and innumerable costers' barrows with flaring lights. I purchased dear old *Ally Sloper's Half Holiday* and *Sala's Journal* and retraced my steps.

We were about three times during the night attending to our little charge.

Sunday 7 August. We got up, indulged in matutinal ablutions and then disposed of a nice breakfast, had a smoke and wrote this: and now, Baby being dressed, we are going to sarah forth ('sally' is slang I believe).

Passing the Pump Room we turned on to 'Ye Pantiles', which brought back memories of a happy day we spent here together when boy and girl we rambled through the town on a day's holiday. Then we decided to make for home; we just escaped a heavy downpour. A snooze each, and *Ally* and *Sala*, has brought us to 4.15.

The die is cast. The Rubicon is passed, it is decided. Let all the world listen. Cuthbert Henry Peerless, it is decreed, shall be short-coated, and Mill is writing to Fanny to oblige us by sending, *per* Her Majesty's Parcels Mail, some of his apparel.

Monday 8 August. Looks finer. We strolled to the Pantiles, listened to the strains of a really good band and perused the morning's news as delineated by the graphic writers of the *Daily Telegraph.*

During the morning we had made overtures to Miss Head, so at 2.30 she appeared on the scene as our nurse. She carrying our precious infant, we started off and soon saw an enormous crowd of people who had assembled to pay a last tribute to Alderman Waymark, a large and influential draper who is buried today.

We had a most enjoyable drive to Southborough, and then home.

The time now is 25 minutes to six. 'John—where's Beageley? Is Ned in the yard? Put in the books. Now let me see, what about the morning?'

Seven o'clock, I must write to Kate. So lighting a cigar, I make my way to a stationer's and expend twopence in the purchase of paper and envelopes. By Jove! the muse is on me tonight, I am writing powerful letters I can tell you. Poetry flows from my pencil like water from a half-inch HP cock. Then supper and to bed. Little Toby wakes at regular intervals all night.

Tuesday 9 August. Millie is washing our first attempt, and a band is discoursing sweet music under our window. I have been writing several letters, one to the Governor, one to Benton, one to Charley Feldwicke about coming up here—and now I have lit a cigar, extravagant idiot, and I think we shall go out, but the weather is queer.

We started and posted our letters on 'Ye Pantiles'. It is a quaint old-world place, now tenanted by hundreds of gaily dressed promenaders and loungers. The band is playing and we perambulate up and down, stopping to look at some of the fancy goods in the shops. Some of the Tunbridge ware is really most ingeniously made up—the colours and designs being most sweet. Then home to dinner.

After a rest, with Miss Head carrying Sir Cuthbert, we made our way to the common to the cricket ground. There was a match in progress but I never saw such a slow affair. We waited about but I never saw a ball bowled.

Good sleep all night, *i.e.* not disturbed by little Cuthbert Esquire; dream I am living in Duke Street again, and find door leading into Dukes Passage unlocked late at night, and communicate same to the Governor who all the time looks like Cuthbert. I suggest arming with revolvers and feel much excited, then I wake and distinctly feel a fluttering under my head, as though somebody was feeling under the pillow, rouse up a bit, listen, and as I hear the watches ticking, think it must be all right, as if anybody got in they would take those first. Think perhaps leaving the window wide open at the bottom, the room being on the ground floor and a lane running at the back, is a rather unsafe proceeding.

Wednesday 10 August. Haddock for breakfast. Feldwicke's letter saying he shall arrive Sunday at 10.52; Kate's letter saying she shan't. Then we start out and stroll to the Pantiles. Some of the people are most amusing. The proper study of mankind is man, and for material, let me suggest 'Ye Pantiles', Tunbridge Wells, at twelve o'clock in the day, for you will find some queer characters there.

Then we engage a cab for an hour's drive, round by outskirts of Eridge Castle (seat of the Marquess of Abergavenny), on to Mount Ephraim and home. Proper fare is two shillings; the driver demands 2*s* 6*d*. I reason with him. He departs with two shillings, grumbling; I hope he won't go and commit suicide. He was a queer, fat little man, with a quantity of boils on his neck, which were quite interesting to look at as he drove along, perched above us on his little seat.

Steak and tomatoes constitute our midday meal, and then we take the path leading to the High Rocks. We pass a good many hops, and now the air is laden with an astringent smell, which has a peculiar appetising effect. We look at some men washing the hops with soap-suds, which they pump through a rose at the end of a hose.

The High Rocks are curious formations, well worth a visit. Go into the summer-house, and regret deeply that we cannot find our names that we wrote on the wall when here last. Everybody writes on the wall or ceiling, and I can only think it must have been whitewashed over since we were here. However, *nil desperandum*, we write them again.

Thursday 11 August. Up early and to the baths. They are open to the air, with dressing-boxes half round, and the water is from three to ten feet deep. It is very nice, but like all water in baths it has a green, slimy, greasy kind of feeling that to a sea-bather is very unpleasant.

Now Mill, Cuthbert and I have mounted a brake and are off to Southborough again. It is a beautiful drive. We debrake, and little Cuthbert proceeds to assimilate some nutriment into his constitution, then off again to the Wells—late for dinner, by Jingo.

Friday 12 August. Up at 8.45—we must be off to meet Charley F. We get there just in time, hail a cab, get the luggage in—laugh very much at the porters who keep on putting two or three screens in the cab that don't belong to us—then we all take train to Tonbridge. This is a quaint old-world town; we go into a church, then down to the grand bridge. One old tub looks very safe, and soon a queer dried-up fossilised man comes hobbling up.

'How much an hour for that thing?'

'Shillinanour, zir.'

We embark and off we go. No words can describe the glorious beauty of the river this grand afternoon. Honestly I never enjoyed anything so much.

Saturday 13 August. Breakfast at 8.30, then Feldwicke, Hilda and I out, nearly buy a clock for £25, then a shave and home. Then all out over the common, how lovely it is. Whew, look out, confound the dust. Then to Pantiles, but on the way we stop and see Sanger's Circus, which is encamped on the common; the lions were really grand animals, then the kangaroos, bears etc. A man was being photographed in the lions' wagon as we got up to it. Then he patted them all round.

Sunday 14 August. We breakfast together, then all start for the recreation grounds. Hilda feeds the cygnets, then up Camden Road we see a fireman starting off. We glean that it is an outbreak at the sewage-farm, High Brooms. Presently we arrive at the fire station. Outside is the engine, which emits so much foul smoke it well nigh chokes poor Cæsar. There is a crowd of people, but dear me, we in Brighton are so used to seeing the firemen brush about and get away in a few seconds that it made our fingers itch to see them fooling about, strolling up, and generally humbugging instead of setting at it smartly. No horses yet and we have been standing here nearly a quarter of an hour. Dear me, they have come at last, and the first symptom of bustle has commenced. They are a couple of good animals and evince some objection to being shut to. They are half in, when up jumps a jet of dirty water over all the people—laugh—they wipe the water out of their eyes and then at last a fat old man mounts the box, and off they go. Poor sewage-farm, it must be all burnt down.

We recline on the common, and hear the Salvation Army, then pack up and off we go to the station. 'Tis a beautiful evening, so calm, and the air is sweet. What a lovely journey it is from Tunbridge Wells; to the lover of nature, the fields and hops are beautiful sights. Where shall we go next year?

Paris

1893

Saturday 1 July. At six o'clock we get up, call a cab and reach the station. I try to telephone to the yard, but the girl will not put me on until I pay.

Kate has now arrived, and off we go. At Lewes we wait and wait. Train after train comes in crowded with beanfeasters and excursionists. They swarm out and dash down for a drink, and rush back as though running a race.

At Newhaven we board the steamer. Presently another train arrives with the luggage, which is stacked in a huge pile and covered with a tarpaulin.

We go swiftly, and soon glide into Dieppe Harbour and catch our first glimpse of *monsieur* on his native quay. Ding-ding-ding—'*Le train pour Paris*'—and away we go. Boys run alongside for coppers, up springs a policeman armed with a sword and gives chase, boy dodges behind a hut, and then breaks away followed by the policeman, and overturns him. We laugh heartily, and settle down to our journey. It is very close, and the dust intensely disagreeable.

At St Lazare we claim our trunks, and the officer orders us to open ours. He puts in both hands, kneads it, and chalks it off. Away we go for our hotel, and I buy this book—15 centimes.

Sunday 2 July. We awake, we are in Paris, we know it, there is a peculiar smell all over the city.

The waiters certainly love us. They hang on our lightest word, and the assiduity they display in waiting on 'Missie' (the name by which they address Kate) is wonderful. We *do* eat.

After breakfast we proposed going to Eiffel Tour. But *'L'homme propose, Dieu dispose.'* The hall porter has some tickets for ride to Versailles. The fountains play this Sunday, and we are beguiled, and slap-bang goes another 15 francs.

All through the Bois de Boulogne we bowl along, then draw up at a café and start drinking—I should say we have been more thirsty here than we have ever been in our lives. We drink till we burst, and then we are awfully thirsty, so we drink again. We walk through one street and drop down outside a café, and say: 'Don't bleed us, give us brandy.' The waiter is astonished. He shrugs his shoulders, but we say: '*Trois limonades et glace*

or *une bouteille de vin ordinair,*' and then we drink, and they do charge us, but we want drink—drink—drink, and must have it.

Our guide is a cute fellow and very jolly, full of fun, and we make quite a friend of him. When we remount our coach, our driver keeps whistling and shouting to his horses and cracking his whip.

Hullo, here we are at the Trianon. Here we see the rooms occupied by Napoleon Bonaparte, touch the billiard-table on which he used to play, and see some most valuable furniture and china. To the coach-houses, where we are shown the State carriages, and a gaudy collection they are; then to the Petit Trianon where we see the private rooms and jewel-case of Marie Antoinette, the latter mutilated by the Communists.

Lunch in the open air under some trees. We are a jolly party. We begin to fraternise and thaw to each other. There are four young Americans, jolly nice fellows, two Australians, nice men, older, and our three selves—Lord, how we laugh. We are besieged by itinerant vendors of photographic views, fans, flowers and opera-glasses to look at the fountains. One man asks £1 for a pair, and then by easy stages keeps lowering the price till he finally sells to one of the Americans at 10 francs, a considerable fall.

Then we go into the Palace of Versailles. The guide says, 'Stick to your umbrellas, they will take them if they can, and we shan't come out this way.' I clench mine, and resolve to keep it or perish in the attempt. I push on, and up rushes a Frenchman in a cocked hat and bars my progress. I prepare to sell my life dearly, when suddenly it dawns upon me that I am smoking, and that that is what has upset him. I feel I am in the wrong; I go out and throw away my cigarette. Mutually apologising, we are friends again.

We pass through the palace, and admire a looking-glass where you cannot see your own eyes, then out to the gardens. We listen to a military band, and up spring the fountains. They are certainly very fine. Then we remount our vehicle back to Paris.

After *dîner* we go out to the Champs Elysées. This is Sunday evening, but there are several café concerts in full swing, and the lights are dazzling.

Monday 3 July. On a steamer to Notre-Dame, then to La Morgue. There are four poor things lying here dead. They look ghastly. After a good look we go up Rue de la Roquette, by the prison, into Père la Chaise—a lovely place.

I at last succeed in getting *numéros* for an omnibus. Up one comes, the conductor shouts out the numbers, and in we go and reach Place de la Bastille. Then I go to get some *numéros* to the Madeleine. After going to about three *bureaux*, they tell me you don't want *numéros* for Bastille to Madeleine. Curse this system of omnibuses.

After dinner we started off to the *concert d'Ambassadeur*, the

Ambassador being a café. Although we could not understand the songs we enjoyed it very much.

Tuesday 4 July. Make my way to the Pont de la Concorde, and paying 50 centimes, enter one of the floating baths. But the water is not nice—it has that greeny kind of taste, and the steps are coated with a slimy deposit.

Home, then to the Louvre; here we inspect statuary and mosaics of the highest worth, and are slightly struck by Van Dyck. Back by boat to Concorde and home, then drink till we can only just stagger to the lift and ejaculate '*Troisième étage*,' and fall into bed, where our stomachs rattle like waves beating on the seashore.

Wednesday 5 July. Commences and continues to rain. Having spare time, I am going to put down a few impressions that I have gained of this sprightly people.

Taking Sunday: now, nearly all the shops were open. Some building operations were going on. Heavy horses were drawing loads of merchandise. Men were digging up the streets just as usual. Theatres and circuses a blaze of light. Café concerts etc. in full swing. Then the horses here are all driven the right-hand side of the road. The cabmen wear white high-hats, glazed, and red waistcoats. The policemen are dressed *à la militaire* and carry swords. The bread is in some cases a yard or more in length. A great number of the people shake their left hands. Whole families sit in chairs on the pavement outside their houses in the evening. They all seem to imbibe immense quantities of drink. The openness of their WCs etc. in the streets. The number and magnificence of their buildings and statues—and at every turn you are confronted with the motto of the République, '*Liberté, Egalité et Fraternité*', and they make a lot of fuss about '*Gloire*'.

Still, they are not a bad lot, and we have met with nothing but politeness and courtesy. For instance yesterday we were on a steamer; I was smoking a cigar. Opposite me were two working men, dirty from toil, and one of them, lifting his hat, with the air of a prince, and his '*Pardon, m'sieur*,' asked for a light. Now in England, the same class of man would most probably have said: 'Give us a light, guv'nor.' So I knocked off my ash and drew it up full alight, the Frenchman lit his cigarette from the Englishman's cigar, and a mutual good feeling was established. But how those two did argue with the steward of the boat, 'twas about the number of the bridges, and they talked, grimaced, and gesticulated like mad, and then every now and then a man down the other end would chime in, but at last they got quieter and I began to hear '*Très bien*' and '*Oui oui*' and as we got to our destination they had calmed down.

I have not bought any drink for myself all day, and the girls have only had a cup of milk each. Kate says rain is much cheaper for us because we don't buy drink.

After dinner I prowl about the *fumoir* and the hall. There are three or four guides trying to get parties for a run tonight. One or two lots go off, but one guide is left without a job, and he is the best got-up of the lot. His hat and coat look superfine, but appearances are deceptive. He tells me 'tis an old hat, got up. Petroleum or something they put on it. He is a most conceited hound and a regular sharper, I should think, especially as he talks so much about being square.

Thursday 6 July. Run in the Morgue: only two bodies today, one old and one fresh. On now to Palais Luxembourg, the museum and picture gallery. The sculpture, although a small collection, is very beautiful. One subject called '*Le nid*' attracts our attention most, and we go back to it again: it is in marble and represents two beautiful children, one about fourteen months and one about 2½ years, asleep in each other's arms. It is so simple and yet so lifelike. Then through the picture gallery, the work of living artists only. Some were very good, but some to my mind were simply daubs. About seven tenths of the subjects were from the nude.

On to Tomb of Napoleon, but we cannot get in, though there is a notice saying it is open. At last we find a gate and stroll in. Up rushes a decayed veteran, one of the old National Guard or something, and carries on like steam. He talks so sharply that we don't understand, but we know it means 'Get outside,' so out we go. The first piece of discourtesy we have received.

Home to *dîner*, then to the Olympia or Nouveau Cirque. Awful price to get in, and awful prices for refreshments: bock, an inferior kind of beer, 50 centimes for a very small glass not more than three parts full. Seeing this I determine not to have anything to drink, especially as we had been drinking heavily at dinner (a bottle of Claret, three bottles of lemonade, and about a quart of water between us). I upset the waiters terribly. They keep trying to explain that as there is a table I ought to have *consommations*. But I steadily decline and at last they give it up. A really splendid performance is given, including a white ballet and a serpentine dance by limelight which is superb.

Home to bed. Got out about 1.30 a.m.—five or six steam-engines, steam all up, and horses harnessed in two or three, in our street. I think they are fire-engines but can't see very well. Somebody locked out of the hotel keeps knocking. I go back to sleep.

Friday 7 July. To the Halles Centrales, an enormous meat, fish, flower and vegetable market. It does stink. Out and up Avenue de l'Opéra and Rue 4 Septembre to the Bourse. The shouting, hustling and crowding is awful.

Away to Pont Concorde. Here I give Mill my watch and all my money except 60 centimes, and have a swim. Water is warm but not clear. It tastes nasty, and when I dive down deep (the water is nine feet) it is quite thick. I should say it was unwholesome to bathe in.

It has been hot today. *Dîner* discussed, we go to Champs Elysées and look at the *cafés chantants*. It is a most brilliant scene. I never saw so many gas-lights before. Then for home; we hail a cab by hissing. You don't call to a *cocher* here, you hiss at him.

Saturday 8 July. We buy some fruit in the street, cigarette tubes etc., then back to shops opposite Tuileries. It is the hottest day we have had.

Sunday 9 July. Mill is bilious and sick. I give her brandy and then order up coffee and toast (dry).

Kate and I start for Eiffel Tower by steamer (fares today are double). By lift up to *premier étage*—theatres and restaurants all round—then we get in lift for the top. Write and post two postcards, then a bell rings and we descend.

Across the road into the Trocadéro Palace; we enjoy this, especially upstairs the groups representing the clothing and pursuits of different races, tribes and nations. Then into another building containing models of large public works. In the middle was an enormous cone-shaped mass of glass prisms. What it represented I do not know.

Today, although Sunday, they were unloading barges all up the Seine. Heavy cart-horses at work and a great many shops open. Two men opposite our hotel have been sitting outside their shop, playing cards, for hours. Funny people, aren't they.

Monday 10 July. Mill decidedly better. Tip two of our waiters, jump into cab, and off.

Reach Gare St Lazare, and into a carriage like a small room, with eleven places all round the sides, leaving the centre open—a nice airy carriage. The journey down is better than expected, not so dusty and dirty.

Out and aboard our boat, the *Seine*, launched in 1891. She is fast, but something queer about her. Although not a bit rougher than when we came, this boat pitches three times as much, with the natural result that a good many people are ill.

We have a French captain, and I don't like him half as much as I did our English captain going. We have aboard a very fat, exceedingly queer-looking monk or friar, at whom everybody laughs.

At Brighton we descry Mr T. Garrett coming down the wrong platform. Kissing and shaking hands all round. We have travelled a long way without any accident, and we are extremely thankful as we lie down in our own bed once again. Dear reader, *bon jour* or *soir*.

Malvern

1894

Saturday 4 August. This morning we are going to start for our holiday. We have decided to go to Great Malvern—in fact I have already got the tickets.

We breakfast, call a cab, and in a few minutes are seated in the train and speeding towards London. How green all the fields look, and how brown the corn is getting, proclaiming the approach of harvest. I only hope we may have harvest weather.

The first notification of our contiguity to London is forced to my notice by a remark from Cuthbert: 'What a lot of chimneys, Papa.' You see what it is to have a child with an observant mind; he noticed at once that the great feature of London was chimneys.

The train stops and we charter a cab: 'Paddington Station.' 'All right, sir,' and off we go—over Waterloo Bridge, along Oxford Street and we are there. An official ensconces us in a through-carriage to Malvern, and off we go with a long, sweeping kind of speed—little or no vibration. At last we are only a few minutes after time on a run of 3½ hours, quite long enough to be cooped up.

We jump in a cab and drive to the bottom of the street where our house is situated. The driver deposits us in the road—explains he can't drive up there, pointing to a hill like the side of a house—takes his fare, and away he goes as brisk as a bee. Ten minutes afterwards we are refreshing ourselves with tea.

We put the little boy to bed and then go out to reconnoitre. Grim and scowling are the hills, 1,300-odd feet above us, covered by black clouds, so that we cannot see their heads. There is a misty drizzle, making it unpleasant to be outdoors. We buy some soap, a cake for tomorrow, a guide to Malvern, this book etc., and then stroll back.

Sunday 5 August. The sun is shining brilliantly, so up we get, and are soon discussing our matutinal meal with an appetite that is almost appalling. Then we turn up towards the hills.

A little way up we see a shed fitted with mangers—a donkey-stand. No donkeys though. Evidently here the donkeys are Christians and observe the Sabbath.

Taking a circuitous path we trudge slowly up. At our feet, Worcester

Cathedral stands out prominently; above us the hills frown grim and terrible. Heavy clouds are collecting round the hilltops, the wind freshens. Plash, a drop of rain, and we start as quick as we can to make the descent. To dinner: loin of hot mutton, peas and potatoes etc.

Baby goes to bed, and after a smoke I go to sleep also. At four o'clock we all get up, and Cuthbert stands on a hassock at the open window and looks at the large quantity of people coming down from the hills. Then we all three go for a walk to find the baths. They belong to the Imperial Hotel, a fine building, and the baths are some distance from the main building. We see that both ladies and gentlemen use it at stated times.

Monday 6 August. I woke about four o'clock—surely it is raining. I looked out, and my worst suspicions were confirmed. It was raining in that dogged, determined manner which means lasting. Up and to breakfast: then we watch the people climbing by our window to the hills.

With that recklessness so characteristic of bank-holiday pleasure-seekers, they go up in fair numbers, the majority of them carrying lunch or dinner, and many of them already appear wet through—what they will be like when they come down I cannot imagine.

We have lounged, slept and messed about all morning, and now they are commencing to lay dinner.

After dinner I have a most painful attack of toothache, and go to find a dentist and have it out. Bank holiday: no dentists at work, so I go in the Belle Vue Hotel and have a drop of whisky.

After Cuthbert is put to bed, Millie and I go for a long walk. We find ourselves at Malvern Link—crowds of people, steam-roundabouts, swings, and coker-nut shies are in full swing, and the public are evidently enjoying their bank holiday. I have seldom seen a prettier sight than the common as we came upon it this evening.

Tuesday 7 August. Gorgeous sunshine; we all three go out to the donkey-stand. We charter three asses—Cuthbert has a special one fitted with a basketwork pannier, and he is strapped in. 'Pull up! Now then! Pull up!' and off we go.

We are accompanied by a little boy, William Coombs or Coomber. His age is ten. He tells me he has been four years driving the donkeys up and down, so he began at the mature age of six.

I don't hardly like going up on a donkey—it seems cruel—but when I talk to the boy he pooh-poohs it altogether. 'Carri yer! I should think so, w'y he's tuk up over 20 stun.'

'Over 20 stones? Never. Man or woman?'

'Ooman, zir.'

By circuitous paths we wind our way up the hill. Our goal is the Worcestershire Beacon.

Remembering that the 'merciful man is merciful to his beast', I dismount two or three times when we get to an extra-steep incline. Then I lead the donkey. When I remount, the animal appears to resent it. The boy says: 'You shooddent git down, zir, he doant like startin agin wen yew gits oop.'

About half-way up the young rascal met another donkey-boy, and stopped to talk to him, and let Cuthbert's donkey go on alone. (Hitherto he had been hanging round Cuthbert's donkey's neck all the way up.) Mill was in front, I was next and Cuthbert last and it was nearly five minutes before I discovered he was not there. It seems rather dangerous for a child barely over two years of age to be strapped on a donkey's back up a precipitous hillside, without an attendant.

At last we reached the top. The view to the other side of the range is much superior to the side on which Great Malvern stands—it is indescribably beautiful. I begin to see that there is a charm in mountaineering.

It is a sight that will for ever be impressed on the mind's eye, and here is one of the charms of a holiday. The time may come when you have become incapable of stirring from your own fireside: but if your mind has not gone, you can call up the scenes you visited in your youth, aye, when you were in the plenitude of your manly strength and vigour. The little

a sight to make the angels weep.

child who was with you then may be a middle-aged man—you may perhaps be nursing a child of his on your knee, but in the mind's eye you can revisit the scenes you visited with him, and thus enjoy again your youthful jaunts.

We descended, and came upon St Ann's Well, and then I left Millie and Cuthbert and went to see Mr Midgeley, the dentist. I was ushered upstairs and took my seat in the chair of torture. I will not lift the veil on this trying episode: let it be enough to know that my tooth is out. I paid the dentist 2*s* 6*d*.

Now at 7.20 p.m. it is raining fast. There have been hundreds of excursionists here today; they keep coming down from the hills, wet but jolly. They are evidently imbued with a Mark Tapley spirit, for the wet has no effect on them.

After supper we took heart of grace and went out. The streets were deserted. It seemed to me as though I had been here by dark before; it must be the fact that the place seems like Lewes by dark.

Mill says, 'Yes. The fifth of November at Lewes.' The streets are damp, and it seems for all the world like a November night.

Wednesday 8 August. We are going to Worcester today, but how about the rain? We stayed at home all the morning, and then off to the railway station, hot-foot.

Now, I am on the loose this afternoon. Usually before I go into a strange place I work everything out mathematically. Today, I don't care a cuss. I don't ask for ticket to Foregate Street or Shrub Hill; I take what they give me like a child. I am in a plastic mood, like clay in the hands of the potter. When I get in the carriage I see the tickets are for Foregate Street. At Foregate Street we get out. I don't know whether Foregate Street is the best station for the cathedral and the porcelain works, but we shall see.

Into High Street, and by Jove we are right. We go through the market, and there is the cathedral. It is a magnificent old pile. The new organ cost

£8,200. A magnificent new reredos is to be seen—a grand new pulpit—King John's will—pieces of skin flayed from people in very early times, and a host of other things.

Then we go out to the towing-path. The River Severn flows on its way, and of all the pretty landscapes I have ever seen, this stands high in the list. In High Street we purchase some views, then to a very old house where Queen Elizabeth stopped; note the balcony from which she addressed her subjects.

Then at the Cross we take a tram to Shrub Hill Station, and have a chat with the driver. He has been fighting, has our driver, and he has two lovely black eyes, but he is a good sort and tells us a good deal about the city. There are large railway-signal works here, employing seven to nine hundred hands; Perry Wood on the right is where Oliver Cromwell concealed his men when fighting against King Charles, and he tells me Foregate Street ran knee-deep with blood. Then we go back to New Street and Friar Street to see the oldest buildings I ever saw. Our driver repeated time after time that 'Worcester was an old ancient city,' and so it is. I like Worcester very much, but those houses are as old as can be.

Thursday 9 August. At eleven o'clock we go by four-in-hand char-à-banc round the hills, through the Wyche Pass to the British Camp: a rough place with entrenchments and a prætorium, made when the Romans invaded Great Britain. Home through the village of Malvern Wells. We passed the kitchen-garden of the late Jenny Lind who died near the British Camp.

After we left the char-à-banc, I said: 'Tom and Fanny are here.'

'How do you know?' said Mill.

'I can see their footsteps.'

'Don't be so silly,' said Mill.

We turned up St Ann's Road, and I said: 'Well, there's Tom anyway'—and there he was, 'as large as life and quite as natural'. We were delighted to see each other, and in a moment we were shaking hands with Fanny and Dottie.

After snatching a hasty dinner we go up to the donkey-stand, and off we go. Tom, on a pony, soon got at our head and kept his position all the way; as for us, we were a mass of donkeys, nearly always in a scramble.

About fifty yards from the top, Tom's pony suddenly stopped for a natural purpose. Tom had no idea what he had stopped for, and flicked him up with his umbrella. 'The beggar won't go any more. What's the matter with him, are we up top?'

We were bursting with laughter, the bystanders were splitting their sides, I noticed two or three matronly females squirming as they laughed. Then it dawned on Tom, and he blushed to the tips of his ears.

The pony, having finished, gravely resumed his march to the top.

After a smoke, I convoy them to St Ann's Well. Here amongst a little crowd we make our way to the fountain to drink the water. It is a room about nine feet square, white tiled walls with blue dado, and it looks beautiful. The water is very cool, but I do not think it tasted irony at all.

Tea, and then off we go for the station. Fanny has been harping on the beautiful sleep she will have, stretched on the seat going home to Bristol, but in a moment their carriage is full up. We pity them. The engine whistles—'Take your seats,' shouts the guard—and off they go.

Friday 10 August. To the station, and start through Malvern Wells, Upton-upon-Severn, Ripple, Ashchurch and Tewkesbury. At Cheltenham we wait till I am nearly sick of it—off at last, Cleeve and then Gloucester.

I pressed Tom to meet us at Gloucester today, and rush to the cathedral to see if he has been there. A verger produces the visitors' book—people from the USA, but no 'T. Garrett'.

This is the finest cathedral, I believe, in England. Unfortunately we get in with a large party: a nice old clergyman with twenty-one villagers on an outing.

The verger starts us. He is deaf, and I can't help laughing at him. He starts like this: 'Now, gentlemen, yew sees that 'ere star in the middle of the tower—that's the centre of the tower—you see.'

Then to the crypt. 'You see—this yer floor wus all boans, you see.' Then the regular guide takes us in hand. He does not say, 'This is so-and-so,' he says, 'This would be the Lady Chapel—this would be something else.'

Then out, and make our way to Gloucester Docks. Here are immense warehouses, and large ships alongside the quays unloading, and all is life: but the entrance to the docks has a lock, and Mill has no eyes for anything else. She does enjoy it.

Then to the station, and into a train. We rush into a compartment, pull down the blinds, stand at the window, and secure the compartment to ourselves. The guard looks at us like thunder when he goes by, but off we go all alone. Rains like steam.

Saturday 11 August. After breakfast we charter two donkeys, and a pony for me, and 'orf we do' as Cuthbert says, up the hill. About half-way up we stop and are photographed.

We have a splendid journey up. My pony stopped up top just the same as he did with Tom, but as we were in the know, no hilarity was occasioned.

We ride down in gallant style. I prefer riding up, but both are very pleasant.

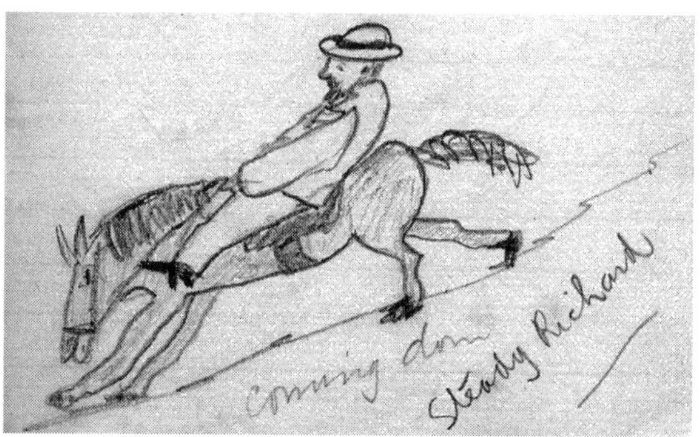

After dinner we send Cuthbert out with a niece of our landlady's, and Mill and I go to find the swan pool—a charming spot. Then it rains.

Sunday 12 August. Cuthbert, Millie and I go down to the swan pool. Cuthbert enjoys himself exceedingly with the swans and ducks. Soon after dinner it rains in earnest; needless to say we don't go out.

Nothing pleases Cuthbert better than to smoke a pipe, so when Millie and I were in Gloucester she said, 'Buy Cuthbert a pipe.' We bought him one, and now ever since tea he has been smoking with me. It is quite company for us both to sit down and have a smoke together—why, I remember when I was a little boy I used to enjoy a pipe too, and Uncle Heathfield at Lewes always kept one specially for me when we used to go over there at no. 7 Lansdowne Terrace or Place.

Truly we family men live our lives over again in our children. God bless them. This rain is miserable.

Monday 13 August. Very fine. Having paid our bill, we depart amidst a shower of adieux to the station, and were soon on our way home. We stopped at every station in this list, except those marked with a star: Malvern Link, Bransford, Henwick, Worcester Foregate Street, Worcester Shrub Hill; here we changed, then Pershore, Fladbury, Evesham, Honeybourne, Campden, Moreton-in-the-Marsh, Chipping Norton, Shipton, Charlbury, Oxford, Reading, West Drayton,* Hayes,* Ealing Broadway, Westbourne Park and Paddington.

At Reading we passed Huntley & Palmer's large biscuit factory, and Sutton's seed stores. A very large area of land alongside the rails is used by Sutton's for a test-field for the cultivation of plants from their seeds.

Arriving at Paddington and hailing a hansom we were soon careering through the city traffic, over London Bridge. Catch the train beautifully and reach Brighton Station, and here I will bid you farewell.

Weston-super-Mare

1895

Friday 26 July. Year by year people who go away are met with the difficulty of 'where shall we go this year?' It is a knotty question and like the poor it is always with us.

After considering the rival claims of numerous places, Weston-super-Mare, 'finely situated on the Somersetshire coast of the Bristol Channel, open to the invigorating breezes of the Atlantic Ocean, distant from Bristol 20 miles, Bath 32, London 139,' as the advertisement says, finally secures our patronage. So at about eleven o'clock Friday morning I sent the following despatch to Millie:

> ARRANGE EVERYTHING TO START FOR LONDON TONIGHT
> HARRY.

She set to work, and after dinner deposited little Cuthbert at Queen Square where he is to stop for a few days; then in Ellen Freeman's charge he is to proceed to Warnham.

At 7.30 p.m. we started from Brighton Station for Victoria. No light in the carriage, which made the latter part of the journey rather dismal.

Arriving at Victoria about 9.30, for our train was very late, we took a hansom to Ashton's Temperance Hotel, nos 29 and 30 London Street, Paddington. We discussed a bit of supper with relish, and then to bed.

Saturday 27 July. About four o'clock there was an enormous amount of wheel traffic, the principal part of it being the Royal Parcels Mail vans—they have a large depôt just above the hotel. A little later the London papers arrived in vans and were deposited at the station. Then by six o'clock it was all quiet again.

Up and into the station, and at 8.27 off we go: through Westbourne Park, Acton, Ealing, Castle Hill, Hanwell, Southall, Hayes, West Drayton, Langley, Slough, Taplow, Twyford, Reading, Theale, Aldermaston, Midgham, Thatcham, Newbury, Kintbury, Hungerford, Bedwyn, Savernake, Pewsey, Woodborough, Devizes, Seend, Holt, Bradford, Freshford, Limpley Stoke, Bath, Tiverton, Saltford, Keynsham, Bristol, Bedminster, Flax Bourton, Nailsea, Yatton, Puxton, Worle, and then our journey ends at Weston-super-Mare—a run of four hours and 23 minutes. 139 miles.

We detrain and start out for the Railway Hotel. Giving our portmanteau to a lad, who becomes our guide, we are soon at our destination. We then have a wash up, and are soon seated at table.

The waitress says, 'Would you mind carving three lots, one for a gentleman downstairs?'

'Certainly.' First course, salmon. I cut off three lots.

Waitress takes one lot downstairs, then comes back. 'Would you mind if the gentleman downstairs joined you at this table?'

'Not at all.'

Up he comes. He was a young man—'Haw, haw' style of chap. Heavy—put it on a lot. We fall to conversation and laughter. He is rather an amusing member.

Second course, roast duck. Next come roast lamb, cabinet puddings, blancmange and stewed blackcurrants and Devonshire cream. Cheese, butter and lettuce. We make a good square meal.

I arrange to meet our newly found friend at eight o'clock tomorrow morning to go for a swim together in the baths.

Sunday 28 July. I rise and find my man ready to start; away we go to the baths. We are soon swimming about. It is a small bath, open to the sky—water looked rather thick and muddy.

Breakfast, then out for a long walk along the sands. Lots of men and boys undressing on the sand and bathing. Back to dinner at two o'clock: salmon, roast duck, roast lamb, pudding, blancmange and stewed plums, apricots, grapes, cherries, gooseberries, not forgetting cheese etc.

Read and sleep in drawing-room, then out to the sea-front. Crowds of people sitting on seats, on the walls, any and every where promenading.

By Anchor Head, watch the lighthouse rotating light in the distance. See the finest shooting-star I have ever seen—it fell with a stream of light like a sky-rocket.

Monday 29 July. On to the Pier, toll twopence each; take two tickets *per* the steamer *Waverley* for Cardiff. In about three quarters of an hour we are entering Cardiff Harbour or Docks.

The amount of shipping lying in the open and at the quays is enormous. I counted ninety to a hundred steamers and sailing-ships, but in the whole docks I should think there were over double that quantity.

We disembark and pass in the gates of the Bute Docks—men of all nationalities in all directions, coal-dust everywhere. Several steamers were taking in their coal.

After a good look round we go out along a street crowded by captains and seamen of all nationalities. Then on a tram to Broadway. We pass some warehouses, shops devoted to maritime matters, and a large statue which says 'JOHN BATCHELOR, THE FRIEND OF FREEDOM.' I must confess that I never heard of him before.

On, and now the houses are villas, and semi-detached villas, beautifully kept gardens etc. We have left the business part of Cardiff behind and have got into the aristocratic part of it.

Then we commence investigating on foot. There are numerous arcades through which we stroll, looking at shop after shop, then we see in the distance Cardiff Castle. It is a stone building of recent date, the residence of the Marquess of Bute. An old man at one of the gates said people are admitted every half-hour, one shilling each. I did not think it looked worth it, and murmuring 'Dear at the price' we strolled away again.

To the Great Western passenger station; on the cab-rank outside were a number of horses, and I was surprised to see that not one had a nosebag as we are accustomed to in our part of the country, but all had a tin or galvanised iron bucket strapped on them for a nosebag.

Then we remounted the tram to the docks. The tram company enjoin their customers most earnestly 'to keep their seats while going under the bridges'; it certainly is a tight fit. One we went under, they were painting, and the fellows had to draw their legs out of the way pretty smartly.

When we got to the docks, the crowd of stevedores, watermen, labourers, sailors, pilots, loafers etc. was enormous—knots congregated round some pertinacious cheap-Jack or other Hawkins etc. Two o'clock makes a clearance and then we go aboard the *Waverley*—on come the people, old, young, rich, but very few poor, and away we go.

Music, oh! ye shades of Beethoven and Mozart, what a prostitution of thy sweet art when music is relegated to the tender mercies of a trio of steamboat musicians. One artiste? presides at the piano, which he thumps as though he were trying to break every bone in its body.

What the cornet lacks in musical skill he makes up by speed. The rate at which they play is extra double express—the violin is just as bad—but the worst of all was the vocalist. Oh heavens, his singing. His voice he had evidently left at home, and I could have wished he had been left at home too.

He gravely assured an imaginary Tommy Atkins 'that he was a good 'un, heart an' 'and', and also mentioned 'that we were proud of him and loved him' etc. etc.

Landing on Weston Pier we rambled off to Kewstoke Woods—simply lovely—then back to a stone quarry. No signs of blasting; I am rather disappointed.

After dinner, to the railway to see train times to Bristol and London. The man gives us a printed card, which is excellent—but if we return Friday we shall have to pay 5*s* 2½*d* each. Oh how fearfully and wonderfully constituted are railway companies—if I had my way I would make them 'sit up'.

Tuesday 30 July. We take the 11.30 a.m. boat for Ilfracombe. At 2.45 we pull up by the pier and file through the gate, paying twopence each. A most disagreeable man collects the money and one of our passengers had a heated discussion with him, culminating in our passenger moving him aside pretty sharply.

The cause of quarrel appeared to be through our passenger having paid for two, having got parted from his wife, and then the fellow wanted to make her pay again. However I think our passenger beat him.

Out in the street—a line of dining-rooms—a woman rushed up to me and said, 'Dinner sir, 'am, lam', roast beef, peas and beans.' Well, I thought, this is handy, in we go. 'Goo oopstairs,' says she, 'moore retired like oop thare.'

Upstairs we went, into a scrupulously clean dining-room containing about six tables. About seventeen other passengers by our boat were with us, and we all seated ourselves.

After a long time the woman came up with two beefs. One woman wanted lamb. 'Very sorry, mum, lamb's all gone.'

I noticed signs of impatience amongst us. One man rushed downstairs to give his order in the kitchen. Then more grumbling: 'How long are you going to be?'

'Give you yours in a minute. Can't serve ye all at once.'

Things went from bad to worse—I laughed and laughed. At last I nailed the woman. She said, 'You can have lamb, all the beef is gone.'

Another pause, then I heard a commotion downstairs, and the woman burst in the room with: 'Very sorry but there ain't no more dinners.'

How we roared. Up jumped three or four women. 'So this is Ilfracombe, is it,' they said, and downstairs they went.

'Now then,' I said, 'have you got any cold ham?'

'Yes sir.'

'All right, two plates cold ham. Then send and get me a pint of bitter, will you?'

She said, 'We are awfully busy. I will if I can.'

Presently an ancient-looking boy appeared with it. 'Fivepence,' he said.

'What, fivepence for a pint of bitter?'

'That's what they charged.'

I said, 'This really won't do, you know.' But I always think of a few lines in *She Stoops to Conquer*, when Hastings says, 'Ah, travellers George must pay in all places,' and I am reconciled to these petty swindles.

After dinner we climb to the Capstone Parade, where I make a sketch; then on to the steamer for the return journey.

We had just cast off and started backing, when up and spake an elderly man with a long beard: 'Oh, Captain, put me ashore please, I only came to see my daughter off.'

The captain said this was rather awkward. 'I know it is,' said the man, 'but I've engaged my bed here, all my luggage is there, what shall I do?' Well, our captain decided to put him aboard the *Alexandra* who was layering off ready to come into our berth, so we eased alongside her, and whirr goes a line from our peak, and we are soon locked together; then a gangway is put across from our paddle-box to the *Alexandra*'s, and the foolish man solemnly walks across it.

Our captain is as handsome a man as you will see if you search for a long time—about 34, with a bronzed red face, tall commanding figure, bright blue eyes, and a dainty moustache, he is the beau ideal of a naval commander; his name is Campbell, and a passenger tells me there are two brothers Campbell and they are very popular indeed. The line of steamers is called P. & A. Campbell Ltd.

Right forward it is blowing fairly hard. Two or three hats go overboard like pieces of paper flying away.

At nine o'clock we are alongside Weston Pier. Gangways to another steamer and right over her to the pier; dark, both steamers crowded from stem to stern, and a good deal of confusion. Then along front to Madeira Cove—quite the fashionable rendezvous.

Wednesday 31 July. We stroll along the sand, which is crowded with people, amusements and donkey-riding in full swing. Then a drive to Uphill. A crowd of people when we get down, and on investigation I find an inspector of police had struck a little boy on the leg with a stick and drawn blood. All the people were up in arms against him. Two or three clergymen took up the case and talked earnestly to the chief inspector about it. The boy's mother was very voluble and tried to get two policemen to take him into custody, but this was 'no go', so she was advised to summon him.

The crowd hooted him and shouted: 'Who hit the boy with the stick? Coward!'

He looked as silly as possible and very uncomfortable. He certainly had a very ugly stick, having numerous jagged points or thorns branching out on it. I trust he will be brought to account for his conduct.

Thursday 1 August. Up early and off to railway station. At Bristol we get on bus for Clifton Down, and over the suspension bridge. Bang goes a blasting charge in one of the quarries, then the heavy rattle of falling stone, and the clink, clink of the crowbars as the men loosen masses of stone which go hurtling down to the depths.

Back down Whiteladies Road, Millie says: 'Hullo, that's Mr Wise's shop, and there's Alan, wonder if he knows me—don't he stare.'

Suddenly he saw who it was and, rushing for his hat, came out. He pressed us to go and see his mother, and off he came with us to their house. Annie, Dottie and Beattie come forward, round comes the trap and in we jump: over the Down to Coombe Dingle, then through Henbury and Westbury back to their house, through very pretty country. Then hot-foot to the station.

Dinner at 6.20: salmon, roast duck, lamb chops, French pancakes, apple pudding, cream, potatoes, marrow and French beans. Then Millie plays in the drawing-room and I get in a song or two edgeways, and once more we seek our virtuous couch.

Friday 2 August. We rise early and indulge in our usual matutinal ablutions—I can never understand anyone electing to be dirty. Oh! the refreshing pleasures of a bath.

I pay my little bill and with a lavish hand dispense *backsheesh* among the domestics, and then we are marching on to the station. 'Boots' has got there with the luggage, and off we go at 8.50 a.m.

At Paddington we hail a hansom to Victoria, where we catch train for Horsham. The scenery from London to Horsham would want a lot of beating.

Arriving at Horsham we have an hour to wait, but what does it matter? 'Time was made for slaves,' and we are free. It is this reckless feeling, this entire freedom from control that has its own subtle charm when holiday touring.

I interviewed a cabman, but finding he wanted four shillings to take us to Warnham, I decided to wait.

After about half an hour the cabman came up and said he would take us for three shillings—but 'I'm not a "gal" of that sort'. If he wanted to take us for three shillings he should have said so at first—cabmen, and the system on which they conduct their business, are both mystical and incomprehensible. Why a man should ask an exorbitant sum, and stand idle hour after hour, when by asking a reasonable and fair amount he might be at work, is 'one of those things that no fellah can understand'.

At Warnham we found that Alice and our little son had gone to Horsham: so Mill and I started through the fields to meet them. Presently in the distance we espied Alice pushing Cuthbert in a mail-cart. She saw us, and we could see her tell Cuthbert, and then he looked round and grinned at us like a Cheshire cat.

After the salutations were over, back we trudged: and about three minutes from home, down came the rain. Presently we settled down to a game of nap, and it rained in torrents.

Sunday 4 August. Do people as a rule think enough of the great boon that they enjoy in the possession of a weekly 'day of rest'?

Sunday is good for man and beast, and although I would always oppose anything that tended to continentalise our English Sunday, still I view with pleasure the advance that is being made in the present day, towards the opening of picture galleries, museums, etc.

Having discussed breakfast, we shaped our course towards church—but good heavens! Alack-a-day, by Gis and by Saint Charity! and all other 'sweet oaths', I have missed Saturday—so now I must hark back.

When we met Alice coming to Horsham was Friday night. Next day was Saturday, and it rained in torrents. Uncle Fred and I went up to the Village Institute and Club and read the papers, then dropped in the Oak for a friendly glass. Rained all the afternoon, rained all the evening, and this was the night we settled down to nap as before mentioned.

Now I take up the thread of my narrative again.

After tea the whole garrison paraded and marched on Warnham Court to see an aloe which is blooming this year. Now an aloe only blooms about once in a hundred years—but if what I saw was a fair sample of aloes in general, I should not 'rend my garments' or 'put on sackcloth and ashes' if in future aloes did not bloom at all.

Monday 5 August. Mill and I went to order a trap to take us to Horsham tonight, but 'no go': the village boasts of two but they are both engaged till 10.30 p.m., being a holiday. Well, we shall have to walk to Warnham Station.

Our hosts kindly press us to stop one more night, but I know that we must go. So after tea we pave our way to Warnham Station. Tonight there is a grand carnival etc. at Horsham, so Alice and Fred accompany us. Our luggage we have sent on in a truck propelled by an elderly rustic.

It rained all the way. I carried Cuthbert part of the way, then Fred took him, I took him again and then Fred finished him, and I can truthfully say I was not sorry when we got there. Then it rained with renewed vigour.

At Horsham we waited for an hour and a half. Alice and Fred saw us into the train.

A man under the influence of drink was in our carriage, which was a saloon carriage, so Mill jumped out at one station and got in next compartment, and I handed Mr Cuthbert over and then got over myself.

At Brighton the station is literally choked with people, and elbowing our way through we gain a cab and are off on the home stretch. We draw up at our door and find all well, and Lily waiting to receive us.

I regret to add that we had about reached home when a terrific explosion of a bomb and mortar took place during a display of fireworks at a Foresters' Fête in Preston Park, injuring nearly twenty people, several of whom have since died. We were of course ignorant of its happening until the next morning and I have only entered it here now, because if I or anyone else should happen to read this years hence it will serve to localise the date in one's mind.

Jersey

1896

Friday 21 August. Today we start on our annual holiday: Mr and Mrs Thos Garrett senior, Millie and myself. Our destination is Jersey.

After tea we started for the station. Reaching Victoria, we chartered a four-wheeler for Ashton's Temperance Hotel. Mr and Mrs G. took room no. 5 and we took no. 6—the same room that we slept in last year.

Saturday 22 August. The traffic commences soon after three o'clock and keeps up continuously till about six. Soon after seven o'clock we get down. All appears confusion—people rushing in and out, and the attendants have considerable difficulty in coping with the demand for breakfast. After settling up, off we march to the station.

Our train runs in, and we settle in the four corners. Then an old woman gets in, looks askance at the luggage on the rack, and tells us that she has had two trunks fall on her head at different times. She keeps repeating this, so we move our trunks.

At Weymouth Town our train runs right through the streets like a tram, no protection at all, no fence, and thus we go right up the quay, till we stop opposite a magnificent steamer named the *Ibex*.

We force our way on board and sit down to dinner—bump, whirr, she is starting—the tables shiver and shake, and Millie after one spoonful of soup decides to go up on deck.

When we get on deck we light up cigars and look around. Just then a little boy is sick all over the place, then his brother also, and then the women begin. Presently Mill rushes to the rail and pays tribute also to the dreadful *mal de mer*, and there she stops and retches for about an hour.

Presently we run into St Peter Port alongside the quay. Here is a very busy scene—people lined all along the piers, and up spring a lot of women carrying baskets.

'Beautiful grapes!' they cry. 'Sixpence a bunch,' and they do a brisk trade. A lot of our passengers disembark at Guernsey, then the fruit-women rush off and we are off again.

Now Jersey looms larger. Innumerable rocks jut up above the water, and we realise what a dangerous iron-bound coast it is. We are on land again at about eight o'clock.

There are buses from all the hotels, and boys attached to them keep shouting the names of the hotels they represent. Shortly I hear the cry 'Pomme d'Or!' and in a moment we are up in a wagonette. A rocket shoots up high in the air, and a fellow passenger says: 'That is a signal from the boat from France, announcing that they are about to enter the harbour.'

In a few minutes we reach the Pomme d'Or. I am well pleased with the hotel; the courtyard is better than that at the Hôtel St Petersbourg, Paris, and more trees and shrubs.

After dinner we sally out, and the cigars claim my attention: very heavy Manillas, ten for a shilling. I buy one shilling's worth, and wandering on I see a tobacconist selling off ten cigars for fourpence. I have four pennyworth of these also.

Sunday 23 August. After breakfast we go out into Royal Square. We find the soldiers are in church, and we decide to wait and see them. As we are strolling round the churchyard out rushes a verger, and says to me: 'You must put out that cigar.' I say, 'Certainly,' and walk out of the grounds. Subsequently I see him pounce again and rush someone else out.

Presently the soldiers troop out and off they go to Fort Regent, situated on a rocky frowning height. We notice they are the Northampton Regiment.

Back to the hotel for a wash. We find a letter awaiting us from Cis, saying Cuthbert is quite well and happy. This pleases Millie exceedingly.

After dinner we go for a stroll. We are much surprised by the size of the harbour—for such a place, it seems far and away too large. We suppose they know their own business best, but this work was not carried out for nothing, the Victoria Pier costing £61,000 and the Albert Pier £200,000.

Monday 24 August. Awakened by the report of a cannon. A lot of cabs and buses hurrying off to the harbour. Mill and I go off up the quay and see our steamer the *Ibex*, also her sister ships the *Gazelle* and the *Antelope*. Then up come the people, some walking, some riding bicycles, some in cabs, all making for the *Ibex*.

The streets are full of cars; the Royal Blue and the Royal Paragon are the strongest companies, and the rivalry between them is intense. As we go along, one of the Royal Blue men accosts us and gives me a book of times and routes, but the weather being queer we will not decide.

Then the weather seems inclined to clear, so we go back to where the cars start from. In a moment we are surrounded by about six rival touts: but sticking to the man of the Royal Blue we decide to go by him, and he carries us off in triumph—to the disgust of the others, who reproach him with poaching on their ground.

Some of the cars have four horses, some three, some two. We go on a two-horse. It takes some time to fill up, as so many seats are ordered here, so many are to be called for at this hotel, etc. At last we are full up with about sixteen passengers, then off all the cars go in a string, at least fifteen cars.

We are going to the Grève de Lecq, the north-west of Jersey. Here I may tell you that the population of the whole island is about 60,000, of whom 30,000 are in St Helier. Tobacco is free, and as was silver in the time of Solomon, so 'cigars are counted nought in Jersey'. You rarely see a pipe. Everybody smokes cigars, early and often. The average annual revenue of Jersey amounts to £50,000, derived as under:

Duty on wine and spirits	33,400
Public house licences	2,000
Anchorage and harbour dues	13,000
Markets	750
Balance in sundries.	

The country is very pretty: apples in abundance, Jersey cabbages by hundreds (these stalks they make into sticks, and shops display large numbers of them), a good many Jersey cows. Each cow is tethered down; I never saw one loose. Our guide says the reason they are tied down is to prevent the wind blowing them off the island—our guide is a fraud. The cabbages he calls 'a field battalion of the Royal Jersey Militia'; a haystack, 'a Jersey beehive'; terribly plain women in the gardens and fields, 'some more of Mrs Langtry's cousins'; cows, 'some more specimens of our famous Jersey antelope'. As he fires off these exclamations every time we pass either of the objects, it becomes a little monotonous. Then he distributes bogus five-pound notes; on the back is a description of an 'Exciting and Novel Game. The Tourist's Roadside Whist'—scoring as follows:

	Points
Open gate	1
Goat	1
Pump	1
Ladder	1
Wheelbarrow	1
Windmill	1
Pig in a sty	5
Woman milking a cow	10
Man on ladder	2
Catching a lizard	20
White horse	5
Magpie	5
Cat in window asleep—game	
Policeman in uniform—game.	

The game is 31 up. One party takes the right-hand side of the road, and the other the left, but it seems to hang fire.

I notice that all the gateposts to fields and gardens are simply pieces of squared-up granite, a good thing for the purpose as it is everlasting. Nearly all the houses are of stone; not very high-pitched rooves, and not exceeding four storeys.

At the Grève de Lecq, Mr G. and Millie have some lunch, while Mrs G. and I go on to the shore—the most lovely stretch of sand I have ever seen. Here is a little range of buildings for the use of soldiers who practise shooting here.

Presently we stroll back, and the people are photographed in three groups. We find two of our party are missing, but the desire of our party being to go on without them, we do so.

Tuesday 25 August. We get a train which goes as far as St Aubin—the prettiest place we have come across without doubt—then back to station and to the famous Corbière Lighthouse. Inside it is most interesting to see the different burners, fog bell, sheets of all passing ships etc. Mounting right up to the lantern, we find the light is surrounded or enclosed in prisms, and the man goes inside and presents a most horrible sight, being distorted most grotesquely.

Wednesday 26 August. French breakfast at *dix heures*—very large, say six courses—then off on a three-horse car, first halt Princes Tower.

This tower was built in the eleventh century. According to legend, a Lord of Hambye came to kill a terrible serpent, and while resting after the combat, his rascally servant slew him, and told the fair Gisla that her husband had succumbed to the wounds he had received during the encounter with the serpent, and that while dying he had charged him to tell her to honour with her hand the faithful servant.

After the wretched man supplanted his master, he used to mutter in his dreams during the night: '*O, moi misérable, misérable que je suis d'avoir tué mon maître.*' This ultimately led to the condemnation of the false servant. Mortified, Gisla heaped over her husband's grave a tumulus, and on the top erected a chapel of sufficient height to be seen from her castle at Hambye.

Then on to Bouley Bay. Here is a grand view of the Ecréhous Rocks. One, called the 'Rocking Stone', is nine feet long, ten feet wide, weighs ten tons and is easily rocked. A man called Philippe Pinel, born in 1820, lived on them forty years and was called 'King of the Islands'.

Away on cars again to Gorey, and back to St Helier. Then Mr G. and I go out alone to find a very old friend of his, a Brightonian named Mr Kine, who is a brewer. We had seen a public house in Charing Cross, St Helier, with W. KINE on the lamp, so we went in and enquired for him.

'Oh,' said the man, 'he has left this place five years, he lives next door to the brewery in Springfield Road, but you wouldn't find your way there tonight.' Mr G. thanked him and left. Two or three men were drinking in the bar, and as we went out, one of them shuffled after us and said: 'I can show you the way.'

We said: 'No, thank you,' and left him disconsolate. We did not want his help, you see.

At last we saw the name up, W. KINE'S BREWERY, but found he was out, gone to the theatre. So Mr G. left word where he was staying, and would he call at hotel in the evening after the arrival of the French boat.

Thursday 27 August. As the clock struck six, Jersey time (eight minutes 42 seconds slower than Greenwich time), we were on our way up the quay, and were soon aboard the steamship *Victoria.*

I never saw a boat toss more; for such a sea it was absurd. I heard afterwards that she was a round boat amidships, no keel at all, and that accounted for it. When she rolled we could not see over the rail. But although many were bad, we were all right, and smoked in peace. Into St Malo after a run of 2¾ hours.

St Malo is a walled town, surrounded by ramparts. We walked round a long way, and watched the bathing from a lot of machines: wooden frame of battens, wooden roof, canvas sides and ends, and little solid wooden wheels. Bathers male and female. Then down into the town, into a buffet, and a good lunch of bread, butter and prawns, beefsteak and chips, *petits pois*, Camembert cheese and five bottles of bock. They swindle us a bit as we pay in English money.

We go on to the Pont Roulant or rolling bridge, running on rails on the bottom of the sea between the Avant Port and the Port de Marée; then we board our steamer. We find Mr Kine has called twice at hotel while we have been gone.

Friday 28 August. Directly after breakfast we go up to Mr Kine's. He was exceedingly pleased to see Mr G. He is getting an old man, about 67 I think, but is a big hard old chap, and could talk a donkey's hind-leg off. He cuts us a few roses and a little heliotrope. Then we go in and are introduced to his wife and married daughter, and her little boy.

Then off to secure a car drive to the Plémont Rocks. By the proprietor's offices, Mill and I look round the stables and workshops; they keep 120 horses, do all their own shoeing, coach-building etc., also shoe for the public. It is a pretty big concern, and I hear is going to be floated as a company.

Hark, a bell rings, and we are ushered up into a beautiful little wagonette built to hold four inside, and one on box with driver, and drawn by a pair of beautiful horses, so we are to be all alone today, which is very nice.

Vinchelez Lanes, entirely overhung by trees each side, are charming; Plémont Rocks awfully grand. In such places, man feels so small. We are exhilaratingly happy. Then on car again to St Mary's Windmill, Arsenal headquarters of Field Batteries Royal Jersey Artillery, Jesson Watermills, St Lawrence Vineries, St Aubin's coast road and home—the weather perfect all day, and the prettiest drive we have had. Dinner at 6.30, then along comes Mr Kine, and we go for a walk.

Mr Kine talks incessantly—he is a most entertaining old chap. He lived in Florida for years, and tells tales without number. One was not bad. He says Jersey people are not to be matched anywhere for sharpness, lies, cunning, etc. A Jersey man died, and he knew he was not good enough to go upstairs (pointing to the sky), so he went down to the other place and knocked at the door. Old Nick opened it, and said: 'Hullo, where do you come from?' 'Jersey,' says the man. 'Wait a minute,' says Nick. 'You can't come in: this place isn't bad enough for anybody coming from Jersey!'

I must say, so far as our observation goes, we cannot agree with him, but he has lived here forty years. He was telling us about a woman who wanted him to marry her. She said, 'I have enough to keep me, you know.' On enquiry he found she had exactly £100, producing £5 a year. Needless to say, he was off.

Saturday 29 August. Today we shift to Guernsey. We have a beautiful passage, and dear old Mill is as jolly as a sandboy, which makes us all happy, as it pains us to see her feeding the congers and wasting her breakfast in the prodigal way she did coming over. In 1½ hours we are in St Peter Port, Guernsey. Walk to Channel Islands Hotel, and off for a drive again.

The driver is a good fellow, and tells us everything very distinctly. Guernsey is divided into farms of 25 to 30 acres, but most of the farmers are turning their attention to grape- and tomato-growing growing under glass. There is 200 miles of glass in Guernsey. One greenhouse we passed was on rails, so that they could move it when they wish. Here are plenty of cows, all tied down again for three reasons: first, because they should not blow off the island; second, because in many instances they grow two crops in one field at the same time; third, because the fields are small, and if loose they would spoil more than they would eat. He says Guernsey can beat Jersey in everything except 'telling lies and bank failures'. Land commands £10 to £12 per acre, and you raise three crops in fourteen months. 'One farmer who had a range of greenhouses for grape-growing planted a lot of sixpences one day, and in three weeks they had grown to two-shilling pieces, so he gave up grape-growing and went in for that instead.'

One thing strikes the visitor at once, and that is the excessive blueness of the water round Guernsey. Our driver says it is caused by the washerwomen using so much Reckitt's Blue and emptying it into the sea.

Home, then away on electric tram, twopence each to St Sampson Harbour. The car is driven by electricity: the current runs through a wire suspended on posts, and is conveyed into the machinery of the car by a long arm, having a wheel which runs under the wire. Very fast travelling.

Sunday 30 August. Out to Castle Cornet. Coming back we are much pleased with a large basin for sailing toy boats. As it has a wall about two feet high, there is no danger of slipping in.

After lunch, go for walk along Esplanade, then it begins to spatter and we get home. Here all is excitement over an accident to one of the cars. The horses took fright at a steamroller standing wrapped up in canvas as they turned a corner; the car turned completely over on a little bank, and shot out the whole of the passengers, 21 in number. It is marvellous how easily they have escaped. The most injured was a lady staying at the Royal Hotel, and an old gentleman staying here: they seem to have supported the whole weight of the car as it lay on its side, enabling others to crawl free. It has been a great shock to them all. Yesterday when we were out I must say the way they went around corners was something terrific—almost shot you out every time. In Jersey we never had anything like it.

We are very thankful we did not go, as we might have done; the car started from our hotel door.

We lounge, smoke and sing during the evening. In the hall is a musical automatic machine set to the 'Old Hundredth' and they keep putting in pennies till the people seem really to have had enough of it—and after a long time we prevail upon them to put in another tune, a march, which they would not do before as the 'Old Hundredth' was the only sacred tune they had.

Monday 31 August. A beautiful morning; it bids fair for a good passage. On to quay, where we find our luggage. The *Gazelle* lies alongside, loading thousands of baskets of fruit for Weymouth. After a time the *Ibex* steams in, and we stream on.

Millie has decided to walk about all the while. So she takes off her hat and puts up her hood, and the wind plays havoc with her generally. I keep close attendance, and talk to her all the time. Mr G. and I still peg away at our cigars. Presently the luncheon bell rings, and Mr G. makes a feint of rushing down as if he was starving, whereupon we laugh muchly. I should like to go too, but Millie will not release me. Neither she or Mrs G. can be persuaded to go down.

Millie on board "The Ibex"
August 31/96

Presently I descry England, and lo we see the White Horses on the hill and are close to Portland. We run in under the Bill, and are soon alongside Weymouth Pier: thankful that Millie has not been sick.

Then into the train—Paddington and Victoria—and reach Brighton about 12.15. Mr and Mrs G. having offered us a bed for the night at 13 Queen Square, we charter a cab from Brighton Station.

From the time we left our house on Friday 21 August, till we sit down in Mr Garrett's house, we have been by rail, steamers, cabs, 'buses, cars, electric and steam-trams, and on foot, at a rough computation over a thousand miles without a scratch, and a deep feeling of thankfulness wells up in our hearts to Him who has guided and protected us through all our wanderings.

Warnham and Taplow

1897

Saturday 31 July. On this day we are shaking off the cares of business, resting for a few days from the race for wealth. Cuthbert and Millie drive off to take train for Warnham. I am going to ride up on my bicycle. It is a superb morning and the machine bounds along like a thing of life.

It is absolutely surprising what a prominent part the bicycle plays in modern life. Ridden by all, young and old, rich and poor, gentle and simple, male and female, it has come amongst us, conquering all, and bids to remain for all time—unless the motor-car should supersede it, but at present the motor-car seems to lag dreadfully.

At Cowfold I have a large soda-and-milk. On through Horsham, and at the Dog and Bacon another large soda-and-milk goes down sweetly—then in a few minutes I draw up outside Mr Freeman's at Warnham and find Millie, Cuthbert and Uncle Fred in the garden; been in about twenty minutes. Alice and Ellen are both well, and the first news I hear is that Mill has left a piece of smoked salmon in the train.

After dinner we all took a stroll in the fields towards Warnham Court, playing with Cuthbert with a racquet and ball.

Sunday 1 August. Alice and I have arranged to ride on our machines to meet her brother Fred who is riding up from Worthing. We get away soon after 7.30, but the roads are very loose and full of small flints, which makes me think a good deal about punctures. After we had been riding about an hour, Alice said she had taken the wrong turning, when confound it, my hind wheel punctured. I soon had the machine upside down and took a flint out of the tyre, and the wind hissed out. After a little trouble I find the puncture and patch it up.

Meanwhile Alice rode back to the crossroad to wait for Fred. No sign—we can't make it out. We go home, just as the others are starting for church. At about twelve o'clock Fred and Harry come along—Fred's tyre punctured after he left Worthing and he had been pumping it all the way, delaying him about 2½ hours. However, lucky it was no worse.

Then a long walk, supper and bed. All day we have been trying to repair Fred's tyre, but it completely baffles us.

Monday 2 August. Alice, Harry and I mount our machines. The others follow us in the trap from the Oak. At the top of Leith Hill we all have dinner, picnic fashion. Cuthbert is very happy.

Then off; the trap went a different way. As we rode along, Harry Freeman fell over and bent his pedal. We tried to straighten it, and broke it, so he rode one foot the rest of the way. We reached home before the trap—no key, so got a ladder and got in the landing window.

Tuesday 3 August. Alice has decided to ride with me to Stedham to look at some ash-trees. In the saddle about ten o'clock and make a start. Not got more than thirty yards when Alice falls over while arranging her dress. So we go to a blacksmith, and he straightens her pedal and away we go. Alice is guiding. To avoid a hill she takes a turning which eventually landed us about two miles wrong; however, we canter into Billingshurst and have soda-and-milk. The publican directs us to follow the single telegraph wire, which we do, to Wisborough Green, then Petworth, and on through a grand park, to Stedham. We find the timber, and selecting about ten trees, remount and make a grand entry into Warnham soon after a quarter to eight, having gone 53 miles.

Wednesday 4 August. Millie and I catch the train to London; Cuthbert is to stop at Warnham. It is terribly hot today. At Leadenhall Street, a little business, and then cab to Paddington and take two third-class tickets to Taplow.

At Taplow Station I get a cab and say: 'Do you know the Dumb Bell Hotel?'

'Yaas, all right.'

Only a short ride. They are able to put us up, so we are shown to a very nice airy large room.

Then a stroll down to the river—it seems like fairyland as the boats glide along. We have a good look round and see several very large boat-builders' and boat-letters' sheds—they appear to have hundreds of boats and punts and steam and electric launches.

Then we stroll back to the hotel, and have a nice little dinner of roast beef, potatoes, marrows, stewed pears, cheese etc., washed down with some splendid Scotch-and-soda.

Thursday 5 August. A glorious morning. At ten o'clock we are on the river in a single sculler, a nice mahogany boat—a piece of cocoa-matting in the bottom, a pair of sculls, a little boat-hook, a nice cushion in the stern for Mother and cane-work for her to rest on, and a piece of goat or sheepskin tied on the seat for me, which completes a really creditable little turn-out. We row along to Boulter's Lock—here I pay threepence. This is the first time I ever took a boat through a lock.

Upstream to Cookham, then a peal of thunder rolled and reverberated. The heavens darkened—we were certainly in for it. I gave with all my might, and in a few minutes ran in alongside the landing-stage of the Ferry Hotel.

A man received our boat, and we had our cushions, matting etc. out in no time, and made for the hotel dining-room. Now the rain fell in sheets, the lightning flashed, the thunder rolled, and a perfect deluge of large icy hailstones fell without intermission for about ten minutes. The way the hailstones lashed the waters of the Thames was a sight not to be forgotten in a lifetime. We hugged ourselves excessively at having reached shelter in the nick of time, and ate our luncheon with great gusto.

In about an hour the sun came out again, so the attendant baled out and swabbed up our boat with a mop. He told me that two gentlemen were sheltering under a tree, in their punt, when a large bough was struck by lightning and fell, narrowly escaping them.

At Cookham Lock the boat runs up an inclined plane on rollers, and a little trolley running on tram-rails receives the boat, which is then pushed along till you reach another inclined plane, down which the boat glides into the water. We pull leisurely and watch the rats by dozens running along the bank. Then back to Maidenhead Bridge and to Bray, immortalised in song. We pay six shillings for hire of the boat all day.

Home, a jolly wash, and dinner at seven o'clock—boiled fish, roast lamb, roast chicken, blancmange and stewed pears.

Friday 6 August. To Taplow Post Office to draw some money. Money on holiday is a very necessary evil—you will remember the Scotchman 'wha hadna been in Lunnon five minutes before bang went saxpence', and if a Scotchman bangs saxpence in London in five minutes, how much must you bang in Warnham, London and Taplow in, say, seven days?

Then to Taplow Station—two single thirds to Slough—and stroll away to Eton. Eton College from the outside does not appear to be up to what people have led me to expect.

Then we go over the bridge and are in Windsor; the castle certainly stands up quite nobly.

We make friends with a policeman and enter two chapels, then get two tickets at the Lord Chamberlain's stores office. We are conducted through the State apartments—very nice but nothing out of the way. Mill not fancying the climb up the Round Tower, we get make our way to the Windsor Great Park Long Walk.

Beautiful tea in the Bijou Café, then back to station. When we arrive at Taplow Station, we can see there is a bubble and fever of excitement. Three or four flags are hung in the station—a piece of red carpet is laid down.

'What is the matter here, my man?'

'Oh, this is ready for the arrival of the King of Siam. He will be here in a few minutes; he has taken a place here, Taplow Court, for a fortnight.'

Outside was a little detachment of Bucks Hussars forming a guard of honour, three or four policemen bustling about, a few gentlemen waiting to receive the king, a crowd of about two hundred people, at least fifty bicycles, and a few little flags stuck on a fence.

We wait, the time being beguiled by a 'funny' man in front. In every crowd there seems to be a Joe Millery kind of individual, who seems to enliven the dreariness of waiting. We also have a good deal of amusement in watching a Sergeant of Police, who struts about as though he was 'Lord don't know who'—he had a face, well, it was enough to make a cat laugh.

Presently the train steams in, and the King of Siam and several other coffee-coloured individuals, all dressed in black frock-suits and top silk-hats, get into the different carriages in waiting, the Hussars dash off and the whole cortège make their way to Taplow Court, Mr Grenfell's residence.

Then we make our way to our hotel, and see Mr Thos Garrett standing outside. We find he and Mrs Garrett have arrived about an hour: a telegram announcing that they had started from Brighton is waiting for me at the bar.

Saturday 7 August. Take a boat at Bond's and up the river to the Quarry Hotel, Bourne End.

After lunch we proceeded to re-embark, and Mr Garrett lost his balance: the boat careered a good deal, her stern shot away, and he was nearly in the water. He clutched the landing-stage and was at full length, and gradually drew the boat in with his legs, damaging his shins on the gunwale. The waitress rushed down, much frightened, and the boat attendant came up: but we paddled away, glad he had escaped a ducking.

Downstream to Maidenhead Bridge, where we see a tremendous excitement: there are punting races in progress. It is a gay scene—boats, punts and launches everywhere, the ladies' dresses bright and attractive, smart people drinking tea on the lawns, and the banks and bridge lined with people, making a very pretty picture.

Anon three muscular-looking young fellows in punts arrange themselves to start. They are off—the crowd shouts till they disappear round a bend and are lost to view.

Presently they heave in sight again, one leading by about three lengths. Suddenly three cannons fire and the regatta is over.

Then Millie and her mother go home and Mr G. and I walk to find a chemist's shop to buy some Goldbeater's skin for his damaged leg.

Maidenhead is alive with people and traps and bicycles, as numerous as rabbits in a warren.

Sunday 8 August. We all four go in a landau for a ride to Burnham Beeches: exquisitely pretty, drives all through it—Sir Henry's Drive, Duke's Drive and Moat Drive we notice, painted on iron noticeboards—then through the village of Burnham, Bucks, and back to hotel about six o'clock. A beautiful drive.

Monday 9 August. We got up early and packed 'beautifully', Mother says, ready for breakfast. Then Mr and Mrs G. come with us to the station—full of people, and bicycles by the dozen. At 9.7 to the minute the train draws in, and we are off again, sweeping along with that kind of underlying consciousness of strength that I never notice on the London, Brighton & South Coast Railway, by which I gather that these engines of the Great Western are much heavier and more powerful than our company's.

In half an hour we are at Paddington—not a stop anywhere—45 miles an hour. We jump in a hansom and glide along to Victoria Station. Here I purchase some fish for our friends at Warnham; I have it neatly packed in a rush-bag, and then into the train for Horsham, over the South Downs. How grand they are, covered with trees, brake and heather.

'Horsham, Mother, jump up!'

We go over the fields, and just as we come through the last field, we spy Cuthbert coming to meet us.

Alice and I ride up to Warnham Lodge, Sir Henry Harben's, to see a cricket match. Back to tea, and then I start to ride home. It is a beautiful evening and a grand ride. I pedal easily into Brighton and reach my own door exactly at twelve minutes past eight o'clock. Millie and Cuthbert are not home. Jack is, and he barks a welcome and frisks about to show how pleased he is—ah, ''Tis sweet to hear the watchdog's honest bark, bay deep-mouthed welcome as we draw near home, to know one eye will mark our coming and look brighter when we come.'

Presently Millie's cab draws up outside, and we are all home again safe and sound. So one more year's holiday is over—soon the pleasant jaunts of summer will be but a thing of the past—and by and by the traveller lies down to rest for ever. Good night.

Norwich and Warnham

1898

Some time ago we decided that this year we should have to get to Norwich, and that it would be too far to take 'Baby'. Now Baby is between seven and eight months old, so he is over-young to be an eminent traveller.

I set about to find companions, and decided that Tom, Burt and I should go to Norwich together. In the meantime Millie had made arrangements with Ellen and Alice Freeman to go to Warnham with Cuthbert, Reginald and Lily.

Then at almost the last day we hear an alarming rumour. Tom and Burt expect to be called as witnesses in a law case—what is to be done? Nothing definite is known, but at all events they decide to START.

Saturday 23 July. I woke at a quarter to four and, being afraid to trust myself with another forty winks, got up at once. Mounting my machine I rode to the yard and locked my watch and chain and our silver spoons in the safe, and then off to Burt's house. 'Ding-a-ding' tinkled my bell, and then I see at the window Burt's delicate little hand waving.

Off we go and arrive at station. Tom comes along, and at 6.25 our train steams out. At New Cross we change, and arrive at Liverpool Street.

Now we are off through Forest Gate, Manor Park, Ilford, Chadwell Heath, Romford, Harold Wood, Brentwood, Shenfield and Hutton, Ingatestone, Chelmsford, Hatfield Peverel, Witham, Kelvedon, Marks Tey, Colchester, Ardleigh, Manningtree, Bentley, Ipswich, Bramford, Claydon, Needham, Stowmarket, Haughley, Finningham, Mellis, Diss, Burston, Tivetshall, Forncett, Flordon, Swainsthorpe and Norwich Thorpe Station. Putting up our luggage in the cloakroom we jump on our machines and, passing over Foundry Bridge, ride off to Mannering's shop. Saturday is cattle-market day and the streets are full of sheep and cattle, bucolic farmers and drovers by the hundred. We take a wrong turning and get landed in the thick of the cattle—have to walk a bit. Some of the roads are execrable—cobbles and pitchers.

Mannering is not back from dinner, so ride off to his house, Earlham Road. On the way I see Mannering riding down on the 'bus—we ring our bells and give him a shout but I don't think he sees us (although I find afterwards he did). On and find Cis. The house is a corner one and stands on a lot of ground—nice garden in front, double-fronted house, side entrance to house, another side entrance in Caernarvon Road, greenhouse at back, scullery and outhouses, nice little lawn and back garden. The hall is very spacious and the house most conveniently arranged, downstairs dining-room, drawing-room, kitchen and scullery all on one floor—upstairs five bedrooms and a very tiny bathroom all on one floor—staircase rather narrow for the spacious hall and landing upstairs—a very convenient, most airy house, two storeys high. In fact all the houses seem but two storeys high except the hotels. Rent £40. Taxes very heavy, double what they are in Brighton.

Then out to the Great Eastern Hotel. We engage a large bedroom containing one double and one single bed.

Sunday 24 July. Ride down river towing-path. Tom starts a watercolour sketch, then on again till we get to Wroxham Bridge. Here was a large boat-builder's and boat-letter's shop, so we spoke to Mr Press, the owner.

He was a short, stoutly built man of about 53 and seemed a good sort. He showed us the interior of a pleasure wherry we could hire—£8 a week, or 30 shillings day.

We took her for two days. He supplies two men for crew: we victual them.

Then off to Cromer. Splendid roads the bulk of the way, but a little loose in two places. Arriving at Cromer, which is springing up into some repute as a watering place, we ran on asphalted roads to the sea-front. The pier was washed away a little while ago, so the town is at present pier-less.

Burt seemed a little off coming back. When we got to the city proper we found it so full of people that we had to keep dismounting, in fact I walked the last 500 yards. People utterly disregard your bell and get in your way terribly, yet there are a lot of cyclists about and several cycle-shops.

Monday 25 July. Rail to Wroxham and to our noble craft. When we arrive, the owner's daughters are getting our stores aboard—a mountain of beef weighing 10 pounds, four loaves of bread, a pound of tea, sugar, two pounds of butter, tin Nestlé's milk, potatoes, salt, pepper, mustard, one dozen lemonade, one dozen soda, one dozen Bass, one bottle of whisky, two great chunks of bacon, 18 eggs. Are we going for a year's cruise, I wonder? Anyway stores cost about 34 shillings. We step on board, hoist sail with a two-handled winch, cast off and away we sail with a little jolly-boat about 8 feet long towing along merrily behind.

What a sail ours is when hoisted! I take it to be 40 feet high by about 25 feet wide. Our craft is named the *Alma*, owned by Mr Press, a noted builder in Norfolk. She is 54 feet long and about 12 feet wide. In her bow is a deck about 9 feet long, with seats furnished with red plush velvet cushions on which we lounge round the mast, then the roof of the cabins, with a deck each side about 16 inches wide, then a half-deck and well at the stern in which one man stands and steers and works the sail which is like a black tarpaulin. The mast is pitch pine about 12 by 12 where it is stepped into the tabernacle, and about 45 feet high, weighted at the foot with an enormous piece of iron which just balances it to lower it if necessary under a bridge.

Tom sketching in
the fore of the
Alma on the
Wensum July 25/98
HP

About half-way along deck are the companion-ways facing each other. Descending you enter the saloon which is about 5 feet 9 high, 9 feet wide. At the stern end is a sliding panel through which the cook hands in the hot things at mealtimes. There are five shelves with holes in which the glasses slip—hooks on which the jugs hang—looking-glass, clothes-brush, chair, two beds, then two lounges upholstered in red plush pile velvet, a table of varnished pitch pine with two extending leaves, four cupboards of varnished pitch pine (two each side), then the companion-ways—sliding windows all round, with chintz curtains, the ceilings covered with a kind of felt striped red and violet, floor covered with linoleum, a rug, and lockers all round under the beds and lounges—then a partition with sliding door, covered with thin oil-cloth imitation cane-work pattern.

Passing through the door on your right is a nice WC with two handles to pump water in and out; on your left an enclosed lavatory basin (into which you pump the water with a beer-pull handle), hanging mirror, velvet frame, wire sponge-rack, soap-dish and toothbrush-rack, three towels. Then another sliding door. Passing through this door you enter another cabin about 9 feet long by 9 feet wide, 5 feet 5 high, fitted with open cupboard, three shelves, two beds, mirror in oak frame, large washing basin with enclosed cupboard under with two doors, rug and linoleum, two brass candle-brackets, beer-pull for water, soap rack, glass bottle and tumbler, sliding window with curtains. Passing up the companion-way and walking aft you get to the men's cabin. It is a snug little hole, fitted with a beautiful little galley range on which our cooking is done. Here the men sleep.

As soon as we are fairly under weigh we have a bottle of beer apiece and the crew attack their stone jar of beer. Unfortunately wind and tide are dead against us, and it really pains us to see one of our crew pushing for dear life with a long quant. These quants are about 24 feet long, thus

Sticking this into the bank or bottom, the man places the truck end against his shoulder and presses all his might and walks aft—very fatiguing.

Our skipper is a study—a rather tall, rather gaunt man of 68—as hard as nails, sailed this river for over fifty years, knows every crook and turn and is a freshwater sailor every inch of him—dirty, I confess, but a good honest simple sailorman and a steersman that it would be hard to beat.

Our other hand is a man about forty, a good chap and not at all a bad cook. But we like the skipper best, and among ourselves we call him 'the old 'un and bold 'un'.

Plodding along we seem a long way off Acle—but patience is a virtue, and at last about 6.30 we reach our destination. There had been a regatta all day at Acle and what a sight the boats are; moored along each bank there are 150 to 200 craft, dressed with flags and gay with people. There is a steam-organ, swing-boats, shooting-galleries and cocoa-nut or coker-nut shies, all the constituents of an old-fashioned country fair.

We walk to the village of Acle about 1½ miles to get a twopenny cake of soap—then back and aboard. The cook has gone to the fair, so we invite the skipper down into our cabin, fill up our pipes and our whiskies, and sit and yarn till past eleven.

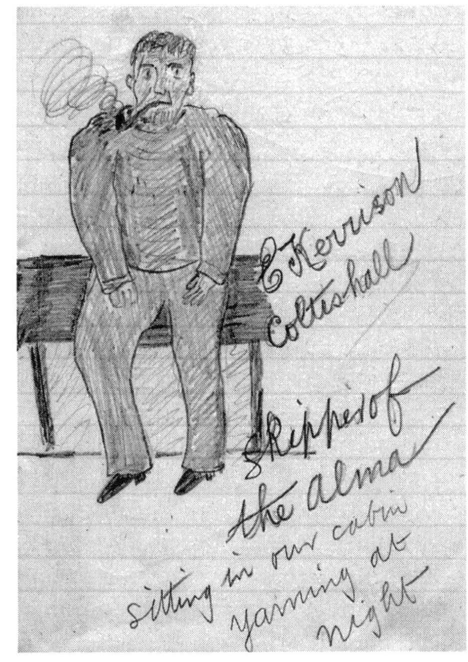

C Kerrison
Coltishall
Skipper of
the Alma
sitting in our cabin
yarning at
night

Tuesday 26 July. I wake at four and peep out—the river reflecting every detail of the craft on her bosom. I get in the jolly-boat and have a row, then

undress and plunge into the river—much warmer than I expected.

Then we quant off, and the cook and I hoist the sail with the winch—very hard work. After bit the skipper lets Burt take the tiller, then Tom has a turn, and then I get quite a long spell at the helm. This is jolly. We are getting quite nautical men.

Behind us the black towering sail of a wherry bowling along, at our right hand the enormous white sails and dainty spars of a yacht, and every now and then an inlet to a little broad, or a dyke, or an eel-fisher's hut, and wherever you cast your eye you can see half-a-dozen windmills; without a windmill no Norfolk landscape is complete. Then a pleasure-steamer, the *Pride of the Yare*, a very ugly craft, steams round us to give the passengers a chance to see how picturesque a Norfolk wherry is.

We moor on the bank for tea, then cast off and are soon back to our starting-point, Wroxham Bridge. Mr Press comes along and we settle up and tip our crew. The men collar our goods and chattels and it is a very quick march to catch the train.

Back to Great Eastern Hotel, Norwich, and we get our old room, which feels like home to us.

Wednesday 27 July. We ride over Foundry Bridge to Thorpe, then heigho for Yarmouth. It is a new road, made almost entirely straight, quite flat and uninteresting. Large quantity of cows on the marshes—plenty of windmills—once I counted eleven in sight at one time.

Nearing Yarmouth now and paying a halfpenny each we go over a railway bridge and are soon running along the front. We are exceedingly pleased with it—here are very pretty ornamental gardens for promenading and a bandstand. Then there are circular tents on the sands in which *al fresco* concerts are held two or three times a day. Farther on is an aquarium, a large circular bicycle-riding railway and a switchback.

Turning our wheels we wend our way to see some of the old rows—there are hundreds of them, all numbered, narrow, squalid, dirty little courts, lanes or alleys. Then away for Lowestoft, ten miles away.

A man driving a trap seems to pit his horse against us, so we let go a bit, but I must say he held on wonderfully, as we could hear the music of his feet for at least four miles. Then we ease up and by Jove a mile from Lowestoft we hear him coming along again, so we put on a stroke or two and there we are.

On our left, as we go through the older portion of the town, we notice what they call 'scores', very narrow lanes leading down the cliffs to the beach.

Making our way to the fish wharf, we are staggered to see the number of masts—it is a forest. In a large arm of the harbour lie the fishing-boats; they are moored tier upon tier, bow on to the quay, packed so closely that scarcely a bit of water was visible. Boat upon boat appeared to be fitting out to go to sea.

Then round to the pleasure part of the town. The low lighthouse on the beach near the Ness is the most easterly point of England. It has been recently removed a little farther inland in consequence of the encroachment of the sea. We watch the bridge swing open to let a ship pass through. How beautifully these swing-bridges are adjusted.

Then heigho for Norwich, through Oulton, Somerleyton and St Olaves, and have a gin and ginger beer at a quaint old-world hostelry. We cross the River Waveney—a beautiful sight—then on to Loddon, a very pretty village.

At the hotel we find our letters, and are glad to hear that the lawsuit is now definitely settled not to come on this week.

Thursday 28 July. To Ely to look at the cathedral. The exterior is the most beautiful I have ever seen, very similar in style to the Houses of Parliament. Here is a grand view over a very flat country.

Then mount our machines and steer for Cambridge, distant sixteen English statute miles. Passing through the outskirts of Ely we pass several lots of chicken, roaming with the usual reckless stupidity of the British hen. I said, 'Who is going to kill this chicken?' as I saw one rather more foolish than the rest, but we managed to steer through—then we were amongst another lot, and one was fleeing to and fro, first across my front wheel and then Burt's. Suddenly it turned round to clear Burt, and darted under my front wheel headlong—bump, I was over him with my front wheel, bump again harder with my back wheel. I was very sorry, as I am afraid he was mortally hurt. I did not look round, but Burt and Tom said he just managed to pick himself up, very much damaged. There were a lot of men standing about, so I hope they killed it.

Now it begins to rain. We see a beer house, but it is such a poor poverty-stricken house that we push on and in a few minutes sight another. We go for all we are worth, and dash up just as it begins to rain in earnest.

There was only an old woman at home, and we asked her if we could have a bit of dinner. 'Oi ant got anny then,' she said in very broad dialect.

'Well,' we said, 'there wouldn't be time to kill and cook a fowl, would there?'

She did not seem to fall in with that.

'Well, cook us some eggs then.'

She went to shift a large saucepan in which she was boiling some potatoes, when off came the handle, over went the pot, and the old lady carried on right and left. We cleared out into the little quaint old tap-room, and we could hear her crooning and grumbling away to herself.

After a while she brought in our eggs and bread and butter and gin and ginger beers. We fell to. Then we tried ringing the bull for a bit, and went into the kitchen to see the old lady feed two little pigs with milk.

Then we envelop ourselves in macintoshes, and in this order we enter Cambridge over greasy and slippery roads.

We push on to the station. Here we essay to put up at an hotel, but the lad we accost gives us to understand they object to cyclists. Much disgusted, we turn off sharply and go a little way back to the Great Northern Hotel, where we find most excellent quarters.

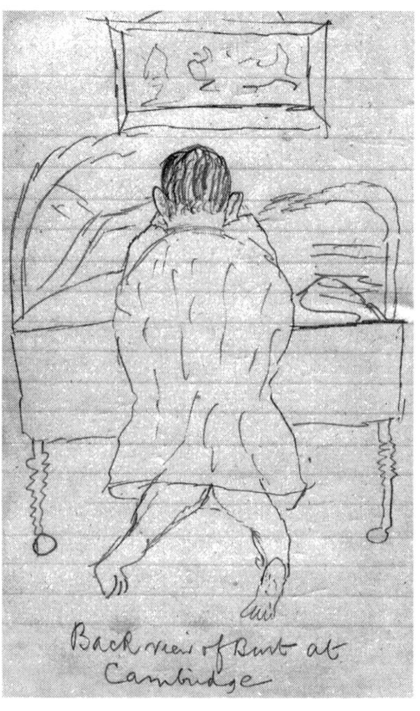

Calling in at the post office we are astonished to find a letter from our young lady Miss Kent, the waitress at Great Eastern Hotel, Norwich, saying that in taking our hotel bill out of a £5 note she had given us £1 too much change.

Tom is sure she only gave him £3; she says she gave him £4. We spend the next hour in thinking over and jotting down all our expenses and then add up our monies, and somehow it does seem as if Tom has £1 too much, and yet we can't understand it, and so we speculate and discuss, always unable to come to any definite understanding.

Friday 29 July. Braving the elements we put on our macintoshes, and a pretty sketch we look. My two chums find an old chap who is desirous of guiding us round the colleges, so we fix him at once and away we go. Trinity and St John's and King's are the best.

Trinity Chapel is very fine. In the cloisters at Trinity is a most curious echo—there is a door with a knocker one end of the cloister, standing opposite to this at the extreme end you stamp your foot on a flagstone and you would swear the knocker moved and knocked twice. The flowers in the quads are beautiful—every window with a box full of flowers in full bloom.

A strange thing in three or four principal streets is a stream of water running down the channel alongside the curb. Our guide tells us that formerly the colleges used to have dip-wells, from which the water was dipped out for washing etc.

When colleges begin to pall upon us, we pay our guide and go on alone. Outside the Fitzwilliam Museum we are deeply disappointed to find that on Fridays the public are never admitted, it being reserved for university students and their friends.

Then we catch the 2.35 to Liverpool Street. Away, away, with a roar and a rattle, the iron monster speeds on its way.

Nearing London we pass Cheshunt, and are astounded at the miles of glasshouses where they raise tomatoes etc. for the London market. From Liverpool Street to New Cross, then we catch a train for New Croydon, where we intend to put up for the night and ride in on our machines tomorrow.

Arriving at Croydon the weather seems so cheerless that we decide to rail on home tonight. So Tom and Burt take tickets for Brighton and I for Three Bridges and catch a train directly.

At Three Bridges I mount my machine and away. I fall in with a bicyclist bound for Worthing, and we ride together. He tells me he once rode last year 135 miles in one day, during which he drank fourteen pints of tea. About half a mile out of Warnham I meet Harry Freeman just come to meet me, my telegram having only been delivered about ten minutes. In a few minutes I arrive and am welcomed by my bonnie little Millie who looks blooming, Ellen, Cuthbert and Baby, and very soon Alice and Fred come in from a bicycle ride. Then supper, and then Millie and I go for a delightful stroll together—like old courtship days.

Saturday 30 July. Fred and I ride on our machines into Horsham and back to deliver a telegram. After dinner the house generally melts into laziness and sleep.

Sunday 31 July. All except Ellen go to church. The afternoon is spent in rest, and all keep to the house till about 8.15 when Millie and I go up to call on Mrs Massey. Millie plays while Nellie sings, and I am presented with several of Nellie's paintings to pass judgement on. Mrs Massey is full of fun and frolic as usual.

Monday 1 August. A perfect English summer morning. I take off Millie's gear-case which Saturday evening had given us some considerable trouble as the chain ground and squeaked against it in a most distressing manner.

At 10.30 Alice, Fred, Mill and I started for Guildford, some nineteen miles distant, and putting up at a temperance hotel have a cold dinner.

Then we are off again for Dorking. The first place we stop at is Shere. We particularly wished to come here as Millie's mother was either born here or lived here as a girl, and always waxes enthusiastic over Shere and the neighbourhood. It is certainly very pretty. Here we taste a kind of chalybeate water like Tunbridge Wells.

Then on, and after descending the worst hill I ever saw and pushing up another the other side almost as steep, we land in Dorking. There are so many people that we turn at once homeward. We pull up at a confectioner's for four sodas-and-milk, and a funny thing happens. I came out to see if the machines were all safe, and as I stood there the proprietor came and shook hands and said, 'I used to go to school with you at Pyemont's, Mr Peerless.' I recognised him then, and looking over the door saw his name, Jones. He tells me his grandfather left him the house and business, and two or three other houses up to the next corner. He tells me he's getting on all right, only unfortunately he is still single. I think this is a thing he might easily remedy.

Tuesday 2 August. Millie and I start on our machines for Brighton. We have arranged for our luggage to be delivered to St James's Avenue, and Lily, Cuthbert, Reginald and the mail-cart to come by rail.

Millie and I career along together like birds on the wing, to Henfield and on till we get to Dale Hill. From the Plough we find a strong head wind is blowing this side of the Clayton Hills. Clouds of dust till we get to Patcham—then there is a little more shelter, and we spin into Brighton gaily and arrive home all safe soon after 1.30 p.m.

We are eating *al fresco* when Lily and our two sons arrive, and then we are all home again—thankful for the kind providence that has guided us out and home without the slightest mishap.

Ireland

1899

Saturday 22 July. Soon after four o'clock I had a cold bath, then off to the station. We were in time to receive Tom and Fanny; soon after Mr and Mrs Garrett came up, and then away for London. At Victoria we chartered one cab for the lot, five inside and Mr G. on the box. On the way our horse slipped down, and Mr G. jumped down and examined the horse's knees—not cut a bit—so off again and arrived safely at Euston Station, the London & North Western Railway Company.

At one minute past eleven o'clock the train starts—on through Willesden, Wembley, Harrow, Pinner, Bushey, Watford, Kings Langley, Boxmoor, Berkhamsted, Tring, Cheddington, Leighton, Bletchley, Wolverton, Castlethorpe, Roade, Weedon, Welton, Rugby, Brinklow, Shilton, Bulkington, Nuneaton, Atherstone, Polesworth, Tamworth, Lichfield, Armitage, Rugeley, Colwich, Milford & Brocton, Stafford, Great Bridgeford, Norton Bridge, Standon Bridge, Whitmore, Madeley, Betley Road, Crewe, Chester, Flint, Rhyl, Llanddulas, Llysfaen, Colwyn, Llandudno Junction, Conway, Penmaenmawr, Llanfairfechan, Aber, Bangor, Menai, Llanfair, Gaerwen, Bodorgan, Ty Croes, Valley and Holyhead.

Just after Stafford we hear the dining-room attendant come along the corridor; he stops at our door and says, 'Party of six for luncheon,' and up we start, eager for the fray. We follow our guide and squeeze ourselves into a compartment with a natty little table down the middle. Salmon mayonnaise, cold lamb, then cheese and biscuits. We feel very nice after this little collation, then the three lords of the creation indulge in the pipe of peace.

At Holyhead we jump aboard our boat, a powerfully built paddle-steamer with triple engines of no less than 4,075 horsepower. She is very high out of the water and gives one the idea of being built for rough weather.

We go up on deck and muffle ourselves in overcoats and cloaks. We are disgusted with one young fellow who is an arrant fool, he looked like a warmed-up corpse, suddenly he was sick to windward and it blew all over a gentleman standing by—the most filthy sight I ever witnessed.

Several children are sick by now and the mop is busy.

At sunset we see the lighthouse, and enter Dublin Harbour. A friendly sailor having volunteered his services, we load him with part of our baggage and make our way down divers steps, under subterranean passages etc. till we emerge into the street.

Here is a crowd of Irish jaunting-cars. We charter two, and are soon being tooled along over the vilest road of granite setts you ever saw. We stop at a swing-bridge while a ship passes through, then off again into crowds of people and scores of jaunting-cars till we draw up at the Royal Exchange Hotel, Parliament Street.

Sunday 23 July. Breakfast of salmon cutlets followed by bacon and eggs. After this we sally forth to Dublin Castle at the top of our street. While we stood here the guard was relieved by soldiers in Scotch uniforms, kilts etc. and black busbies with tails—a very pretty sight.

Leaving here we cross the river and see Guinness' noted brewery—an enormous place—and we soon after enter Phoenix Park, at the western extremity of the city, where the Lord Lieutenant lives in summer. The first object that attracts notice is the Wellington Memorial, built of Wicklow granite, 200 feet high, costing £20,000.

After a long stroll we make our way to the adjoining zoological gardens. What interests us most is an enormous elephant to whom we throw pennies. He searches for it with his trunk and then hands it to the attendant, who gives him a biscuit in exchange.

Later we go to Sackville Street. Here is one of the most busy scenes I have ever seen—crowds of people and at least twelve to fourteen tram-cars in sight at one time. People crush and push to get on them. In Sackville Street is a high monument to Nelson—closed today, but we shall go up it another time.

After several unsuccessful essays we succeed in getting on a tram going to Donnybrook. Everyone has heard of Donnybrook Fair which is held here.

On the way there is some excitement caused by a disagreement between our conductor and a man who persists in going on top against his orders. At last he lets him go up but stops the tram in a minute and sends a policeman up to bring him down—I don't quite understand what it is all about.

At Donnybrook we come back again directly. These trams are electric, driven from overhead wires against which a long arm from the top of the tram just touches the underside.

We go on to look at Christ Church Cathedral, and back through the most poverty-stricken tumbledown alleys I have ever seen.

Now, what is the impression of Dublin? I think it has some extremely fine buildings, but that they are spoiled by the squalid surroundings; there are many terrible rookeries about.—

That the service of trams is an excellent one.—
That the soldiers are very much in evidence.—
That the jaunting-cars are very numerous and very nice.—
They drive recklessly.—
All the horses are good.—
That Sackville Street is a fine street.—
That the police are a grand body of men and we notice that they all carry their truncheons outside.—
That the Royal Irish Constabulary are very smart.—
That we have never seen so many people barefooted in the streets—seven children out of ten have neither shoes or stockings and very few any head covering.—
That the Liffey is dirty; that at low tide it lets you know it is there if nature has provided you with a nose.—
That all the roads are laid with granite setts.—
That many of the jaunting-cars have pneumatic tyres.—
That some of the tyres have balls of India-rubber all round, thus—

That the majority of the people are poor and rough-looking.

Monday 24 July. To Kingsbridge Station; caught the 9.15 a.m. train. At Mallow we change, and at last reach Killarney at 3.15.

We passed scores of little Irish cabins: thatched roof, and sides of mud and stones. Very few had chimneys, generally one little window only, and all looked much the worse for wear. We kept passing also peat, dug and cut into little briquettes, and stacked up for drying before being burnt. A good many cows and goats.

When we get to the Palace Hotel they only have two decent rooms, so Mill and I go up the street to another hotel called the Park Place, and fix a room just for the night. After dinner we take a wagonette to Ross Castle, and get our first view of Lough Leane. The sun was shining brilliantly, and the green-clad hills made it a superb picture.

Tuesday 25 July. Down to the Palace Hotel for our first drive: through pretty scenery till we reach the Gap of Dunloe. The cars do not go beyond here, and the journey is continued on ponies.

Here between the mountains are wonderful echoes, which are awakened by peasants with bugles and by the discharge of small cannons. When we get off our ponies we pay one shilling each, enter the demesne of Mr Herbert, and pass on to the lake and boats. Here we find our luncheon sent up by the hotel boat.

As we get along it gets considerably rough, but we get ashore all right at Ross Castle. Our coaches and cars meet us, and home we go.

Wednesday 26 July. Away to the Abbey of Muckross, then on through the most beautiful scenery: yet even while sunshine is at its best, every now and then there is a misty fall of rain from the mountains.

The view from Torc Cascade is certainly one of the finest in Ireland.

Descending, we are accosted by two old Irish crones and I have a drop of potheen filled up with milk which is delicious.

After lunch, three or four of us stroll down to a cricket match but it is a slow affair. They are bowled and caught out, one after the other, with monotonous regularity. Then they lose the ball and about ten of them poke about all over the field, and when it is found they decide to leave off, so we stroll back to dinner. Being Mr Garrett's birthday he stands a bottle of champagne—'May his shadow never grow less.'

After dinner we gain access to a nunnery; it is recreation time, and about ten of them sit outdoors knitting lace.

Note: on the way up our street I regret to say my coat caught in a nail sticking out of a barrel on the pavement and gave it an ugly tear—a new coat, too.

Thursday 27 July. Stroll through the Earl of Kenmare's demesne, then to the station and get in the train for Cork. Our stopping-place, Golding's, is an old mansion containing very large high-pitched rooms. We have a large drawing-room to ourselves and dine privately together. Then we rush off and take train to Queenstown.

Directly the train starts, a man in the carriage with a fiddle starts playing and singing—very unpleasant. We let him finish one song, but when he begins another we really cannot stand it so we ask him to be good enough to leave off, and Tom gives him a penny. This seems to incense the fiddler, as he throws the money on the floor and gets out at the next station.

We arrive at Queenstown and are much taken with it.

Going to the steamboat pier we take tickets for Cork—one of the most extensive harbours in the United Kingdom, and large enough to afford shelter for the whole British Navy. We stop at several piers till we come to a place called Passage and enter the station: without exception the most filthy hole I have ever seen, worse than a cattle-shed.

Off to Cork, and home to a dinner in which fowls form a very important part. Then we go out and ride on electric trams all over the place.

These trams have been in use about four months and are the best I have ever seen. They run incessantly and the fare is only a penny, and people patronise them wonderfully. They are driven by overhead trolley system, and a splendid idea also is this—the standards which carry the overhead wires are utilised for the street-lamp electric lights. The only place at present in the United Kingdom. It is really a perfect system, and they carry twenty inside and twenty-four outside.

Friday 28 July. Off to the Cork and Muskerry Station in Western Road—six return tickets to Blarney. This is a light railway and runs through the streets and out on the country road.

Blarney Castle is a very old ruin to which threepence admission is charged. Here is the celebrated Blarney Stone, which to him who kisses it imparts such a power of persuasion that he becomes irresistible. Hence the expression 'soft blarney speeches now'. The real stone is now enclosed in iron bars, and as it is about eight feet down the outside of the castle wall it is impossible to get a good kiss at it, so we kiss it through our sticks.

When we get back to Blarney Station we start weighing ourselves, and the following is the result:

Mr Garrett	12 stones	11 lbs
Mrs ditto	8 —	7 —
Tom	10 —	9 —
H.H. Peerless	9 —	12 —
Millie	10 —	1 —

Fanny happens to have strayed away. We find her at last, but then she absolutely refuses to be weighed. We entreat, beseech and threaten, but to no purpose. She comes away unweighed. This is a striking example of the truth of the following lines:

A man's a fool who strives by force or skill
To stem the current of a woman's will,
For when she will, she will you may depend on't
And when she WON'T, she WON'T, so there's an end on't.

Then home and luncheon. After this we go along a filthy quay to see the steamers, and get alongside the *Innisfallen*, a large boat carrying cargo and passengers. Her crane is working like mad, hauling in and lowering huge packages of cases, all going like clockwork and yet done at very high pressure—you can see it is a race against time. Now that is the last, and almost before it has been slung, the labourers are hauling in the platform, the donkey engine is hauling in the cable, and with a discordant screech she has started.

After dinner, go for a stroll to a place called the Mardyke—here is a bandstand, but the stream that runs alongside, from which I presume the place takes its name, smells stagnant.

Saturday 29 July. We took train to Passage and then caught the steamer to Queenstown. One of the islands in the harbour is Haulbowline, on which large quantities of stores are kept for both naval and military. Spike Island is used also by the Government. The scenery is beautiful.

Arriving at Queenstown we toil up to the Roman Catholic Cathedral, a grand building, not really finished yet. The interior is beautiful but the lighted candles at the different shrines seem distasteful to me, as do the confessional boxes.

Then home and to lunch, and at 3.30 p.m. we leave for Dublin. It is so hot and so dusty and dirty that by the time we reach Dublin we are covered with smuts and dust from head to foot.

Piling all the luggage on a jaunting-car, we send Millie and Fanny to take care of it, and we other four walk to our old hotel, the Royal Exchange, Parliament Street. Dinner came very welcome to us, and we did pretty fair homage to the drink, as the heat had given us all an immense thirst.

Sunday 30 July. We take a tram for Douglas, fivepence each, one of the grandest rides you can imagine, through Merrion, Booterstown, Blackrock, Monkstown, Kingstown and then our destination Dalkey. Then back on the tram.

After dinner we all go to St Patrick's Cathedral (Protestant), a grand pile, then away to Phoenix Park. We have a definite objective this afternoon, our destination being the spot where the ill-fated Lord Frederick Cavendish and Mr Burke were cruelly murdered on the evening of 6 May 1882 by the gang of Invincibles.

At last we come to the very spot—here two rude crosses are cut in the turf, and a filthy crew of poverty-stricken men, boys and old crones try to sell relics to passers-by. I forgot to mention that just before we reached the spot where the murder was committed, we came across a herd of graceful stags and deer.

After tea, out again to the Roman Catholic Cathedral in Marlboro Street off Sackville Street. On the wall outside is a font of holy water, and a constant stream of men and women go to it, take off their hats, dip in their fingers and cross themselves with it, and pass on.

Monday 31 July. Walk to Sackville Street. Tom goes to the post office to enquire for letters, and then he buys a fishing-rod for Sidney, then down to the harbour and embark on our steamer the *Violet*, the self-same boat that brought us over.

Bells ring as we pass the fog-shrouded lighthouse, and fog-horns hoot from the opposite pier, and we proceed cautiously on our way. Lookouts in the bow strain with all their eyes, and five officers are on the bridge, and we seem to be feeling our way along.

Now one of the officers from the bridge runs forward and consults the lookout. Boom, boom from guns on our starboard quarter—hoot, hoot, from somewhere else.

At intervals I go below and consult the dial in the engine-room and look at the steam-gauge. Once I see the dial at 'stand by', and we hoot with renewed vigour. 'The fog is thickening, then,' says a friend we have picked up, who has been an engineer on shipboard himself. But all goes well, and the dial is shifted to 'full ahead'.

Now we hear the ding, ding of the bell at Holyhead Harbour, and we creep along till we are in our berth, safe and sound. Small boys on the quay shout 'Hurrah!' and now the gangway is lowered, and grasping my bag I get off fourth or fifth and fly to a carriage and secure a smoking compartment to just hold six.

At about 2.50 p.m. we start, and perhaps we go to sleep. How is it that ninety-nine out of a hundred people, after lying back with closed eyes and nodding heads for half an hour, when you say 'What a nice sleep you have had,' look at you and say, 'I haven't been to sleep, I never can sleep in the train'?

On, on, and we say, 'After all, this England of ours is a fair countree.'

At 8.45 p.m. we run into Euston, then crowd into a four-wheeler with 'yours truly' on the box.

How bright and gay London looks tonight. I have a confidential talk with the driver, and he lets me into his views on privileged railway cabs, also the little rankling sores that exist between licensed drivers and the powers that be at Scotland Yard, also narratives of bilking, also he discusses with keen disgust the growing habits of rich Americans to patronise 'buses and underground instead of cabs—he also shows me his two-and-elevenpenny watch which keeps as good time as one costing £20. We also discuss different methods of road-making, and at last arrive at Victoria Station.

We reach Brighton with the exchequer getting rather low. Goodbyes all round, and jumping into three cabs we part at last. Safe home—hurrah. Not a scratch after a round of at least 1,400 miles. 'God save Ireland' is our last cry—and goodbye.

The New Forest

1900

Saturday 30 June. Millie, Cuthbert, Reginald and Mr and Mrs Garrett left Brighton Station at 10.15 a.m. for Lyndhurst Road. I understand that when they arrived it was raining.

As they knew no other address, they drove first to the Fox and Hounds Hotel. The children seemed to be a slight obstacle, but it was agreed they should stay that night and see afterward what should be done.

After Millie was gone I had the pleasure of dining with my father at Portland Street, and then he and I returned to the office and finished the June quarter's bills, and the bonds were riven and I was free.

It was about six o'clock when I made my way home to 12 St James's Avenue.

It is a dismal feeling to enter a house where there is always a loving greeting for you, only to find it empty: but Jack the dog overwhelmed me with caresses and gambols, and I bustled about to get my tea and supper combined.

On looking at the state of the commissariat I found that it was somewhat depleted, so I sallied forth and bought four eggs and a quarter-pound of the best Dorset butter, and soon had a good meal.

Sunday 1 July. At 1.30 a.m. I was awake, and at 2.20 came a ring at the front door, and I found a policeman had come to call me up. He had been sent by the electric-light extinguisher of the street-lamps, whom I had asked to call me, but he not being on duty had sent the policeman instead.

'Bobby' said it was a dirty morning and a high sea running—not very promising for me.

I packed sandwiches and two bottles of milk in a cardboard box and strapped it on my machine, and at 3.10 was ready. Just as I opened the front door came another ring. This was the electric-light man come to call me. He was too late, however, having overlaid nearly an hour.

At 3.15 I was off, right along Western Road on the wood and up Sackville Road, Hove. Here a train happened to be passing over, and the engine-driver and fireman leant over and gave me a hearty cheer.

Along Upper Shoreham Road to the old bridge. The white-haired custodian was nodding asleep in his box, but a few sharp peals on the bell roused him and he hobbled over the rails, opened the gates and let me through.

All well to Sompting, where I have to ease up behind 44 cows going to be milked.

About three or four miles east of Arundel I commence driving rabbits, sometimes single spies and sometimes in battalions. They flee before my irresistible advance till I almost reach the town. I pelter into Arundel, a city of the dead, at 5.25, and dismount at the Norfolk Hotel to push up the hilly street.

Into Chichester at 7.14, and now milkmen begin to be in evidence. A strong wind takes all the life out of my machine.

Havant is reached at 8.24, and now people are all up and about.

On again to Burlesdon Bridge over the River Hamble. I enter the inn and have a glass of milk with an egg beaten up and a glass of port in it.

In saddle again and grind merrily away, till the tall spire of Lyndhurst Church is in sight, and then to the Fox and Hounds Hotel—safe and sound after covering say 72 miles at 1.10 p.m. I find my people just commencing luncheon, and I do my fair share of execution on chicken and ham, roast beef, salad, peas, potatoes, cherry tart, cream, butter, cheese, and a brandy-and-soda.

The weather is dull and stormy, and we rest all the afternoon.

Monday 2 July. Grandpa and I mount our machines and ride to the station. When we get our newspapers at the railway book-stall we are horrified to read of the terrible catastrophe at Hoboken, New York, by fire destroying docks, steamers, and awful loss of life. Thank God we and ours are safe. Truly we know not what a day may bring forth. One minute the cordial greeting of friends, the jocund song—then a spark, a column of smoke, the hellish tongues of fire lick up, men turned to fiends, discipline lost, manhood disfigured—alas!

It rains all the afternoon, and about seven Mr G., Cuthbert and I go for a walk into the forest—then on comes the rain again.

Tuesday 3 July. Mr G. and I get on our machines and ride to Cadnam, then to Castle Malwood, Stoney Cross where we walk to the famed RUFUS STONE, planted on the exact spot where the oak tree stood from which the arrow shot by Sir Walter Tyrrel glanced and killed King William Rufus. Then ride back, change and dinner.

At two o'clock a wagonette comes round and away we go in grand style for Beaulieu (pronounced Bewley locally) and Lord Montagu's modern mansion, adapted from the old abbot's lodging. On by Hatchet Pond, Lady Cross Lodge Woods and Brockenhurst Station—a beautiful road home.

Wednesday 4 July. Mr G., Millie and I have a grand ride to Brockenhurst Station, then over the moor watching the rabbits.

Thursday 5 July. A wagonette appears as per order, and away to Boldrewood. Very fine trees here—two large hoary-headed giant oak trees are called the King and Queen. Then to the Knightwood Oak, fenced round and said to be the largest tree in the forest; I should think it was about nine feet in diameter. Then through Gritnam Woods by Miss Braddon the novelist's house, and home.

Dinner at seven o'clock—roast ducks most beautiful—in fact they have really loaded our table at every meal—and here it may be as well to tell you that we are still staying.

As I said before, at first they did not jump at the idea of having children about, but when it came to definitely saying 'stay' or 'go', I fancy the thought of turning trade away hurt them, so they came and held a palaver with us all, and it was finally decided we were to stay at an inclusive charge of six shillings per day for each of the four adults, and the children thrown in for nothing, a very liberal and satisfactory settlement.

Friday 6 July. Mr G. and I mount our cycles and ride gaily away for Lymington. This pleasant town of nearly 5,000 inhabitants at one time had a reputation for yacht-building, but this industry seems at present to be in a state of suspended animation.

Saturday 7 July. Just as the clock struck five, Cuthbert and I got out of our respective beds, crept out of the hotel and made our way along the Beaulieu Road to see the rabbits. The other morning we counted 121—this morning we saw perhaps double that number.

Breakfast despatched, we wait about to see if Fanny and Tom would run down here for the Saturday to Monday. No letter, so Mr G. and I ride to Lyndhurst Road Station and telegraph to Tom, asking him to wire reply; then back to hotel, where we find telegram saying they are not coming.

Dinner, and then is the Fox and Hounds lively, with two motor-car loads from Bournemouth, and after that five or six brakes which called here this morning call on their way back to Southampton. After they have gone appears the New Forest Brass Band which plays outside the hotel.

Sunday 8 July. A glorious bright morning. Children objected to going to church, and not only that, but objected to anyone else going, so we went for a beautiful walk instead.

Monday 9 July. This morning the shadow of the end is creeping on us. We have all been very happy here—the landscape is so lovely that he must be a misanthrope who did not feel his heart lifted up and say: 'Oh come out in the garden my love, for spring is at hand, and the sound of the turtle is heard in the land.'

A most enjoyable ride to Romsey. In the market-place is a fine statue to Lord Palmerston. At Romsey is also Strong's Brewery Co. Ltd; they must own an enormous number of public houses, as for miles and miles every public house seems to have up

STRONG'S ROMSEY ALES.

In the market-place Mr G. and I had an amusing little *contretemps*. As he stood close to the Palmerston statue, holding his machine, he let it overbalance and went over with it, sitting down on the hind wheel. I should not record this, only if Millie and I should live another thirty years and we should still have this book, if we should happen to come across it and read this passage, we should say: 'You remember that day when Father fell over his machine at Romsey.'

Well, we have a nice ride back, and at two o'clock our wagonette draws up and we have our last drive—away to Burley, and back by Wilverley Post and Markway Bridge.

To the Knoll, and Cuthbert and I go away over the heathery common to see some of the finest rabbits I have ever seen. Then homeward we trudge, when lo I see a lady cyclist and say to Cuthbert, 'Surely that's your mother,' and I see a hand go up and wave. I say, 'What's on now?'

'Oh,' she says, 'Miss Ings is coming down to try a little ride with me.'

By and by along comes Miss Ings (Mabel), so I run alongside and help her on, and she gets on famously.

Tuesday 10 July. Tears almost at parting: then comes the brougham, and we start for the station. I see everyone safe on the platform of Lyndhurst Road Station, and then mount my machine and hark away, tally-ho, yoicks, hark forward for Brighton.

Now what about the New Forest? Here are a few particulars. At present it may be said to form a triangle some twenty miles long and twelve miles broad.

By the last century, what with neglect, encroachment and the drain of wood to supply both the Royal Navy and the ironwork furnaces that then glowed hereabout, the forest had fallen into great decay, but it has now been to a great extent restored and is carefully administered under the Woods and Forests Department by a deputy surveyor who has his headquarters at Lyndhurst.

The chief woods are oak and beech, besides flourishing plantations of

Scotch firs (a modern innovation). There is a notable absence of elms and willows.

More than a fourth of the original area has come into private hands, by means which perhaps will not bear looking into, but now the Government shows itself vigilant as to its rights.

About a thousand acres are let out on leases. Among the leaseholders is Sir William Vernon Harcourt, whose modern house at Malwood represents the hunting-lodge from which William Rufus went out to his death.

The population of the forest is about 7,000, many of them belonging to the independent class of 'commoners' or small proprietors who contrive to wring a decent livelihood from this grudging soil.

Many gypsies are to be met here, and they have a large winter settlement near Fordingbridge.

Foxes are in sufficient abundance to give good sport, there are otters in the streams, and here and there may be unearthed the rare specimen of the badger. The deer were nearly exterminated by order of the Government in the middle of the century.

Shooting and fishing over the government property is a matter of licence, which costs £20 per annum.

Pigs are turned out at certain seasons to feed on the mast. A shaggy bunch of Forest ponies abounds, and the donkey is ubiquitous. Butterflies are a notable feature, and numbers of people are to be seen trudging along with their nets etc. in pursuit of specimens.

The New Forest fly is a very persevering little member of society.

The forest is a celebrated hunting-ground for the smooth snake, hardly known elsewhere in England. Quite a character is an old native called 'Brusher' or 'Brusher Mills', who does nothing but catch snakes and adders. Up till recently he used to supply them by the dozen to the Zoological Gardens, London.

He is to be seen any time almost slouching through Lyndhurst with a tin can in which he always has some snakes. He poses as a snake-charmer, and the way in which he handles them is a caution.

To sum up, I am prepared to say, without fear of contradiction, that for a quiet holiday which shall improve your health, the New Forest, like Captain Cuttle's watch, 'is ekalled by few and bettered by none.'

Shanklin, Isle of Wight

1901

Friday 2 August. The day breaks gloriously and we are early astir, and at about a quarter to ten I mount my bicycle and ride to the Palace Pier; Millie and Cuthbert walk. Trott takes our luggage on a truck.

Alongside in all her glory lies our boat the *Brighton Queen*, and we trip on board. (Fancy Trott tripping.) What is this stealing over us? It is freedom, which we draw in with the ozonic air.

Just as we have cast off and are under way, Cuthbert tells us that Grandpa Peerless was on the West Pier. Why he did not tell us before, so that we could have come forward and greeted him, is a mystery.

At Worthing Pier I notice Mr Crouch come aboard, and he tells me that he has ordered some teak from us this morning. Then we fall to talking of the fire, and he shows me a handsome gold pencil-case presented to him by a lady and gentleman who were sleeping at the hotel when it caught fire; it had engraved on it '*Presented to Captain Crouch, Worthing, for saving life at a fire on May——*'

It appears he carried the lady downstairs and saved her. Both were singed by flames, and at foot of staircase were overcome by the smoke. The gentleman he put on a balcony and afterwards got him down a ladder.

At Ryde we disembark. Making our way across the pier to the trains, I purchase tickets for Mill and Cuthbert, make my way down the pier wheeling my bicycle, and start for Shanklin. I do not think a prettier ride could be found. In some places the trees overhang the road completely, like the green lanes of Jersey.

I pass through Brading—very pretty—through Sandown, and then reach Shanklin. I see a sign 'Clarendon Mews', and just opposite is my port, the Clarendon Hotel. Millie and Cuthbert have arrived about ten minutes ago, and I am soon with them in the bedroom—very clean. We think we shall be very comfortable.

Saturday 3 August. Jumping up, Cuthbert and I make our way to the Undercliff, and Moorman's Bathing Office. I purchase some tickets and we get into a machine, a horse is hooked to it, and 'Hold tight, sir!' and off we go bumping and shaking over the sands. We are soon undressed and sporting in the beautiful water, in company of about fifty others, ladies and gentlemen, as what is called 'mixed bathing' is practised here.

Now, nothing is more pleasurable than mixed or family bathing, and although an innovation in England, it is a practice that is sure to increase, now the 'ice is once broken'. That any harm can come of it is absurd, as properly carried out mixed bathing is quite decent and moral, and much to be commended.

But if I leave myself in the water all this time while I am preaching on mixed bathing I shall get cold, so running to our machine we rub down and dress. 'Ready to go back, sir? Hold on then.' Splash goes our horse, bump goes Cuthbert's head against the side as we start off. Creak, creak goes the machine, a fearful lurch when we stop, and then we hurry home to breakfast, which we devour with a relish.

After breakfast I telegraph to John about the good ship *Sirius*, and then we take our way up the Upper Chine and away over the glorious downs towards Luccombe Chine and the Landslip—face to face with nature some 700 feet above the sea.

After lunch I go and have my hair cut, always a great resource in hot weather.

Dinner at 7 p.m., and Mother chums up with a Mrs Stark, or Sterk, a young married lady of seven months' standing, staying here with her husband and a large Russian hound (Rex), and a dear little black spaniel (Bounce). As she and Mill are I think 'companions in misfortune', being in what is delicately expressed as an 'interesting condition', they exchange notes and confidences and get on a friendly footing.

Sunday 4 August. Cuthbert and I go for a bathe; quite a rush for machines this morning. Then away we go to church—St Saviour's on the Cliff, a large modern church. It soon fills up, and numbers have to go away as there is no room left.

Monday 5 August. Bank holiday. To the Isle of Wight county cricket ground to see some bicycle sports and running races. We get very cold sitting about, and before it is over we start for home. Put Cuthbert to bed, and Millie and I go for a quiet stroll down to the green, where we listen to a troupe of singers. They have a pitch illuminated with about a dozen Japanese lanterns, and about a hundred chairs for which they charge a penny each person.

Tuesday 6 August. Letter from Mr Garrett this morning. Sorry to hear Burt and Maude's twins are still very ill.

I get a paper and find Empress Frederick is dead. Then we walk to the Chine, pay threepence each and enter. It is a very pretty sight—bold rocky chasms covered with ferns, and a tiny waterfall meandering down.

After lunch we seek pastures new on the road to America Woods, and eventually retrace our steps and enter Shanklin by the gasworks.

Back to dinner at 7 p.m. I am able to see the time by my watch again, as on Saturday at 11.25 p.m. its spring broke. Sunday of course I could not get it repaired, Monday was bank holiday, but I found a jeweller and watchmaker's open and left it to be ready Tuesday at six o'clock, and now I have it. What a comfort it is—to be without a watch in a strange place is very trying.

Wednesday 7 August. I get out my machine to ride to St Helen's. No country could look prettier. Through Brading (here is an old lock-up containing the old stocks), I push on to St Helen's and get there just as Millie and Cuthbert are toiling up the hill out of the station. Then we commence our walk to Seaview.

A friendly native tells us we had better go across the fields, so lifting the bicycle over a gate, away we go through turnip-fields, corn and clover. Cuthbert gambols along with his ball, and opens the gates for us as we pass from field to field. At last we go down a steep rough hill and get on the sands.

Here is a sight indeed—hundreds of people sitting, strolling, playing cricket. On the left are rows of bathing-tents, two and three deep, crowded with people dressing and undressing, ladies and gentlemen, boys and girls, running, swimming and attempting to swim, others boating—a bright scene of life and gaiety.

Making our way along the sands, we see jutting out a thousand feet into the sea an ugly suspension pier, looking like a cousin of the old chain-pier at Brighton—a poor-looking structure. Along comes a crowded steamer and disembarks a lot of people.

Cuthbert and I paddle for some time. Then a lovely walk back to St Helen's, where I leave Millie and her first-born, and mounting my machine reach home about twenty minutes before they do.

Thursday 8 August. After breakfast we decide what to do for the day. I want to go 'round the island' on the SS *Cambria*, but Cuthbert seems afraid of being sick, so it is decided that I am to go alone. Parting from them at the pier gates, I pay my penny and march to the end.

From the fort belches out flame and smoke; far out to sea, where the shell strikes, the water leaps up, and then comes the report to our ears—boom-oom-oom.

Anon we cast loose, and away we go. At West Cowes I was struck by the number of American yachts; Vanderbilt's was one, supposed to be the most costly yacht in the world. Then away on the home stretch, a glorious run of say 66 miles—three shillings all the way.

Friday 9 August. Stroll to Old Shanklin Church, extremely pretty, then back to lunch. After that is despatched, we hurry down to the pier to meet *Brighton Queen*, for we expect Millie's father and mother. She runs alongside full of people, and for a time I give them up, when Cuthbert says, 'There's Grandpa and Grandma!' and there they were.

Saturday 10 August. At ten to ten, Mr and Mrs G. and I might have been seen making our way up the hilly High Street to the post office, outside which a keen observer would have seen us climb up to the top of the four-horse coach *Island Queen.*

There were only eight of us: on the box seat, what we conjectured was a newly married young couple—then Mr and Mrs G. and I—then two ladies and one gentleman. Ta-ra-tu-tu-tut-ta goes the horn, let them go, and away we crawl up a steep hill for I should say nearly two miles, then downhill, and so we go on, most difficult work for cattle.

At Ventnor we are surprised to see how large the Consumption Hospital is. On through the beautiful Undercliff till we get to Blackgang, where we shut out for 1½ hours. Mrs G. buys a walking-stick for Cuthbert, and tells us they have a large skeleton of a whale in the bazaar.

Now our horses are led out and shut in, and off we go to Carisbrooke. After a steep climb to the castle, we make our way to the well-house. Here is a strongly framed wooden wheel to draw up the water. The attendant addresses a donkey, and tells him to get inside the wheel; this he does in a very intelligent manner, and immediately begins walking for dear life, like on a treadmill. Round goes the wheel, and up comes the bucket filled with water.

Then doth the man lower the lighted candle down the well until it reacheth the surface of the water, and the visitors peer down into the depths thereof, and they do see the tiny light flickering a long way down.

Then doth an elderly female woman ask, 'Is the well straight, because it looks as though it goes this way?'

And the attendant gravely answers, 'It is as straight as they could get it, madam.'

Now round comes the coach, the guard makes the welkin ring with his horn, and away we clatter. Six miles from home it comes on to rain. Up go umbrellas, rugs are pulled up, and for four or five miles it patters down.

Presently a brilliantly defined rainbow appeared, stretching over the sky as we cantered along. Soon after we pull up and dismount, having covered 32 miles through beautiful country.

Sunday 11 August. As Cuthbert and I jump out of bed this morning, 11 August 1901, it is borne to our minds that our days of careless ease are nearly over, so we must meet our fate like men. While these thoughts are running through our heads we dress and go down for our last bathe. How fond one gets of the ever-restless sea—the element which as a child one dreads.

After breakfast we all stroll along the high cliffs towards Sandown, and scan with anxious eyes through the field-glasses to catch a sight of the good ship *Sussex Belle* by which we have arranged to return—but it is a fruitless quest.

As we expect John to come down on the *Sussex Belle*, as soon as I have eaten dinner I make my way to the shore, and soon have the satisfaction of seeing John marching down the pier. After a hearty grip, we get on board before the crush. Goodbye, beautiful Shanklin.

Let go the cables, stand by, ding-a-ding, full ahead now, and away we sweep with the methodical beating of the engines below, stemming our way towards the English mainland.

Now do we see a gradual change creep over little Cuthbert's face, and anon I find him sitting in the stern sheets, a solemn little figure. Taking his little cold hand in mine I lead him back to our seat, when suddenly he gives a convulsive heave, and the deck is disfigured with his dinner. Then do I roam the ship to find a man to clear it up.

Then we have a cup of tea.

Then does Millie make signs to me to lead her away, and I guide her to the ship's rail, and she also gives a slight convulsive movement. Then do I see her fingering wildly to detach her veil, and then do I say, 'Throw the veil away,' for I see that as a veil it will never more be useable—then do I see several people move hastily away from her, and I lead her back to her seat.

Then does she consume a brandy-and-soda, and becomes once more in her right mind.

Then does Worthing appear, and soon the battle day is past, and we are once more ashore.

Here we find Grandpa Peerless on the pier steps to welcome us and Mrs Lindo, Miss Percy and Arty. Kindly hands help us with our luggage, and I struggle with my bicycle down an unearthly length of pier, through a crowd of people. You would never realise how long the Palace Pier is without you carried a heavy portmanteau or tried to steer a bicycle through a crowd of people on it.

Thank goodness that's over, and they are in a cab and I on my machine. A few minutes and we are safe inside no. 12 St James's Avenue, drinking a drop of the 'crather', and toasting to 'our next holiday'—and now goodbye.

The English Lakes

1903

Saturday 20 June. For some days we have been in negotiation with Messrs T. Cook & Son, tourist agents, respecting a tour to the English Lakes, and yesterday we received the tickets. This morning we caught the 7.30 train for London Bridge and, chartering three hansoms, dashed pell-mell through the Borough, blocked with market-gardeners' wagons and strewn with cabbage-leaves.

Our driver then begins a system of short-cuts which I think in the end prove much longer. Passing through a very narrow street blocked at the other end by a brewer's dray, our 'Jehu' essays to pass. First we collide on the near side against the wheel of the dray, and backing out we try again and knock our off wheel against a post; but the brewer's car-man, now taking hold of our off wheel spokes, guides us through, down we come with a bump—slash goes the whip, and away we bound and dash up to St Pancras with a minute and a half to spare.

Burt and Maude were already there, and at the last moment in rushed Tom and Fanny. We were bundled in separate carriages, our luggage hurled in after us and away we went—too much of a hurry to be pleasant. We communicated with each other by the corridor.

At Chesterfield we notice a curious twisted spire to the church—quaint but not pretty. At Hellifield Junction, Maude and Millie complain that the motion of the train has upset them, but they pretty soon recover—brandy-and-soda for Millie. We get another train to Carnforth, change at Ulverston, and get to Windermere (Lakeside) at 5.30.

We were billeted at the Lakeside Hotel. The lawn slopes down to the edge of Lake Windermere. On the opposite side of the lake are rugged mountains rising one above the other, a noble view.

What gives us some surprise is the weather—in a district, mark you, noted as the wettest in England, what do we find? A land dusty and parched; not one drop of rain for the last three weeks. Never has fortune smiled on us more.

Sunday 21 June. The longest day. After borrowing some books of prayer and hymn, we take our way to Finsthwaite Church, a quaint little edifice with the hand of time heavy on it. We have a quiet impressive service, the lessons and prayers read by a patriarch of about eighty with a long white flowing beard, in the best way we have ever heard—every word given the right emphasis, making it an intellectual treat to listen to.

After lunch we charter a rowing-boat and row to Nicholl, where we toil up a mountain. No words can describe the rugged grandeur of the scene. We build a little cairn and place a newspaper in it, as a guide for us to see where we have been.

Then we commence the descent, and Millie occasions some amusement by coming down the steepest part on her hands and a part which shall be unmentionable.

Monday 22 June. 'Boots' takes our luggage and we embark on board SS *Swift*, and steam away up the lake till we reach Ambleside. Here all is hurry, bustle and confusion—buses, coaches and drags by the score. We take the Queen's Hotel bus, the landlady meets us and we are shown to our rooms.

Now off we go on the Round of the Langdales ride—21 miles through such scenery as a southerner never dreams of.

A fine dinner, and then pay threepence each to see the Stock Gill Face. This is a waterfall renowned for its beauty, only it lacks a volume of water through the drought.

Tuesday 23 June. At ten o'clock mount on our drag for ride to Ullswater and back. Leaving Ambleside with six horses we toil up such hills as we never dream of. Most of us have to get down, and for three solid miles we tramp up and up to the Kirkstone Pass, 1,480 feet high. Here is a sign:

KIRKSTONE PASS INN
ANTHONY CHAPMAN
THE
HIGHEST INHABITED HOUSE
IN ENGLAND
1481 FEET ABOVE LEVEL OF SEA.

Passing down the other side, very steep, we soon come in sight of the 'Brothers' Water'. This tarn obtains its name from the fact that on two separate occasions, two brothers were drowned in its waters. We then run along the valley of Deepdale, and drive into the grounds of the Ullswater Hotel, Patterdale. It is most splendidly appointed, and here we lunch.

About a quarter to four we resume our seats on our char-à-banc, through Troutbeck, passing the Mortal Man Inn, and to Ambleside.

Wednesday 24 June. On a coach to Rydal, and then from Grasmere we have to walk up Dunmail Raise. The counties of Cumberland and Westmoreland are divided on the summit of the pass, and we obtain a grand view. Here are pieces of rock which look like a huge organ and a lady playing on it.

We now reach Wythburn Church, reputed the smallest in England, get on to the wall and look inside.

Leaving Wythburn we reach Thirlmere Lake. This has been bought by the Manchester Corporation, and is their chief source of water, is three miles long and just over a quarter of a mile wide. The water is conveyed to Manchester, 95 miles distant, by a series of huge aqueducts. This lake was originally 112 feet deep, but a huge dam 800 feet long has been erected, which has raised the lake considerably, and our driver tells us it is proposed to raise it 17 feet more. The road here has been diverted in several places by the Manchester Corporation, and two new bridges built.

On till we ascend a terribly steep hill, and drive to the Keswick Hotel, close to the railway, with the platform of which it communicates through a long conservatory. It is a palatial place, electric light, lift etc.

Lunch, then we make our way to Derwentwater and hire a boat. There is on this lake a floating island, which occasionally rises to the surface, buoyed up by gas from decomposed vegetable matter.

When we came out of the boat, we discovered it had been making water—it had about three inches deep over the stern floor, and Fanny and Maude got a bit wet. The man said four young fellows had had her off, and they must have damaged her.

Thursday 25 June. I made my way to the Derwentwater, paid fourpence, and a penny each for drawers and two towels, and was soon undressing in a wooden bathing-house, containing twelve dressing-boxes. Walking out on a springboard, I plunged into the water, and had a good swim.

After breakfast we took a char-à-banc for Buttermere and back. We have to get down and walk up a mile and a half up Honister Pass—terribly steep. Arriving at the top, in front of us is Honister Crag, a producer of excellent slates. The quarry employs 100 to 200 men and turns out 300 tons of slates per month. High up in the sky we hear the men working, and a constant shower of waste pieces of slates descends into the pass.

Most of us walk down, and I never saw so steep and rough a descent. The skid was buried, and right over the felloe was sunk into the stones.

Friday 26 June. Got up to find mist rolling over the rugged tops. We take the 9.32 a.m. train, and at Penrith take the Crown 'bus to the Crown Hotel. We find our rooms engaged for us, and at once start on a tour round the town.

First we see the ruins of Penrith Castle, built of red stone—very poor—now used as a nursery garden. Then we meander to the old parish church, and see the giant's tomb—very old stones at head and foot, about 15 feet apart, covered with nearly obliterated Celtic designs.

Then it rains like steam and we get back to hotel. Lunch, and then we walk over Eamont Bridge and on through Lowther Park to the Yeomanry Camp. Wet and woebegone looks the camp, and a dismal overcoated sentry marches to and fro in the rain.

Then back, and we note the Beehive Inn. The sign runs thus:

In this hive we all are busy
Good liquor makes us funny.
If you be dry walk in and try
The virtues of our honey.

When we got back, there there was a telegram waiting for Burt, from Mr Garrett, telling him to see Liverpool.

Saturday 27 June. We paid our bill, and got off on the Cockermouth, Keswick & Penrith Railway. At Hellifield, Tom and I dash out and find the station-master, show him our tickets, and say we wish to go to Liverpool.

He was a nice-looking, rather fine man, upright and well groomed. When we had finished our explanation, with a dignity which became him well he waved a ticket-collector to him, and spake thus:

'These gentlemen are a party of six, and they wish to take Liverpool in their tour, I think it will be all right, but just take down the numbers of their tickets, will you.'

The collector saith unto him in reply, 'Yes sir, of course if they had come from Carlisle they could go and break at Liverpool.'

We pressed a shilling into his responsive hand, and rushed like mad to our carriage—train on the point of starting, and Burt rushing pell-mell down the platform with a bag of buns. All in, and away we go. Hurrah!! We shake hands all round, elated at our success.

On through Chatburn, Langho, Wilpshire and Blackburn.* Here we hear the cry 'All tickets ready please,' and along comes the ticket-collector.

We hand ours up, and he exclaims: 'Well, this is a game. You're going to make a delay. I shall have to take these numbers.' So he gets out a book and laboriously writes them down. We replace the tickets in our pockets, and the train moves on, running into Liverpool Exchange Station at twenty to four.

Here we march out to find the Washington Hotel. Fanny slips down like a ninepin, for the pavements are greasily dirty and there is a slight fall of rain.

*While we were rushing along in the train we suddenly saw something fly by and could not think what it was. Later on we discover it was Millie's ruffle which blew right out of our carriage. We laugh at this. (Author's note.)

I give over my portmanteau to a boy, and Tom gives his to another, and in this order we reach the Washington Hotel, Lime Street, Liverpool, engage our bedrooms and sally forth.

Coming as we have done from a close communion with nature in its loveliest form, the crowds of people, the hurry and drive, the bustle and confusion, the noise of innumerable electric trams, the dirt and the barefooted boys jar on us. The misty rain too damps one, and into my mind come the old words so true: 'God made the country, man made the town.'

Well, we jumped on a tram with a covered top, so that we had a roof to keep off the misty rain, and away to Pier Head. Electric trams in every direction—crowds of people.

Arriving at Pier Head, we went down a covered gangway bridge, to the Prince's Landing-Stage. We saw the *Lucania*, an immense steamer, start for America.

Up Walter Street we file into an underground restaurant—very stuffy indeed—a good many people. Now on to the Town Hall: passing under the archways, we are on the Exchange Flags, in the centre of which is a splendid monument to Nelson by Westmacott. It cost £9,000 and weighs 22 tons.

Then Tom takes counsel of a friendly policeman, and acting on information received from him, we mount a tram in a slight drizzle and traverse many squalid parts of the city.

Returning, we retrace our steps past St George's Hall—outside which is a large crowd being harangued by a demagogue—to Walker Art Gallery. We hear a terrible clatter, rattle and noise, and a fire-engine and escape dash by to a fire.

We wind up the eating for the day with poached eggs on toast, cup of chocolate and ices. I go next door and have my hair cut.

Sunday 28 June. Look all round Lime Street Station, a very fine place, then go and inspect St George's Hall.

This is really a noble building. In it are two assize courts, an immense hall for public meetings, and a fine concert-hall. There are seven miles of pipes beneath the floors, and hot or cold air can be admitted at pleasure. In front of the colonnade are four colossal lions which cost £200 each. Opposite is a monument to Wellington, cast from cannon taken at Waterloo.

Making our way to the landing-stage we saw an immense crowd, and scores of vans and drays carting mail-bags out of the *Etruria*, a very large steamer. Passing on we see the *Cedric*, White Star Liner, just coming in from America. Four gigantic gangways are hauled up with tackle, two at the bow and two at the stern, and they commence to throw over the trunks.

The gangways are very steep, the trunks are pushed on to them from the ship, and the law of gravitation makes them run down very fast; in many cases they run right across the landing-stage. On the landing-stage a sailor stands with a rope fender, which he whips under each trunk to arrest them a little.

On the stage are perhaps a hundred porters with luggage-trucks, and they jump on each box and wheel it away to the Customs. I counted our end of the ship 494 packages.

While this is going on, a gangway has been run over from an elevated stage, level with the deck amidships. A double row of stewards line this gangway, and light articles of luggage are passed from hand to hand for about an hour. When all the luggage has been disembarked, off come the passengers.

After dinner we go by Mersey Railway under the river to New Brighton, then to the pier. We have six plain teas at ninepence each, and make our way to Eggs and Ham Terrace, and thence to the Perch Rock Battery and a most gorgeous sunset. The steamers are leaving for Liverpool packed with people from stem to stern.

After a while we stroll home. On the way we suddenly hear screams and shouts, and see people jump out of a tram-car. A crowd collects, and we hear that a little girl of eight or nine, noticing something wrong on the tram she was on, had jumped off top to the ground. She was picked up very much injured, and we waited about ten minutes till a horse ambulance came up and took her to the hospital. Meanwhile the car stood in darkness, and several more pulled up behind it.

We got back to hotel soon after ten o'clock, to find it religiously shut up. The porter was outside talking to a girl, and he rang the bell and had us admitted into the back saloon—a drink, smoke, a few biscuits, and to bed.

Monday 29 June. We pay our bill, and I go to Owen's, Stanley Road, and have a look round, but I am unable to come to business. Then take overhead electric railway to Canada Dock, Irvin & Sellers; again can't come to business.

We walk to Lord Street and enter a café. Dinner was the worst-served meal I ever had. They had no licence, and sent out for Bass and stout, which did not arrive till we had finished. Then we walked to station.

Before we left we purchased a basket of strawberries, half a pound of caster sugar and a pound of biscuits, and at intervals of ten minutes we serve these round. We have carriage to ourselves all the way.

At Leicester we get six teas handed in, and then have a grand finish of the strawberries.

To St Pancras, and reach Brighton 10.51, after arranging to all go to Scotland next year, if all is well.

Now, a few facts about the English Lakes. One rather strange custom is that farmers, in taking a hill farm, rent flocks of sheep from the landlord.

One thing we thought rather dangerous was that in every drive—and perhaps these drives are the most dangerous and require more skill in manipulating the reins than any other drives in England—there was never but one man, the coachman, who had to do everything—get down many times and put on the skid, leaving the reins in the hands of a passenger who perhaps hardly knew one end of a horse from the other. I think there ought always to be two men sent.

To sum up, I believe there is no better holiday to be had than a run through the English Lakes. The scenery is magnificent, the air is beautiful, and no one can go (if they get fine weather) without coming back reinvigorated by the change of air. We were all charmed.

To turn our attention to Liverpool. First, it has very fine railway facilities—in what is known as the Liverpool district there are no less than 108 stations. The city also boasts the terminal stations of the London & North Western, Cheshire, Midland, Lancashire & Yorkshire. Lime Street Station, Central Station and Exchange Station are very fine.

It has the most perfect system of street electric trams I have ever seen. Universal fare for all or part of the journey is a grand piece of work.

The ferries plying from Liverpool to Birkenhead, Eastham, Egremont, New Ferry, Seacombe and New Brighton, running every five or ten minutes at fares ranging from one penny to fourpence, are cheap, useful and well appointed.

The city has some very fine buildings, notably St George's Hall, Walker Art Gallery, Exchange, Town Hall, Custom House etc., and some very fine theatres.

It possesses several large parks, containing over 800 acres, and over 150 churches and chapels of all creeds.

It struck me as being as great commercial centre for shipping, but like all shipping ports it appears to have a deep lower stratum of squalid poverty. It makes one's heart grieve to see so many barefooted boys running the streets, and one cannot help thinking what they will develop into as they grow up.

I am very pleased to have seen Liverpool, and it has a closer similarity to London than any other place I have ever been in.

Scotland

1904

Friday 17 June. Today Henry Heathfield Peerless and Amelia Sarah his wife caught the 7.30 p.m. train from Brighton, and were conveyed to London Bridge Station. On arrival we chartered a hansom to St Pancras (Midland Railway) Station.

Giving our luggage to a porter, and telling him to reserve us two places third class for Edinburgh in a through-carriage, we wended our way to the refreshment room; Millie had two hard-boiled eggs and one small Bass, and I had three sardines on toast and one small Bass also. I purchased a bag of sandwiches to take with us, and found our porter, with two corner seats secured in a very nice carriage with a lavatory in the compartment.

I despatched my friendly porter for two pillows at a cost of sixpence each. A large number of people came to see friends off, and as at one minute past ten we began to steam out, they gave a parting cheer, and handkerchiefs were waved in farewell.

We begin to settle our pillows, and our two fellow travellers do ditto. The man was about fifty, dark and very bald-headed, and when his wife covered his head in a cloak and he laid down he was rather a sketch. The wife was a rather full-blown specimen.

As we get farther along we pass furnaces belching out flames, which look very pretty indeed.

Saturday 18 June. By now the short night has waned and day is with us, and we rattle along. Hellifield is reached at a quarter to four, and I have a smoke on the platform till we start off again. We finally draw up in Edinburgh (Waverley) Station after a run of 10¾ hours.

We collar our belongings and struggle up hundreds of steps into Princes Street, where we jump in a hansom, and are driven to 39 Melville Street, Nicol's Private Hotel.

We ring the bell and are ushered in, and up comes another cab with a lady and gentleman. We go up a stone staircase with iron balusters and a mahogany handrail to our bedroom (really the ante-drawing-room). They put us here, they say, 'so that we shall be near our friends', they having got into their heads that the people who arrived with us were friends of ours.

After lunch we walk down King's Stables Road, with Edinburgh Castle towering above, to the old part of the town, and enter the Grassmarket, originally the place of public execution and now poor and squalid. Passing on we reach St Giles Church, commonly styled 'the Cathedral'. Close to this a stone in the paving is marked

I.K. 1572

believed to cover the remains of John Knox.

Continuing our way down High Street through extreme poverty and squalor, and meeting dozens of drunken men and very rough characters, and exceedingly dirty barefooted children, we reach the ancient Tron Church, and then to Canongate, passing John Knox's house. All here is poverty, the street having narrow closes or courts each side, from which crowds of dirty neglected unkempt children and frowsy women pour out in shoals. At nearly all the windows they have a wooden pole arrangement projecting, on which they hang out their clothes to dry.

It is marvellous to reflect that these houses years ago were the residences of the flower of Scottish nobility—the mansion of the Dukes of Queensberry is now a house of refuge for the destitute.

We emerge in front of Holyrood Palace and enter. In Queen Mary's bedroom we see her bed and some chairs in the last stages of decay. In this room Darnley, the Queen's husband, murdered Rizzio, the Queen's favourite, and the floor is said still to be bloodstained, but I can't say I saw it myself. Still, it was rather dark just there.

By chance we run against Mr and Mrs Dawson, the lady and gentleman staying at our hotel, who came same time as we this morning.

Sunday 19 June. To breakfast at 9.30.

Imagine us seated around a round table—present Mr Stacey (grey-haired old gentleman from Cardiff), Mrs Stacey (very fine and large), Mr J. de Mont something (a young man, rough hair, from Guernsey, an electrical engineer), Mr C.W. Dawson (partner in a coal company at Great Yarmouth), Mrs Dawson (his wife), myself and Millie. We keep up agreeable conversation while we consume breakfast—then Millie and I sally forth.

Never have I seen so many monuments as this city has erected. Public buildings of noble appearance absolutely abound in all directions.

As the trams pass us, Mill sees one labelled 'circular route', and being mad on circular routes she must and will go, so we mount up top, and have a delightful ride. We dismount at the post office and climb up Calton Hill, opposite the prison (a very large pile). The National Monument on Calton Hill to commemorate the Waterloo heroes was begun but never finished. Twelve gigantic columns rear their heads to heaven and make a striking object—£12,000 was spent here and then the project fell through.

We pave our way back to 1.30 dinner, catching sight on the way of his dusky Highness the Alake of ——, accompanied by a field officer in full uniform and escorted by mounted police, drawing up in a carriage and going into the North British Hotel.

After dinner Mr Dawson and I climb up Arthur's Seat—somewhat of a tug—then Mill and I make our way to Edinburgh Castle. The buildings are principally modern and consist of barracks for about a thousand men. Then down into Princes Street and enter gardens, and here the bald-headed man and his wife who came in our carriage on our journey from London come up and shake hands. They say they are getting on all right, but from what we can gather they have not seen much.

Now Edinburgh strikes me as being:

A fine old city, combining very old parts with very new, the newer portion containing innumerable grand buildings.—

Full of monuments. They put up a monument on the slightest provocation.—

Paved with very hard granite setts on the roads, except Princes Street which is wood.—

There seemed to be an unusual quantity of drunkenness.—

I was much interested in many of the door-handles, all brass, and the enormous brass figures on very many doors, thus

XXXI

in about five-inch figures.

The new streets are very wide indeed. Melville Street where we are staying has a clear space from one row of houses to the other of over a hundred feet.

Monday 20 June. We breakfast early with Mr and Mrs Dawson, and Mr J. de Mont something, the Guernsey man. We are all going to Glasgow.

Our intimacy with Mr and Mrs Dawson is rapidly ripening. We are beginning to feel as if we had known them for years, and have arranged to 'split' a cab to station.

At 9.5 a.m. train starts, and we gaze regretfully at Edinburgh and say farewell. We go via Forth Bridge, and are on tenterhooks to get a view of this famous structure, so that when one of us says 'There, it's in sight,' Mr Dawson jumps up to look out of the window, and, the window being up, knocked his head against the glass and smashed it into atoms.

Now we laugh long and loudly. We shut the window down and no official discovered it.

At Stirling we cross the platform to another train, and proceed to Buchlyvie where we get in our third train. On the way, Mr J. de Mont ——'s portmanteau suddenly falls off the rack, brushing Mill's head and landing on her knees. Another prolonged laugh.

Arriving at Aberfoyle in torrents of rain, our spirits sink to zero. We mount a char-à-banc, seats and rugs wet through, and no cover overhead, and under a forest of umbrellas streaming with water we drive a short distance to Aberfoyle Hotel and a very decent luncheon.

After lunch we mount the char-à-banc again, and I manage to get a dry India-rubber cover for our legs. Much amused with one old American lady who asked the driver about a dozen times for a dry rug; when she sees him coming with one she shouts out: 'Ah! You are a jewel, you are!'

Off we go through grand mountains and titbits of scenery all the way. At Loch Katrine we embark on a small steamer to Stronachlachar, then by coach to Inversnaid on the shores of Loch Lomond, the finest of all the Scotch lakes. On a steamer to Balloch, where we get into a train for Glasgow, which we reach about a quarter to 8 p.m.

Here we shake hands with Mr J. de Mont ——, as he is going to Baikies Hotel. Mr and Mrs Dawson and Mill and I charter a four-wheeler and drive to Hotel Balmoral, 222 Sauchiehall Street, where we find our rooms reserved. We see Glasgow is a very busy place indeed—it has 761,700 inhabitants.

Tuesday 21 June. To George Square, a grand open space full of monuments; I think the Scotch break out in monuments. The centre is the Scott monument, 80 feet; east and west are equestrian bronze statues of Queen Vic and Prince Consort; also statues of James Watt, Sir John Moore (a native of Glasgow), Lord Clyde (also a native), Dr Thos Graham, formerly Master of the Mint, James Oswald MP, Dr David Livingstone, Thos Campbell the poet, Sir Robert Peel, Robert Burns—and a very fine large statue recently erected of W.E. Gladstone MP.

We pass on to Glasgow Cathedral. The stained-glass windows are only forty or fifty years old and not very good.

Coming out, we took the wrong tram, so they let us get off; gratuity to conductor for his civility. On tram to Botanic Gardens—tour through palm houses till they get too hot for us—then to Glasgow Art Gallery and Museum, a most grand pile. Back and to Cook's office, 83 Buchanan Street, to take four tickets at 12*s* 6*d* each for a tour tomorrow.

Wednesday 22 June. On a tram to Broomielaw Glasgow Bridge Quay and on the board the *Lord of the Isles*, a large steamship carrying 1,600 passengers. We steam down the Clyde, by the great shipbuilding-yards, with iron ships being built, and we see them in every stage—some only just laid down, some almost ready to launch, some launched and being fitted in stream—rivets being driven in every direction makes a continual din of hammering and a lively scene. To me, fond of shipping and ship construction, a great treat and a sight I should have been sorry to have missed.

At Dunoon we get on a coach through lovely scenery to Inverchapel. Here we embark on little SS *Fairy Queen*, then on coach to Lochgoilhead and board the SS *Edinburgh Castle*, a dirty boat like a collier. We steam into Loch Long, and at the union of the two lochs, looking back, we get the prettiest picture of the day.

Past Ardentinny, we are brought down from the sublime to the sorrowful by seeing a really handsome man aboard drunk, and taking out a flask and drinking more whisky, so strong that it makes him blink. A little dog coming along, in his maudlin way this young fellow pulls the dog's legs about as he lies on the deck—but to my great satisfaction, after a while the dog resents these liberties, and showed a fine set of teeth, which seemed to tell our young friend to keep his hands off, which he did.

When we stopped at Blairmore, a crowd of women and children came on board, and were certainly not an acquisition—they crowded the boat, and the children raced all under your feet.

We reached Glasgow with the last five miles' stink of the Clyde in our nostrils. I must say it was a bit 'whiffy'.

Thursday 23 June. I get up and write my diary till 7.15 when I rouse the lovely angel that shares my couch, and she rises and makes her 'twilight', over which I shall draw a veil.

I decide not to go out of town today, as I want to see a little more of this busy bustling place. We take a tram and go west to its extremity, Whiteinch—then back on same tram, east to Glasgow Green, the proletarian park of Glasgow. It has in centre a heavy stone column to Nelson.

Then Millie selects a tram ride, and we ride up Cowcaddens Street and Garscube Road and presently land at Possil Park right on the outskirts of Glasgow. The park was merely a rough playground as far as we could see, and Mamma began to think we were stranded.

We followed the tram-lines to try and get back some other route, but finding they ended in a tram depôt for the cars, we retraced our steps to the hotel and supper.

When we had nearly finished, Mr and Mrs D. came in and had their meat tea—they gave a glowing account of the Falls of the Clyde and Tillietudlem Castle.

Then a smoke in the smoke-room with Mr D., who tells me some very strange anecdotes of a haunted house at Norwich, which he knows are true as he was intimately acquainted with the people.

Mother is cross when I get to bed because I have been so long.

Friday 24 June. Quarter day. Catch the 10.5 a.m. from St Enoch Station, detrain at Greenock and on board a nice steamer named *Mercury*. We stop at Colintraive and take on two cows who are very difficult to get aboard.

Now the scenery is magnificent, and as we enter Loch Riddon and steam to Ormidale it is perhaps the sweetest part of the whole route.

At Tigh-na-bruaich, very pretty, we disembark our cows after some violent struggling.

On the return journey the weather looks very threatening. We land at Greenock in pools of water, and take train to our hotel. Entrance strewn with rice; they have just had a wedding.

Pay the bill and say goodbye, and make our way to Queen's Street Station, to catch 8.20 p.m. train for Edinburgh.

As we arrive very early, Mr D. goes in station-master's office and gets them to wire to Edinburgh to reserve us four corner seats. The Hotel Balmoral hall-porter brings our luggage, and we are off.

Arrive at 9.30, and soon gain our other train, and guard labels our carriage RESERVED. A very comfortable corridor carriage.

Having hired four pillows we settle our luggage and then watch a small crowd next door to our compartment, who have come down to see off one of our passengers, a young Scot.

They carry him shoulder-high to the carriage, and when he has kissed the girls all round, and got in, the men keep on shaking hands with him till I think they must pull his arm out of its socket.

Then they sing very nicely a Scotch song, the refrain being 'Will he no come hame agen,' and then join hands in 'Auld lang syne' style.

The train is now on the point of starting, and one girl gets a last hurried kiss. One girl forces through crowd and strokes his face through the forest of hands which now grip him, so hard and so frequently, that two or three men in the train have to hold him up and back.

We have some strawberries all round, which do not seem to agree with Millie as later she goes out in the corridor and is sick out of the window. Then we all get to sleep, waking up at intervals to show our tickets.

Saturday 25 June. At about five to eight o'clock we run into St Pancras. Hearty goodbyes to Mr and Mrs Dawson, and then I go and have a wash and brush-up, twopence.

After that we charter a hansom to Victoria Station. A little way on, the India-rubber tyre comes out of the iron bed on the wheel rim, so cabbie says he's very sorry but we must shift into another hansom which draws up alongside us. 'Bad job for me, sir, too, as it's my first job this morning.'

I give him threepence for a drink, and we get in the other cab and arrive at Victoria Station, put our luggage in cloakroom, and have our boots cleaned. Then on 'bus to Earls Court.

Arrive soon after ten, to find it does not open till twelve o'clock. Take another 'bus and go for a ride, and then it rains in torrents. Of course my hat must blow off in the mud.

Sit down in Westminster Cemetery, and at 12.1 o'clock enter Earls Court. Being early, the place has a deserted appearance: but we start the round and get on very nicely. Millie is much taken with the electric staircase up which we are both taken. Then we go and see the airship in full swing, and fairly revel in the sight of the Canadian Chute. Mill says she has never seen this before, and laughs so much at one old gentleman in the front that I thought she would burst herself.

We listen to the Lancers Band 21st (Empress of India's) in the Imperial Court, then a tour through the Italian Village, then listen to band of HM Grenadier Guards in Western Gardens. Mamma has another pennyworth of electric staircase elevator, then a last look at chute and out on to a 'bus to Hyde Park Corner.

Get off 'bus here in a block caused by a demonstration marching into park—walk down to Victoria Station. Tea at Aerated Bread Company just outside station, then a vain search for a shop to buy a doll, and into the 5.45 p.m. train for Brighton, which we reach at 7.45 p.m., jump in a cab and away for home.

Pull up at a toyshop in St James's Street and Millie jumps out to buy a doll, and while she is gone, I see Reggie and Cuthbert come up and Baby on other side with Harriett, shouting out, 'Papa! Papa!! Papa in 'e cab!!!'

Millie jumps in, and Reggie and Cuthbert, and away we go again and reach home at last safe and sound.

We have been on foot, rail, coach, steamer and tram about 1,115 miles, and now we must settle down again into everyday life—but although our holiday for 1904 is over, the remembrance of the grand old Scottish hills, and the placid lakes, and rushing rivulets, and hurrying dashing waterfalls, will long remain engraven on our memories.

Naples

1905

Friday 24 February. Thomas Garrett senior, Mr W.C. Bartlett, his son Mr E.C. Bartlett and myself had agreed to meet at Brighton Station at 7.15 a.m.

I got up about four o'clock. Trott called for my portmanteau, and Millie and I started to walk to the station.

Arriving, I found I had utterly forgotten my field-glasses, so took advantage of Mr G.'s offer to let their man drive to St James's Avenue and get them. It seemed a sporting chance whether there was time or not.

Messrs Bartlett then came up and we took our seats in the carriage. Millie waited outside carriage, and Burt undertook to run the glasses up the platform if they came in time.

We were already in motion when he dashed up with them, and we clutched them through the window. Goodbye, goodbye.

All the way to London it was lowering and foggy, and on arrival at Victoria it looked like night—dark, and all the lights alight.

We went by underground railway to King's Cross, and then on foot to St Pancras, and at 10.55 our train started for Tilbury Docks. It was a dreary marshy expanse of country we passed through, misty and miserable.

At last we pulled up at Tilbury Docks and passed across to our ship—the RMS *Ophir*, 6,814 tons, bound from London to Australia. We are booked to Marseilles. I went up to see the purser, who turned up his book and found I was to have no. 60 berth. My cabin-mate is a sergeant in the Royal Garrison Artillery, going out to Colombo.

After dinner we went up to the smoking-room, and had just settled down when we heard a long grinding noise.

I thought it was a heavy packing-case bumping down from deck to deck, but on running out I found we were in collision with a ship and anchor. We had smashed a boat which we were carrying on davits, the strong teak rail was smashed in two or three places, and the stairs leading to the first saloon deck had been pushed out of the upright.

Every precaution was at once taken; the watertight doors were lowered, and the first officer came rushing on the scene to inspect the damage.

On again, and the next incident was a wreck we saw on the Goodwins—two masts pointing dumbly to the sky and telling perhaps of valuable lives lost. Rather encouraging for the beginning of a voyage.

At six o'clock we sat down to a very good high tea—haricot mutton and mashed potatoes, beef and salad, toast, bread, butter, jam, marmalade and good tea. We are seated at the centre table, and these seats we are to retain all the voyage.

After tea we go up on deck and find it dark. Ship now moving much faster. She is a large boat, and is certified to carry:

1st-class passengers	334
2nd " "	136
Steerage	197
Crew	270
	937

After a while, cards are suggested. We try to buy a pack, but are told they are all under seal (something to do with the Customs officers) until arrival at Plymouth, when—that being the last port she touches in English waters—the Customs take off their seal and they can sell them.

We were half-inclined to wait up and see Brighton lights, but while we were cogitating eleven o'clock came, and out went the lights on decks and in saloons, so we went to our respective cabins.

I found my cabin-mate in his top bunk reading a new book on gunnery, so I undressed, leaving on my two pants and two vests, and crept into my little cradle, switched off the electric light and laid down. Somewhat disturbed by someone partly drunk in a cabin not far off.

Saturday 25 February. A beautiful morning. I roamed all over the ship and watched the sailors pouring water from a hose copiously over the decks and companion-ways. They seem very strong on water-cleaning aboard.

At eight o'clock sat down to oatmeal porridge, haddock, roast mutton, toast, bread, butter and tea. Then I wrote to Millie and sent off several postcards of the *Ophir*, posting them at the post office.

We now had a panoramic view of the brown ragged esoteric cliffs of Devonshire; we glided in by the breakwater and hived off to Plymouth. Here we saw an ugly three-funnelled man-of-war, the *Cornwall.* A tanker soon came alongside bringing local newspapers, letters, parcels etc.

Close to us lay the New Zealand shipping company's fine steamer, the *Turakina.* Mr B. and I devoted a little time to studying the Lascars or Coolies who were shifting packages. They are rather picturesque as they shuffle along, with a cloth like a red petticoat to just below the knees, and a piece of cloth roughly thrown over their shoulders. They seem a stunted race, very puny in appearance and devoid of any male dignity. All the dirty jobs in the ship appear to fall to their lot.

Soon after 2.30 a tender brought out a sprinkle of passengers and luggage. The ship's doctor stood at the gangway and scrutinised each passenger with eagle eye; one man who had a terrible rash on his face he stopped, and told him to come to his dispensary to be examined.

We waited and waited then till nearly five o'clock, when the Great Western Railway tender the *Smeaton* brought the last lot of passengers, and soon we were steaming out alongside the breakwater.

We had a good high tea, and Mr Bartlett gave us his ideas on the different orators in Parliament.

During this time the sea had been rising, and none of us seemed to want any dinner. Mr G. said it really seemed too soon to be eating again, and I said: 'Let's go and get some fresh air.'

When we got up, the wind was much fresher, and they were making provision—covering tarpaulins over hatches and wedging them in for a dirty night. Mr G. tried to interest brother Bartlett in looking for the Lizard light, but he said he didn't care where the Lizard was. Between ourselves he was looking very queer.

I was feeling doubtful of myself too, and turned in. Directly I got in my cabin the floor went all over the shop, and I brought up all the food I had in my body. Crept into bed, after I had rung for the steward.

She was now rolling heavily, and people were retching and groaning all round and children crying.

Sunday 26 February. I woke very queer, got out to dress, and was soon stretched on the floor bringing up bile. The Bay of Biscay was now a wild mass of heavy waves, off which the wind swept the tops in spray, and the ship rolled terribly.

During the morning I found Mr G. stretched on the floor being sick, and Mr Bartlett in bed feeling very queer. Ship rolling violently, and breaking china nearly every time. Only about eight show in to tea.

She rolled heavily during the whole night, and the water was running down the companion-ways and washing about the decks and the saloons and cabins.

Monday 27 February. Up about a quarter to seven, and it was a subdued party we were, and a very limp party, and a party aching at the pits of our stomachs.

I went below and asked for a biscuit and started eating it, but coming across the saloon with half of it in my hand, and the floor running with water, she gave a violent lurch, and sent me sliding down to port-side where I fell under some chairs. A steward helped me up and said, 'You hurt, sir? My G——, you might have broken your arm.'

Yesterday one of our passengers fell in the same place and cut his fingers and made them bleed, and another fell and sprained his hand.

I went in to breakfast in fear and trembling that I should do something dirty. I started on oatmeal, and had eaten about three parts of it when I felt queer, slipped out to my cabin and brought it all up.

The sea is now calming down a little, and we are just able to sight land. This gradually looms plainer as we pass Cape Finisterre. We watch several steamers pitching, tossing, staggering, rolling on their way.

I go into saloon and write up to date in this book, and now I am going on deck at 5.15 p.m. and will let you know what I see there. . . .

I go up and find Mr G. and we sit and watch the waves. We are now off Portugal.

At seven o'clock p.m., I smoke my first pipe for 48 hours.

At 10.45 ship time I find my Sergeant in his bunk reading his gunnery book, so I undress entirely and only wear a night-shirt as it is now warmer.

'Are you ready for me to put out the light, Sergeant?'

'Ready whenever you like.'

'Right.' And then I lie down, and fall a-thinking of the girl I left behind me. In my mind's eye I can see Mum's dear old face, and the familiar old room, and perhaps she is handling Wilfred David now—good night, dear wife.

The bed vibrates, and you can hear the steady thump of the engines as they thrust us irresistibly on our way. Other eyes are watching, other hands are working, other brains are thinking for the ship and me.

Tuesday 28 February. With confidence we troop down to breakfast and have a good feed—oatmeal, Yarmouth bloater, toast, rolls, brown bread, white bread, beautiful butter and good tea. There are also steaks, sausages, beef, mutton etc.

We are now just off the River Tagus, on which Lisbon lies—can see the mouth of the river but not Lisbon, although we think through the glasses we can just see some of the towers.

At twelve o'clock the following notice is posted:

SS *Ophir*
Lat. 37.52 N
Long. 9.20 W
Distance run 321 miles
Feby 28/05.

Watch deck quoits and then change for high tea.

We expect to be at Gibraltar very early in the morning. We have on board 58 shipwrights and engineers, who are going out under the Admiralty for five years at Gibraltar to repair ships of the Navy, and we shall lose them tomorrow.

I had a chat with the sailor who has charge of our deck this afternoon, and he says we have 126 Lascars aboard for stokers: three shifts of forty each, and six to cook for them, as they would sooner starve than eat anything prepared by a white man or one who is not of their caste. They are in charge of a head man called the '*serang*'.

I looked at the engines today, and they seemed quite strange; there were two vertical cylinders continually bobbing up and down.

After tea we get our postcards ready to post at Gibraltar tomorrow morning, and now one of the sergeants has just set up a gramophone in the saloon.

Wednesday 1 March. At six o'clock I and a few others are on deck as we glide in the Bay of Gibraltar and gaze up at the renowned Rock. We had breakfast specially early, and at nine o'clock we boarded the tender *Margaret of Gibraltar* and steamed away about 600 yards at two shillings return for the King's Stairs, Gibraltar. Here is a beautiful harbour, crowded with warships and torpedo-boats, coal-hulks etc.

At the stairs we disembarked and, led by Sergeant Sizer, we proceeded to the post office and I cabled home.

Now Mr Bartlett happened to know a Major Cooper stationed here so he went to find him, and presently we met him, and the Major suggested we should have two cabs and view the new works at the harbour.

He explained that the whole Rock is absolutely pierced with the best and newest guns possible to acquire. Numerous caverns and galleries extending two or three miles in length, and wide enough for carriages, have been cut in the solid rock, with portholes every twelve yards, and more than a thousand guns are mounted. The place is full of soldiers and barracks.

The money that has been spent here is fabulous, and they are spending millions more on the new docks, capable of accommodating in dry dock vessels that may be built of increased sizes for the next twenty years.

We happened to be here on a red-letter day for the Rock, for the Major had us driven to where we could see a gigantic battleship, the *King Edward VII*, glide into a maiden dock, one of three new ones under construction. A crowd watched the entry. Various guns were also firing at target practice.

We began to be a little nervous about time, as the good ship *Ophir* casts off at eleven o'clock and will wait for no man. However, we trust the Major, and nothing will do but we must go to his barracks and have a drink. So we nine troop in and an orderly rushes off for whiskies etc., and we pledge our host, and then our cabs drive like the d——l, and land us at the quay with two or three minutes in hand.

The Major comes on board with us and has another whisky, and then we say goodbye heartily. He has been stationed here fifteen years, and is I believe genuinely pleased to see us.

Mr G. throws him one of his cards as he sits below us in his tender but it falls in the water, and then Mr G. throws another. He gets the second one, and the men recover the first from the water, and we see the Major carefully drying it with his handkerchief. Then I throw him my card which he catches, as we understand he wishes to put a paragraph in the Gibraltar papers regarding our visit.

Now soon after eleven o'clock we sheer off—goodbye, hats waving, handkerchiefs fluttering, and in bright sunshine we glide away.

As an Englishman I am proud and deeply gratified to have set foot on such a memorable spot as Gibraltar. Here, surrounded by continental countries, we hold one little bit against the world—the key to the Mediterranean and an everlasting monument of England's greatness. THEY WILL NEVER TAKE IT FROM OUR BULLDOGS NOW. Then on deck and a cup of beef-tea and biscuits.

As we have lost the 58 passengers at Gibraltar, the chief steward has given Mr G. and me a cabin to ourselves, so we have all our things shifted into it. Supper, and then promenade deck and smoke, and now we pass Cape Nega or Negat.

Great fun with an inoffensive gent who has brought a book on board and runs all over the place showing people. Bartlett, Sergeant and the sailor George, our deck-hand, enter into a little conspiracy and try and bamboozle him; Bartlett goes round and gets passenger after passenger to go up and ask him questions about it and they keep him very busy with the book, and we go off at intervals into dark corners and explode with laughter and still he does not smell a rat.

Thursday 2 March. There is no doubt that for utter change and rest one ought to go for a sea cruise. As a passenger, mark you—a sailor's life is a dog's life. No set hours, and exposed to tempest, boiling heat and deadly cold. But we passengers—why, we are simply lazy. We eat, drink, sleep, smoke, and forget what the date is, and don't care a cuss generally.

I got up about 6.30, without waking my father-in-law, and found a steward who made me a bath, then went on deck. The little man with his book is already at it again.

The coast of Spain is still in view and very mountainous.

After dinner I see a notice stuck on the board: 'There will be a tug-of-war on the second saloon deck at three o'clock.'

Mr G. is the starter and judge. They have three pulls, one side winning two.

There was considerable discussion afterwards, each side appearing to have many excuses and recriminations, but all very good-natured.

I go to our cabin and write a letter to my wife—what a world of meaning is conveyed in those four letters! The mystical union of two human beings, to cherish and comfort each other in this life. Love . . . and by a singular coincidence this is also a word of four letters. My advice to a married man can be summed up in three words: love your wife.

I could preach a sermon on this theme, but while writing I heard the sudden loud ringing of a bell, and thought, 'Hullo! What's up?' I got outside, and see stewards hurrying up the stairs with cork jackets on.

'What's up, eh!'

'Oh, only fire- and boat-drill.'

This is a weekly fixture; at a given signal—the bell—each man goes to his post. Some go to the hydrants, others get the hoses out, others go to the watertight doors, others take provisions to the boats, others stand by the boats to lower away. All done like clockwork.

Then I make a tour of the ship and look in at the engine-room doors, the washing-up department, the bakers' ovens, etc. Here it is like a busy hive of bees, all at work. Lascars carrying water etc. Some Lascars begrimed with coal-dust and wet with perspiration come up off duty from the stokehold.

Mr G. has just come upstairs, and I find during fire-drill he was shut in the saloon a prisoner, as the watertight doors were put down and he was caught in a trap.

Have my hair cut, and then on deck watching dancing. Lightning appears at intervals, and it is cooler.

Friday 3 March. Woke up feeling very queer. The ship is now rolling a great deal; we are in the Gulf of Lyon, and it is nearly as bad as the Bay of Biscay.

A cup of beef-tea helps me to feel better, and I go on deck. We pass a lighthouse and enter Marseilles roadsteads. Along comes the tug-boat tugging another boat containing the pilot. They cleverly run under our stern and alongside our lea, the pilot hops aboard, and off we go.

We enter the harbour, then off come tenders etc., but it is now 4.30, and we are to sail at six o'clock, so we decide it would be useless to go ashore. We remain on deck and watch the bumboats alongside.

There are eight boats, laden with shawls, lace, clouds, opera-glasses, postcards, knives etc. They carry two or three men and nearly all one young woman.

They hold on with a boat-hook to the ship and then begin to trade with our passengers. The salesman or saleswoman has a long bamboo rod, on the end of which a bag is tied. When they make a sale, they put the goods in the bag and hand them up, and the purchaser takes out the goods and puts the money in the bag. Their charges seemed subject to considerable reduction if the purchaser bargained.

Through the glasses we can see the cathedral, and electric trams just like ours running along the front.

Started at 24 minutes to eight out of harbour. George recounts interesting scraps of information respecting sailors' discharges, the bad ways of the old crimps who a few years ago used to victimise poor Jack ashore.

Then as I sleep top, I say good night and Mr G. gives me ten minutes' law and I get to bed. Mr G. then comes down and retires.

'Good night.'

'Good night, sir.'

I lie and picture Mum's face. Good night Millie dear, God bless you.

Saturday 4 March. Steward brought us tea in cabin, then on deck: and now a curious thing happens. They suddenly swing the ship right round and we describe a circle. On enquiry we find they do this to test the compasses.

Watch the isle of Elba where the great Napoleon was imprisoned—a mountainous wild rugged sterile island.

Now we are in the Tuscan Archipelago. Porpoises sporting around. Mr G. has gone to have his hair cut.

We expect to get to Naples fairly early tomorrow morning. Notice exhibited that all letters for Naples must be posted by 10 p.m.

We agree that we are sorry to have to leave the ship tomorrow, also many of the passengers with whom we have become friendly.

Sunday 5 March. Up at six o'clock, and on deck. We were entering the Bay of Naples, and Mount Vesuvius looked grand in the distance. The summit was covered with snow, and dense smoke belched forth.

We had a good breakfast, and then in a babel of confusion got into a tender. We were swarmed all round by dirty crowd of villains who tried to sell things to us, begging, etc. The ship was crowded round with boats and it was all confusion.

On landing we were immediately surrounded by crowds of touts and beggars who almost took us by storm. We fought our way to the Customs and got our luggage passed, after some difficulty with some of Bartlett junior's cigars which they demanded duty on, but after his refusing to pay and saying they could keep the cigars, they gave them over.

We chartered a cab to Hotel Continental, unloaded and entered. Then out to the aquarium—a terribly dark dismal-looking place—and for a long walk along south-west of bay. We are much struck by the general air of dilapidation on all sides; it looks like a fine old place, letting its buildings decay for lack of repair. Electric tram back to hotel.

Never in my life have I heard such a noise as the people made during dinner, to which about sixty sat down. Each one seemed to be trying to out-talk the other, a game in which the ladies seemed to be very proficient. But the ladies' voices seemed to me hoarse and strident. Upstairs, and early to bed.

Monday 6 March. Breakfast and then to Cook's office, very busy with clients. Find a very nice young fellow and work out the route home. Mr G. and I cashed a letter of credit each and we all paid up—very pleased indeed with the way the man put it through. Then in train to Pompeii.

Arriving there we are besieged by guides, touts, beggars etc., but push our way on. Pay 2.50 each and go in. The money here is lira; 2 lire 50 centimes = say two shillings.

It is a subject for deep thought, this city of the dead; here are its roads and houses which once teemed with life, the streets worn by chariot wheels, the stone fountains worn where they held on to drink, the lead pipes still there; brothels, baths, temples and the street of tombs. We have a thorough examination, being taken in hand by official guide after official guide, and handed on from one to the other.

Some of the paintings on the walls were very quaint, and the subjects would probably shock the ladies of today. We experience considerable difficulty in finding our way out, as it is like a maze, all the streets alike. We bring away several pieces of lava and stone and some of the original mosaic stones of a floor.

Then to station. After punching our tickets, the ticket-collector comes back and says: 'Train be a two hours a late'—what!

Then up come an American and two ladies: 'I say, sir, can you tell ME, THIS man says the TRAIN will be two hours LATE, SAY can you understand it?'

Well, after a bit of a palaver the ticket-collector says that if we walk to the next station we can get a train at seven o'clock.

'How far is it?'

'Half-past one a kilometre,' he replied.

Well, we four and the three Americans got out of the station and were at once besieged by frantic cab-drivers and touts to drive us to the next station.

Well, of course I don't really know, but I honestly believe that it was a conspiracy hatched between the ticket-collector and the cab-drivers to get us out of the station and then bleed us for cab-fares. To defeat this we decide on principle to walk.

The cabs follow us a considerable distance, but drop off disgusted at last, and except for boys anxious to guide us we go on unmolested.

The sunset was gorgeous. Arrive at next station, one of the dismallest dirtiest places you can conceive, and wait. At last the train comes and we get a spacious first-class carriage.

Watch Vesuvius' fiery glowing top and reach Naples about 8.30 p.m.

Charter two one-horse cabs and drive to hotel.

The roads here are paved with large irregular-shaped stones and are very uneven, and the jolting is terrific. The cabs drive furiously and whips are slashed with great force like pistol-shots, and in places they drive on road or pavement among the people, who have hairbreadth escapes.

Tuesday 7 March. Settle bill. In 'bus to station, and on the train. Run alongside the Appennines and then into flatter country.

We are forcibly reminded of some of Rome's ancient greatness by passing miles and miles of the old aqueduct—it is a stupendous piece of work, constructed on innumerable lofty arches, and must have cost millions.

Arrive at Rome, and on our way to the train for Pisa we see one of Cook's men, so I tell him to lead the way and it's 'Follow the man from Cook's!' He'd heard that before. Then he got us four of the neatest little luncheon-baskets you ever saw, and we ate under the searching gaze of two male and one female Italians.

It is ten o'clock (instead of 9.35) when we get to Pisa. Our first impression is very favourable. We hop into the Hotel Victoria 'bus, and at the hotel are shown to two communicating rooms, airy, clean, well furnished, and not less than 27 by 20 feet.

Wednesday 8 March. Buy some tobacco and matches and a map of Pisa, and go up Strada Maria to the cathedral. The interior is superb. Robed in the full vestments of his holy office sits the bishop on his throne, and in procession pass before him the clergy and choir; they bow the knee as they reach his presence, pause while he blesses them and makes the sign of the † on their devoted heads, and then pass on. We are somewhat surprised at the number of them; at a rough guess, clergy and choir would amount to a hundred.

We stand and watch this holy mummery, and then they unrobe the bishop and we pass away—out to the Campanile or Leaning Tower of Pisa just opposite. Bartlett junior and I ascend 294 steps to the top.

Then to the Baptistry, where there is a famous echo. The sacristan sang three or four notes, and the sound returned like a glorious swell of harmony on a grand organ. The most wonderful effect I have ever heard.

Down Strada Maria we enter an antique-shop and have glorious fun buying goods for Mr Bartlett in a patois of French and Italian. We purchase to the amount of 188 lire = £7.10.5 and give orders that they are to be sent to our hotel at *une heure* when we will pay. Then I go to the Banca Commerciale Italiana and change another letter of credit.

Back to hotel and to *déjeuner à la fourchette*. Nearly done when the head waiter comes and says they have brought the antiques, so we tell them to wait till we have finished, and we will come and talk to them.

Out we go to the salon, and there are three men and the goods. Very amusing lot of palaver, and we have to finish up by giving them 15 lire more to make a case and get a permit from the Município and send off to England. With lifted hats and much bowing and scraping they pick up the goods and depart from the presence.

We leave Pisa with regret. The hotel was very good, the town clean, no beggars, the buildings and statues fine, and every appearance of being thriving.

At station a scramble to get seats in train, then away through innumerable smoky stinking tunnels and get as black as sweeps.

We arrive at Genoa Station and amidst an enormous crowd make our way on foot to Hôtel de Londres, not more than a hundred yards—then a stroll. The number of enormous marble buildings here, the statuary and the general air of well-to-do-ism strikes us pleasingly.

Thursday 9 March. Little unpleasantness about the bill. They almost refuse to accept our coupons, saying we ought to have told them when we first arrived—charge us 2.05 lire too much. However, pay up and clear to station.

We go on through beautiful mountains and snow, change at Turin, and get in the train for Paris.

Soon afterwards we reach Modane on the frontier between Italy and France, and here the trouble begins. We had to leave our carriage and take our baggage across the rails to the *Douanier*'s to examine.

Imagine hundreds of people all on the same errand, and all anxious to get back to the train, with a babel of chatter in a foreign tongue, and you may have some idea that we had to look sharp.

I got out first, for they never looked in my trunk at all, and made my way back to our carriage where we had left our umbrellas and overcoats, rugs etc. Directly I got there, several Frenchwomen or Italian women and a man tried to take our places. I tried all I could to keep them out but to no purpose. Then the others came up till we were absolutely jammed in, people and luggage.

They refused to get out, and called the guard, and all five of them talked to him at once. When I could get a word in I told him it was our carriage all the way from Turin; they told lies and said it was theirs first.

Neither side gave way, so they slammed the doors and off we went, nine sitting down and four standing, and luggage all over the place. It was an uncomfortable packed position, and as we had about thirteen hours still to go in the train we were not over-pleased.

At last we drew up at a station and one of the women called the guard and went on nineteen to the dozen, gesticulating, chattering, gabbling and well nigh crying, all most dramatic. We sit solemnly and look on.

The guard says in about another hour he may be able to find them three seats.

Later, when we stop at Aix-les-Bains, they get out after much scrambling and sorting out of luggage. We were glad to see them depart, and we English settled down for the night.

Friday 10 March. At about six o'clock the shade is pulled back from the lamp and we have a smoke.

We are very dirty with smoke and dust, and at 6.35 we reach the Gare de Lyon, Paris, after being in the train for about 22 hours, take a cab and go to Hôtel St Petersbourg. Then we go out—to the Madeleine, Place de la Concorde, Tuileries Gardens, Notre Dame, Morgue, back to Louvre, over to Napoleon's Tomb.

At 6½ *heures* enjoy a good dinner. Mr G. and B. sport a bottle of champagne to drink to the guide. Then out and to the Nouveau Cirque—show not anything better than the Hippodrome at Brighton, and the ladies in the *Promenoir* rather disgust us.

Saturday 11 March. We start very punctually from Gare St Lazare, through richer-looking country than any we passed in Italy. At Dieppe we pass across to the good ship *Brighton*, a fine turbine steamer. There is every appearance of things having been made snug for a rough passage.

I am not sick, but believe I could have been if I had tried. I confess to being a little pleased to see the white cliffs of the tight little island, and as soon as we are berthed we rush ashore and through the Customs.

Mr Bartlett has found a masonic friend who is a manager of a number of railway restaurants, and he has us in a private room and provides tea. Then we march to the Newhaven town station, and find there a French doctor who attached himself to our party earlier. He ought to have gone in the London train, but he is so fond of us I suppose he can't leave.

He is in trouble, having lost an umbrella. We send a porter back to try and find it for him, and on cross-examining Monsieur, find it is a stick he has lost, not an umbrella. Back comes porter, and we give him the address Monsieur is going to in London, and he is to forward it.

Away to Lewes. Hearty handshakes and we drop Messrs B. at London Road. At Brighton Station we are met by Mrs G., Millie, Tom, Fanny and Sid and Burt. To Clarence Square and supper, then home we go to 12 St James's Avenue, and dropping the role of a traveller who has traversed by steamer, train, cab and on foot about 3,794 miles, I take up my conjugal duties, and the curtain descends on the history of the 1905 holiday tour.

Switzerland

1906

Friday 1 June. There is an old saying that 'the man who hesitates is lost'. If this is so, I am lost, for never have I hesitated so much as I did over this Swiss tour.

However, at last Millie sent Gladys and Wilfred in charge of Harriett to her aunt at Bishopstone, Sussex. Reggie we had sent to Mrs Thompsett at Keymer, and Cuthbert we had arranged should stay at Mrs Peerless', Portland Street, Brighton. So having disposed of our family, we shut up no. 12 St James's Avenue, and prepared to start. We had all our tickets and coupons through the Polytechnic.

Arriving at Brighton Station I find the others already there, and away we go. At Newhaven we troop on board the SS *Dieppe* (the last new turbine) and take our quarters in the second class.

Mr G. went to enquire for a fellow mason, a Captain McGee, captain of one of the Newhaven–Dieppe steamers. In a few minutes a broad-shouldered open-faced man of about 43 hurried up and was introduced all round. He seemed very pleased to see Mr G., and showed us all over the ship, then calling a ticket superintendent he told him to pass us in the first class. So we changed our seats, and tinkle, tinkle, 'Cast off there,' we were off.

I lost sight of Mr G. for a very long time, and when Fanny and I found him, we three started to walk forward.

'Look out for Pup, Harry,' said Fanny.

'No fear,' said I. 'He's a mariner.'

How true it is that when thou thinkest thou standest, take heed lest thou fall. We had been shipping a lot of water, and no sooner were the words out of my mouth than we both slipped and fell in a sitting posture on the deck, side by side.

At last Dieppe came into view, and we prepared to disembark. Fighting our way with luggage we pass the Customs and race for the train. The whistle shrieks and away we crawl through the streets of Dieppe for 'gay Paree'.

We reach Paris at about a quarter to seven o'clock, and in a few minutes we reach the Hôtel Terminus. Millie and I sleep in no. 28: unfortunately two beds instead of one, and the pillows were enormous.

Saturday 2 June. Down to a poor breakfast of bad beef, then off we go for the Gare de l'Est and start for Lucerne.

Little tales cheer us up, and ever and anon a ripple of laughter runs over our party. Dull carking care is thrown to the winds, and a very little makes us laugh, we feel so free and happy.

The country was flat and well tilled, being divided into very small holdings.

We take seven lunch-tickets from our conductor—then with dismay I discover one of the rubies in my ring has dropped out. Oh what a wicked world it is, when even stones in their rings refuse to keep in their appointed places.

Looking out, we see great bunches in the foliage of the trees, and speculate as to what it may be. Some say it is mistletoe, some say it is not. But 'wisdom is justified of her children', and on enquiry the mistletoites are pronounced to be right.

As the scenery improved, we began to get out in the corridor to get a good view, and Dottie discovered how to play the great new game which she promptly christened 'rubbing tummies in the corridor'.

This can be played by any number of players. About a half of those taking part range themselves along the corridor, and the other half perambulate up and down, and as the space is limited, a great deal of fun can be extracted, especially by those who are inclined to *embonpoint.*

At last we reach Lucerne and tumble out, a terrible crowd of us. As we march out of the station, I hear a voice crying 'Polytechnic party this way!' and it seems familiar. Pressing up to him, I say: 'It's Mr Fellingham, isn't it?'

'Why, Mr Peerless,' says he. 'How are you? Hurrah!'

We shook hands heartily, and he explained that he had been at the chalets a fortnight, and had volunteered to come down tonight to receive the party.

Hastily saying adieu, we secured a porter and told him to find the Hôtel de l'Europe 'bus, and were soon driving alongside the lake to our hotel.

A wash, then through the vestibule to dinner. We enjoy it muchly, and under the cheering influence of the grape Tom begins to develop brilliant powers of conversation.

Sunday 3 June. Millie, Mr and Mrs G. and Dottie, like good respectable people, go to the English church, and Tom, Fanny and I explore the old part of the town: quaint old frescoed buildings, queer signs, crazy overhanging gables, old fountains etc.

After lunch we go up to Seeberg to keep our engagement with Mr Fellingham at the Poly chalets.

He took us under his wing, and showed us all round the chalets, originally an old monastery. Then we board a steamer to Station Pier, Lucerne, and go to see the famous Lion of Lucerne, carved out of an enormous rock close to the Glacier Garden. It is a memorial of the valiant defence of the Royal Family of France by a legion of Swiss Guards who nobly sacrificed their lives while defending the Tuileries on 10 August 1792.

I, a foreigner, cannot look upon it unmoved, for so it is that noble courage will always compel recognition from men of every age and country. The wrinkled brow of the lion, wrung with pain from his mortal wound, is a grand triumph of the sculptor's art.

Reluctantly we turn our faces towards our hotel and dinner. Music and singing delight the ear during this meal, and is then continued in the grand vestibule.

Mr G. and I go out in a pouring rain and stroll down-town. It was sloppy and dirty, and after listening to the strains of a fine band in a bier-garden, we decide to get back.

As I say goodbye to Mr G. at our door, Millie comes out with an alarmed face and says: 'Oh! Harry, there's some Frenchwoman in one of our beds, and I can't get her out, I can't understand what she says.'

A couple of quick strides and I was in the room. There, in the bed nearest the door, I saw the black head of a woman, her white night-dress just peeping out of the bed-clothes.

Rapidly running over in my mind the proper French phrases to use on this rather singular occasion, I advanced towards the bed to commence the attack on the fair foreigner. As I got closer, and was just about to commence with, '*Madame, je—*,' my eye detected a fancy comb embedded in the black head of hair, and that comb seemed familiar to me.

In all my experience I had never seen women in bed with combs in their hair, knowing well that the arrangement of their hair at night is a lengthy operation. This gave me pause for a second, and then I shouted out: 'It's Fanny!'

How we all laughed at the *dénouement.* Millie says the expression on my face when she first told me was a picture.

Fanny jumps out of bed, pulls off the night-dress which she had drawn on over her clothes, and wishing each other good night, Millie and I woo sweet sleep.

Monday 4 June. Whit Monday. Day-excursion for Vitznau.

On the steamer I get into conversation with a nice motherly Canadian lady who is going to Flüelen. She is a well informed woman, and appears to have been nearly everywhere. She talks on a good many subjects, politics etc., Alaska award, and when we compare watches she informs me that 'I did have an American watch, but it went back on me, so I jest bought anuther in Geneva.'

At Vitznau we made our way to the mountain railway adjoining the landing-place, and had our first sight of the queer-shaped mountain engines.

Climbing very slowly, we reach Rigi Kulm and get out. Then up several zig-zag paths we gain the highest point, crowned by a wooden belvedere. It is snowing quite fast, and the crowd are snowballing. One varlet hits Millie's umbrella, the silk of which it rents, to my disgust.

Down to the station, the snowflakes blowing upwards. As we get lower the snow ceases, and we arrive at Vitznau in a heavy downpour of rain.

Our steamer is very crowded, and Mr G. and I have an amusing conversation with a talkative man from Birmingham. Had we had time, I think we should have known his birth, parentage, education and everything else about him—as it was, he crowded in a lot of detail in a short time, telling us his baby weighed 16 stones 10 lbs, that he had been under the doctor 17 weeks, that he had left his best watch at home, that it was a presentation watch costing £30 and given to him for saving the life of a boy who was drowning in one of the locks of the Manchester Ship Canal.

He was a jolly old boy, and we left him with regret.

Tuesday 5 June. By steamer to Flüelen, then crowd along to the railway. At Göschenen about eight wagonettes were waiting to convey those who did not wish to walk to Andermatt, and Mr and Mrs G. and Millie took their seats at once.

Tom, Fanny, Dottie and I were made of sterner stuff. The roads were rough and zigzag, and we had to climb up an iron ladder set in the rocks. Then we passed over a bridge built by Napoleon to get his artillery across the torrent. We found fortifications in the mountains, and massive iron gates, which in time of war would be used to close up the pass. Then through tunnels, from the roofs of which streams of water dropped, necessitating my putting up an umbrella. The dirt was horrible.

As we pass barracks, and soldiers exercising on a plateau, how crisp the air is, and how light and happy we feel.

Now we enter the old village of Andermatt, and join about 140 persons in the vestibule of the Grand Hôtel, waiting to get into the luncheon room—but another party is there, and we have to wait patiently.

At last the doors are opened and in we rush, and are soon partaking of Irish stew, roast beef and diplomacy pudding, washed down with Suisse bier.

Feel much better, and go out into the quaint old-world village. All the houses are of wood, and nearly all are covered with little shingles made of fir about 2½ by 2¼ inch thick, giving the same appearance as armour or gigantic fish-scales. In some cases these shingles had dropped off from old age.

Andermatt is reputed to be the highest village in Europe. This little place possesses two churches, and wending our way to one, I am absolutely bewildered at the richness of the interior, which seems to bear comparison with a cathedral. Where did the money come to pay for it? Then into a chapel, and here on shelves were scores of grinning skulls.

Back to Flüelen, where we rush on board the SS *Victoria* and take tea in the saloon. We pass Schillerstein, and ahead of us the golden orb is tipping the snowy mountain-tops with a copper radiance, and a little solemn touch steals over me as I watch the day dying—a day's march nearer home. Now the last bright ray is gone, and a chill runs over me.

Many of our passengers begin to take great interest in the engines now. 'Cold? No, thought I'd have a look at the machinery, that's all.'

Reach Lucerne at nine o'clock, and dress for dinner.

We were going along the verandah to the dining-room, when I heard a cry and a clatter: Millie had fallen backwards and measured her length on the stone flags.

I assisted her to rise. 'Hurt, my dear? Take my arm.'

Limping a little we gain our seats, thankful that no bones are broken. I may say in a day or two she had a bruise as large as the palm of my hand.

After dinner, go for a stroll alongside lake and watch the moon, feeling that we have had a glorious day, and years hence shall we say: 'Do you remember the day we went to Andermatt?' 'Why, it was 1906—how the time does go.' 'By Jove old man, your hair is thinner than it was then, eh?' And we shall fight all our old battles over again by the fireside.

And that is one of the good things about a holiday like this, if you are careful to look at things with discerning eyes, you can call up mental pictures of scenes at will, which is beneficial.

Also in company does it give one a better chance in conversation— 'Have you ever been to—' 'Oh yes, we went so and so—' And away you go comparing notes, and both find out what deuced clever fellows you are, don't you know.

Wednesday 6 June. Go and look at the Lion, which we introduce to the notice of Mr and Mrs G. and Millie—Tom, Fanny, Dottie and I, having seen it before, assume a kind of proprietorship in it, and point out its noble beauties as though it belonged to us.

One by one we steal off to ⊖⊖. Now I don't think I ought to put this in, only ⊖⊖ did strike us as a peculiar sign, used as we are in England to see 'Gentlemen Only,' 'Ladies Only,' or in France 'Pour

Messieurs,' 'Pour Dames'—here we see ○ ○ and ⊖⊖. Well, 'one touch of Nature makes the whole world kin', and if we made a little joke of it we meant no harm.

Then we take a tram to Emenbrücke, and walk alongside a river. The air is laden with the fragrance of the hay which they are making in the adjacent fields. We pass a gentle fisher who no doubt reviles us in his heart—but what do we care? We are free, we have no work to do, let him curse.

At last we retrace our steps, troop into the Restaurant Flora and order lunch. A dainty little waitress with her broken English captivates the male portion of our party, and even the females agree she is rather pretty. Calves' head, beef and plenty to drink puts us into a most amiable state of mind.

Having been on the tram to one extremity of the line, we now decide to go to the other, so take one to Kriens. When we reach the end we find a car about to start up a mountain.

We came here without any idea of going up, but the natives seem to expect us to go, and appear to be delaying the car for us.

As it seems the proper thing to do, we hastily take tickets for we don't know where, and off we go, up a steep incline like the side of a house, 2,638 feet high.

Mr G., Tom and I make a tour around the mountain-top, and eventually find the ladies, who seem to be a wee bit snappy, as though we had been away too long, and they make little innuendoes such as, 'It's a wonder we didn't go back a long time ago,' and so on.

We enter the next car, and get beautiful views of the lake as we slip down. Tram right to Hôtel Europe.

After dinner we walk to the chalets. It appears to be a custom for the 'Polys' staying at the chalets to invite the 'Polys' staying at the hotels in Lucerne to come up to a social evening every Wednesday, so togged up in our best we are on our way to accept of their kind hospitality.

On arrival we are shown into the large dining-hall, and a singing concert, recitations etc. are in progress. Empty chairs are difficult to find, and we are all divided.

It was rather interesting to sit and scan the faces, many of which are now getting familiar, as we keep on meeting each other on steamers, up mountains etc.

I listen to two or three songs and a recitation, then as the room is insufferably hot I get outside in the fresh air, and smoke.

Then the room is cleared for dancing, but it is far too crowded and hot for me to trip on the light fantastic, so Mill and her mother get into a wagonette, and Mr G. and I walk back. It was one of the most perfect nights: all around rose the mountains, peak on peak, the air was soft and sweet, and the waters of the lake glistened in the moonbeams . . . but what is that sound that falls on my ears?

'Is that a nightingale, Mr G? Listen.'

'Nightingales? I'm afraid your nightingales are frogs.'

And frogs they were no doubt.

Thursday 7 June. Steam away to Alpnachstad, and on the cog railway to Pilatus Kulm. At the top, lunch is the first thing we do, and I fancy we do it pretty well. The hotel was evidently covered all in with snow not so very long ago; now it is about nine feet high, banked all round the walls with places cut out of it to let light in to the windows, and tunnelled out for people to walk through. It presented a very strange appearance.

Now we used to be a party of seven, but I begin today to see that we are getting to be a party of eight. A Mr Dolding evidently finds Dottie's company very attractive, for he is gradually becoming one of us.

The man in charge of our party now begins to round up his flock so that they can be photographed as a group, but as I have a rooted objection to being photographed with a crowd of strangers, I slip off up to the summit of the Eisel, and train our field-glasses on the Poly crowd as they line up and face the camera, and discover Mr and Mrs G. well in the front.

A few adventurous spirits are going to walk down half-way, and Dottie and Mr Dolding start with about twenty-five others on this rather rough pilgrimage.

With the glasses we follow their movements for some time. We see them approach a large stretch of snow, and Dottie gets on it, takes two or three steps and falls headlong.

We six take our seats in a descending car, and on reaching *terra firma* 'make tracks' for SS *Victoria* and back to Lucerne. Dottie gives us little details of the walk down, narrating that at one point Mr Dolding slips, his heels go up in the air and he lands backwards in a ditch. We see him directly after, and find he has put on an overcoat to hide the dirt on his clothes.

Friday 8 June. Soon after ten, away we go under the guidance of Mr Thick, a very bright fair-haired young man who conducts us nicely through the old town. On the wall of the old Apothecaries' Hall we see an inscription: '*Amor medicabilis nullis herbis*,' which being interpreted into the vulgar tongue meaneth: 'Love cannot be cured by medicine.' Our conductor hazards that many of us have found out the truth of this axiom, and a laugh goes round the throng. Then we all troop into the Hofkirche for an organ recital. One of the selections, delineating a storm on the Alps, was very realistic: the rain sounded very real, and several people told me it made them feel cold to hear the wind blowing so naturally.

After lunch, T.G. senior and Fanny go off to buy some lemons and come back with some collars instead. They appear to have had a bit of an escape as a runaway horse was pretty close to them.

Saturday 9 June. This morning we have to leave Lucerne, and in our hearts we moralise a little on the mutability of human affairs, and feel that 'man fleeth as it were a shadow, and never continueth in one stay'. We walk to the station, and off we go.

At the Brünig Pass we get out and walk to a spot renowned for a beautiful view, but it is not clear enough to see it properly, so back we go and study the inscriptions posted up in our carriage:

NICHT RAUCHEN
NON FUMEURS
È VIETATO DI FUMARE

MAN BITTET NICHT IN DEN WAGEN
ZU SPUCKEN

ON EST PRIÉ DE NE PAS CRACHER
DANS LA VOITURE

SI PREGA DI NON SPUTARE
NELLA CARROZZA

So you must not smoke and you must not spit, and my eyes wander, and out in the station another sign strikes me:

and I am glad to find something that you may do.

Then we start off again, and Tom stands in the open corridor outside our carriage talking to a man who seems to know all about everything we pass, and I hear Tom say in a patronising way: 'But you speak English very well.'

The man quietly rejoined: 'Yes, I'm a Scotsman you see.'

And now we find out that this Scotsman is in charge of the Poly party for the remainder of our holiday and that his name is Mr Wallace. He wore a black Alpine hat and a flowing black Alpine cloak, and turned out a very decent fellow with a fund of dry quaint humour which gave us many a laugh ere we parted company.

At Meiringen we walk to the Reichenbach Hotel and join the throng which surrounds Mr Wallace, who holds a lot of paper slips and calls out the different names written thereon. I find I am no. 18 room, second floor. 'So far, so good,' as the boy said when he ate the *first* pot of his mother's jam.

It was done in a businesslike way, and I like a businesslike method of doing things, but alas when I try the door I can't open it. It appears to be locked inside, and I hear someone in there moving about.

I turn the key this way and that, and then the woman in charge of the floor bustles along. 'I am number 18,' I say, 'but I can't get in.'

Now I hear someone inside trying to open the door, and knocking, and I laugh to myself with fiendish glee as it dawns on me that I have locked the villain in.

The woman says, 'I'm very sorry, but if you will have number 21, it's a beautiful room, only it won't be vacant till a quarter to four.'

Mr and Mrs G. kindly allowed us to wash in their room, and then we went down to the worst-served meal that I ever had the honour of assisting at. I am not a gourmand, but I like to feel that the management are not watching every mouthful.

After lunch we walk to the Gorge of the Aare, which the guide-book tells me is considered one of the wonders of Europe. The clerk of the weather having come to his senses, we walk along a narrow wooden platform supported on light iron bracket girders let into the side of the rock and protected by a light railing on the left hand to prevent us falling into the rushing torrent. Retracing our steps we meet Dottie and Mr Saunders, on whose shoulders Dolding's mantle seems to have fallen.

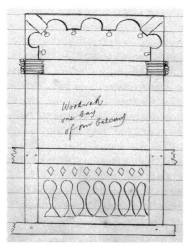

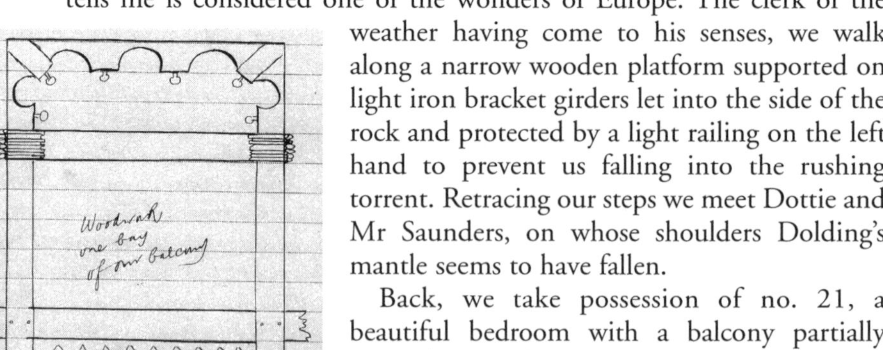

Back, we take possession of no. 21, a beautiful bedroom with a balcony partially covered in with carved wooden posts and a fretted fence of wood, and picked out with electric-light lamps, somewhat after the style of the woodwork on our Palace Pier.

Wash, dress and to dinner—hardly enough to go round, and I believe they have to collect some of the plates from those first served and wash them for those they keep waiting. When the fish course comes, as revenge I take a large piece as they serve me first. When they come to poor old Tom, they have to cut it up into little pieces and he gets two little mites, whereat I laugh amain.

After dinner we walk to Meiringen, and then to bed. When Mill and I pull down the blinds we are astonished to see how beautifully they are painted, representing in vivid colouring a Venetian scene.

Two beds with eider quilts encased in white linen not less than fifteen inches thick; these we promptly throw on the sofas, and get into bed.

Sunday 10 June. There is no time like the morning: the air is different, and as I take deep draughts into my lungs, I seem to enlarge and feel fit for anything 'from pitch-and-toss to manslaughter'. Scrupulously carrying out my matutinal ablutions and arraying myself in the best sartorial triumphs that I have at my command, I descend to breakfast.

Seated at the end of my table, my eyes rove round, and I note how fresh and nice some of my countrywomen look. I always think it is a pretty sight to see women sit down to breakfast in a hotel on a sunny fresh Sunday morning. Their hair looks nice, their blouses are clean and fresh, their cheeks glow and sparkle after their morning's wash.

It was a bit of a scramble for rolls, butter, honey and jam, but I am 'death' on everything that comes my way for I am on my mettle with this hotel.

After breakfast, stroll round grounds and look at a glass-house, built very quaintly, as if it were composed of hexagonal bottoms of glass bottles. The clouds envelop the mountain-tops like a bridegroom embracing his bride.

Opposite our hotel is a magnificent waterfall called the Alpbach, and at the back of our hotel is another equally fine called the Reichenbach—wild and rugged. After lunch we go to see the Alpbach Falls up close. I put up my umbrella to keep off the spray.

Dinner, and then going into the vestibule find the whole place in confusion at the supposed loss of three of the Polys.

This morning a considerable number of Polys started with the guides to go to the Reichenbach glacier, about an eight hours' job *pour aller et retour*. These three waited till two o'clock and then went off same journey on their own, certainly a foolish thing to do.

The two guides began to be 'as busy as bees in a tar-tub' and, accompanied by a few men, started off in different directions to search for the missing ones. It was quite dark and we could hear the guides cooing as they went along. Tom and I went a little way up the mountain, and about a quarter of an hour after the search parties had started, two ladies and one gent came by.

'Hullo! Are you the three lost ones?'

'We're all right—what do you mean?'

'Well, they think you're lost and have gone to look for you. You'd better get down and report yourselves.'

They hurried down, and we are told the wife of the gentleman quite broke down when she saw him and he had to lead her away upstairs. It appears they telephoned to our hotel once or twice to say they were all right, but the messages were muddled or not understood.

One guide, Mr Thick, came back soon, but the other, Mr Wallace, was out till nearly twelve o'clock.

The electric light on our balcony was not switched out till midnight, and I believe it was kept on till then to guide them back; anyway it hindered us getting off to sleep. They are always very prodigal with their electric light, and on enquiry we find they pay so much a year and burn what they like, so this accounts for it.

Monday 11 June. Got up and packed. Tom and I walk to Meiringen Station, calling on a watchmaker on the way and asking him to straighten Tom's spectacles which have become bent. He tinkers with them, for which Thomas forks out 10 centimes, and then to the station and meet the others. We proceed to Brienz where we all go aboard a steamer.

We converse with Messrs Wallace and Thick, mentioning to them a notice in English which we laughed at in the Glacier Garden, Lucerne, which ran 'One is requested not to surpass the bordered ways.' They said they had seen on the box of a shoe-black at Territet, near Chillon Castle and Chamonix, an inscription in chalk: 'English spoken, American understood.'

On arrival at Interlaken continue our journey by mountain railway, skirting the river till we reach Grindelwald, and walk to our hotel rejoicing in the names 'Schwarz Adler' or 'de l'Aigle Noir'. Our room smells stuffy and is dark and old, and has an enormous warming-stove in it.

Presently Millie and I go down town, and as I am getting rather shaggy, I go in a shop and have my hair cut and beard close-trimmed. 'How much? Good heavens, 1 franc 80 to have your hair cut.' However, travellers, George, must pay in all places: sound philosophy, and has reconciled me many a time to some extortion or other.

Back to a good dinner, well served. At the conclusion of the repast, the guide gets up and says: 'La-adies and gentlemen—may I claim your attention for a few moments. Tomorrow, tho-ose who wish may join an excursion to the Mer de Glace. This takes about eight hours there and back, and there will be a cha-arge of two shillings each for guides.'

Well, I have had no experience in walking on ice, and whatever betides I've got to be back into business on a certain day, and if I should break an arm or a leg, should I feel that I was justified in going? No.

The mention of the word 'walk' is quite enough to put Millie off it; Mr and Mrs G. are off it too.

Dottie wants to go, and after dinner I see her boots handed over to the hall-porter. They come back later studded all over with vilely ugly hobnails to keep her from slipping.

Going out in the grounds we see the prettiest sight I have ever seen: the setting sun, colouring the snow a beautiful pink. Mr Thick comes along

and says: 'Oh! This is the Alpine glow, you don't often see it so good. I must go and get the others.'

To bed, thinking we are in for a wet day tomorrow.

Tuesday 12 June. Lounging outside hotel, I notice the mountain guides framing about waiting for the walking party. They carried ice-axes and a coil of rope, and looked rather businesslike.

We say goodbye to Dottie and Mr Saunders, then walk to the upper glacier. A man gives rugs to the ladies, and we enter the ice grotto. This is a crooked tunnel hewn out in the solid ice by this man, and although there is a hundred feet of ice above the roof, it is quite light, only it is a peculiar white light, and looking round at the others I see their faces are like corpses.

It ended in a little square chamber, in the centre of which a large block of ice had been left, like a solid table, in which a little fir tree was stuck. It was very cold and we did not stay in long.

On our way back we passed two men taking a swarm of bees that had settled on a wall on the roadside—also a peasant stationed at the side of the road blowing a queer-shaped arrangement, about eight feet long, producing bugle-like sounds which echo and re-echo in the surrounding mountains.

Then Tom and I go to the post office to get a strap of mine sent on from the Hôtel de l'Europe where Millie left it. On the way a horse runs away, dropping things off the van as he rushes madly along, knocking the wheels against the legs of a horse being led along the road.

Back and to dinner; then we all go to the Bear Hotel, and in the large hall see cinematograph pictures of Alpine views and climbing

Wednesday 13 June. Shake the dust of Hotel Adler off our feet and proceed to railway station. Train is divided into sections and hauled up the gradient on a cog track in the centre of rails. Wild flowers surprisingly profuse.

At Scheidegg we detrain, and I climb up steep snow about eighty yards, take off overcoat, sit on it, hold all the loose ends in my hands tightly, push off and glissade down the snow. It is a job to keep straight, and nearing the bottom I spin round and finish up head first instead of feet first.

Then, hearing a roar like thunder, I look up, and am fortunate enough to see a huge avalanche of snow fall from a mountain into the depths below.

After we take the first train to Lauterbrunnen ('clear springs'), where Tom sketches a house he has fallen in love with. Return to station, and through lovely scenery to Interlaken, where we walk to our hotel, the

Bellevue. Dinner splendidly served by waitresses in Swiss costume.

Thursday 14 June. Out on our balcony, watch River Aare and look at the cows with different-toned bells hung round their necks crossing the bridge. Then down into the garden where one of the Polys excitedly shows the Jungfrau with the sun shining on the pure snow.

At ten o'clock we all walk to Heimwehfluh, and I dig up a baby fir-tree to take home. Spend the afternoon in and out of shops along the Höheweg, buying presents.

Back to dinner, after which to the kursaal; very fine band. At the intervals they display a card 'PAUSE'. They play 'God save the King' during one selection, and we English all stand up.

Friday 15 June. By steamer and train to Berne. Here we enter the Hôtel de France and have a good lunch. Warm welcome from the motherly landlady, and she and I are soon as thick as thieves. Then to the famous Bear Pits at the end of the main street across the Nydegg Bridge; the town is said to take its name from these animals, a supply of which has been maintained in the town for nearly 500 years. In the lower town the bulk of the women seem to be engaged in washing in the streets, beating the clothes violently on a board.

Very hot and close, so after a while we climb up an old wooden staircase and regain the upper town. Nearly all the streets have heavy colonnades over the pavement and it seems to pen me in after the open mountain life.

Back to dinner at Hôtel de France, and then by 8.17 train we depart. The ticket-collector pops up like a Jack-in-the-box at intervals, and at Delle the *douaniers* board the train to examine the luggage. The chief officer opened the door of our carriage, stood at attention rigidly and gravely saluted. I saluted in return. Stepping forward he asked if we had anything to declare; I said no (all this in French).

He stood motionless and his eye moved all round, looking at each package, then he saluted and withdrew. I thought the show was over—but no. Close on his heels followed two men who seemed to me to be his familiar spirits, both armed with a long iron rod. One entered our carriage, solemn and dumb, and proceeded to rake under one seat, then under the other, then coming right in he solemnly raked in the other direction, and then stalked out like Hamlet's ghost.

When he was gone we burst into peals of laughter, till we were brought to our senses by people next door, who wished to go to sleep, knocking the partition.

Saturday 16 June. On arriving at Gare de l'Est, Paris, we charter two cabs. Our horse is a bag of bones.

I have been in a good many dangerous positions, but I don't think I ever stood more chance of a broken neck than I did on that ride. Our cab slipped on the tram rails, we got inextricably mixed up in the traffic, once he drove so close that another horse got his head right in our cab and I took hold of his shaft and pushed him off with all my might—but we reached Gare St Lazare safe and sound, and got in the train. At Dieppe we got aboard the same ship as we came over in.

We have a nice passage, except that the blacks from the funnel are very offensive.

Arriving at Newhaven, we take our seats in the train for Brighton. *En route*, I point out items of interest and antiquity to Dottie, who I have no doubt is highly edified. Finally reach St James's Avenue and find all well.

As I write these lines I have heard of a horrible accident to the Plymouth Boat Express, and when I think of those poor creatures cut off in the heyday of life, I cannot help thinking that we have much to be thankful for.

The New Forest

1907

Sunday 9 June. Having disposed of the olive branches that cluster round our table (viz. Cuthbert Henry, Reginald Leslie, Gladys Amelia and Wilfred David; young children are like arrows in the hand of the giant, and happy is the man who has a quiver full of them)*—I, Henry Heathfield Peerless, timber merchant, and Amelia Sarah Peerless, the faithful wife of the above-named, arose from their virtuous couch, mounted on bicycles and rode to Brighton Station. While labelling our machines, the inspector told us Abbey's malthouse had been burnt out in the night.

It was a glorious morning, and as we got into the country all nature seemed to laugh with gladness. At Havant we mounted our cycles and sailed on our way.

Arrived at Woolston Floating Ferry and crossed the Itchen. On the opposite bank we pedalled away on the Western Shore Road, and thus escaped the traffic, trams, and the narrow road under the Bar. A mile further on rain fell heavily, and we took shelter under a splendid shed—reaching Lyndhurst all well at 12.45 p.m.

Mrs Ings junior welcomed us at the Fox and Hounds. After tea we go for a walk on the heath, and Millie suddenly gets worked up into a kind of mild botanical fever, and keeps me busy digging up roots of young oak trees, mosses etc. which she carries in her *mouchoir.*

Coming back we see Mrs Ings senior in her shop, and then Mabel came forward. Mrs Ings was in widow's weeds, and we then knew that our old friend Mr Ings must be dead.

We were really very sorry, and as she told us a long tale of all the trouble she had passed through, commencing with the loss of her dear husband thirteen months ago, it did seem that troubles never come singly.

Poor Mabel had lost a dear little two-year-old daughter, who—in perfect health, while Mrs Ings and Mabel were both ill in bed at Lyndhurst with influenza—got at some of the quinine tablets, was sick and dead in twenty minutes.

We felt quite brutal to remind them of their sorrows.

*Being from home I have not a Bible to refer to, but I know this is the sense of the passage. (Author's note.)

Monday 10 June. Mamma went out to the draper's and got a cardboard box for her botanical specimens. Showery still, but we walk to Bank—get some more roots, and send off the box to Cuthbert. Then we rest one hour, mother unrobes and climbs on the bed.

Dress again and walk to Emery Down—Millie greatly interested in a farrow of thirteen pigs a week old. Dinner, and then a walk to look at the outside of the Bench View Private Hotel on the Southampton Road, which Miss Shipman has taken.

Tuesday 11 June. Get our cycles and away we go, heigho for Romsey. The road is nearly straight for miles, the wind is behind us, and Millie thinks under these conditions she should become an ardent cyclist.

When we get into the Market Square, we see a huge poster announcing a grand pageant to be held 25, 26 and 27 June, in commemoration of the thousandth anniversary of Romsey Abbey.

Through lovely scenery we get to Hursley, and thence to Winchester. A long steep hill, where we have to keep both brakes on hard, and we are entering the city of Winchester through one of the ancient gateways, the West Gate.

No English city is richer in legendary associations than Winchester. One of the Saxon bishops was that St Swithin whose funeral is said to have been delayed for forty days by rain, giving rise to a familiar superstition. Canute hung up his crown in the cathedral, after the traditional scene on the seashore at Southampton.

We descended the steep High Street until we reached King Alfred's statue, and admired the rugged nobility portrayed. Then, pushing our machines, we turn into the Close and note a grand avenue of aged elm-trees going up to the main entrance of the cathedral. Today the beauty of the facade is spoiled by a network of scaffolding, as extensive repairs are in progress.

Then look at shops, old houses etc., particularly noting the George Inn, one of the oldest in England, having flourished here under the same name since the days of Agincourt.

Wednesday 12 June. Decide not to cycle in such a strong wind, so walk to Queen's Head Inn at Burley, where we have lunch. The rain kindly abating, we walk over a windy heath to Holmsley Station, catch the train to Brockenhurst, and walk the four miles to Lyndhurst. With clouds threatening, we come to the Crown Inn just outside Lyndhurst and call in for refreshments.

A customer is, I think, somewhat of a *rara avis*.

The landlord, a young fellow, seemed quite alone in the house, and was whiling away his time by strumming on a piano when we arrived, and before we were out of hearing, on our departure, we heard him resume his occupation of torturing the piano.

Thursday 13 June. During breakfast we read a letter from Mr Garrett, saying that he, Mrs G., Tom and Fanny will come on Saturday in Tom's motor-car. At 10.25 we mount our iron steeds and have a delightful ride to Beaulieu.

It is impossible to give a worthy description of the beauties of the countryside. Fancy two or three miles of undulating heather-clad plain, then we pass Beaulieu Road Station, through grand old woods, then the river on our left hand widens, till when we reach Beaulieu it has become a lake, and is sweetly pretty.

We admire Lord Montagu's beautiful mansion, then go and look outside the ruins of the old abbey: but as we have been over it on two or three former occasions we do not visit it today. We head up the old village street in the teeth of a gale. As we pass Hatchet Pond we see some Royal Engineers constructing pontoons, and the strong wind agitates the water into little waves.

For eight miles we plug along, striving every inch we go. When we reach Lymington we cross the bridge at a cost of a halfpenny each, then sail away through lovely country to Brockenhurst and Lyndhurst.

Dinner at 7.25, and then my sweetheart and I walk to Bench View Private Hotel and call on Miss Shipman. To say she was pleased to see us is putting it very mildly—she was genuinely overjoyed. Buxom and jolly as ever, she did not seem a bit altered, and we sat and talked over old times.

Friday 14 June. We walk to Emery Down and look at our litter of white pigs, then we penetrate into the thick forest. The beautiful mosses and ivies are sweetly pretty, and I feel I should like to put some of the mosses under a microscope, they are so delicately constructed.

After lunch I go and have some of my superfluous hirsute adornments removed. Mamma meets me as I emerge from the hair-cutting saloon, situated at the back of a small tobacconist's shop, and arm in arm, closely attended by a dog who has fastened on to Millie, we go to Bolton's Bench, on our old Knoll, and watch golf being played. The dog sits and looks at me with his liquid expressive dark-brown eyes.

He is a black dog, a cross between a retriever and a spaniel. I examine his collar and find 'Holmfield, Lyndhurst' on it.

Coming home, closely attended by our new four-footed friend, at the bottom of Lyndhurst Street I see a gate marked 'HOLMFIELD'. A gardener and a boy open it, whistle shrilly, and shout 'Coom 'ere.'

The dog looks up at me appealingly, as much as to say, 'Must I go?'

I am no stealer of dogs, and I consider it a very bad fault in a dog to follow anyone but his master, so I give him no encouragement, although I am convinced that at a word from me he would have bid them defiance. But I was unbending, and slowly he crept unwillingly towards his gate.

When he got within range, the man threw his cap at him, and slam went the gate, and the dog was trapped, and no doubt got a sound rating.

Dinner at 7.15, as Agnes our waitress is going out. Agnes is a nice girl, and studies us in every way.

Saturday 15 June. The rain was falling in torrents, and we never left the hotel all the morning. I did not know how weather might be in Brighton, and kept rushing to look at every motor that came along—'That's Tom'—'No, it isn't.' 'Here he is.' 'No.' It quite got on our nerves.

Lunchtime came, and then weather seemed better, and we walked three miles to Lyndhurst Road Station, hoping to meet Tom. We had several false alarms as cars came dashing by, and I think we made the occupants of some quite uncomfortable by our close scrutiny. At the station it began to rain, and we walked back.

Mrs Ings met us as we stepped over the threshold, and said, 'Oh! Just after you were gone, a wire came for you.'

I tore open the envelope and read: 'Raining, trip abandoned till early morrow. Garrett.'

Sunday 16 June. The finest morning we have had. I go for a walk, and meet the motor, containing Tom, Fanny, Mr and Mrs Garrett, on the road about a mile from Lyndhurst. They pull up and give me a lift back.

They have had a good run, in just under four hours. Tom having deposited the car under a shed, and instructed the ostler to pour water over her wheels, we three males go inside and have a drink.

Monday 17 June. Tom, Mrs G., Millie and I get into Tom's motor, 'pup pup' goes the horn, and away we go. Bournemouth is our objective.

Through beautiful scenery, her machinery purring like some giant cat, skilfully and carefully guided by Tom, we spin along, as Tom says, 'like a swaller'.

Nothing comes amiss to her, hills scarcely check her, and with irresistible thrust we pave our way, and reach Bournemouth, nineteen miles in about fifty minutes. Then through glorious rhododendron ornamental drives to Canford Cliffs, where Tom pulls up and lets us admire the Canford Cliffs Hotel, and over the architectural beauties thereof the while he waxes eloquent indeed.

As Brightonians I think we feel sorry to see so much evidence of prosperity in Bournemouth and neighbourhood, when we at home are certainly passing through a dull and trying time.

Of course Bournemouth is new compared to Brighton, and their houses are more modern, and it has natural beauties that have been conserved and made the most of, but as I say, our greatest asset still is that only 52 miles separates us from the great metropolis.

Then we turn our iron steed's nose for Christchurch, and draw up outside its grand old church. It would take a day to properly examine. Some of the carvings on the choir stalls are very quaint. Here a friar, disguised as a fox, preaches to a flock of geese; there a baboon, with a cowl on his head, lolls on a pillow. Leaving here deeply impressed, we descend to the mundane by driving to a garage, and giving our trusty steed a drink of two gallons of petrol = 2*s* 8*d*.

On again to Hinton Admiral and pull up at the Cat and Fiddle, an inn 600 years old. Refreshments, and then we whirr on our way, timing one mile in two minutes ten seconds, and reach Lyndhurst all well and delighted with our spin.

Here I may say that I have never seen in any district more motor-cars than there are in and around Lyndhurst. From morning till night they pass up and down our High Street, and we are never many minutes without them.

Cycling is also universal, and hundreds pass every day. Add to this a large horse traffic, both riding and driving, tradesmen's carts, farm wagons and carts, private traps, coaches and wagonettes, and you will readily see that Lyndhurst High Street is very busy for so small a place.

We now discuss lunch, and after that Millie and I start off on our bicycles to Ringwood. The other four are to catch us up on the motor.

The condition of the road was very bad—loose and stony—and I mortally feared one or both of us must puncture.

About 2½ miles from Lyndhurst we met the first person we had seen. He came along in the middle of the road, peering about as though in doubt: a respectably dressed short man, inclined to be hump-backed.

As we approached he shouted to us, 'Oh! I say, I've missed my party. I got out to look at some trees, and missed my party. Can you tell me where this road goes to?'

I said, 'Yes, the way you are going will bring you into Lyndhurst.'

Half a mile further we met a coach conductor in a white top-hat. He hailed us, 'Beg pardon sir, but I've lost one of my passengers, have you seen anything of him?'

We replied, 'Yes, was he a short humped-back man?'

'That's the one sir.'

'Well, he's about half a mile further back. Walking into Lyndhurst, I think.'

He murmured something and went on, and we pursued our way.

A quarter of a mile further on we see a four-horse coach, stationary and blocking nearly all the road, so that we can only just squeeze by. Seeing us, the passengers—who are seated on the top, and visibly impatient—get on their feet, and in a chorus demand if we have seen their conductor and a lost passenger he has gone back to find.

'Yes, passed the passenger a mile back, and your conductor has gone to try and find him.' I doubt if he ever did, though.

We pass on, and at a sharp double turn in the road I get out my mariner's compass to see which direction we ought to take. Soon after we hear a motor purring along.

'That's old Tom'—'No it isn't.'

Whirr, whirr, dust and stench, and it flies by.

Soon after purr, purr, and Tom sweeps along. 'Hullo,' Tom shouts. 'I say, this is a beastly road, old man.'

Away they go, and soon after we get to Picket Post, an inn with an enormous tea-kettle hung up outside, and then run down and enter Ringwood. We find the motor waiting for us, and Fanny discovers a nice old confectioner's, and we troop in to tea. Three dear old ladies minister to our wants.

Then we limber up towards Burley, and eventually get on the Bournemouth Road, which bristles with notice-boards on the sides, thus:

Home at a quarter to seven, a really good dinner, and Millie plays piano to us. Then we disperse, and as we get our candles, hear sounds of a domestic storm in progress. Someone is getting a jacketing, and we hear Mrs Ings in shrill tones, saying, 'You're a mischief-maker, that's what you are here, a mischief-maker.'

We creep up to bed.

Tuesday 18 June. Knowing Mr G. is anxious to get away early, Millie like a good daughter begins to rouse the house by ringing our bell loudly, and we are soon rewarded by hearing sounds of the servants beginning to stir.

At 25 to eight, the motor creeps out of the stable-yard and draws up outside the hotel door. The mechanism begins to purr, and she seems to stand there panting, as though impatient of the delay.

Up get Tom, Mr G., Mrs G. and Fanny, and Mill and I frame around saying goodbye. I manœuvre on the side step of the motor, to get a kiss from Fanny at parting, but she is not so readily responsive as I should have expected, and her hat sticks over so far, and it is also tightly encircled with a motor veil, and she is rather high on the seat, that I have to reluctantly abandon my sinister design.

We suddenly seem very quiet in our room after the bustle of departure. Millie and I walk up to Bank, and get into the grand old woods. We are quite alone, like babes in the wood.

Going along I spy a tree which had grown up with two stems, one of which had been cut off about five feet off the ground. 'There's a lovely seat for you, Mill.'

'No, I can't get up there.'

'Yes you can. Come here.'

So picking her up I deposit her on it, and there she rests like Patience on a monument while I smoke.

Just as we leave the wood, we come across a very pretty object which I had half a mind to bring away, only it was an awkward thing to carry—an old boot, worn out and tossed into the woodside. Not pretty, you will say—but when it was thus thrown away, nature received it, and moss began to grow upon it, until it came to be a real thing of beauty, encrusted with a delicious fairy-like covering of a lovely tint of green, and when you looked closely the delicate formation of mosses was almost a sermon.

Now we get on the road, and alongside it stretches for miles, lying loosely on the ground, a rubber-covered field telegraph and/or telephone wire, laid by the Royal Engineers who are camping in the district.

Anon an officer and a sergeant ride by. The sergeant's horse prances sideways and requires a lot of riding. Frequently he dismounts, and the officer holds his horse's bridle while the sergeant tinkers about with the wire: and as he remounts, and the horse curvets about, he leers at us, as much as to say, 'Don't you think I am a grand horseman to manage a bag of fleas like this beast?'

They stop so often that we keep up with them all the way to Lyndhurst, and then clapping spurs to their horses they clatter gallantly away to their camp, way up on the road to Romsey. Fine figures of men both of them, which they seem to know perfectly well.

Home to a luncheon of pressed beef, potatoes and salad, gooseberry tart and custard, bread, butter and cheese with biscuits. Then watch boys play cricket with manly zest.

Wednesday 19 June. I get out my cycle and ride through beautiful forest to Bartley, then on as far as Netley Marsh, and home by the Romsey Road, coming out at Misslebrook and Westons Corner. A stroll winds up a quiet day, as Mum is not fit for violent exercise.

Thursday 20 June. After breakfast I interviewed Mr Ings on the QT, and asked him to let me have a nice little pony and trap, to be ready at 10.30.

I manœuvred Mamma till 10.20, passing the time in writing and letting her knit. Then I said, 'Come on, we mustn't sit here all day—get ready. You'll want a coat.'

We get outside, and Mum starts up the street.

'Come back, Mummy.'

Then she essays *down* the street.

'Shan't go down there.'

'Where are you going to walk, then?'

'Not going to walk at all, my dear. I'm waiting for my trap.'

'You haven't ordered a trap.'

'Yes I have, it'll be here in a minute.'

In very doubtful tones, 'But you can't drive.'

'Hush, that's all right.' Clatter, clatter, and up comes our little trap. 'Jump up, Mammy.'

It was a sweet little turn-out, painted red on wheels and shafts, with varnished birch body, and spick and span as a new pin—rubber-tyred wheels, and looked very nice.

The pony was a dear little chap, and gathering up the reins I climb into my seat and we go off in fine style.

Millie's nervousness soon wears off when she sees how we spin along, and when we have passed a motor or two, and she sees we are still intact, she settles down, and I think rather fancies we make a pretty picture.

The first time I bring the whip into use, and our steed bounds forward, brings her heart into her mouth, but at last all her anxiety is gone and she is as happy as a queen, driving being her greatest idea of pleasure.

We drive up hill and down dale to Minstead, the Trusty Servant Inn with its quaint sign; on then to Stoney Cross, close to Rufus Stone, where I dismount and caress my little horse's muzzle. Then remount by the Compton Arms Hotel and turn for home.

We partake of lunch, then walk round cemetery, searching for the tomb of the late Mr Ings. It is nearly the last one we come to, and we read the following inscription:

In loving memory of
Alfred
the beloved husband of Eleanor Ings
who died
May 20th 1906
aged 54 years—
Thy will be done.

It was another old association gone—poor old chap—we always liked him and found him a good sort.

Friday 21 June. For weeks people have been saying, 'We shan't get any summer weather now till the longest day—it'll be all right then.' Well, it is a very fine morning.

A four-horse coach from Bournemouth draws up, and the passengers come in for lunch, and we are very busy. After lunch we walk to Whitley Wood to get a fern we noted the other day, and Mill sits on a felled oak. The best evening since we came here.

Saturday 22 June. I go and get my oil-can filled at the cycle-shop, and go all over our two machines, oiling every part and examining and testing all the brakework. Then we say goodbye all round, and the wind absolutely blows us on our way.

We leave Lyndhurst with regret. The forest has a fascination and a subtle hold on me, and for weeks before I came, I said I felt it calling. The English Lakes and the Swiss mountains have the same sort of power over me. I think it is the fact of being right away from the bricks and mortar that pen one in, in towns and cities, and being able to go for miles without seeing a human being, so that you feel you are at 'grips' with nature. These places get you in some mystical way in their power, and when you are away from them, a feeling which becomes at last almost irresistible impels you to revisit them.

Pedalling but little, and freewheeling a lot, we meet scores—I might say hundreds—of cyclists, with hard grim set faces, struggling against the wind, and I believe some of them feel almost nasty to us, as we sail majestically on our way.

At Fareham we stop at our old dairy, and as it is blowing hard, and a small boy is struggling with the shop blind-pole, and the pretty young woman in the shop goes out to help him, and seems rather at a loss what to do, I go out, with that natural gallantry which characterises my every action, and mount the pair of steps, and take it down for them, for which she thanks me sweetly.

Into Havant and on to Chichester. As Mamma's 'sit-me-down' is by now getting tender, we decide to rail home the remainder of the journey. We stable our machines at a confectioner's, and have two boiled eggs each, and Millie avows she has never eaten two before at one sitting.

We then roam about and look at 41 Tower Street, where Harriett's father dwells, and into the cathedral. It is undergoing repair of course. I have had the pleasure of visiting a great many of our English cathedrals, and I think they are nearly always under repair when I honour them with my presence.

At 6.22 p.m. we jump in the train, and arrive at Brighton Station at 7.15. Coming down Queens Road we get blocked in by the Rifle Volunteers and Cyclist Corps marching back from an inspection.

Cuthbert comes up the street, and explains he just happened to meet the railway van at our door half an hour ago, and received the luggage. Bravo! luck again.

Once more we have to be thankful that we have gone out and returned without a scratch—not even one puncture, although we have ridden many miles, and at times over very loose roads.

Goodbye.

Matlock

1908

Tuesday 2 June. I sent to Cook's office for a copy of their 'Holiday Tours', and went and interviewed my friend Johnson, Cook's manager: 'Now then, how about Matlock?'

Well, this fitted in, so I ordered tickets for seven days' residence at Matlock House Hydro, breakfast, luncheon and dinner, and about a hundred miles of coaching on three days.

> Monday: Haddon Hall, Baslow and Chatsworth.
> Wednesday: Wingfield Manor via Matlock Bath.
> Friday: the Via Gellia and Dovedale.

Inclusive fare from London, £4 8*s* 0*d* each.

Saturday 6 June. A fine day but cold. We reached Victoria, jumped in a hansom, and were duly landed at the Midland Company's fine station at St Pancras.

St Albans was our first stop. We were getting colder and colder, and Millie began to worry in a most pertinacious manner for a cup of tea—but 'divil a bit', would the train stop again till we reached Leicester.

Then I secured tea and bread-and-butter for two, and bought a Midland time-table book with maps etc. which I sorely needed, as without a map on a long railway journey I feel like a sailor without a compass.

At Derby, into another train. We have a very amusing conversation with a manufacturer of 'lasts', and I am sorry to lose him when we get out at Matlock. I charter a little boy to carry one bag, and we wend our way to the cable tram.

Before us is a very steep street, said to be the steepest tramway in the world, the gradient being 1 in 5½, or nearly 500 feet in half a mile. This tramway was presented to his native place by Sir George Newnes. As we go up we notice Smedley's Hydro, very barrack-like in appearance.

Our destination is the Matlock House Hydro, where a young lady hurries forward. 'Mr and Mrs Peerless?' she says. 'Would you be good enough to sign the visitors' book? You'd like some hot water, wouldn't you.'

We enter a very nice bedroom on the ground floor, and far away I see a dark building which I find is Riber Castle. We soon wash off our travel stains. 'Well, Millie, I think we shall be all right.'

'Yes,' says Mother, 'that's what I say about Cook's, you can always depend on their sending you to a good place.'

We then find our way to the dining-room, which to my surprise had a stage on which a theatrical sketch was being given. We were thus lucky in being in time for the silver collection, which the male performer now proceeded with limping amble to gather in.

Sunday 7 June. Millie and I set out to explore Matlock Bath, and meander along the river until we reach the Fish Pond Hotel. Opposite is a pond swarming with fish, whose antics are watched by a crowd of people. A notice states that the fish must only be fed with the food from three or four automatic machines which are placed here.

Putting a penny in the slot I procure a matchbox-shaped box of food, and see them dart in confused shoals to secure it. Having exhausted the contents, I close the box and throw it in, and derive great amusement by watching the fish dart at and open it.

We then turn back and toil up our hill, as the trams do not run on the Sabbath. We look outside the Rockside Hydro where our old friend Feldwicke always stays.

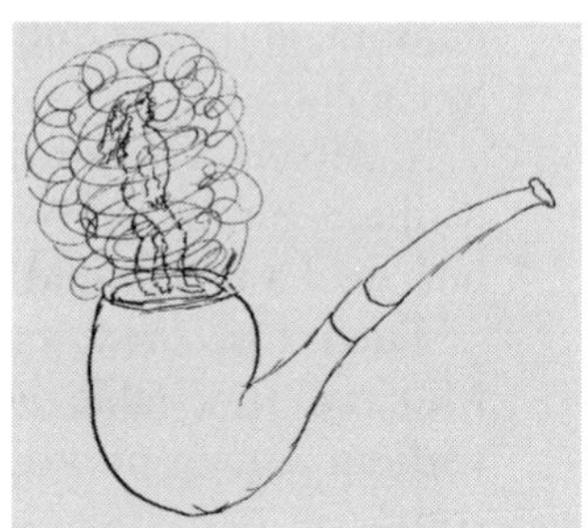

For a time I commune with My Lady Nicotine, returning with appetite to partake of supper. Everybody then adjourns to the drawing-room and adjacent lounges and listens to music on a grand piano. A Mr Davies, an old gentleman of 74, sang with great fervour, and we find he has been a rather prominent singer in his day, having toured for several years with Sims Reeves and other notable figures in the musical world. That he has a genuine love for music, no one who sees him can doubt.

Monday 8 June. We go to Smedley Street and climb up into a char-à-banc belonging to Messrs H. Hand & Sons and drawn by two nice horses. Our party consisted of Mr and Mrs Goldspink who sit at our table; Mrs Lennon, a rather quaint old widow of a Liverpool tugging company; Mr Sweeney, something at Whitehall; a young Frenchman; and two young men whom we did not know.

A band commenced to play, belonging to a school treat, and our horses did not seem to appreciate the efforts of the man who dealt gigantic strokes on the big drum. To pacify our horses the driver drove up Smedley Street and back, much to the disgust of some of the older ladies, but at last we did start in gallant style, the horses stepping out well, and their feet rang out like music as they strode along.

At length reached Chatsworth House and looked round on a mass of holiday-makers, innumerable char-à-bancs, wagonettes and traps, and the largest number of bicycles we had ever seen in one place. The people waiting to gain admission formed up in a long queue four abreast.

One of the estate men handled them as follows. Close to the entrance gates was an enclosure, like a pen or pound, with a movable piece of scantling as a bar at each end. Closing down the bar near the entrance gate, he proceeded to lift up the bar at the back end, and when the people to the number of about fifty or sixty had filed in, he closed the bar again, raised the bar at the front, and the people passed through the entrance gates.

At the house we were received by a superior-looking maid-servant who became our guide. The sculpture, I think, appealed to me most: but being Whit Monday, and so many people, we were hurried through where I could gladly have lingered, so that we had no time to examine anything at any length.

Through most beautiful gardens to the stately glass-house and a fountain in the form of a weeping-willow. We then came to a rocking-stone weighing seven tons, and a stone block weighing three tons, used as a turnstile, so nicely balanced that it can be moved by a child. Back, and drive away to the model village of Edensor. The church contains a monument to Bess of Hardwick, a buyer and seller of estates, a money-lender, a merchant of lead, coal and timber. She lived to a grand old age and died immensely rich and without a friend in 1607.

Passing from here, a girl on a bicycle, trying to avoid us, loses control of her machine and is thrown off rather heavily on the side of the road. On through pretty country until we reach Bakewell.

Now the impression that a chance visitor takes away of a town he visits (and when I say 'he', I embrace 'she' as well, a thing which I am told 'he's' do to 'she's' sometimes) depends so much on the aspect under which he sees it, that it is never fair to judge it by one visit. You might rattle into Bakewell 364 days in the year and the impression would be of a staid sleepy old market town, but today is Whit Monday, and this old place is alive with people; hundreds of horses are in the square, cavorting about as their owners run them up and down and try to sell them, heaps of cheap crockery lie on the ground and the owners thereof shout its praises, cheap-jacks in parti-coloured raiment harangue open-mouthed rustic audiences to whom they try to sell shoddy knives and razors, and the crack, crack of the rifles in the gipsy shooting-galleries keep up a running accompaniment. Altogether it is a kind of Babel.

We rein up our steeds outside the Rutland Arms Hotel, and as there is a shooting-gallery in full swing, the aforesaid steeds begin to execute a few fancy steps and resemble a pea on a drum.

I regret exceedingly that the six luncheons served to the Matlock House contingent must have left a very small profit to mine host of the Rutland Arms. The young Frenchman certainly did heroic feats as a trencherman, Goldspink did himself well, Millie is never very backward when food is about, Mr Sweeney ate on slowly and methodically (I suppose being at Whitehall he has long since eliminated all the 'hurry' he might ever have had in his composition), and even old Mrs Lennon did full justice to everything that came her way.

After lunch we strolled out amongst the crowd, and listened with considerable amusement to a comical cheap-jack selling knives and razors who kept the people in a continual roar of laughter.

Leaving him, I feel I must have six shots at some balls which are suspended in the air on jets of water. I manage to dislodge two out of six. Then we leave the noise and uproar, and off we go again merrily for Haddon Hall.

Purchasing tickets at sixpence each (the guide-book says fourpence, and the young Frenchman who has been reading his guide-book all day seems inclined to kick at this, but I say 'It's all right, holiday prices, come on'), we make our way through a little portal gate in the doors. First impression is that here you have a real old gem in a decent state of preservation.

Then we stroll about the grounds, regain our char-à-banc and have a beautiful drive home.

Tuesday 9 June. Walk to Matlock Bath. On our way we pay threepence each to go into Long Tor Cavern. A little boy takes us in hand, and giving us each a lighted candle in a candlestick, we penetrate some distance into the mountain.

Then pay a penny each and enter a petrifying well, a very quaint sight. The water comes from iron pipes in the roof and gently sprays over a basin hewn in the floor about nine feet in diameter. This basin is packed with the most heterogeneous collection of articles conceivable: old hats, eggshells, bird-cages, pipes, balls, kettles, teapots, bird-nests, candlesticks etc. These are subjected to the falling water for about twelve months, by which time they are coated with a strong layer of limestone. They are then sold to visitors.

Home to lunch, after which I work in bedroom on the estate accounts till the dinner dressing bell clangs out.

Coffee in drawing-room, then all troop down to dining-room to see *tableaux vivants* on the stage. There is a deal of waiting between each spectacle but they were not bad. 'The cheat,' after the picture by ——, a

lady who has cheated at the bridge table, evoked great applause. 'The gypsy,' 'Other woman' etc. etc. But the *pièce de résistance* was in several *tableaux* 'Home they brought her warrior dead'. Mr and Mrs Goldspink figured with many others in this set.

Wednesday 10 June. Char-à-banc drive to Wingfield Manor, where Mary Queen of Scots spent nearly sixteen years in captivity.

We were received by the daughter of a farmer who lives in a small house by the entrance. She sold us a nicely written guide-book, and then left us to wander at our own sweet wills until the pangs of hunger assailed us, and we trooped into the farmer's parlour to lunch. In an adjoining room we see quite a number of curios laid out like an old curiosity shop.

At our hydro I plunged into estate accounts again. Then dinner, and after coffee in drawing-room we joined in progressive whist—Millie is a gentleman on this occasion. We neither gain a prize, although Millie was nearly highest gentleman. Mrs Lennon won the lady booby, a hat pin. Gents' booby won by a girl, box of cigarettes. First ladies' a loving-cup. First gents' a very nice little match-holder arrangement.

Millie having resumed her normal sex, I consent to take her to bed.

Thursday 11 June. Up into the baths, and find the attendant is a young man, smart, civil and obliging. He made a hot bath for me, in which I revelled—then under the spray needle shower, which he graduated by easy stages from hot to cold. Soon after I might have been observed consuming breakfast.

As soon as this is over I 'make tracks' for our bedroom, get out my pen, ink, papers, and estate accounts book, and settle down with a grim determination to try and wring the neck of this job today.

I worked steadily till eleven o'clock, interrupted at regular intervals by the 'alarms and excursions' of the chamber-maid. Each time I tried to coax her in, but before I could get a word in, she was off like a startled hare. I thought, 'Well, this is really too bad, the poor girl wants to tidy up the room, and I must give her a chance'—so I lit my pipe and strolled out into the grounds, watching the hall-porter painting the wooden balustrading in front of the raised terrace outside the drawing-room.

As I sat there conversing with him he was called away; when he was gone I could not resist the temptation to paint one or two of the balusters myself.

'Well, time's up,' I must get back to work. Gain bedroom again and find silly girl has not taken advantage of my absence. Settle to work again until I have to go down to luncheon. Then up to bedroom again, and just after four o'clock I thankfully write the last item in the copy of the estate accounts. I feel like a schoolboy released from school. Millie helps me to pack it up, and I watch her deft little fingers and think: 'Blessing she is: God made her so, and deeds of week-day holiness fall from her noiseless as the snow.'

Walk to Victoria Hall, sit in grounds and watch girls play tennis—then down town and have my beard trimmed. The barber had recently been partaking of a hearty meal of onions, so I was not sorry to regain the open air, catch up Millie, and then toil up to our hydro—wash, change, and march down to dinner.

After coffee, a number of us trooped upstairs to attend an electrical demonstration by Nurse Payne. I was surprised at the number and costly nature of the electrical appliances that this hydro possesses.

Nurse, who was a dark, pleasing little woman, proceeded to show us the radiant heat bed; this is supposed to be an improvement on the Turkish bath. The patient lies on the bed and is covered by a sheet steeped in a solution of tungstate of soda to render it non-inflammable. Four powerful electric radiators run along the sides of the bed and provide the heat. A coverlet, supported on iron standards so that it does not touch the patient's body, is placed on top; in this coverlet is a circular hole through which the patient's head is placed.

The body is thus exposed to enormous heat which of course produces profuse perspiration, but the head being outside the coverlet the patient breathes the normal air of the room.

The next was a vibrator for stirring up the liver—and it is claimed by its friends that it is equal to horse-riding exercise. Nurse asked if anyone would like to try it. I said, 'I would please,' and quite enjoyed the sensation. Several more then had it applied; Millie at last consented and made such a comical face when Nurse first put it on her back that the whole company were convulsed with laughter.

She showed us a Dutch oven-like arrangement for giving radiant heat locally to a foot or an arm, then came the 'high frequency'. This is electrical current at an enormous voltage automatically controlled by a mercurial brake. Nurse said: 'Will anyone please try it?'

I said: 'Yes, I will, but don't you touch me while I am having it.'

'Ah, you know something about it, I see.' Nurse then asked me to lie down on a couch, handed me a metal cylinder and pulled on the switch. I felt nothing. She said, 'Touch the frame of that glass on the wall beside you.' I did so, and a tingling sensation pervaded my fingers and green fire flashed forth from my fingers and danced round the frame.

She then placed her hand about four inches from my boot, and green fire leapt from the leather of my boot into her fingers. 'Here, don't you burn up my boots,' I shouted.

Then she showed us the Finsen burner used for lupus cases, and then a most interesting collection of x-ray photographs, and wound up by showing electric massage on the face and neck. Several ladies submitted their faces to this operation, and to see them was irresistibly comical.

Friday 12 June. On our ticket we have a drive today to Dovedale. I went out and had a careful look at the weather, wind, clouds etc., and at last made up my mind to chance it. We mount our char-à-banc in Smedley Street, and on *per* 'Via Gellia'—this is the Latinised name of the walk made by the late Mr Philip Gell along the beautiful ravine between Cromford and Bonsall.

We clatter into Tissington, a very pretty village, and put up at the Peveril Peak Hotel. A good lunch, and then tramp to Dovedale—one of the sweetest pieces of scenery I have ever seen. Mrs Goldspink tells Millie that she is on her honeymoon. Speculation has been rife as to whether they were a newly married couple or not.

After dinner a number of us go downstairs and have a ping-pong tournament. Dr Duncan begins to blossom out and at regular intervals calls out in a cheery voice, 'Well played everybody.' He crawls under the stage to find missing balls, and we hear a muffled voice say: 'Shall I stop under here?'

Mr Goldspink, who played a good game, was in the final with Dr Duncan, and won—prize a nice little flat silver pencil-case.

Saturday 13 June. Millie and I go for a walk alongside river. After lunch, rains heavily and blows a good half gale.

Mrs Olliff and I against Dr Duncan and Millie at bridge. Mrs O. and Dr D. are players by book and rule. They worry Millie by asking, 'Do you discard from weakness or strength?'

We play till perilously near dinner-time, then rush off to our rooms, and the way we wash and scramble into our clothes for dinner is 'a caution to snakes'.

After dinner we assemble in the drawing-room and quaff coffee, then to the dining-room and play children's games. I never thought that I should descend to such puerile amusements, but 'a little nonsense now and then is relished by the wisest men'.

We played musical chairs, then four rows of four potatoes were laid on the polished wooden floor and we were provided with a teaspoon and had to pick up one row of potatoes without touching it with anything except the spoon, a most difficult task. To see Mrs Lennon on her knees struggling with the potatoes, and ever and anon stopping to talk to a specially refractory one, made us laugh so that I quite hurt my stomach and made my cheek-bones ache.

Then gentlemen stood up in a row one end, and ladies faced each the other end—ladies ran up to gentlemen with a needle and thread, gentlemen had to thread needle, give it to lady again and lady run back; my partner and I won this. Then we sat in two rows on chairs, and one gentleman and one lady were blindfolded and started off to find each other—the gentleman continually calling out 'Rachel, where art thou?'—lady replying, 'Here I am, Jacob.' When my turn came I groped about, and at last the girl and I banged our foreheads together with some force.

Soon after we retired, and the wind howled round the house as though it would like to tear it down.

Sunday 14 June. Mixed a Seidlitz powder and administered it to Millie, then went and had a spray shower.

After breakfast we went for a walk above Rockside, returning in time for dinner. At five o'clock we walk to the Wishing Stone and Matlock old parish church. Supper, after which we all sit in drawing-room listening to music and recitations.

Monday 15 June. Knock croquet-balls about, then catch the train to Buxton. Leaving the station we make for the Pavilion, pay sixpence each and enter the grounds—plenty of people, and quite a gay scene—tennis-courts, croquet-lawns, skating-rinks, water for boating, swans, ducks etc. A very fine concert-hall wherein we listen to a first-class band of about forty performers and a conductor whose mop of hair shaking here and there as he frantically conducts amuses us greatly.

Tuesday 16 June. Millie and I went down to station to see Mr and Mrs Goldspink off. They press us to stay the night with them on our way home.

Home to lunch, during which Miss Fishbourne (a Sheffield lady who is at our table) tells us she knows Mrs Grey of the Steyne Hotel, Brighton, and is very friendly with Lord and Lady Jonas.

In the afternoon we were to have had a garden-party in the grounds, but the weather being threatening it is decided to postpone it, and Dr Duncan who is elected Master of the Revels suggests ninepins first, then we play deck-quoits, then billiards, and we wind up in the drawing-room with a grand ping-pong tournament.

Dr Duncan and I come out top, and amidst rival shouts of 'Go it Bournemouth!' 'Go it Brighton!' the Doctor wins.

After dinner we settle down to bridge. We hear there is a fire down town, but we are much too busy to see about fires.

Wednesday 17 June. Pouring in rain. Dr Duncan gets up a concert-party which we dub the Cracksmen, and we are to wear black masks. We spend nearly all the morning rehearsing.

Afternoon Millie and I start bridge, but have to leave it and go rehearsing again.

In the evening we form up on the stage (without our black masks, as Miss Lacey who wears glasses cannot see with a mask on), up goes the curtain and the show begins. A most unqualified success—everybody says they would like to have it all over again the next night.

Thursday 18 June. Mill and I climb up the Heights of Abraham and the tower. We then find the guide and enter the Great Rutland Cavern, the largest and one of the most interesting of the many caverns in Matlock—when lighted by gas, its great chambers and dome-like roof make a very effective scene. It is said to be large enough to shelter 10,000 men.

After a considerable distance we came to a pool of water called Jacob's Well. Glasses were lying around it, and our guide filled two for us, and we both drank what seemed most excellent water.

Catch a 'bus home and partake of luncheon, after which we converse with a Mr Kay. He lives not far from Lyme Regis, and tells us that recently a kind of volcano has broken out there close to the cliffs. He also descanted at some length about Cornwall, having been invited there when Sir William Treloar went down some little time since. He said Sir William had quite a triumphal progress in his native county.

I go and have my hair cut, and on my return find Millie playing ninepins. Mr Kay and I play bowls; after several rounds the gardener comes and plays with us, and a very good game he plays too. We play on to the last minute and then scramble into our clothes for dinner.

A Mr Boam now sits at our table—he is a farmer, a tall, black-bearded, loose-limbed giant, as pale as a ghost and as weak and nervous as a child. Never laid up in his life, some months ago he contracted influenza, got about too soon, relapsed and had to keep his bed for sixteen weeks. He has been sent here for treatment and I hope he will be restored, as he is a rough diamond.

Friday 19 June. When we wake we are filled with the consciousness that today we have to depart, and some little thought comes to us that we are only sojourners as our fathers were, and that some day we shall make that last grand departure to 'that bourn from whence no traveller returns'.

Down to breakfast and make a tour of the room saying goodbye. Poor old Boam at our table, when we say we are going, pleads with us to stop another week, but we say, 'No, we have to get home now.'

Soon after we mount the cable-car, and at bottom of the hill we purchase a little piece of 'Blue John' formed into a vase as a present to take to Mr and Mrs Goldspink.

Reach St Pancras all well, tube to London Bridge, and thence to

Streatham Hill. We ask a policeman about a tram, and in a short time are deposited at the end of Becmead Avenue. Mr G. is outside no. 54, fixing a spring on the gate, and he is very pleased to see us.

It is a new house, not really out of the builders' hands, as the stair-treads have to be painted. It is very nicely arranged—bright and well decorated and every stick of furniture is new.

After dinner we four stroll out, buy an alarum clock and go for a pretty walk. The common is really like country, and no one would believe they were so near London.

When we return, Mr G. shows us some excellent photos on lantern slides which he took when on a holiday in Spain. With these slides he has given a lecture on his travels.

Saturday 20 June. We awoke to a good lot of ringing of bells. We hardly know what to make of it—turns out later to be workman trying to get in to paint the stair-treads.

Say goodbye to Mrs Goldspink, and with Mr Goldspink board a tram for Victoria. He gets off before we reach our destination and we say goodbye. No one could have given us a heartier welcome. Although our acquaintance has been but short, we feel like old friends.

Jumping on a 'bus we go to Marble Arch, and get another 'bus to the Franco-British Exhibition. We pay our shilling each and traverse several long buildings filled with trade exhibits, then go for a tour on the lagoons on a swan boat. A man pedals this along and we get a good idea of the outsides of all the buildings. We gaze at the Flip-Flap, and then through *Daily Mail* building and enter Ceylon Village.

Into several of the palaces. Some diamonds marked up at £18,000 and £22,000 each, very fine. Much taken with Parisian and English frocks and hats displayed to great advantage on wax figures.

At about four o'clock we make our way out through shoals of people coming in, and eventually land at Victoria, and have a nice tea at the Aerated Bread Company.

Pick up our luggage and away we go, and reach home all well. Children come in and we are reunited, and ready to settle down into the old lines once more. Goodbye.

Lynton

1909

Perhaps no one was ever more undecided about a holiday than I this year.

The timber trade, after six bad years, was in a worse condition than ever, and it was a grave question whether one ought to incur the expense of a holiday. Buying was difficult, and after months of negotiations I had only contracted for a small part of our requirements, at prices that gave me no pleasure.

A cargo which I was anxious to buy had come to nothing, and then news came of a great strike in Sweden in the timber trade; all sawing was stopped, and it was forced on me that it would be impossible to buy what we wanted this year.

In consequence of the strike, chartering a ship became difficult. After an experience of nearly thirty years, I have never had so much trouble as when I eventually chartered the good ship *Albertha*, at a higher rate than I wished to pay, to load what we had bought.

Then Millie and I had relied on sending the children to Keymer, but when we made enquiries it was not convenient for Mrs O. Thompsett to have them, as she had let her rooms. However, Mrs J. Thompsett of Oakdene, Western Road, Hurst, no doubt would be pleased to do so.

By this time I had nearly made up my mind not to go away at all, but I did not like to disappoint the children, who for weeks had been talking of what they were going to do when they went to Keymer. Also I have always felt that a woman should be taken right away from her children and her home duties for a short time every year. Every night when we went to bed, poor old Mother would say: 'Have you decided anything yet? We shan't go this week then'—and how many times she sent word to her laundry that she must have the washing home by Thursday, as we might be going away, I should not like to say. I began to think the laundry people would be justified in thinking we were lunatics.

Well, one evening Millie and I took the rail to Hassocks, got the 'bus to Hurst, and found Mrs Thompsett, who was most willing to have our little people. 'Send them just when you like, Mrs Peerless, I am sure I shall look after them all right.'

We decided to send Gladys and Wilfred up on the Saturday, and Reggie was to go to Warnham. The road being now clear, I got another copy of Cook's 'Holiday Tours', and then got Millie to ask her father and mother if they could come with us, which they agreed to do. Millie went to Beal's, East Street, and bought me a guide-book to Lynton and Lynmouth, and I arranged for Cuthbert to get his meals somewhere in the town and sleep at 12 St James's Avenue during our absence.

Friday 27 August. Trott loads our portmanteau, and we pave our way to the station. Mr and Mrs G. are already there, and we commence our journey to Victoria and away through St James's Park to Waterloo.

Having a good hour in hand, we stroll about the station, gaze at soldiers going from platform to platform, and watch the moving panorama of people coming and going in unending streams.

At 10.45 we enter the train for Barnstaple, and away we go. Past Byfleet, Maybury, Woking, Brookwood for Necropolis, Purbright, and then the welcome call to luncheon comes; we enter the bright dining-car, and partake of a very well served meal. Millie goes to sleep and looks the picture of well fed contented repletion.

Millie asleep in the train after luncheon.

We pass Wilton, which brings to my mind a very happy day Millie and I and Charley Feldwicke spent there before we were married. At Exeter our compartment is invaded by a lady and gentleman. She has a strained look in her eyes, caused I fancy by looking after the old gentleman. He strikes me as being a little eccentric; he has lived in India, and from his face I fancy he has held some kind of judicial position. He rambles a good deal about trees and grass—asks me several times whether trees do not spoil grass.

I notice that the earth here is very red, and as I believe 'Adam' means 'red earth', I think this must be the kind of earth from which Adam was made.

On again to Lynton by the 'toy railway': in order to avoid the expense of long embankments and bridges, the line has been made to turn and twist, and at several points the turns are so sharp that the lines are almost parallel with other parts to be traversed.

At Lynton Station I push about in the crowd, and at last espy a thick-set pleasant-faced man with 'Imperial Hotel' on his cap. I hail him, and we clamber into a little 'bus drawn by two horses. We are quickly full up, and they pile luggage on top till I think they will break the roof.

We now go through lovely wooded scenery with the West Lyn river a long way below us. Nearing Lynton we descend an awful hill, then drag up another, and stop outside the Imperial Hotel.

At 7.30 we sat down to dinner in a large room like a greenhouse, with continuous windows all round the front and side, looking out upon the sea. Under the glass roof were white linen or thick muslin sheets, stretched tightly and pierced at intervals by electric wires from which depended Osram electric lamps, and it made both by daylight and when illuminated electrically a very pleasing bright room.

After dinner, Millie and I stroll out to the cliff railway. This is the iron link between Lynton and Lynmouth, and is one of the steepest water balances in England, erected at the instigation of Sir Geo. Newnes in 1890.

The two cars are fixed equidistant on an endless wire cable. A tank beneath the top car is charged with water (of which there is a plentiful natural supply) and the tank of the bottom car simultaneously emptied. The brakes are released, and then by the law of gravitation one car runs down and the other is dragged up. The whole car is made to slide off the platform, so that heavy merchandise, loaded carts or motor-cars can be placed on the lift and 'shot up', but it was not my privilege to see this.

Cars run every few minutes daily from 7 a.m. to 8.30 p.m., and during the season and on Sundays later. The fare for a passenger is up threepence, down twopence, return fourpence, motor-car up ten shillings. Gazing down the abyss by dark it certainly looked very dangerous.

We then strolled back to hotel. Our bed was d——d hard, and Mamma growled 'like a bear with a sore head' when she got in, and said it made her back ache.

Saturday 28 August. We were roused by a knock on our door, and a cheery bright pleasant voice saying 'Hot water please mum.'

We breakfasted, and then 'Boots' waylaid me and persuaded me to go for a char-à-banc drive on Exmoor to Simonsbath, a special inducement being that we are sure to come across the stag-hounds hunting.

At eleven o'clock the char-à-banc drew up, and behind a nice pair of horses we descended a terrible hill to Lynmouth. A very tall and stout gentleman of our party began to get into a 'mortal funk', expecting every minute to be thrown out over a precipice.

On the open moor a number of horsemen and horsewomen and traps are waiting to see the stag-hunt come by. Our driver pulls up, and for about an hour everybody strains to see them come over the hills on our right—but several false alarms end in nothing, and our driver gives it up as a bad job.

We put up at the Temperance Hotel and have an indifferent lunch. Two of our party, a Miss Hart and her brother, who elected to have bread and cheese, were kept waiting an unconscionable time. They were remonstrating with the waiting-maid, when the other waiting-maid chimed in and informed them: 'We have something else to do beside waiting on you.' This struck me as fairly impertinent for such a one-eyed place.

We found Simonsbath to be a poor little village. The post office was part of a small quaint cottage.

We started for home about 3.30. After about a mile of uphill I heard a motor struggling after us, and said: 'Look out, there's a motor behind.'

Motorist shouted to our driver, 'Am I right for ——?' (I could not catch where.)

'Naw sir ye must go back tew Simmonsbaith, ye're quite wrang.'

The motorist muttered 'Oh damn,' and it seemed wrung from him, after struggling a mile up the hill.

We now begin to meet disappointed horsemen and women returning from waiting for the stag-hounds, and after safely negotiating several awful hills, we arrive safely at our hotel.

Dinner is enlivened by wasp-hunting. Bridge in the lounge, and to bed. Millie swears at the pillows.

Sunday 29 August. Knock at door, 'Hot water please mum'—Millie's treble answers 'Thank you.'

At breakfast Millie affords us some amusement by her ejaculations every time a wasp comes near. Millie and I and the stout gent then go along the North Cliff Walk. Hundreds of feet below is the sea and the face of the cliff is precipitous. There is no railing or protection of any kind, and I should not recommend it as a walk for one who had dined not wisely but too well.

We had not proceeded more than fifty yards on this path when the stout gent who had been hugging the left side and planting each step with great care, grunted, stood still and jibbed. 'I can't go any farther,' he said. 'I feel giddy—this is too precipitous—I never could look down from a height even as a boy. Will you please give me your hand and lead me back?' So I took his hand in mine, and with great deliberation, planting each foot with such care, I got him to a seat just inside the gate where he anchored and said he would wait for us to come back.

Leaving him there, Millie and I revel in the fine view. We are now fairly in the Valley of Rocks, Castle Rock behind us, the Devil's Cheesewring on the land side, Ragged Jack and several more.

Pursuing our road, we gain our hotel in a slight shower. The stout gent, finding we did not return, and that it came on to rain, had gone back to the hotel, and soon after we all had tea in the lounge. Then a smoke and dressed for church, which is next door to our hotel.

A very aristocratic clean-shaven clergyman was in command, assisted by a very young curate; he read the lessons in a nice voice but stumbled at times and harked back. He also preached from the text 'Possess ye your souls in patience.' He looked very nervous as he stood in the pulpit, and although time may give him confidence I must say that at present he is not 'peorful'.

Afterward we adjourn to the lounge and Millie plays the piano, but failing to get any of the others to follow suit it fizzles out and we get to bed. Millie does a growl at the mattress.

Monday 30 August. A beautiful drive to Hunter's Inn, where we have very good cream. Then Mr G., Millie and I and the stout gent started down a narrow lane to Heddon's Mouth.

Millie and Mr G. soon got ahead and I had the stout gent on my hands—he grunted a good deal and took great care where he planted his feet, but I got him to within a few hundred yards of the sea where there was a bridge over the river. I advised him to wait there.

Pushing on quickly, I found Millie and Mr G. sitting on the hillside. Having just had the pleasure of seeing a man slip in the shallow river essaying to cross it on stepping-stones, they particularly desired me to try as they wished to see someone else fall in, they enjoyed the first so much.

I crossed in good safety, whereat they ironically clapped their hands.

The shore was a grand sight. The waves broke over the rocks, as one of our party remarked, 'just like the roll of musketry volley firing'.

With reluctance I turned back and picked up the stout gent, and together we strolled back to our hostelry. I was surprised to see the quantity of char-à-bancs standing outside. We went into the hotel garden, and watched one young fellow play lawn-tennis with a strapping girl. Our time being up we remount our char-à-banc, and reach our hotel exceedingly well pleased.

Directly Mamma gets into bed she bewails her hard lot, but as her voice gets weaker and finally ceases I conclude Titania sleeps.

Tuesday 31 August. Take cliff railway to Lynmouth and walk along the East Lyn river to Watersmeet (the aborigines call it Watersmitt).

We pass several anglers whipping for trout, and where the houses at Lynmouth abut on the riverside, we saw one catch a fish, give it to his friend, who climbed a ladder to the house, and handed it in, we presumed to be cooked. It seemed to me a kind of 'boots mended while you wait' style of fishing.

Passing happily along, we reached a refreshment place called Myrtleberry and were pounced on by the proprietor who gave us a small book and leaflet:

Important Notice to VISITORS . . .

> **Having come up the Valley to see the Watersmeet and Falls, do not go back without seeing them, which a great number of Visitors are doing this Season by going past them on the wrong side.**
>
> The path is open to all Visitors wishing to avail itself of its use, **perfectly free and without solicitation of any description.**
>
> Visitors desiring Refreshments will, I feel sure, please themselves where they partake of same, and I respectfully point out that the Myrtleberry tariff will be found on the cover of the little illustrated Guide to the whole district presented with this, or obtainable gratis at Myrtleberry, and ask you to kindly note that **Myrtleberry is in no way connected with any other house in the Valley, or with any person distributing blue leaflets opposite my premises.**
>
> **W.G. ATTREE,**
> (Proprietor Myrtleberry), 1909

I was rather surprised at this man's solicitude as to our welfare, but thanking him in a courtly manner we resumed our pilgrimage. Crossing a stone bridge, we were in view of Watersmeet. I now saw why the man at Myrtleberry had been so solicitous about our going a certain way, as on the other side I saw another place called Watersmeet Cottage where refreshments were provided.

Having gazed our fill we hark back and enter the grounds of Myrtleberry, which the proprietor with native modesty dubs 'the prettiest green spot on earth'. I think the continuous use of superlatives should perhaps be guarded against.

We ordered two ices and sat down alongside the river to await their appearance.

Now if Millie has a weakness for anything it is for ices, and she is a considerable connoisseur of them too. When Millie attacked hers, she waxed enthusiastic, declaring they were 'rale old Varginny grit', and had it not been for the ill results that would have followed, I would have given her as many as she could eat.

Glancing at a few shabby specimens of birds in an aviary, which the proprietor pressed us to see, we tramped into Lynmouth, crowded into the cliff railway and arrived at our hotel. After lunch, sit on the little terrace and watch steamers.

Millie having noted the deadly lively boredom which seems to impregnate the atmosphere of the lounge in the evening, and having in mind the busy merry evenings we spent at Matlock last year, had been in communication with the young woman in the hotel office with a view to getting up a progressive whist party this evening, but the project has fallen flat, entirely I believe through the young woman's lack of effort. I did rather pity the others.

Millie having given vent to her animosity against the bed we settle down, and the world forgetting, by the world forgot, sleep.

Wednesday 1 September. Stroll out shopping, as Millie wants a pair of warm gloves for driving. She certainly buys a pair long enough, as they go nearly up to her shoulder.

At eleven o'clock, seven of us get on one of the hotel char-à-bancs and start for our drive, through very pretty wooded hills till we stop and water the horses at Rockford—a very sweet spot with the tumbling noisy little river on our left. We push on to Badgeworthy Farm House, Malmsmead, where we partake of mutton, stewed fruit and clotted cream *ad libitum.*

After lunch, with a cheery 'Now then horse' from our driver, we clatter off. In a short time we reach Oare Church, famous as the place in which Jan Ridd and Lorna Doone were married, at the conclusion of which ceremony readers of *Lorna Doone* will recollect Lorna was shot by Carver Doone through the church window from the branches of an old oak-tree in the churchyard. Several of us tried to get into the church, but we had to content ourselves by peeping through the windows.

By Glenthorne and through the village of Countisbury, an episode occurred which might have had a very unhappy ending.

We were driving down carefully with the skid-pan on the wheel and the brakes on, when a motor came struggling, puffing and blowing up. To pass each other required care because of the narrow space. We drew in alongside an excavation on the hill on our left hand; the motor, nearly spent with the tug up the hill, stopped also, and a lot of steam escaped from the fore part of the car.

Then our near-side horse refused to pass, and our driver shouted out to the motorist: 'It's the steam she is afraid of, shut if off can't you, then she'll go by.'

'It'll lie down presently,' says Mr Motorist.

Well there we stood, and our horses began to plunge and swerve, bringing some of the passengers' hearts into their mouths. Our driver was very skilful and quiet, and in two or three minutes the steam subsided, and with a slap of the whip we were by and the danger was passed—but I should not expect to get off Scot-free in similar situations.

We ultimately reach Lynmouth. It is too much of a drag for our horses to take us up to Lynton, so Mr G., Millie and I walk up the zig-zag path and find it a trying climb. The opinion seems to be 'never again'.

Thursday 2 September. To Glen Lyn, perhaps the prettiest spot we have ever been to. The guide-book says: 'No words can do this paradise justice. Its charms are inexhaustible.'

Lunch, then Millie and I go out to town hall. This is a very nice pile; it cost just over £15,000 and was given by Sir George Newnes, whose beautiful house is perched on top of Hollerday Hill, at the back of the town hall.

After a climb we reach the summit—the view magnificent. Then home and dinner, and after sundry grumbles at pillow and mattress Millie gives over and I presume sleeps.

Friday 3 September. Board the char-à-banc for Ilfracombe. It seems to me they have booked one seat too many, or say half a seat, as he was a little French boy accompanied by two very large fat women and a slim man, whom I put down as his mother, aunt and father. It was a tight fit, and the Frenchwoman volubly informs all whom it may concern that she 'book her seats yesterday, the best seats, the box-x-x seat-t-ts'.

However, off we did went, and we were very comfortable, except that when one of the large French female women stood up, Millie complained about her hat being knocked by the lady's abdomen.

We were soon in the midst of a pack of hounds and three or four scarlet-coated huntsmen on their way to meet at Lynton.

Through pretty scenery we go till we reach Parracombe, where we men get down and walk up a very steep hill. We now rattle on our way to Combe Martin and pull up at the King's Arms, which is also known as the Pack of Cards, and it has some resemblance to a house built by children with cards. The village street is over a mile in length and comprises a quaintly picturesque conglomeration of farms, cottages, residences and shops. All seem to possess large gardens and orchards, and I do not think I have ever seen more plums and apples growing than I did there.

Leaving here we pass Watermouth Castle and clatter down High Street, Ilfracombe. After luncheon at a Swiss café we sit on the Capstone Parade. Then we start on our homeward journey. Mr G. happens to mention that a musical doctor had committed suicide at Haywards Heath, a Mr Jordan, he thought.

Our stout friend said, 'Not Warwick Jordan, was it?'

Mr G. drew out the *Sussex Daily News*, and sure enough it was Warwick Jordan.

Our stout friend knew him well, having sung in a choir at Lewisham years ago when Jordan was organist there. We thought it a strange coincidence.

Saturday 4 September. Lounged about in the hotel till lunchtime, during which meal it rained in torrents.

At teatime our stout friend gave us a conundrum: 'What is my name which signifies what I can do to my clothes?'

Millie guessed 'Darn', which was wrong, so she had another shot and said 'Patch', which is correct, so now we know his name—James Patch Esq. He has travelled nearly all over the world and is always telling us interesting bits about New Zealand, America, Africa etc.

He amused me when he was telling us about a journey he made to the hot springs in New Zealand. He said if you have a Maori girl guide and a Maori to look after her—that's ten shillings. If you take her alone it's £5.

Sunday 5 September. The air was like champagne—a steep descent through Lynmouth, and then a stiff climb up the zig-zag path to Lynton.

Dinner at 7.45, and after that to the lounge, where the company is so deadly lively that we go off early to bed. Wind rising after sunset.

Monday 6 September. Hurricane blowing. Cliff railway to Lynmouth and walk along the esplanade. Find a row of little wooden boxes on the side of the road, which we discover are bathing-machines.

Bathing being in full swing I decide to have a swim, and enter one of the little hutches and get into a bathing-costume. Coming out I miss the steps down to the shore, much I imagine to the surprise of the lookers-on, of whom there were a goodly number.

The bathing place is a narrow strip where the rocks have been cleared away. On either side are cruel rough jagged black rocks—not at all a cheerful spot to one accustomed to Brighton's fair beach. However, I found the sea was wet and much like ours at home, only not so clear.

Clothed and in my right mind after my bath, I hold Millie's hand as she walks on the tops of a wall of larch posts driven into the ground. Ascend by the railway and enjoy a cup of tea in the lounge.

We are about the only occupants, as everybody else seems to have gone to the town hall to a violin recital by the brothers Hambourg. The usual grumble closes the day, and as there is a high wind I plug the window-sash with a duster.

Tuesday 7 September. To the lounge where an old lady who is on a driving tour is playing the piano with great skill. Directly lunch is over, *per* cliff railway to Lynmouth and watch some men tarring the good fishing-smack *Three Sisters Cove.* Finally mount stairs to bed; Millie indulges in imprecations against all hard beds and uncomfortable pillows.

I dream of a fire in New Road, Brighton, and the people seem too slow for me—I wake myself by shouting in a loud tone 'Move'—get out of bed and find it is 3.25 a.m., the sky full of bright stars and the street quite lighted by brilliant moon. To my surprise several cocks are crowing and the rooks on Mount Sinai cawing as though they were restless.

Wednesday 8 September. I knock up Mr and Mrs G. and Mr Patch and say we had better do the Minehead drive today.

At 9.15 a pair-horse landau draws up outside our hotel, and I clamber up on the box beside the driver.

He was a clean-shaven wiry man, a typical coachman, and I found him a most excellent driver. We had two good willing horses, the near-side one rather slight for the job but full of life and go, and until recently he had been a gentleman's hunter; the off-side one was rather heavier and, although not so showy, a real serviceable animal.

We started in fine style down the diabolical hill to Lynmouth, and at the foot of Tors Hill we three gentlemen got down and walked, as did also nearly all the passengers on the Minehead four-horse coach which was close at our heels. The road was loose with stones and deep in mud, and Mr Patch huffed and puffed along like an amiable Sir John Falstaff.

After about a mile we remounted and proceeded, accompanied by quite a crowd all bound for a meet of stag-hounds. By and by we came to the meet and picked our way through people, carts, carriages, motors, horses, horsemen and horsewomen, straggling over the common in a confused heterogeneous mass.

Having got through we bowled on again, meeting scores of horsemen and horsewomen, then had to pull up again to let the hounds and scarlet-coated huntsmen pass, followed by a dense crowd of horsemen and women, and for two or three miles we keep meeting little companies of hunters all hastening to the meet.

I was surprised at the number, and at the lowest computation should say we saw 350 horses; people come from all parts of England and put up at Minehead to participate in the kingly sport of the chase of the wild red deer which abound in this district. In the season 1903 and 1904 the Devon and Somerset, the Quantock, the Barnstaple and the Tiverton packs accounted for no less than 381 deer. In addition many calves were killed when they were getting too numerous.

The runs given are unequalled for pace, length and excitement, and not infrequently has a stag taken a leap over the cliffs into the sea, followed by the foremost of the pack, unable to pull up in time.

Having assisted at this important function we push on and descend a terrific hill and pull up outside the Ship Inn, Porlock, a very quaint old-world village. We partake of some refreshments, then away again on more level roads, and presently pull up at the Beach Hotel, Minehead. Entering a luxurious lounge room we interview the chief waiter, who I believe is an earl in disguise, and are ushered into a very fine dining saloon.

We have the best clotted cream we have struck on our travels. Four or five waiters hover around us, and the whole thing was done with tone and style.

At 3.30 our carriage drew up outside, the rain falling pitilessly. I hardly liked to face the box seat, so got them to let me go inside; but it was an awful squeeze and I could see very plainly they would much rather have my room than my company. So when we got to Porlock and pulled up again at the Ship, I got out and says I to myself, says I: 'I shan't get in there again if I get drowned on the box going home.'

The Ship Inn was besieged by hunters returning, and was so busy that I thought it useless to attempt to get some tea—so enveloping myself in a macintosh, I left directions for the driver that I had gone on walking, and started up Porlock's steep hill.

For about three miles I strode on, getting hotter at every step till I was bathed in perspiration from head to foot. A young huntress rode by and cheered me up with intelligence of the chase: two kills, she said, and the best day's sport she had ever had except once at Plover's Barrow.

Looking back I saw our horses struggling up and a cloud of steamy perspiration floating up ten feet high from them.

Soon after they overtook me, and our chariot—which had looked so spick and span when we started—was now covered in red mud, and the horses looked dishevelled and dejected. I mounted the box and we rolled on.

The steep red road was like a ploughed field, but the horses behaved admirably, and reaching Lynmouth in good safety our driver deposited us at the cliff railway. We were all sleepy, and I think Millie's objurgations against the bed were neither so vehement or so prolonged as usual.

Thursday 9 September. Lounged about while the ladies went shopping. After tea in the lounge, Millie played piano and then Mr Patch gave us specimens of Gregorian chants and a piece of his own composing which he styled the Patch March.

He has become so attached to our party that he has decided to go to London with us tomorrow and has written to his housekeeper to prepare his chambers for Friday evening. I get our bill so that I can correct it, to save time in the morning.

Friday 10 September. We started from Lynton Station and reached Barnstaple Town at about 12.20. Here we say goodbye hurriedly to Mr

Patch, bustle him in his train, and 'so much for Buckingham'. We adjourn to the Castle Hotel opposite and look at the barmaid's hair.

At 1.9 our excursion train runs in and away we go. I order two double tea-baskets to be supplied to us at Templecombe.

In due course we made Templecombe and no tea-baskets came to us. Just as we were starting I heard some little fuss next door and fancy they were brought there, however off before I could investigate.

It is a great shame that it is not a corridor train on a long journey like this, and I have almost made up my mind that the London & South Western Railway Company will in the future be deprived of my distinguished patronage. It was a good job we had brought some sandwiches.

In our carriage were a boy and girl, perhaps nineteen or twenty years of age, who created some amusement by the open way in which they cuddled and canoodled each other.

Mr G. put his arm round Mrs G. and said, 'Come on Mother.' Mrs G. shook him off. 'There,' says Mr G., 'that's the difference the ring makes.'

The other people in the carriage nearly burst with laughter and the young lady blushed all over, and the lad looked as though he hadn't seen it and wondered what it was all about.

After repeated stops we did eventually reach Waterloo, and chartering four-wheeler no. 16669 started away for Victoria. London really looked very pretty as we went over Westminster Bridge, but the air was very stuffy to us who had so long been inhaling the sweet pure air of mountain and moor.

We boarded the 9.5 train, and soon after eleven o'clock we were once more in our native town, and reached our baronial mansion—all well. Cuthbert is in bed, and Mamma bending down to kiss him, and he rising to kiss her, they bump their heads and laugh.

Millie and I then get to bed, and Mum 'purrs' about how nice and soft it is, and stretches about like a young tigress on soft bed of grass.

Saturday 11 September. In the afternoon Millie journeyed to Hurst and got her bairns—all well except Wilfred who has contracted whooping-cough.

Barmouth

1910

Wednesday 6 July. Millie and I meet Maude at Brighton Station. Burt has gone to London to see a gentleman about a job in Regency Square, Brighton.

At 7.30 a.m. our train glides off, and we reach Victoria and wait for Burt. Anon he comes, and 'Jehu' tools us to Paddington. Here we secure a compartment to ourselves. Looking out of the window we notice the portly form of Dean Hannah, who climbs into a train opposite to ours.

At Birmingham we stop for the first time. The impression Birmingham gives a railway traveller is a black and gloomy one indeed, and a light rain makes the picture more dismal—it may well be called the Black Country, and today I think it looks blacker and more forbidding than usual.

At Ruabon we change into another train, and finally at 5.10 p.m. reach our destination, Barmouth. The estuary of the River Mawddach looks like a desert; and our quarters, Hendre Hall, turns out to be a quaint place decorated with a miscellaneous collection of old pewter utensils, old roasting-jacks and a grandfather's clock.

Thursday 7 July. We sally forth and walk by the sad seashore. The foreshore has a general air of being uncared for, unkempt, dishevelled and poverty-stricken.

The parade is well paved with a tar granolithic compound which is dry and clean. At the south-east end is a pavilion for concerts, also a few second-rate shops; at the north-western is a wide expanse of fine sand into which your feet sink at every step.

There are numerous hotels and boarding-houses, all built of a grey stone which does not produce a very bright or warm appearance: but they look very clean and well furnished, and appear to have a large number of strangers within their gates.

During the night I wake in a fright, fancying that something ran across my face. I light the candle, but cannot discover anything.

Friday 8 July. We make our way to the railway station and get a copy of excursions arranged by the Cambrian Railway. Sauntering off we get detached from our young ladies, and Burt—admonishing me to secrecy—drops into a barber's shop to have his beard shaved off. I stroll on to the quay, where an old boatman named Roberts, owner of a boat called the *Victory*, points out the pleasure we should experience if we were to hire his boat.

I find the girls, then Burt comes up, and for a few minutes the removal of his beard is the sole topic of conversation; great astonishment at the plumpness of his face now that it is exposed to the gaze.

After a considerable amount of fussing about by the coach people, we start off on a four-horse char-à-banc, being part of a freight of about 22½ persons. Soon after the third milestone, a house on the left called Caerdeon is pointed out to us as the residence of Darwin while he was writing the *The Descent of Man*.

We are now among hayfields, and the scent of the newly mown hay is very sweet, and he or she would indeed be a misanthrope who did not feel his or her spirits rise, as he or she snuffs in the sweet air, and hears the galloping horses' hoofs strike rhythmatically on the road, and feels the exhilaration of rapid motion. So you see we had several of our senses gratified: smelling, seeing, hearing, feeling.

We get down about twelve miles from home, and Burt and I stroll down to the river which is very wild, large blocks of stone lying about in all directions. Burt tries to rearrange several of them, as he seems to think he can improve waterfalls and rivers by shifting stones here and there, but as all but the smallest seem to resist his efforts, we stroll back and look at the sheep-shearing.

About fifteen men are ranged on seats, with a kind of stool in front of each of them, on which is laid a sheep, and with swift movements their fleeces are shorn, and they are carried away to await the attention of an old patriarch who slowly and feebly brands them with an iron dipped in hot tar. Then their feet are untied and they scamper off to join their brothers and sisters, no doubt feeling very thin after losing their thick jackets.

Then we start off for home in grand style. Safely negotiating the Fiddler's Elbow, a dangerous bend in the road, we pull up at Bont-ddu, water our horses and give up our tickets, and rattle into Barmouth.

After dinner we stroll down to Barmouth Bridge. The iron portion was recently reconstructed at a cost of £30,000; a part of it swings aside for the passage of ships.

At the entrance we pay a penny each, and sit in a little covered seat that will just accommodate four persons. We decide not to go off the other end, as it seems silly to pay to come on again. But man proposes and the Barmouth Bridge Authority disposes: for marching in all innocence through the turnstile where we entered, we are met with a demand of one penny each before they will let us go off—and we discover that there is not a toll-gate at the other end. You pay to come on or off, both at Barmouth end.

Saturday 9 July. Breakfast, then reconnoitre to find a vacant lavatory, which is not always to be accomplished in a hotel just after breakfast. But if at first you don't succeed, try, try, try again, and once inside you smile grimly as you hear other applicants try the door and go away sorrowful.

We then write letters. Burt seems to have a letter which like the poor is always with us. At odd moments he gets it out and pegs away at it, and we say, 'Writing to Arthur, Burt?' and he says, 'Yes.'

'Haven't you finished that letter yet?'

'No, not quite.' Still, Rome was not built in a day.

Then to the coach office, and on a char-à-banc to Dolgelley. Soon after we started the conductor pointed out a little girl seated a few seats in front of us, and informed me that she was a beautiful singer, who had won prizes. 'I do like to hear her sing,' he said. 'I shall get her to presently.'

We stopped at Bont-ddu, and when we were ready to go on again, Burt and Maude—who had gone to see a waterfall at the back of the hotel—were not back, so the conductor went in through a gate and blew his horn to hurry them up. Being a comical fellow, I understand that as there was a pig loose, he put the horn close to the pig's ear, and scattered the pig.

The truants having returned, we start off with a flourish on the horn.

The little Welsh singer had now perched herself on a little seat at the back, where the conductor would sit ordinarily; he stood on the steps, and they commenced singing together very prettily. The effect was rather spoilt by the girl, who would burst out laughing at some critical point. The conductor sang on steadily, and one could see his whole heart was in it.

He had a busy time—one moment you would hear them singing, the next he would be blowing on the horn, the next he would hop down and put on the skid-pan, back singing, down again to take off the skid, then at each hill he would run and urge on the leaders with a green bough or a light branch which he would pick up as he ran. Back on the steps, a peal of laughter, a whispered consultation, and then they are singing again.

The little girl's pure young voice rose and fell in bursts of melody, and the conductor singing seconds followed her conscientiously. I could not help comparing her with a songbird: God had given her the gift of song, and sing she must, no matter how, where or when. And then her youthful animal spirits spoilt it all, just as we were thinking how pretty it was.

The songs they knew were legion. One after the other, some grand musical Welsh melodies like hymns, then the next moment 'Yip-I-addy-

I-ay'. One they sang frequently was very quaint, somehow like this:

> I had a sister Arabella,
> She had an umbrella,
> And never would go out without it.
> Did you ever see,
> Did you ever see,
> Did you ever see such a funny thing before?

Then hark they are singing in Welsh again, like a hymn.

And so with the rattle and clank of horses, the grinding noise of our wheels and a blast on the horn in grand style we prance into Dolgelley. Millie squirms as we escape the corner of a house by a hair's breadth.

Of all the quaint old-world places that I have ever seen, this is one of the quaintest. It has narrow crooked streets which seem to lead nowhere. The best description of Dolgelley was once given by an old gentleman after dinner with the aid of a decanter and a handful of nutshells. 'You see this decanter,' he said—'That is the church.' Then taking the shells, and dropping them promiscuously around the decanter: 'And these are the houses.'

When we find the Ship Hotel we seat ourselves under an awning. Our conductor teaches me a little Welsh. He is very proud to tell us he is a father and that his baby is two weeks old today.

Now the little Welsh singer strolls up, and we find her name is Dolly Richards. The conductor is her cousin. I try some of my newly acquired Welsh on Dolly, and am gratified to see she understands what I say.

At ten to four we start off home. Dolly and the conductor giggle and sing.

After dinner we go down on the front to the Royal Magnets, a troupe of performers like our Highwaymen, but it was rather poor. At the conclusion of the entertainment, we stroll in the town and take our physic at the Last Inn.

Sunday 10 July. We start for St John's Church, reputed to be one of the finest structures in Wales. It was consecrated in 1890. The tower fell in 1893, causing much damage to the fabric but luckily no personal injury.

It has seating accommodation for about a thousand persons, and although it was not full, it was very comfortably filled and we enjoyed the singing and the elderly clergyman's discourse.

After dinner we climbed to top of Dinas Oleu, alongside Barmouth High Street. I lost a lot in perspiration, and our faces were like beetroots.

Burt and Maude go to 6.30 service at St John's. Millie and I go out to meet them, but unfortunately miss them; the whole street was full of people coming out of churches and chapels.

Monday 11 July. Go down town and buy a sponge and a washing-glove, for 'cleanliness is next to godliness', and we do try to be clean.

We return to hotel, and I cannot believe my ears. A man has come up from Davies Coaches with a huge motor, to know if we will go on a day's motor drive, 12*s* 6*d* each. No, certainly not. We are going today the Cwm Bychan Lake drive as arranged.

By and by up comes a char-à-banc with a clergyman and his wife seated therein; they wanted to go some other drive but Davies inveigled them on to this one.

So we start off along a high coast road. At Llanbedr we dismount and purchase six sticks with iron points which prove a great comfort to us. I have hitherto always looked on these sticks as being a bit affected, as though the persons carrying them were trying to look like mountaineers, but I have now changed my opinion. They are extremely useful.

The clergyman's name is Conolly or Conolloy, and he was for ten years in a 'living' in Jersey; he is now at Exton Rectory, Hants. He poses as a wag or wit, and is always telling stories of a laughable nature; in fact his conversation is a medley of words impeded by laughter. His laugh is not a good manly laugh, but has rather an effeminate character, and I think in time would pall on one.

His wife is a short, plump, tubby woman, but I feel 'as good as gold'. She can be humorous too, and tells us a story of a little girl who used to steal fruit: her mother said, 'When you feel Satan tempting you, you must say, "Get thee behind me, Satan."' Shortly after she was again detected pilfering the fruit, and the mother said, 'Mary, you know what I told you, you must tell Satan to get behind you.' 'So I did mother,' said the child, 'but when he had got behind me, he pushed me into the currant-bush.'

Five miles from Llanbedr we pull up outside the farmhouse of Dolwreiddiog. We all troop into a very pretty room crammed with little knick-knacks and curios and some shells for guns—they were blacked over except the brass ends with black lead. Our clergyman picks one up and examines it carefully, and in the process blacks his hands very nicely, whereat we smile in our innards.

The table is briskly and profusely laid and we sit down with a nice middle-aged lame lady, and enjoy a luncheon fit for a king, composed of cold roast chicken, ham, tongue, salad, gooseberries, stewed junket, cheese, butter and bread, for which we pay only 1*s* 6*d* each. Fate cannot harm us, we have lunched today.

We now walk to the Roman Steps, which are said to have been made by the Romans to facilitate the ascent and descent of their sentries to and from the pass, Bwlch Tyddiad. They are said to number over 2,000, but I felt I had been walking up quite 20,000 at the very least.

Back again by the coast road and draw up at Hendre Hall. Miss

Williams, the daughter of the hotel, says: 'We are getting up a party to go to the Olympians—will you join?' Yes, we will.

Dinner despatched, we hurry down town to a large tent erected in a rough field close to the railway station. A large audience—electric light, bless you—a cramped stage with most brilliant electric footlights.

I had had a dose of Magnets on Saturday and I expected but little better tonight, but I was most agreeably surprised. It was a light play entitled *Old Virginia*, with a thin plot, and the major portion of the show was singing: but each performer was an artist, and I came away well pleased.

After the show we sit in the open field and see a series of moving pictures of scenes from *Oliver Twist*—not very good but highly appreciated by the juvenile population of Barmouth, who crowd around the railings and sneak into the field in the dark in large numbers. A man goes round with a box, collecting money, and announces if they make it worth his while he shall exhibit a fresh set of pictures every evening.

Tuesday 12 July. Four return tickets to Snowdon Station—a combined rail and coach excursion by the Cambrian Railway. Stopped at Dyffryn, Llanbedr, Harlech, Talsarnau, and by this time our carriage has cleared a little and I am able to look round at those who remain. One is a young fellow dressed in black and a top hat, a shabby-genteel commercial who confesses his utter inability to get on in the pronunciation of Welsh names.

A young fellow and lady, dressed in white sweaters and heavy nailed boots, told me they were going to ascend Snowdon and return to Barmouth tomorrow. I said, 'We are going to Snowdon Station and shall go up by rail.'

'You can't go up by rail from there,' the young fellow said. 'The railway up Snowdon starts from Llanberis.'

'What! You don't say so, then I have read the railway description of today's excursion wrong. Well, we shall have to walk up.'

'Oh, you'll manage it all right,' he said.

The others looked rather glum, as they had counted on getting up Snowdon by rail—especially Millie.

At Portmadoc we jumped up on a char-à-banc. I was on the box seat, and at Tremadoc our driver got down and handed me the reins.

Off again, and our driver repeatedly throws newspapers (which appear to have come by post) skilfully into gardens or lodge gates and grounds of houses as we pass. The scenery culminates in as pretty a scene as can be imagined, viz. the Pass of Aberglaslyn. I have no wish to see anything different—it is really good enough.

Eight miles out we stop at the Royal Goat Hotel, Beddgelert, a very nice hotel. After luncheon we get into a wagonette and pass Pitt's Head

Henry Peerless as a boy, with his younger brother Charles.

A spread from the 1904 diary. Henry Peerless filled the pages of his notebooks with tickets, bills, postcards and pamphlets.

Having hired 4 pillows

NORTH BRITISH RAILWAY.

PASSENGER'S TICKET.

C

No. 7899

190

From EDINBURGH (Waverley)

To

Via Carlisle.

PASSENGER'S PILLOW TICKET.

6D.

PAID.

A separate ticket must be issued for each pillow.

This ticket to be given to the Passenger.

The Pillows must be placed in the netting when done with, or on arrival at destination.

The issue of this Pillow ticket does not entitle the holder to occupy more than the seat for which he has paid his fare and holds the fare ticket.

we settle our luggage & then watch a small crowd next door to our compartment, who have come down to see off one of our passengers, a young Scot.

They carry him shoulder high to the carriage, & when he has kissed the girls all round, & got in, the men keep on shaking hands with him till I think they must pull his arm out of its socket —

Then they sing very nicely a scotch song the refrain being "Will he no come hame agen" & then join hands in 'Auld lang

Peerless family group, Brighton, circa 1900. *From left to right, sitting*: the diarist's stepmother Esther, and his father David John Peerless. *Middle row*: Charles Feldwicke and Minnie Feldwicke, née Peerless; Walter Mannering; Charles Peerless; Amelia and Henry Heathfield Peerless, the diarist. *Back row*: Minnie Peerless, née Garrett; and the diarist's sisters Kate, Emma Cecilia (Mrs Walter Mannering) and Lily.

Left: Garrett family group, 1890. Henry Peerless's brother-in-law and travelling companion Tom Garrett is shown standing behind his father and his grandmother, who is holding Tom's son Sidney.

Below: Tom Garrett, who ran a building firm, was also an accomplished draughtsman. His sketch of a house at Lauterbrunnen in Switzerland was pasted into Henry Peerless's diary (see entry for 13 June 1906).

The Peerlesses arrived in Glasgow on 22 June 1904, as Henry Peerless wrote, with the 'stink of the Clyde in our nostrils. I must say it was a bit "whiffy".'

Sir Hiram Maxim (1840–1916) had made the world's first practical machine gun, and later designed a steam-powered biplane, which managed to leave the ground but otherwise failed to fly. Afterwards he turned his hand to creating fairground rides, including the 'captive airships' which Henry Peerless saw at Earls Court in June 1904.

The Grand Hôtel de l'Europe at Lucerne, Switzerland. Henry Peerless's caption reads: 'Verandah on which Millie slipped and fell.' (See 5 June 1906.)

Bern. Der Bärengraben
Berne. La fosse aux ours
Ernst Selhofer, Phot., Bern Dép. 250

'To the famous Bear Pits at the end of the main street,' Henry Peerless wrote on 15 June 1906, in Berne, Switzerland. 'The town is said to take its name from these animals, a supply of which has been maintained in the town for nearly 500 years.'

Horse-drawn vehicles outside the Fox and Hounds in Lyndhurst, in the heart of the New Forest. 'You will readily see that Lyndhurst High Street is very busy for so small a place,' Henry Peerless wrote on 17 June 1907.

At most seaside resorts, entertainment was provided by minstrel troupes, pierrots, German bands or light orchestras; but Henry Peerless felt that Barmouth's Royal Magnets were sadly inferior to Brighton's Highwaymen. (See 9 July 1910.)

Above: Henry Peerless visited Berry Pomeroy Castle on 3 June 1912, but the ghost was not in evidence.

Left: 'This very woman came by our hotel this morning,' Millie Peerless wrote to her son Reginald in May 1912. 'There are not many of them about now, only a few very old ones.'

Ascending Mount Snowdon by its 'queer little railway' on 6 July 1915, Henry Peerless wrote about its 'dilapidated, neglected station', and the hut at the summit 'for foolish people who desire to sleep up here. . . . I wonder how many people who do stop the night ever see a good sunrise next morning. More probably it is raining, or misty, or blowing so hard that it would blow your hair off.'

The High Street at Clovelly, which the Peerlesses and Garretts visited on 8 July 1916. Henry Peerless felt sorry for the 'ancient donkeys waiting for customers. They spend their lives carrying people and goods up and down the precipitous street, and they seem very solemn over it.'

Beauty Spot of the Forest—EMERY DOWN,
½ mile from Lyndhurst Church (keep to the right).
GARAGE
The bottom part of the Historic Oak House was originally a Caravan left in the Forest by the French after one of their raids. The Old Room and the Forest House (adjoining), is full of rare ANTIQUES and Art Treasures.
NEW FOREST INN. THE FOREST HOUSE, annex.

The New Forest Inn, Emery Down. 'The landlord . . . did not favourably impress me,' Henry Peerless wrote on 29 May 1917. 'He muddled on about the old inn having originally been a caravan left by the French, and pointed out several antiques in the walls. We had quite a difficulty to shake ourselves free.'

The Compton Arms Hotel at Stoney Cross (see 1 June 1917). According to one of Henry Peerless's favourite writers, Miss Braddon, Stoney Cross provided the finest views in the New Forest. A six-lane highway now runs through it, and the Compton Arms has been taken over by a fast-food hamburger chain.

Peerless and Garrett family group, Charleston House, September 1913. *From left to right, standing*: Arthur Garrett; his parents, Maude and Burt; Millie Peerless; Tom and Fanny Garrett; Henry Heathfield Peerless, the diarist. *Seated*: Sam Garrett's housekeeper, Miss Ford; Harriett and Thomas Garrett; Sam Garrett. *Sitting on ground*: Sidney Garrett; his cousins, Geoffrey and (*lying on carpet*) Edwin Garrett; Gladys Peerless; Marjorie Garrett and her brother Walter; and the diarist's sons Wilfred (*leaning on elbow*), Reginald and Cuthbert Peerless. Writing in December 2000, Marjorie Fox (née Garrett) recalled the occasion. 'It was my Grandfather's and Grandmother's Golden Wedding,' she wrote. 'I remember he put a gold half-sovereign under all our plates. The other thing I remember is I fell in the pond.'

Rock—a large rock at the side of the road, bearing a remarkable resemblance to William Pitt. At Snowdon Station we cross the narrow railway track, and commence our walk up.

Millie drops out at about three-quarters of a mile, and Burt, Maude and I go on without her. But when we have been walking hard 1¾ hours, we decide as time is getting on that we had better return. We go a short-cut and get in a springy bog in which Maude sinks.

All safe on the road again, we see Millie and exchange signals with her.

I feel a little guilty at leaving her all this time, but when we arrive I am agreeably surprised to see how cheerful she is, and pleased to hear her say that the good woman at the refreshment room lent her a pair of opera-glasses and she has been watching us up and down the mountain. 'Come along,' she says, 'I ordered tea when I saw you coming.' And as brisk as a bee she pours our tea and we are all very happy.

A train is in the station, and at the last moment—hot, red and breathless—up runs a fat clergyman. 'One hour five minutes from the top,' he gasps, and I should not have been much surprised to see him drop on the ground in an apoplectic fit.

We get in a wagonette, and by and by draw rein outside Portmadoc Station—rather a dirty dismal little station we find it. Our train pulls up, and we get a fine view of Harlech Castle as we clatter along. As I gazed, I thought of the pride some old earl or baron would have felt when he finished building this stronghold—and now I see knights and men in armour, while maidens look over from the battlements—a camp of armed men—horses prancing and pennons flying—and then I hear the strident voice of a porter shouting 'Llanbedr and Pensarn,' and come back with a jerk from the realms of fancy to the prosaic twentieth century.

Home, to dinner and bed, only to be awakened in the night by shouting from a crowd of people. Then we see a light flash in our window and hear someone going about our grounds, and hear a shout—'Who's there?' Then all gets quiet again.

In the morning we ascertain that the disturbance was the result of a lot of people waiting up to hear the result of some election, or the passage of some measure or debate in Parliament, in which the amiable Lloyd George was interested, and that our hall-porter, hearing the noise, had got up and took a lantern round the grounds to see what was the matter.

Wednesday 13 July. A lazy morning. We gently stroll down town, then nothing will do but we must all four have our photo taken in a group, as a souvenir of our happy holiday together, at a shop on the front in the pavilion block where they say they take ladies in Welsh costume, i.e. a tall hat and a shawl.

We interview the young lady at the counter, but alack and alas they only possess one hat and one shawl, so after asking innumerable questions and prices we depart, saying, 'If we think any more of it we will call again.' I expect the young lady has heard that tale before.

Burt and I go over to the Marine Hotel saloon and gargle our throats. Home and lunch, then we sit on the lawn and look through a stereoscope at a quantity of Indian views.

At 2.15 Mr Jones comes up in a wagonette, and as we drive down town informs us that we are riding in a vehicle that was made specially for Mrs ——, widow of —— of the great firm of —— when she entertained Princess Beatrice at Barmouth. Then we go touting for custom along the Parade, but and at last Mr Jones gives it up as a bad job, and away we go to Bont-ddu and the gold-mining works.

I enquire for the manager and am sent up a flight of steps to his office, and in a rough office I discover a young fellow at a desk. I have no wish to libel him but I believe I woke him out of a little nap. He said we could not go into the workings as they had just been blasting and they would be full of fumes, but that we could look over the mill, and detailed a pasty thin careworn old young man to guide us.

Once in the mill, conversation was out of the question, for the noise of the stamps was deafening.

He took us up three or four lofty flights of steps, and at the top we saw the rock emptied from skips on to a staging outside. Then it was fed into a hopper or crushing-box, and the iron jaws cracked it into pieces which fell down a wooden shoot. Then to the next lower floor, which trembled under our feet with the vibration of the machinery. The man explained as well as he could in dumb show what it was all about.

Streams of water were directed into the troughs, and at the next floor the stamps jumping up and down reduced it to a dirty-looking liquid, like cream in consistency. At the lowest floor it came through fine-meshed sieves, and I understood the precious metal was finally deposited on magnetic plates.

When Mr Pritchard Morgan started somewhere about 1860, a discovery of £60,000 worth was made in a bunch. But expectations were not realised, and gold-mining was discontinued. Then fresh attempts were made, with improved methods and modern machinery, but the results so far are very poor and they are crushing tons of stuff only in the hope that presently they may again strike a rich lode or vein. I hope their dogged perseverance will be rewarded.

Thanking our friendly guide, we retrace our steps and interview mine fair hostess of the Bont-ddu Hotel, who is a nice motherly woman of large dimensions, and who sells Burt some tobacco at a reduced rate as it has got musty outside. Then we jump up in our trap and swing along back to Barmouth.

Dinner, and then we hurry down town to an outdoor concert given by the Keith Prowse Entertainers. I was not impressed, and would say the most comical thing was a dog in the audience who barked most vociferously each time the people clapped.

Thursday 14 July. We hustle down to the railway station and take four tickets for excursion to Devil's Bridge and back. This is a very long distance. We stop at Towyn, a rising watering-place of about 1,500 inhabitants, and alight from the train at Aberystwyth, 'the Brighton of Wales'. From here a coach takes us to the Hafod Arms Hotel, Devil's Bridge, a very nice hotel, and I should say recently reconstructed.

Crossing the road we paid a shilling each and began to descend steps alongside a raging waterfall. At the bottom we found a crazy wooden bridge over the torrent, and then before us was a truly appalling flight of steep steps. Up and up we toiled and puffed—Millie stripped off her blouse and went up with bare arms. At the top we entered through a turnstile to the Devil's Punch-Bowl.

This is one of the grandest sights I have ever seen. The waters of the rivers Rheidol and Mynach have scooped out terrific chasms, and their waters still leap wildly in a series of cataracts.

We then turn our attention to the Devil's Bridge. There are really three bridges, one above the other. Two are modern structures, the third is that ascribed to evil agency. The legend is that an old beldame named Megan Llandunach had lost her only cow across the chasm. The devil appeared, and offered to build a bridge on condition that he got the first living creature which crossed it, and which he expected would be Megan herself in quest of the cow.

Up went the bridge, and the artful old lady drew a crust from her pocket and threw it across and sent her dog over after it.

> The devil looked queer and scratched his right ear
> And sprang from the side of the ravine.
> He exclaimed, 'A fine hit: the devil is bit,
> For the mangy old cur isn't worth having.'

We leave this beautiful spot reluctantly and mount the char-à-banc, then the train, and ultimately reach Barmouth after as good a day's excursion as anyone could wish, and considering the distance covered and what we have seen, ridiculously cheap—103 miles for 5*s* 6*d* each.

Dinner at 8.15, very nice—telegram waiting to say ship's papers have arrived.

Friday 15 July. A little shade of melancholy is over us, for Burt and Maude are leaving for home. Their departure makes a blank, but we revive and walk to Arthog, a charming little village standing amidst most picturesque scenery, the crowning feature being the celebrated mountain Cader Idris.

Home and dress for dinner. After this has been disposed of, out down a lane between two stone walls to the sands. Beastly windy and rather cold, and the sand sweeps along like in a desert. We make our way to the esplanade and look at the Magnets awhile.

As we pass the Olympians tent on our way home, it shivers and flaps in the gale as though it were a ship at sea.

Saturday 16 July. A gentleman who travelled all night and arrived here this morning is placed at our table for breakfast. We find his name is Bond, that he is something to do with a Billingsgate firm; he had been an old Volunteer and had been shooting at Brighton on the old Sheepcote Valley range.

He was rather a peculiar pleasant-looking man and had rather an impediment in his speech. However, we got on very well. During breakfast we got so far that he showed us a piece of Klondyke gold that a friend gave him.

After breakfast Millie and I go by rail to Penmaenpool, a sweetly pretty place. We walk along the road leading to Arthog, then turn up a path on a tree-clad mountain, and come to a long flagged conduit conveying water from the mountain to the George Hotel.

I have heard it stated that water will not run uphill, and Millie has the same characteristic: she always jibs if you try to get her to climb. Today, although I am sure the beauty of the scene is enough to tempt anyone to go on, she cries off as usual, so we turn back to the George Hotel and on to a wooden balcony overhanging the river, perhaps as pretty a scene as one might ever see.

On the balcony are several callow youths in clerical garb who are very much in evidence in the district. A large number have come to a home on the Llanaber Road, and I believe they are being trained for service in the Roman Catholic Church.

Getting into conversation with the landlord, he tells me the river is full of fish. 'Why, a little while ago I was in my boat and a salmon jumped right into my boat. He weighed eighteen pounds and we had him cooked for breakfast next morning.'

I asked the landlord about the 5.25 train, and he said, 'Well, she'll be very late, because the 4.45 is half an hour late now.'

'We had better go by the 4.45 then'—so we say goodbye to mine host, and in a few minutes the train arrives, and we arrive at Barmouth.

Little fuss outside our hotel—a motor-car belonging to one of our visitors was standing at our gate, when a car came round the bend in the road and ran into it and did some damage to the front portion. No one was hurt, and next day our visitor sent his chauffeur with the car to Coventry to have it repaired.

After dinner we go into High Street, full of people shopping, and I buy Mother a pair of sandals. Hugging our purchase, and hoping great things from it, we dawdle home. Wind blows very high all night.

Sunday 17 July. Walk the most windy dusty walk I have ever taken, along the Llanaber Road to attend service at Llanaber Church—about fifty people in the congregation and a very short service. A nice sermon from the eighth chapter of Romans and the fifteenth verse, 'Ye have received the spirit of adoption, whereby we cry Abba, Father.' I do not think I have ever heard anyone pronounce his words so painstakingly as the clergyman did. He gave to each word the pronunciation of each letter it contained: A-D-O-P-T-I-O-N, not adopshun.

I learn that under Roman Law, a man who adopted anyone could not disinherit him, and an adopted son had greater legal rights than a son. I was tempted to ask the clergyman, only I don't like brawling in church, whether under these circumstances the old Romans had the hardihood to adopt anyone.

Blown to pieces again as we walk back.

At 8.15 Millie and I to the Olympia tent to hear the Barmouth Male Choir—very slow at starting, but at last the curtain is drawn and we see the stage filled with a motley collection of youths and men, presided over by a strange figure in trousers much too long for him.

Monday 18 July. Catch the 9.40 train to Llanbedr and Pensarn; a boatman meets us, and we arrange for him to ferry us over to Mochras or Shell Island. We pass a lot of wildfowl. The island is deeply covered with shells of every description—there must be many millions, and at every step we crush them. We have a large basket and pick up many varieties.

Back to station and home. Millie goes out shopping and I do some clerical work, then to Olympia tent to see the Comets, a troupe of pierrots and pierresses: very fair, but not so good as last week's show.

Tuesday 19 July. Up at six o'clock, and Millie wrestles with the packing. Clear up account and bid affectionate farewell to Mrs Williams and Mrs W.'s sister, Miss Owen. Laugh at Miss Owen because she takes us for a honeymoon couple.

To station in good time, and a friendly guard puts us in a second-class through-carriage for Paddington, wherefor sixpence leaves my pocket and goes into his. Soon after we are seated, Mr Bond and a young fellow in the petrol trade come along, as they are going to Arthog to ascend Cader Idris. Goodbye, Barmouth.

We reach Brighton about seven o'clock, charter a cab and then see Reggie on the platform staring everywhere but in our direction. Shout to him, but he does not hear, so I jump out and drag him into the cab.

Reach home and find all's well. And now the little play is over, the curtain drops, the band is playing 'God save the King', the lights are lowered and we file off the stage—we are ordinary humdrum citizens again, trying to earn money, not scattering it with a lordly air as we have been doing for the last fortnight.

But the change has done us good, and we have conceived a liking for Wales. I think the greatest surprise was in finding the Welsh language universally spoken. I had an idea that, except for some old toothless dame, it had ceased to exist, but not so: every man, woman and child spoke Welsh and English interchangeably, and the two languages are now taught in all the schools.

The people realise that the attraction of tourists is a valuable asset, and everything seems to be done to induce people to make Wales their holiday ground. In conclusion I can with confidence recommend Wales as a place fitted in every way for an enjoyable holiday.

Ramsgate

1911

For some years Mr and Mrs Garrett have said, 'You ought to see Ramsgate,' and as we had never been further east than Dover, this year I said: 'Very well, we four will go.' Reggie shall stay with Mrs O. Thompsett at Keymer and travel by rail to the grammar school of Brighton, at which seat of learning he sits at the feet of Thomas Read, Esquire. Cuthbert, Gladys and Wilfred we leave at St James's Avenue in the care of our maid-servant Mary Josephine Jouman Crook.

Saturday 3 June. I rose at five o'clock, carefully arrayed myself in an old suit of grey herring-bone tweed, and then sat at my bureau and compiled a specification of repairs to be carried out at no. 20 Osborne Villas, Hove, for the trustees of David John Peerless deceased.

Having finished this I wound up all the clocks, then made my way to 47 Middle Street and was soon engrossed in the morning's letters, having disposed of which John and I ran down to the Bodega together for a 'stirrup cup'.

At 10.20 I marched to Brighton Station. Here I met our man Winton with an empty truck, and he said Mrs Peerless and Mrs Garrett were in the train, and Mr Garrett was on the platform.

We have to change at Lewes, Hastings and Ashford, where we ensconce our good selves in a carriage which boasts of a lavatory. At Wye we see a large crown outlined in chalk on a hillside.

We are now in a fine pasture-land grazed by immense flocks of sheep, with orchards and hop-gardens galore. Finally reaching Ramsgate Station at 4.10 we charter a four-wheeler, and by devious byways are conveyed to our destination: Rock View, Albion Place, Ramsgate. Our room had one window, just under and a little to the right of the W in ROCK VIEW.

We had a wash, and found the water very hard, and then I went out. At the harbour I telegraphed home that we had arrived safely, and then looked at the fishing-smacks, of which there are between four and five hundred berthed in the inner basin. As this is the Saturday before Whit Monday I fancy they have all come in for the holiday.

Back and wait for dinner, which we were told would be at 6.30—but 6.30 passed and no gong sounded, and Mr G. began to get impatient.

'Silly old fool, what did she say 6.30 for if she didn't mean to have it ready?' But everything comes to him who waits, and at 6.45 the welcome sound of the gong dinned out.

Sunday 4 June. Mr G. and I go down to the harbour and descend into the bowels of the earth to a lavatory—it is rather a fine place, and contains hair-dressing saloon and a tobacconist's shop.

Later we might have been seen making our way to St George's Church. There is seating for 2,000 people and it was fairly well filled.

Midday dinner, then listen to the band of the East Buffs, very poor indeed. Back to tea, which being Sunday was embellished with shrimps, which appears to be a hoary custom here.

We had nearly concluded tea when we heard a motor-car outside, and behold, there were Tom, Fanny, Sam and Sidney. They looked very red, and no doubt were glad to have a wash and some tea.

Then we eight sallied forth and boarded a tram for Ellington Park. I knocked my head pretty forcibly against the iron bottom of the roof, and I must say I consider the construction of the stairs very bad, as nine strangers out of ten must knock their heads going up.

Monday 5 June. Fanny, Sid and I go down to the sands east of the harbour and find crowds of bathers besieging the bathing-machines. After a struggle we secure machines belonging to Mr Mumford and have a dip in the briny ocean. Water was very nice, but too shallow for a swimmer who knows the pleasure of taking a header off the West Pier, Brighton, which I should pronounce to be one of the best bathing places in England.

Home for breakfast. A little later the motor comes round, and Tom, Mr and Mrs G., Mill and I jump in. The motor purrs her way to Broadstairs and Margate, and having asked the road from a friendly policeman, we reel off the miles without any apparent effort. It was very hot, so that even motoring one did not require an overcoat.

Sandwich is about 8½ miles from Margate, and in a very short time we pulled up at the Barbican which is the entrance to this ancient town. Here a man in charge of the gate kindly relieved us of a shilling.

The ancient haven of Sandwich reeks of antiquity—the curfew is still rung morning and evening in this old-world place. At present it is as dead a town as you will find in England, except that in the St George's Club golf-links it possesses the finest links in England, and it is the aim of all good golfists to say they have played there.

We made a little tour, looking eagerly at the quaint old houses, then Tom took us to a house he noticed yesterday: Sir Roger Manwood's Grammar School, founded by a chief baron of the Exchequer during Elizabeth's reign.

We moderns gaze on it with reverence, and as we gaze, we seem to be somehow linked with the dim past again in the good old times of Merrie England, when might was right—when all our modern innovations were unknown, and things moved slowly, and men were more content in their quiet way than we of the twentieth century, who hustle and bustle our lives away, pent up in cities and towns, engaged in a feverish race for commercial supremacy, or living in a continual round of excitement or pleasure, and breaking down at forty with shattered nerves and ruined constitutions.

Be sure, high civilisation has its drawbacks and penalties which its votaries cannot escape.

Regretfully leaving this relic of the past, we make our way to an old-world inn, and in the quaint parlour quaff copious draughts of cyder. Next door is a church, and great excitement is afoot anent a soldier's wedding—may they both be happy, say I.

The order is now given to turn the motor's nose homeward, and as if she knew it she bounds off, through Pegwell and home—a most delightful run.

I went with Tom to house the motor, and assisted him to run a quantity of water through her machinery to cleanse it. At first it ran out discoloured and rusty, but at last we got it to run clear. Tom lovingly oiled it and got himself delightfully dirty. I was much struck to see the interior mechanism which was very oily, covered with thousands of dead midges or flies.

We partook of a welcome luncheon, then straggled down to the harbour. Being a bank holiday, humanity was too much in evidence for it to be really pleasant.

We chartered a good strong lugsail boat, licensed to carry fourteen, and with the boatman in the bar to look after the sail, and me at the helm, away we went out of the harbour. The *Prince Frederick William*, a fishing pleasure-yacht with a large party aboard (some of whom were dancing on deck) passed us, and when we caught her wash, Millie expected us to be shipwrecked every minute.

The skipper had a pleasant face, somewhat dirty withal, but a man I fancy who knows his business. Tom took a snapshot of him and we all laughed when he said, 'No, no, skipper, turn your face the other way, you're better-looking like that.'

In the evening we go to the Pavilion, and from the balcony watch skating and confetti-throwing by skaters. At about eleven o'clock the manager orders all skates off and attempts are made by some of the young men skaters to sweep up the confetti, and then dancing is supposed to begin. It did certainly commence, but in such a half-hearted way that we soon tired of watching it.

Tuesday 6 June. Fanny and I go off to bathe—as we are coming out Tom appears on the shore and snaps us in his camera.

After this, a good idea is mooted by Tom: as they are going to pull up at Canterbury on their way home today, why not all meet there and do the city? So the motor comes round and Tom, Sid, Mr and Mrs G. get in, and Sam, Fanny, Mill and I walk to the station, calling in St George's Church on the way to look at the picture over the entrance. But as there was a wedding in progress it was rather a failure, and we stole out in somewhat criminal fashion.

Arriving at the station, one woman amused us as she was dressed up in heavy clothes, nursing a baby also very heavily clad. It was exceedingly hot, and Mill said, 'Don't you feel very hot?'

'No ma'am,' says she. 'We are cooler underneath.'

We sped through a beautiful smiling country and got out at Canterbury West. When we turn into Westgate Street we see old houses by the score. Here is the old Falstaff Inn, with its beautiful ironwork supporting the sign, and a few steps farther the West Gate completed by Archbishop Simon of Sudbury in 1380. This Archbishop Sudbury was mainly responsible for the imposition of the poll tax in the reign of Richard II.

At Dartford one of the collectors demanded the tax for a girl under fifteen, and making an insulting attempt to establish the claim, was killed on the spot by her father Wat the Tyler. In a few days the whole rural population of south-eastern England was in open rebellion and marching on London. They ultimately captured Sir Robert Hales, the King's Treasurer, and our friend Simon of Sudbury, whom they beheaded on Tower Hill. The archbishop's head is still preserved in his native town of Sudbury, and his body lies on the south side of the choir of Canterbury Cathedral with a leaden ball occupying the place of the missing skull. This might make interesting reading for Lloyd George, the present Chancellor of the Exchequer, with his Form IVs etc. etc.

Passing over King's Bridge we go into St Thomas's Hospital, the new post office, new Beaney Institute Museum and Free Library and the old Fleur de Lis Hotel. But we are all agog to get to the *pièce de résistance*, so we eagerly turn up Mercery Lane, troop in the saloon bar of an inn and quaff liquid refreshment and munch a few biscuits: then we reverently step into one of the best cathedrals England possesses. Take off your hats and tread softly, we are walking midst the illustrious dead, and their spirits may still haunt the scene where they ministered, when like you and me they had beating hearts and rich red blood coursing through their veins.

I can hardly say how much I am impressed by all I see. It is too much for one day's visit, and to do it properly I should want to stay in Canterbury a month with a companion who was just as enthusiastic. It seemed to me that amongst our party, Tom felt the most like I felt, and in him I seemed to recognise a kindred cathedral spirit.

The tomb of Edward the Black Prince impresses me. Above the tomb hang his gauntlets, casque, wooden shield and velvet coat: don't it make you feel that history and you are better friends than you used to be? You have seen the remains of the Black Prince, and Edward seems more real than he ever did in your schooldays.

But the motor contingent now seem in a hurry to be off, so we all go into the little square outside Christ Church Gate where their motor-car is standing under the surveillance of a very ancient aboriginal of Canterbury. There appear to be two of these ancient Britons who look after motor-cars while their human freights inspect the cathedral.

Tom, Fanny, Sidney and Mr Sam get in the car, and amid a chorus of goodbyes and waving of hands, hats etc. they speed away on their long journey to Brighton. We four turn up Monastery Street and reach the gateway of St Augustine's College. Leaving Mr and Mrs G. in a small recreation ground opposite the gateway, Millie and I enter the cloisters, crypt and chapel. The last piece in a most interesting round was the museum, a quaint collection sent from all parts of the world by missionaries from this college.

In the gardens we found Mr and Mrs G., who had been pestered to death by the unwelcome attentions of the young fry of Canterbury buzzing round them during our absence.

Making our way through innumerable children, we pass into St George's Street where we enter a clean-looking low-pitched shop and order tea. When it is served we are appalled at the great thickness of the bread and butter. However, we make a show of trying to eat some.

A solitary girl is in charge, and when we ask if and when a 'bus passes the shop to the station, she says 'I'll go and see' and goes out and leaves us all 'lonies. While she is gone, a 'bus passes, so Mr and Mrs G. and Millie get in it and I stay behind to pay.

I began to think she would never come back, but at last she came in and said: 'I've ordered a 'bus for ten to five.'

I said, 'Ah! But they've gone by a 'bus that went by some time ago.'

'Well, I shall have to go and tell them not to call,' said she.

'We're giving you a lot of trouble,' I said. 'How much do I have to pay?'

She names the sum and I tender half a sovereign, being the smallest coin of the realm I have.

She has no change. Says she, 'I must go and get change,' and off she goes, leaving me alone again. I began to think she never would come back this time, but at last she did. I made tracks for the station.

Wednesday 7 June. By tram to Broadstairs. Millie and Mrs G. sit and listen to open-air entertainers; Mr G. and I walk on sands and sit on the pier or jetty. After dinner Mr G., Millie and I go and hear the Yachtsmen concert-party. We forgot to get some cold-cream for Mrs G.

Thursday 8 June. To harbour and get on a wagonette bound for Minster. Our first stop is the Sportsman Inn, Pegwell Bay, and as we have traversed over a mile I presume a stop was necessary.

When we start again, we turn up inland through pretty country and reach Minster, about six miles from Ramsgate. Having de-wagonetted we troop into the inn and refresh.

The church is the 'lion' of the place, and we are very interested. Here is part of the wooden cover of the old chained Bible: it is all that is left of the original book, as ruthless visitors stole it piece by piece as relics.

Then by a different route we return to Ramsgate. On arrival I am pleased to find a box *per* parcels post from Messrs W. Spence & Son containing a light grey flannel suit which will be very acceptable.

Friday 9 June. Away we go on a char-à-banc for Deal. In front of me, beside the driver, sits one of the fattest women I ever saw. Her back was as full as most women's busts, and her stern ran over the back of the seat and cramped my knees.

On towards Sandwich, passing a place on the marshland where experimental boring for coal was being carried out by a German syndicate. In due course we enter Deal. We walk to Deal Castle—a squat gloomy-looming pile close to the sea—and along a beachy road until we get to Walmer Castle.

Now I had been congratulating myself *en route* on having an opportunity of looking over Walmer Castle, but on arrival I am deeply disappointed to find it closed. The janitor, seeing I was sorry, said 'You can stroll over the grounds,' so I fell in with his suggestion, and was very pleased I did. Our thoughts were drawn to Nelson (who frequently came here to confer with Pitt, when England was engaged in war with Bonaparte), and then to the great Duke of Wellington who died here on 14 September 1852.

Reluctantly leaving this fair scene we awaited the advent of a motor-'bus, and were whisked into Deal in no time. As it is time to start, and a cold wind, I cover Millie with a newspaper under her thin coat. It is bitterly cold, and the fat woman in front of me is nearly snatched. We stop at Sandwich to 'water' the horses and 'beer' the driver, and then heigho for home.

Saturday 10 June. By tram to Margate and on to the jetty. We are here ostensibly to see the husbands' boat arrive from London, and in due course the PS *Golden Eagle* swings alongside the jetty, is made fast, and her living freight swarms across the gangways like bees.

The majority are men, and they are met and welcomed by women and children who have come to meet daddy. Some of the women, in fact most of them, were fine and large.

The *Golden Eagle*, having landed all her Margate passengers, is hastily unmoored and away she churns for Ramsgate. Now the *Royal Sovereign*, a two-funnelled boat, comes along: and as soon as she is moored another huge crowd of men rush ashore, and another crowd of plump matrons rush and embrace them. Crowds of people form up in long queues to go back to London by the steamers.

A discordant noise produced by several young men and women lustily blowing cardboard trumpets attracts our attention, and on investigation we find they are seeing a newly married couple off on their honeymoon.

The blushing bride is embarrassed and almost distracted by their attentions, and takes refuge with her bridesmaids in a large covered seat, and a constable considerably sobers the spirits of the wild young men and maidens, warning that if they don't behave themselves he will have the pleasure of marching them off the jetty.

Now the *Golden Eagle* is seen returning from Ramsgate, and hundreds of people crush down the steps carrying luggage, mail-carts etc. and dash on board. Friends shout adieux and wave handkerchiefs, hats, umbrellas and hands as the good vessel starts on her voyage back to London.

We board a tram back to Ramsgate. I find a *Sussex Daily News* addressed to me in the hall, and am shocked to find a paragraph stating that Miss L.A. Whitmore, one of our best tenants in Ventnor Villas, has died suddenly. In a chastened mood do I wash and change for dinner, for Miss Whitmore was a lady whom I held in great respect.

After dinner, nothing will do but Millie must go to Broadstairs to the Bohemians concert, so we all rush out and get on the tram. We find the place in High Street: a garden attached to a large house had been roofed over and asphalted. Rows and rows of chairs and a nice little stage had made it really a comfortable place, and we were agreeably surprised by the quality of the artistes. Back to Ramsgate and bed, and as the moon is so bright we dispense with candles and undress by the light of the moon.

Sunday 11 June. Stroll up on the East Cliff, listening to the strains of the band of the East Buffs. At 6.30 we parade to St George's Church, then adjourn to drawing-room. Mrs Moore of Philadelphia seems very skittish tonight.

Monday 12 June. On a wagonette to Manston, a pretty little village, then to the New Inn, Old Birchington, and thence to Margate and home—a very pretty drive. At lunch Mrs Moore recounts how she has this morning pulled a little girl out of the ornamental water in Ellington Park.

We spend a lazy afternoon, then suddenly Millie develops a strain of 'deviltry' and in a wild fit of dissipation suggests a ride on the tram to Broadstairs. I fall in, and in a setting-the-village-on-fire strain we board a tram and sit on top in pitch darkness.

Broadstairs is practically a city of the dead, and we are not sure that there will be a tram back to Ramsgate at this late hour. I begin to think it means a walk. Then, thanks be, a tram heaves in sight, and with great relief we are rattled along through pitch darkness to our street.

Tuesday 13 June. Train for Sturry, then walk about half a mile south to Fordwich. This is the quaintest old place I ever struck.

Having made my way to the old church, only to find it locked, and finding that the key is to be had at the vicarage, I apply there and a pleasant maid hands me a massive key about ten inches long, armed with which we enter. The pews are of the old horse-box type, and the whole edifice is very interesting to anyone with antiquarian leanings.

Returning the key with thanks we make our way to the lion of the place, the old town hall. The upper storey is a fine example of half-timbered work. There is evidence that it was extensively repaired in 1474.

In the centre of the room is the old ducking-chair in which scolding wives and disorderly women were ducked in the river from the crane which still stands on the side of the building. A corner of the room is partitioned off and was used as a jury room, and above this is a small room where persons who had been ducked were sent to change their wet clothes.

But the inner man begins to clamour, so we enter the George and Dragon Hotel, and mine host readily engages to toss us up a nice little lunch while we sit on the lawn beside the river. We thank God for a keen appetite and the wherewithal to satisfy it.

Well, we must march back to civilisation and the station. Millie and I make a detour and look at a huge wooden watermill, the largest I have ever seen, but it does not look prosperous and is to be sold. Then the train crawls up, puffing and snorting and out of breath, half an hour overdue.

Wednesday 14 June. Letters to answer, then to pretty Broadstairs and have a swim on 'old Father Neptune's bosom'. Lunch, then all four out to open-air concert, Gold's Yachtsmen.

Thursday 15 June. To Pegwell Bay. Millie and I talk to a magpie who says 'Jackie' quite plainly. When we reach home, we go down to the harbour and board the sailing-yacht the *New Moss Rose.*

The crew cut jokes with the people, and we were quite a merry family party. One little episode particularly tickled Millie. Someone had been sick, and Scottie or Curly armed with a mop marched off to clear up the deck. In the bows, gazing intently at the horizon, was a gaunt raw red-headed booby of a boy with a very prominent nose. Curly or Scottie, returning with the mop held straight in front of him at arm's length, just guided it close to this boy's nose and startled him, whereat all the passengers laughed.

When we landed we went up to Cave's in High Street and had tea. Millie is still a little solemn from the boat-trip, and the smell of paint—which we find rather plentiful—she is inclined to take as a personal insult just now.

Friday 16 June. Mr G. and I gravitate to the quay and watch the dredger at work, then have a chat with fine old Captain Watson of the *New Moss Rose.* We gather she is 45 tons burthen, and licensed to carry 172 passengers.

In afternoon all walk under the cliff to the pier, a desolate-looking structure and I imagine a very bad investment. A slight shower, and people stampede from the sands on which they have been lying in all sorts of abandoned attitudes.

In a foolish moment we decide to go to Sanger's Palace Theatre in High Street. The audience is sparse. The play is yclept *The Peckham Pretender*, and is as weak as anything I ever saw.

Saturday 17 June. Pack—a short word, but it represents a lot of soul-stirring work. Then we stroll about aimlessly.

Cab arrives at 1.40 p.m., a very affectionate farewell to all, and away we go for the railway station. Change at Ashford—on to Hastings and Lewes—and finally reach Brighton safe and sound. So on Monday grim everyday work will grip us by the throat, and Ramsgate will be as a tale that is told.

But if all is well, in 1912 we may jaunt forth again into the highways and byways of the world, and for a brief jolly change let our daily life sink into insignificance while we foot it, and revel in pastures new, and spend a fortnight in freedom.

To our next merry outing then we lift our glass—hurrah!

Penzance and Torquay

1912

Saturday 25 May. I awake to find the sun shining gloriously. A pleasant walk to Brighton Station, and enter the train for Victoria, where we engage a hansom (no. 11832), and reach Paddington at 9.45. A porter grabs our luggage, and I tell him we want the Cornish Express.

'Seats engaged, sir?' 'Yes.'

Anon a lady, gentleman, boy and girl get in our compartment, and the gentleman gets out and returns several times with sandwiches, chocolates, bananas, ginger beer in bottles etc.

I noticed the boy fiddling with the wire on the cork of the ginger beer, and we had not gone far before there was a report, out shot a cork, and ginger beer splashed across. They hastily salve what they can and drink it.

The man with the children is a Devonian who has lived in London about twenty years and is going home to see his father. He is a great talker, and the fact of going home seems to excite him. 'There, that's where I was born,' says he. 'Up on the moor. Never saw a lamp-post till I was fifteen.'

We stop at Plymouth, and then get pretty views of River Tamar, Devonport, Saltash etc. So now we are in Cornwall, and soon see hills covered with refuse from deserted mines, and hedges bursting with white may in full bloom. Next stop is Truro—it is the only city in Cornwall, and is very proud of its cathedral, but I think it is too new to appeal to most people.

After starting again there are on all sides tin- and copper-mines—many deserted. Soon after I see St Michael's Mount, and keeping alongside the sea we draw into Penzance terminus, having covered 306½ miles from Paddington, at 5.7 p.m., about two minutes late. A man with a badge on his coat, COOK'S, tells the porter to put us in the Union Hotel 'bus.

The 'bus is not built for tall people, that is clear, but we squeeze in, the luggage is piled on top and off we go, past the statue of Sir Humphrey Davy and down Chapel Street. At the Union Hotel we are escorted to a nice bedroom with a view over the harbour, St Michael's Mount on the left and the Lizard stretching out all across the horizon. Millie, who is tram-sick, lies down; I go to the post office, and telegraph news of our safe arrival.

At 7.30 we go downstairs, through a room which boasts of an electrical piano, and enter the dining-room for a very good dinner. Then out and purchase a sponge, washing-glove, and some soap at Cannon's late Buckett Pharmaceutical Chemist; cotton at Madame Legg's, and a tin of shoe polish. The centre of town is crowded with Saturday-night shoppers.

Sunday 26 May. Whit Sunday. At a few minutes before eleven o'clock we might have been seen taking our way to St Mary's Church at the bottom of our street. Inside I noticed that there were chairs, not pews—always a bad sign. I ought to have retreated, but thought I would follow Asquith's advice and 'wait and see'.

I had not long to wait.

Soon the choir in procession, headed by a boy carrying a censer and another boy carrying a banner, marched round the aisles. The vicar, a most unhealthy-looking villain with a shaven pate, decked out in rainbow-hued robes and with hands clasped in silent attitude of prayer, supported by a fat shaven-pated curate, brought up the rear.

Candles were lit, the organ pealed out, two or three violins screeched above the din, and the choristers sang with fervour—and I nearly choked with the sickening smell of the incense. Even then I did not cut and run.

The service was really awful, the clergymen being principally engaged in putting on and taking off their hats and the vicar repeatedly changing his vestments. At intervals the boy toddled off to get the censer which he swung in all directions, and I expected him to hit the choristers' faces, but he happened to just miss them each time. Then the vicar between bobbing up and down would take a turn with the censer himself and throw it against the candles and the crucifix over the altar.

His intoning was absolutely grotesque, and it almost made one weep to hear a man intone so badly. He was hardly ever still, pacing this way and that. He eventually elevated the Host or blessed the Sacrament, and drank off the first lot and then a second lot of wine as though he meant it. The curate preached, and soon after we got out. How thankfully I inhaled the fresh salt breeze I cannot tell you.

Back to a good lunch with plenty of my particular penchant, Cornish cream, then walk along the shore to Newlyn. Newlyn has of late become a resort of artists, who have transferred its beauty to canvas.

Being Sunday afternoon, the harbour is full of fishing-boats, and the crews are lounging on deck or lifting heavy iron bars. A small boy has climbed up by a stay to the top of a mast, where he is as proud and happy as a king.

I fancy he is the captain's son, and on deck a sturdy band of fellows watch the boy and shout directions for his descent. When he has gained a rope, they lower him till he can swing onto the taffrail and regain the deck. 'Not for fifty golden pounds,' says the captain to the crew, 'can one of you do what that boy has done.'

A strong young fellow clutches the stay, and hand over hand pulls himself up, but his efforts get more feeble and at last he slides down the rope, nearly flaying his hands.

'Now, Jumbo, you have a try.'

A heavily built young fellow is 'Jumbo', and I saw directly that he would never do it. He struggled but did not get as far as the other fellow, and shamefacedly slunk into the background. We left them balancing weights, and several standing around had narrow escapes of a heavy weight on their toes. I noticed directly they began that the captain, evidently a prudent man, hurried up for'ard out of danger.

Retracing our steps we get to the village: small houses placed higgley-piggledey in narrow courts and lanes. The majority have rough rooms or a cellar on the ground floor, and the entrance is on the first floor, which is reached by heavy stone steps outside the house.

We sit outside the Fishermans Rest, then scale a steep lane containing quaint old cottages, and thence to Penzance and dinner.

Monday 27 May. Up early and ring for hot water which does not come readily. Then to the quay and troop on board the RMS *Lyonnesse*, a strong businesslike little vessel. Never I trow was a finer morning for a sea trip, and Penzance looks very pretty from the sea.

Just before we get to Land's End we have a reminder that the sea is not always in placid mood, for there on the rocks is all that is left of a gallant steamer with a cruel rent in her side. Poor dead craft, dost thou remember the first time the sea assailed thee—how you trembled, and then shook the waves off your nose and fought and conquered? Aye, that was but a little storm, and many worse you rode out in after years; and now thy poor old bones lie helpless there. Poor old craft—thy work is done.

Some distance farther we pass the stern of a large steamer which evidently came to grief on a submerged rock, and in the distance we now get glimpses of the islands. Tradition has it that the strait between Land's End and Scilly was once a fertile pasture, and ancient writers tell of some great convulsion which submerged this fair tract and the city of Lyonnesse. There are also legends that fishermen have drawn up windows on their hooks over the site of the drowned city.

Many small vessels used to be built here, but iron steamships crushed out this industry and Scilly devoted itself to potato-growing. The culture of the narcissus is now the staple industry, and millions of bunches of lovely blooms are despatched to the English markets between December and May.

Arriving at St Mary's, and picking our way over a rough cobbled road, we chartered a wagonette and were driven all round the island, passing many bulb farms which are all protected by high hedges of euonymus. Gladioli were scattered over field after field and looked very pretty, but our driver told us they were treated as weeds, and were very difficult to exterminate.

Now the steamer's siren hoots discordantly so we get aboard, and have a perfect run to Penzance.

We were much amused by a band of young men who rushed to get off the steamer first. Having got up on the bridge, one stopped, and looking down on the passengers crowded on deck, shouted two or three times: 'BE BRITISH!' This, as a topical allusion to the terrible *Titanic* catastrophe, 'tickled' me, and I thought it rather clever. Although I deprecate joking on such a serious subject as accidents at sea, I can forgive a lot for a flash of real humour.

On our way home Millie is much excited at seeing a mouse in the basement of a large house. She is more afraid of a mouse than a tiger, and has a greater aversion to beetles, caterpillars, wasps and earwigs than lions. I take this to be a feminine view of life which it is impossible to reason with. She has also an unquenchable antipathy to cows. Now I love to see a field of cows, and how patient they are: but to her they seem to emit a baleful and malignant light.

Tuesday 28 May. Going downstairs, find hotel invaded by workmen about to repaint the hall and staircase. After breakfast we go off on a four-horse coach for Gurnards Head and St Ives, through very pretty country.

Our conductor is the quaintest-speaking man I have ever heard. His delivery is very deliberate, and he intones. He cuts many jokes. Says he: 'Any lady or gentleman ever been to the Isle of Wight?'

'Yes! Yes!!' say two or three.

'Then on your left is a good view of *cows*.' Much laughter.

Through New Mill and Mulfra till we stop at Gurnards Head at an inn, then walk to the coastguard station, noting many birds on our way—water-wagtails, yellowhammers etc. The cuckoo calls insistently.

The coastguard is soon yarning at us. They are a fine body of men, our British coastguards, and this man—bronzed, lithe and sinewy—looks fit to do anything.

Far below was a three-masted schooner lying close in, a total wreck submerged to above her rail. Mr Coastguard says, 'Yes, she came ashore last Easter Sunday in dense fog. We never knew she was there till next morning, when there she was where you see her now, every sail set and her bow pointing out to sea.'

It appears she was loaded with stone slag, and going up channel got in a fog. Captain did not know where he was, took to the boats and abandoned her. The crew ultimately landed at St Ives when the weather cleared.

The owners took out all her sails and gear, and there she will lie till a heavy storm will dash her to pieces. The coastguard says that if the captain had anchored till the fog lifted he would have been quite safe.

At 12.30 off we go again through Zennor to St Ives. It is quaint beyond words—narrow streets and alleys inhabited by fisherfolk. Meandering up Station Hill we watch the harbour and bay, sweetly pretty.

Anon a large steamship bustles up, tugging an old wooden vessel. At a given signal she lets go, and the old wooden ship with two or three men aboard glides right in the harbour and beaches on the strand. I opine she is to be broken up.

At four o'clock our coach toils up the hill and off we go again, by hedges heavily blooming with sweet-smelling may: through Carbis, Hayle, Whitecross, Ludgvan, and home.

Wednesday 29 May. Painters very busy on our stairs. Char-à-banc arrives early, and away we go to pick up at sundry hotels till we have about 26 aboard. At the end of the Parade our driver pulls up and we are photographed. Our driver is the same as yesterday; he looks like an amiable bush-ranger.

We stop at St Buryan which boasts a fine old church, 400 feet above sea level. In the churchyard is a tombstone with inscription, thus:

> Our life is but a winter day
> Some only breakfast and away
> Others to dinner stay
> And are full fed:
> The oldest only sups and goes to bed.
> Largest is his debt who lingers out the day,
> Who goes the soonest has the least to pay.

On till we reach the hill hamlet of Treen. Here we are taken in hand by an old man who is lame and purports to be a guide to the famous Logan Stone.

There is a wonderful air of rugged independence about this man, and he has a pretty good idea of his own value. Speaking very clearly and with an air of proprietorial pride, he points out the white sands of Porthcurno, where the cables of the Eastern Telegraph Company touch the shores of old England.

'I want you to understand,' says he, 'that we have some things of importance down here in Cornwall,' and he rattles off a number of figures to prove what a great undertaking this Eastern Telegraph Company is.

Then to the Logan Rock, supposed to weigh over 65 tons, and yet so situated that a man can rock it with little effort.

Years ago a Dr Borlease claimed that it was morally impossible that any force could remove it from its situation. This statement led to its being overthrown.

In 1824 Lieutenant Goldsmith (a nephew of the poet), inspired by that indomitable spirit which has ever been a distinguishing feature of the British Navy, determined to disprove Dr Borlease's statement. Landing with a party of twelve sailors he succeeded in dislodging the giant rock which hurtled down from its lofty perch. But his triumph was short-lived. Such a wave of indignation swept over the neighbourhood that the Admiralty signified to Lieutenant Goldsmith that he might now set about putting it back at his own proper costs and charges.

The Dockyards lent him the requisite tackle, and after infinite exertion and at an expense of about £800 he got it back, but they say it never 'logged' with the same ease as before. I imagine this was a lesson to our naval friend, and that he curbed his desire to tumble people's rocks about.

I have myself noticed this desire on the part of some people to alter the arrangement of stones and rocks, e.g. Burt and waterfalls in the Lake District.

Well, having finished his recital, our guide says: 'I am going to climb to the top. Who will go with me?'

Many of the party seemed to think they would, and at last one young fellow straddled the rock and assisted six more on it, and then the guide rocked it up and down.

On again to Land's End, and have a good lunch at the Penwill Temperance Hotel. After this, Cook's man points out several curiously shaped rocks—one yclept Dr Syntax's Head has I believe really a likeness to the good doctor's.

Four miles north, Cape Cornwall looks very grand and appears to extend farther to the west than Land's End, but I think that is an optical illusion.

Thursday 30 May. Struggling downstairs by the painters we get to breakfast; then we go for a beautiful walk, skirting the Trevaylor stream which is full of fish, then by pretty lanes till we reach the village of Gulval. The churchyard has many subtropical plants, and the parish is supposed to contain some of the richest agricultural land in England.

Back to luncheon, then we watch tennis in the Alexandra Gardens. The sky looked very black, so we scooted over to a covered seat and down came the rain. Soon our seat was full of urchins, and as time went on, servant-maids called for them with umbrellas and coats and conducted them home. Several middle-aged respectable tradesmen gaze with rueful countenances at the rain and speculate whether they will be able to play some important match tomorrow.

After dinner, stroll all round the harbour and inspect the vessels. Millie terribly disquieted about where she saw a series of pictures of the Seven Ages of Man. I can't enlighten her as I did not see them.

Friday 31 May. Mill and I purchase several lots of cream to be sent to Brighton, then pave our way to Morrab Road where there is a stand for wagonettes, parley with a driver anent driving us to Mousehole and back.

There is a fixed price per person, but for a little extra he will give us the exclusive use of the vehicle and stop at Mousehole for as long as we like. This seems very satisfactory, so with a crack of the whip away we go.

At Newlyn our driver allows an ancient mariner-type of man to get up outside. The driver tells us this strange-looking individual is Mousehole's great guide, by name Matthews, been in the guide business 25 years, and that his 'puff' is bad, which means that he suffers from chronic bronchitis.

It is apparent that Matthews considers Mousehole to be his own particular preserve and us his own particular prey; somehow he had arrogated to himself some such position as Pharaoh bestowed on Joseph, *viz.*—'And Pharaoh said unto Joseph, I am Pharaoh and without thee shall no man lift up his hand or foot in all the land of Egypt.'

'Come on, lady,' says old guide, and he leads the way, muttering. I could not understand all he said, his dialect being strange to my Sussex ears.

Mousehole is an unsophisticated, unspoilt fishing village. It is strange to reflect that when London hardly existed, this little village was a market town of some importance.

Now Matthews says: 'I want you to see the cavern.' This lies a good half mile south of the village, and Millie seems inclined to jib, but he will brook no denial. Matthews insists. 'I WANT YOU TO GO LADY. I always take ladies down here. You can't go back without seeing it.'

It began to be difficult to descend; you had to sit down, grip iron handholds and slide down. Poor old Mother protested volubly: 'I shall never do it.'

'Oh yes you will lady,' says the ancient one.

When poor Mother absolutely put her foot down, the old man reluctantly had to give in. I went a little farther and looked into the cave. What a sight it was: one could fancy it the grotto of some beautiful mermaid.

When we get to Newlyn on our return journey, old Matthews shakes hands with us affectionately and leaves us, to sit on an old bench and see whether the Lord will deliver any more victims into his hand this day. We converse with the driver, and try and ascertain the truth of several yarns the old villain has been telling us. He appears to be known to everybody in the district; many call him 'life-saver', and the life-saving incident is the most ludicrous.

One day two young fellows arranged a plant for him: at the Mousehole cave, one purposely fell in the sea, pretending to drown. His friend ashore urged the old man out on the rock as far as possible, and held him so that he should not fall in, but at a given signal let go and in the old boy fell. Between them they ducked the poor old chap till they thought he had had enough—then lugged him ashore, filled him with hot brandy and water, gave him a sovereign and put him to bed.

Next day the old boy gives out that he had saved them from drowning by his prowess in swimming.

He was still telling the story today, and Millie had asked him if he could swim.

'Yes lady,' says old guide.

'Did you get the Royal Humane Medal?' says I.

'No sir. Too near home.'

'Ah! A prophet hath no honour in his own country,' says I.

'Quite right, sir, quite right,' says old guide.

The driver told us the truth of the tale. 'Can he really swim?' I asked.

'Not a stroke sir,' says the driver.

Our driver knows him well. Years ago he fished with him for about three months. The old man would play the concertina to 'fasten the fish on the hooks'—this being a superstition, as fish have a way of taking the bait without becoming attached to the hooks.

Home and a good dinner, during which our waiter hands me a telegram about a ship. I go out and wire home: 'Forty too much, better wait other offers, ship rather small.'

Saturday 1 June. Get our packing finished, distribute 'backsheesh', then the hotel 'bus conveys us to the railway station. As time progresses, the crowd thickens and there is considerable fuss about reserved seats.

When we have started, the guard comes along the corridor: and, stopping at our compartment, interrogates the occupants as to whether they are occupying their right seats. Two girls snugly ensconced in corner seats are found to have come without a 'wedding garment', or to be more prosaic to have squatted in reserved seats. Guard says, 'One of you must come out at once,' and then the delicate question arises: 'Which?' Both essay to rise, when one finds her dress is shut in the door. 'Well,' says I, 'that settles it,' so the other one goes and the guard says, 'I'll come back and set your dress free presently, miss.'

Three others are shifted at Truro, and the amusing part is that no one comes to claim the reserved seats, so we take them.

We change at Plymouth North Road and Newton Abbott, and arrive at Torquay, where a 'bus takes us to the Petworth Private Hotel. Then out along the front—as pretty a spot as I have ever seen.

We turn into Fleet Street and buy in a stationer's shop, kept by a very angular quaint female, a guide to Torquay and some postcards.

'Something more, I hope,' says the old female.

'No thank you. Good afternoon.' Up Lower Union Street and look at theatre, rather poor, then in an electric tram to Paignton. We are at once charmed with it.

Going down the main street to the sea-front we see a nice-looking place, Deller's Café, and at once a longing for tea seizes us. We are amazed to see such a beautiful interior, all fittings, chairs, tables, cosy nooks, in really good oak, and the place absolutely thronged with a well dressed crowd of good people. Dozens of tall, dark, black-gowned ladylike waitresses flitted here and there, and up in an alcove an orchestra of females discoursed sweet strains of music. I could have imagined I was in a smart London restaurant; outside London I have never seen a place with such good tone or so well patronised.

Then back on tram to hotel. After dinner, watch the lights of about a dozen warships of the 'King's Navee' anchored just off the town.

Sunday 2 June. A little walk—surprised at the number of gardens and ornamental public grounds we keep finding. Back to our hotel for dinner, and as the people are now beginning to thaw a bit, we get interested in a series of arithmetical problems.

I will try and describe the people: Mr Rhodes, a Rochdale cotton-spinner; Mrs Rhodes; Mr Fryer, friend or relative of Rhodes, yarn-spinner I fancy; Mrs Fryer (these four are very free and easy in their manner—a little loud but nice genuine people); Mr Barker, lives not far from Rochdale (i.e. Todmorden), is very sleepy in his talk and manner but knows his way about; Mrs Barker, his wife; Mr Hind, an old gentleman with a bulbous nose; a white-haired widow, cousin to Mr Hind; Mr Alton? a pale gentlemanly young fellow, a bank clerk stationed at Coventry; two spinsters of uncertain age (one affects to be quite a young thing); and the Palmer brothers (one is tall and loppy and a little strange in his manner—nervous breakdown; the other is looking after him).

Supper is welcome; then a general move to the drawing-room, where Millie presides at a grand piano. Mrs Rhodes sang beautifully and I was never more surprised, as in conversation she struck me as not being very refined, but the moment she began to sing she appeared transformed—not a trace of brogue, and quite an artistic touch.

Mr Rhodes, who is suffering from sciatica and is partially lame, sits in the most easy chair and dotes on his wife's singing, ever and anon urging her to sing 'so and so, please, if Mrs Peerless won't mind going on again.'

Monday 3 June. On an electric tram to Anstey's Cove, a tiny piece of sand surrounded by rocky shore. A signboard at the top of the glen says:

> Picnics supplied with hot water and tea
> At a nice little house down by the sea,
> Fresh crabs and lobsters every day,
> Salmon peel, sometimes red mullet and grey.
> The neatest of pleasure boats to let out on hire,
> Fishing-tackle as good as you can desire.
> Bathing-machines for ladies are kept,
> With towels and gowns, all quite correct.
> Thomas is the man who supplies everything
> And also teaches young people to swim.

Having rested we climb up to the Babbacombe Downs, and home to luncheon. Then on a four-horse char-à-banc through pretty lanes to Berry Pomeroy Castle. At one crossroads an enormous mirror had been erected, and it gave us quite a turn, as our horses appeared in the mirror to be driving into us. I think everybody thought we were going to be run into, until we discovered what it was: then of course we all said what a funny effect it was.

Berry Pomeroy Castle is about three miles from Totnes down a road luxuriant with trees, ivies, ferns etc. We paid sixpence each to a female custodian who showed us round. We then walked to view a fine beech called the 'wishing tree'; tradition has it that if anyone walks backwards three times round this tree, he can bring the fulfilment of any wish. It stood on a slope, and it struck me that one would have to be very active to walk three times round it frontwards, let alone backwards, but I was told that a number of people have accomplished it. The trunk was disfigured by hundreds of initials carved on the bark.

Had a nice tea in the lodge, then the horses were shut in and off we went. The roads and fields were exceedingly red, and horses and men going home from farm work were coated with red mud half-way up their legs.

Arriving all safe at Petworth Hotel, we wash and file in to dinner. Messrs Rhodes and Fryer make a terrible to-do teasing Esther, the chief waitress. Although she takes their chaff in good part, I think she is a little sick of it.

After dinner, all except Mr Rhodes, Millie and I go to a picture-palace;

we three play bridge. Then Millie goes up to bed, and I have a chat with Mr Rhodes. With much feeling, he tells me how upset he was during the first week he stayed here.

It appears that the day before he started from Rochdale he was in a taxi-cab, and passing a tram and a coal-wagon, which he explained by a diagram, a little girl suddenly rushed out behind one of the vehicles, and his taxi-cab went over the poor little thing and injured her terribly. He was horribly upset, and the driver was quite unnerved by the sickening spectacle.

Mr Rhodes went to the chief constable of Rochdale and explained that under doctor's orders he was leaving the next day for Torquay, and that he did not wish to be detained on the chance of having to attend the inquest if the little girl should die. He also made a statement exonerating the driver.

They gave him leave to go, but it was with a heavy heart that he set out. For several days he was on tenterhooks, and then he got a telegram to say that the little girl had passed away. I could see that the occurrence had made a deep impression on him, and I liked him better than I had before.

Then we got to comparing notes, and found he and I had been married the same number of years, and had the same number of children, and in the same order as to sex. By this time we were getting fast friends, and after a cordial good night I went up to bed.

Poor old Mum swore something awful about the bed, and I went off to sleep.

Mum got hold of my notebook and put in the following: 'Millie crochet and fidget till 12.30 a.m.—sleep till 1.30—crochet and fidget till 2.30—' Here her notes abruptly end, so I conclude that after 2.30 she succumbed and was in the arms of Morpheus.

Tuesday 4 June. Caught the train for Newton Abbott and there changed. The platform was full of stout ruddy well favoured farmers, all looking as strong as houses.

When the train for Totnes arrives, in we all troop; we have several large farmers in our compartment, one being almost a small Tichborne. All the conversation was agricultural, and each farmer sang a jubilant song anent the recent rain which seemed to please them well. Sheep and oxen then became their theme, and it was pleasing to see how keenly they seemed interested in their own and other people's flocks and herds.

At Totnes we find a lot of cattle, drovers and dogs. Our fat farmer puffs along accompanied by scores of others, and everybody knows everybody and passes the time of day.

We stroll down the old streets to the steamer berth and go aboard, and land at Dartmouth. After a good luncheon we roam up Duke Street, where is the Butterwalk, containing some grand old Elizabethan houses richly carved. Coming back, great excitement—policeman arresting a drunken man. Millie had seen him about, and was glad he was going to be taken care of.

We now go on board the Great Western Railway Company's SS *Meir* to Kingswear, enter the 3.35 train, and arrive at Torquay in time for tea. It seems very quiet tonight, as Messrs Rhodes and Fryer and their wives have gone up to London to go to the Derby.

Wednesday 5 June. We walk to Livermead, then up a pretty lane to delightful village of Cockington. It is a sleepy old-world place, and the *pièce de résistance* is the forge, known all over the world. The blacksmith had an eye to business, as he had a plentiful supply of old horseshoes for sale as 'Cockington Lucky Horseshoes, sixpence each'—not a bad price if you could sell enough of them—what!

We get back to Torquay, and after lunch rush like mad to get a steamer for Brixham. The captain heads out to the fleet lying off the town, and we notice HMS *Circe* as being uglier than the others. I must say that the modern warship does strike me as ugly.

Then away to Brixham Harbour, and moor alongside the stone quay. This place claims to be the mother of the trawl fishery in England. About 300 boats use the harbour, and there is also boat-building carried on.

The first thing we see and smell is the fish-market; the next thing is the statue of William III. We then go up into the town, resisting the blandishments of numerous drivers who are anxious to convey our sacred persons to Berry Head and lighthouse.

Seeing an enormous flight of stone steps leading to the upper town I start to scale them. Millie hangs back, but I want to see a cavern up there, and seeing that I mean business she turns to and follows, and arrives at the top swearing like steam.

I was surprised to find the said cavern right under one of the houses. I knocked at the front door; a nice woman came forward, and I intimated my desire to view the cavern.

'Certainly sir.' She ran into a neighbour's house and returned with a little girl of about twelve. 'This little girl is staying with a friend of mine,' she said. 'I promised she should come down to the cavern with the next party, so if you don't mind sir she can come now.'

'Mind? Certainly not. Come along, my dear.'

The woman unlocked the door, and then each of us with a candle in our hands followed her into the bowels of the earth. I must say it beats the Matlock show-caverns into smithereens.

Regaining the open air we went in the woman's front room, bought a few cards and paid her fees, and said goodbye. Then holding our noses as we pass the fish-market, we get on to our steamer.

Our steamer whistles two or three times as a warning and casts off, and we have got about fifty yards when two passengers dash on the landing-place and signal us. Our captain good-naturedly swings her round in a circle and rushes out a gangway, the two passengers dash on and we are off again for Torquay—very neatly and skilfully done.

Thursday 6 June. Cawdle's coach picks us up: then to several different hotels to pick up others, and off we go.

After a delightful drive we arrive at the Moorland Hotel, quite alone on the moor and I should think an ideal place to recuperate from nervous strain. One might tramp off day after day and return ready for such sleep as cannot be obtained by town people cribbed, cabined and confined by legions of houses.

We have a good lunch, then tramp over the moor to Haytor and get good views over the surrounding country. Millie with her usual lack of energy sits on the turf below.

At five minutes to three o'clock we see the horses struggling up the hilly road, and off we go again through stretches of wild moorland broken ever and anon by outcrops of rocky tors. The conductor bombards us with the names of these tors, but one passing visit is not enough to digest the information properly. It seems to be a place where a party of firm friends, kindred spirits, should wander about and commune quietly with wild nature. There is something in the immense stretch of rough moorland, a rugged passive strength, as though time and the things of time had no significance here.

Friday 7 June. A wet morning; adjourn to billiard-room. Mr Fryer played wonderfully well—I played as usual wonderfully badly. Mr Rhodes is like several other men I have seen at billiards; he seems to have a perfect knowledge of the game, and to know how each shot should be made, and yet never seems to shine.

Then as it was still raining we played bridge, and Mr Fryer and I got up winners of sixpence each. Mr Fryer appears to know all there is to know about cards.

Saturday 8 June. I go into Mrs Symmons' sitting-room and settle up the account—goodbye. We stroll to King's Gardens and watch the children sailing toy boats, then to station, take seats in the express and away. We arrive all safe in London, and suddenly decide to call on the Goldspinks at Becmead Avenue.

Arriving at their house, Mr Goldspink runs out and welcomes us. Millie says we have come to see the baby, and he says, 'Which one?' We are astonished to hear that they have got another little daughter a few days old.

Mill goes up to see Mrs G. and baby, and Mr G. presses us to have some tea, but we decline. Get tram to Victoria, train for Brighton, and arrive home once more.

Again Providence has watched and guided us over many hundreds of miles and brought us safely through all. 'Please the pigs' we will gang roving agen in 1913. Till then adieu.

Ross-on-Wye

1914

In 1913 we did not go away for a proper holiday the whole of the year—the first miss since 1891. Poor Charley Feldwicke's death on 11 July upset us, and Millie had exaggerated fears about leaving Mary to cater for our little branches at 12 St James's Avenue in our absence.

On the occasion of her father and mother's golden wedding on 26 September 1913 we did all go for the day to Mr and Mrs Manby's at Charleston Firle, and Millie and I stayed from the Friday to Tuesday. This was the longest break we had.

In April 1914 we had the shock of Minnie's death, and by May I felt it was quite time I had a change and let Brighton look after itself. As for Millie, I could see she was wearing herself over her poor father's illness, so I was determined to cut ourselves adrift for a fortnight and try and forget the feeling of gloom that lately seemed to have become a settled part of our daily lives.

We packed our large black box and sent it off in advance at a cost of 1*s* 3*d*, and never again do I wish to have luggage with me on the journey.

Friday 29 May. I dressed for the journey and spent the morning at the yard. The Seven Stars sent round my lunch of grilled plaice, and at 1.5 p.m. I marched up to Brighton Station and found my little wifie. At 2.20 we reached Victoria and hailed a hansom to Paddington—then off we go.

Millie now began to interest herself in the railway map. I am very fond of maps, and when Mum looks at them too it seems nicer. She saw the Dumb Bell Hotel, Taplow, as we dashed past, as we stayed there some years ago it was one to her that she saw it and I did not.

At Swindon we stopped for about five minutes, and passengers swarmed out and besieged a little boy in charge of a tea-truck on the platform. In a few minutes he did not know whether he was 'afoot or horseback', but we did get two cups of tea and a couple of sponge-cakes, thanks to Millie joining in the crowd and fighting for them.

On again through Kemble, Stroud, Gloucester and Oakle Street, and arrive at Ross about 7.10. I see a tubby merry-faced man with VALLEY HOTEL on his cap, so I accost him, and he puts us in a little closed-up 'bus, and in due course we arrive outside the Valley Hotel in Edde Cross Street.

In the hall was an open fire burning on a sheet of iron about 3 feet 6 inches long, no bars or stove. There were several people sitting around, and a young man with a heavy moustache and prominent eyes put out his hand and said, 'I am Mr Caws.'

A maid took us down a long passage to our room, from which there is a view of the horseshoe bend of the Wye—only this evening it is very misty. Our black box was there all right; what a good idea it was to send it in advance.

Just a wash and then to dinner—soup, fish (two servings), lamb, mint sauce, peas, potatoes, gooseberry tart, cheese, butter and biscuits—not so bad. Then as we are strangers in a strange land we go for a stroll—getting dark, grey and dull overhead, all the shops shut, and we think it looks rather dismal, and begin to wonder whether Ross is all the fancy painted it.

We wanted to get a few postcards and write saying we had arrived safely, and after passing shop after shop securely closed, we chanced on a little branch post office. Of all the one-eyed dismal little shows I ever struck I think this was the worst—two old women kept it, and they did look to be two queer old sticks.

Did they sell postcards? Yes, they did. We found most had dust on them, so I with my Sherlock Holmes instinct divined at once that they did not have a ready sale. Well, we looked out a few—could they lend us a pen and ink?

My word, it was 'A pen? And what, ink?' and then in a burst of generosity she handed us a piece of blotting-paper about three inches square and very much the worse for wear. We struggled manfully with these indifferent appliances and then asked for some stamps.

She demurred a bit, saying the post office was shut, but she fished out some. I said to Mill 'I must have a drink,' so I poked in a pub and found the bar crowded with a roughish-looking crew, and was relieved to toss off a glass of cyder and get outside.

Back to hotel and get to bed. The electric light switch was on the wall at the farthest end of the room away from the bed, so I had to get out and switch it off and grope back in the dark. Millie restless.

Saturday 30 May. Millie, vigorously combing her hair, hits the electric lamp and breaks it—a good beginning. Anyhow it was hanging too low.

After breakfast, Mr Caws says someone wants to speak to me on the telephone over the road, so I go across into Baynham's Garage, and up into an untidy office—'Hullo, hullo, are you there? Oh, it's Fanny.' Well, Tom, Fanny, Dottie and Beattie had stayed the night at Lydney and had some idea of coming on to Ross to see us. 'We shall expect you then.'

'Time's up,' says the telephone girl.

Back and stroll round the hotel's delightful old-world garden. Over the wall is the River Wye, which here makes its famed horseshoe bend; then into another garden, and this has a brick-built castellated tower, with a flight of wooden stairs outside. Ascending these I enter a little room giving a fine view over river.

Millie and I then stroll up to Ross Church. In the chancel is a stone beneath which lie the remains of John Kyrle, the Man of Ross. This John Kyrle distinguished himself by his philanthropy and public spirit, lending a helping-hand to all and sundry. He died in 1724, but even now his memory is held in reverence by all good citizens of Ross.

One thing in the north aisle struck us as very peculiar; near the east window were two young elm-trees, suckers from a tree cut down outside, which had grown inside the church. They are now dead, but a Virginia creeper around the trunks makes them appear alive.

Back to the hotel, then along come Tom, Fanny, Dottie and Beattie in Tom's motor. We were very pleased to see them, and lugged them in, and told them all the Brighton news. Then all too soon we have to part, for four motor-cars draw up outside for the Forest of Dean excursion. We notice a girl is driving one of the motors; she is Irene Baynham, daughter of the man across the road.

We go in Mr Caws' own motor—Millie in front with Mr Caws—Mrs Brooke and I each end, and Mr Brooke in between us, a tight fit. Our first stop was Staunton, where climbed up to the Buckstone, a piece of red sandstone about twenty feet long. It used to be a rocking-stone, but in 1885 some foolish excursionists overturned it and it rolled into the roadway beneath. It was replaced at a cost of £500, but its former equilibrium could not be recovered. I was much struck with the formation of the rocks as they all contained what appeared to be little pebbles in about the proportion of raisins in a pudding. Then all into our respective cars and heigho for the Forest of Dean.

Now, these forests in England have always appealed to me, and I remember how some years ago I determined that I would go and see the New Forest. I was so charmed with it that I revisited it some five or six times, and hope if I am spared that I shall go again, and see dear old Lyndhurst, Beaulieu, Rufus Stone, King and Queen Oak, Winchester, Mr and Mrs Ings, Miss Shipman etc.

Well, of the Forest of Dean, the most clearly defined thing in my mind appeared to be that Sir Charles Dilke used to represent it in Parliament years ago when I used to be a very assiduous reader of the parliamentary proceedings.

For some years now, with the growth of modern newspaper journalism, the reports in most papers are so condensed that I think one loses that intimacy with individual politicians which in my younger days seemed to grow up in one's mind by the verbatim reports of their speeches in the

House, but now that I am taking *The Times* I think the old feeling is coming back.

Presently we pull up at the Speech House, a large building formerly used for the court-house of the verderers of the forest. After a very good tea we got permission to go upstairs and see two old bedrooms. Each had an enormous old wooden four-post bedstead, one walnut and one mahogany, beautifully carved and no doubt worth a large amount.

Limbering up we have a fast run home. Into the drawing-room—a spacious apartment with new furniture and a central electric light with a Holophanes shade or reflector, which diffuses the light admirably. Mr Caws is going on his motor at eleven o'clock tonight to Gloucester, eighteen miles distant, to meet his brother at the station, as there is no train from Gloucester to Ross so late at night; he expects to get back about two o'clock, and as it is dark tonight we do not envy him.

Sunday 31 May. To church. A large congregation: a squad of soldiers, and a school of boys and girls in a quaint costume—evidently some kind of charity or endowed foundation.

Trinity Sunday, so the vicar gives his discourse from John 14, verse 12, all about the Holy Ghost. He did not impress me as being an able preacher, but I certainly enjoyed the service.

The weather being fine we decided to walk to Wilton Bridge. It consists of six arches and has embrasures into which pedestrians can stand out of the way of passing vehicles. One of the six arches differs from the others because the original arch was broken down by the Royalists to prevent the Parliamentarians passing during the Civil War. On the north wall is a curious old sundial. Quite close stand the ruins of Wilton Castle, burnt down one Sunday morning while the then owner Sir Giles Brydges Bart and his family were at church.

We were about half-way over the bridge when I saw a motor-bicycle coming towards us. I said: 'Keep well in, Mill, motor-cycle coming.'

She stepped into one of the embrasures, trod in a hole and went down like a ninepin. I heard her cry out, and to my astonishment there she was on the ground.

I lifted her up by main force and propped her against the wall. She said she had sprained her ankle, and thought she was going to faint. I kept talking to attract her attention, and the faint feeling began to pass.

I left her in the embrasure and went into Wilton to get a conveyance to drive her home, but it was Sunday evening and a one-eyed place and I don't think there was a carriage or trap in the place.

Back, and then with the aid of my strong arm and strong umbrella we crawled back to the hotel. Then off I went hot-foot to find a chemist.

Success came to me at the Man of Ross House, and Mr T. Matthews soon supplied me with some Elliman's Embrocation, oiled silk and a crêpe bandage. Rush back to hotel, beg some hot water from Mr Caws, foment Mum's ankle, embrocate it and bind it up in the bandage, slip on her stocking and a slipper, and we get down to supper. Then she hobbles up to the drawing-room.

A funny young man has been decoyed up to the drawing-room by one of the young women, and they press him to play the piano. He seated himself at the instrument and began.

It was a strange medley in a rippling rattling style. Once started he did not seem to be able to stop. He would start off a tune in gallant style, falter a bit, say, 'Oh I've forgotten that but shall I play you so-and-so,' and without waiting for yea or no, off he rattled. He kept it up for about an hour. By this time I fancy some of them were sorry they had asked him, but I rather enjoyed it. He certainly had a bold style.

Having run to the length of his tether, he bowed his adieux and went downstairs to smoke and recover from his exertions.

Monday 1 June. Today we motor to Cheltenham. At eleven o'clock Mill and I and Mr and Mrs Brooke jump in a motor-car driven by a fair young fellow, and away we go.

We get a few miles out of Ross when our chauffeur pulls up, looks at our near hind tyre and says: 'Ah, I thought so, she's gone down.'

Out tools, jack her up and take the tyre off, put on another inner tube and cover, pump up, let down jack, and then to our disgust down goes the tyre again.

Nil desperandum we go at it again, but this time we use a virgin inner tube and pump her tight as a drum—make all taut and trim, and bowl off again—enjoying the air, the sunshine and swift movement, all merry as a marriage-bell—into Cheltenham. All the shops are closed, but I should say many of them are fine and thriving, especially the large drapers and milliners. It is a favourite residential town for Anglo-Indians.

In due course it is time for our homeward journey: and as at times I noticed the speedometer was registering 35 miles an hour, we made short work of our journey home.

Tuesday 2 June. Out on the town to purchase a veil and some Epsom salts. Back and write letters to John Feldwicke, Mr Garrett and Annie Hatherell. Feeling exhausted after coming back from the post I go in the Swan, and the presiding goddess in the saloon sells me a small Bass.

At 11.30 we get in a motor-car driven by Irene Baynham, and through lovely wooded scenery to Raglan Castle. The moat looked green and thick and dirty.

Leaving here we went to the Beaufort Arms and were soon discussing a most excellent luncheon served by the courtly grey-headed host with the manners of a nobleman. I fancied he was originally a butler in a nobleman's family. Then off again through Abergavenny—crowded with village carts—and stop at Skenfrith, very pretty. Leaning over the bridge I saw several fish jumping. Then it is heigho for home.

Bridge in drawing-room with Mr and Mrs Brooke. There is much fun at the next table over a game Mr Caws is teaching them, the Sky game, which appears to be all about new moons, full moons, planets etc.

Wednesday 3 June. We spend the morning on the Prospect. At 1.30, into the motor-car driven by Irene Baynham and off in fine style to Ledbury. The church is exceedingly large, and here is a picture of the Last Supper by Titian. It seems to have had a romantic history—many years ago a former vicar named Marten took it home for safety and it appears to have been taken out of its frame, doubled up, placed in an attic and forgotten. Only a few years ago another Mr Marten, a descendant, found the picture in the attic and sent it up to Christie's to be valued. They saw what it was, and valued it at the modest sum of £25,000.

Our Mr Marten, evidently an honourable man, gave it back to the church. It seems rather a luxury, as I understand the verger to say it cost the church £100 a year to insure it.

We regain our motors and to my chagrin I find that someone has walked off with a very nice pair of reindeer gloves that I foolishly left in the car. Rot.

Back again through Malvern. We happen to pull up close to St Ann's Road where Mill and I brought Cuthbert in 1894, so she and I went and looked at the house where we stayed. It was a little altered, and evidently the people who had it are gone.

Thursday 4 June. Down to the cattle market at bottom of our street—one bull is a noble animal. A nice little man and colt attracted us, and we saw it bought in at £10 15*s* 0*d*. Old dog-cart sold for 35 shillings. A large crowd around a cheap-jack selling boot-polishing paste drew our attention—he was a Jew and had a quantity of sovereigns on the ground in a heap on a cloth. He was marching round, talking incessantly, and the perspiration ran off him in streams. He did a roaring trade and was a most comical entertaining fellow.

Lunch, then off at 1.20 p.m.—three boats. The first time we grounded I think the ladies thought we were shipwrecked. However we got off again with a quant pole, and our people began to get used to it.

Home all safe, and to dinner—then Millie and I stroll in the garden, and as I think it is getting dangerous for her to be so near the strawberry bed I gently lead her away.

Friday 5 June. At 11.30 in George Baynham's large motor—fourteen of us including the chauffeur—for Llanthony Abbey in the Black Mountains.

On the road we stop to look at the 'exhaust' which has got a spring adrift. Up comes a very consequential Welshman and says, 'What are you doing? I thought you were going to light a fire, and if so I was going to FORBID you. Where are you going?'

I should say he ought to be muzzled; he was the most interfering poke-your-nose man I ever chanced to meet.

Charmed with the pretty views we arrive at Llanthony, a grand old ruin of a Cistercian priory founded in the twelfth century. The abbot's private apartments are now a hotel, and in a large room upstairs we have a sumptuous lunch of hot fried ham and eggs. Then the men stroll about outside smoking, and the girls go upstairs and we hear someone crying 'Cuckoo!' out of a window in a tower, and looking up we find it is Millie.

There is some considerable fun later about Miss Wilson being left in this room on her knees looking out of the said window, and a curate being shown into the room which is to be his bedroom, and she quite unconscious that he is there.

All ready to start, our motor emits horrible hoots as Mr Dunbarton is missing. Mr Caws finds him sitting outside hotel and dozing.

Off now and it is all tales—a young widow with a little daughter goes to a railway booking-office, taps the window, the booking-clerk slaps it up and widow says 'Two to Looe.' Booking-clerk says, 'Pip pip!' and slams it down.

Another tricky distich, Mr Caws: 'Isn't it much nicer to ride in a carriage and think how much nicer it is to ride in a carriage than it is to walk—than it is to walk and think how much nicer it is to ride in a carriage than it is to walk.' Miss Wilson has several plucky attempts to repeat this, but it is difficult to catch it.

After a while we arrive at Abbey Dore. Entering the church, we attach ourselves to a clergyman who is taking round a widow and explaining the points of interest in the architecture. I think the widow was bored, and we were perhaps a little rude in following them so closely.

Out to the Nevill Arms and tea—we are a merry party. The strangest pair today are undoubtedly a doctor and his wife, an old lady who paints, powders and poses in dress and manner as a girl of sixteen, a kind of Madame Rachel made beautiful and young for ever. The doctor is very courtly in his old-world manner.

Away again, and take the wrong turning. We pull up at a roadside cottage, and a woman standing at the door gives us directions, and we have a rather difficult job to turn our large vehicle round. Away all right now, through Wormbridge, home and dinner—the room crowded with new people.

Saturday 6 June. Stroll to railway station to make enquiries as to the trains to Tetbury. Saunter back by the riverside. A quiet day after all the excursions we have made during the week.

Sunday 7 June. Several letters—one to sign a Power of Attorney *re* C. Feldwicke deceased and sale of some consols. Mr Brooke and Mr Caws witness it for me and unluckily get in the wrong place. To Ross Church, then sleep and dream about Mr Broad and telephones and a grandfather's clock—awfully mixed-up tangle.

A harpist and a flautist arrive as we finish supper, and then all to drawing-room. The flautist's wife sings—Millie at piano—Mr Brooke sings—Mr Caws sings (especially 'The drum major'). A very pleasant evening.

Monday 8 June. Sit in lounge. Several among the group on riddles or problems. The doctor gives one—put down:

1 1 1
3 3 3
9 9 9

Strike off any seven of the figures, and those remaining must make eleven.

I give it up. Mr Brooke finds it in a moment:

~~1~~ 1 1
~~3 3 3~~
~~9 9 9~~

Then motors are at the door. Mr Caws motors for us; thirteen more of our party in Baynham's large motor char-à-banc. Away and away to Monmouth and then to Tintern Abbey where we pull up.

The Beaufort family sold Tintern Abbey to the Crown in 1901. The Crown have carried out repairs to the ruins, and on our arrival the first thing that struck us was the forest of scaffolding and the large amount of work in progress. We roamed all over it, except where we were roped off from the repairs going on, and enjoyed it very much. There was a card in each part stating what it was, i.e.

CHAPTER HOUSE

MONKS' PARLOUR

Having completed our survey, we stroll across to the Anchor Hotel and admire their beautiful garden—some of the finest pansies I have ever seen.

A good lunch upstairs, and while we are eating it comes on to rain heavily. So we all roam about the outside passages and alleyways of the inn—look in at the cyder mill and press. The bulk of the females sit on the stairs, and Molly (a little South African girl) starts telling a story, which is taken up by a young lady, and then by another and another.

Molly is a very precocious young lady and is touring England with her father and mother, Mr and Mrs Noaks. Mr Noaks is in the Civil Service in South Africa and is returning in a few weeks. They were through the South African war. Molly is ten years old and has been somewhat of a nuisance to two of our gentlemen, Mr Seal and Mr Franks. It began by these two taking notice of her, as men will of a little girl at a hotel, but she followed it up too much, always dogging their footsteps and getting them to play with her, till I fancy they wished they had never been kind to her at the start.

Mr Seal is in insurance in London; Mr Franks is an ironmonger at Maidstone. When he arrived I thought that he was a bachelor, but after Mr Seal came to our table at meals, Franks began to blossom, and we understand he has left his wife and family at home. He pretends now to be quite a dare-devil, but I fancy he is a good respectable family man.

When the rain ceases, off we go for Chepstow Castle, where we walk all round the outside. We find a nice-looking dairy where they supply teas, and soon sit down to a sumptuous spread of bread, clotted cream and strawberry jam washed down with some good tea.

Then into Mr Caws' motor, I on a camp-stool mixed up with the ladies' legs. We went so fast that I was nearly overbalanced at times. It now begins to rain heavily, and as we were going so fast, and as motorists always keep going until you are wet before they will put up the hood, we had quite a little pantomime with Mrs Brooke. It commenced *andante*, thus: 'Jimmy (Mr B.), put up your umbrella.'

Mr B. tried to do so, found the wind troublesome and put it down again.

Mrs B., *fortissimo*: 'Oh Jimmy, do put up your umbrella!' Repeat *ad lib.*

Having now got us wet, Mr Caws pulls up and gets the hood over us.

Dashing along, I hear something break adrift, and find it is a nut carried away off one of the hood stays—so for the remainder of the journey I hold the stay in position with one hand and clutch the car in the other.

Tuesday 9 June. Raining. Millie and I go out to buy and send off birthday presents to our eldest son Cuthbert who tomorrow celebrates his 22nd birthday. Then to Matthews the Chemist's; a boy pilots us through the back of the shop to see John Kyrle's summer-house, at one end of a most beautiful garden. The poor old man's chair was repulsively old, the leather covering looking so dirty that I felt I could not sit in it.

Wednesday 10 June. Our first thought is that this is Cuthbert's birthday, and that it is 22 years since he was ushered into this vale of tears in Hanover Crescent.

At 10.30 a.m. the order goes round 'To the boats!' and we all march down to the riverside.

Rather a heated argument between Mrs Seal and Miss Sheppard *re* suffragettes. Mrs Seal is dead against them—Miss Sheppard a little inclined to uphold part of their views. The lady next to me whispers, 'Let's turn the conversation'—so a fish luckily jumping just then, and an extra-lovely reach of the river, we exclaim about it and stifle what began to look like a slight rupture.

We now land and enter a riverside inn. Mr Caws and I have a long drink composed of gin, lemonade and soda: then all crowd into a room and lunch from viands we have brought in the boats with us, sandwiches and a variety of tarts.

At Symonds Yat the majority of us toil up a rugged path to the summit. The view is gorgeous. Then we glide into Monmouth after a row of superb loveliness.

A lovely tea at Skerrets, and then to the railway station. I should imagine that the railway journey from Monmouth to Ross is perhaps the prettiest thirteen miles in England. I was enchanted with the views of the river, and we all vote it has been a glorious trip.

Thursday 11 June. Early lunch. At 1.30 we all start in motors for Hereford. As it is only twelve miles, a motor made short work of the milestones.

Of course the cathedral was our first goal. The thing that took my fancy most was on the wall of the south transept, an ancient map of the world called the *Mappa Mundi*, drawn on a large sheet of vellum in the thirteenth century by Richard de Haldingham and Lafford. It was the quaintest jumble I ever saw.

Then we trooped to an exceedingly old church, All Saints, a hundred yards away. The verger who took us in hand was a very strange specimen of humanity. I do not suppose one could catch one word in ten and get the sense of it. He showed us their chained library—a priceless collection of most ancient books, each fixed with a steel chain to the shelf, with a swivel. I should imagine that the lot would realise an enormous amount of money at Christie's.

All aboard again, and in trying to pass the big motor several times without success, Mr Caws gets we four choked with dust. However, we do squeeze by at last, and go all out for home.

Dinner, then a most jolly game of Newmarket. At ten o'clock up to pack and kill owlets.

Friday 12 June. Out to Messrs Smith's Bookstores to ask if a book we ordered several days ago, *What Katie Did Next*, had come in. 'No, very sorry.'

I said, 'Well, I'm off this morning.'

'Enquire again at any of our branches, sir.'

Back to hotel and say goodbye—walk to station, and arrive at Tetbury 1.27. Annie Hatherell comes running up to meet us—very pleased to see us and talks most loquaciously. She introduces us to a pretty little governess car and a dear little pony. Annie very full of a new motor they expect today.

We turn into the lovely grounds of Sir George Holford, equerry to Queen Alexandra, which Annie has got permission to show us—beautiful trees and masses of rhododendrons. The paths twist about, and we have a good laugh when after driving some time Annie gets us to a place we remember, because we saw the same men unloading two manure carts.

We finally arrive at our destination, Oldbury on the Hill, and Mr Edwin Hatherell gives us a hearty welcome. We have a talk, and sit in a tent on the lawn.

Beefsteak supper. After this, Mr Hatherell says: 'Have a drop of whisky, Mr Peerless.' I thank him and say no. He presses, and finally says, 'When you're at Oldbury on the Hill you must have some, you can't do as you like.'

I know it is all the very best of good nature, and meant in all kindliest hospitality, but I really don't want it, and only sip it at intervals. Millie tumbled and kindly helped me out.

Saturday 13 June. Found Annie in a large scullery, frying bacon and kidneys. We breakfast in fine style, then go for a tour of the farm, and come on the men sheep-shearing. They are using shears, but Mr H. sends for the machine as he wants us to see it. It seemed to be much easier than by hand. The fleeces weigh about eight pounds and fetch about 1*s* 2*d* a pound—fleeces average eight to nine shillings each. I fancy he will get six or seven hundred fleeces.

We admired some of his heavy carthorses, four-year-olds and fine creatures. One with a Roman nose rather took my fancy. Chaff-cutting on today by steam, also cake and corn crusher.

Great disappointment because the new motor-car has not arrived.

On our way back to the house we meet a bucolic policeman on a bicycle. In fun, policeman says: ''Morning Mr Hatherell, I've called to see your motor driving licence. I think you bin going too fast through the street. I should say you was going quite five mile an 'our.'

'I haven't been down the street at all. I went the other way,' Mr H. says. 'I think you had better come in and have a glass of beer, policeman, if it is not too early.'

'Never too urly sir,' says the policeman with a smile.

To cellar with Mr H. to draw the beer. Nice cellar lit by acetylene gas, as is all the house.

On lawn and under tent, then early dinner off half a leg of mutton—then goodbye and many thanks to Mr Hatherell. Governess car now at the door, so off we go to Tetbury Station. We have enjoyed our visit exceedingly, and they treated us right royally.

Into another train at 3.12—corridor fast express to Paddington, one of the crack trains of the day. Jump in a hansom and get to Marble Arch—all the traffic blocked and we cannot proceed.

The block is caused by a Salvation Army meeting, with contingents from all over the world. Our driver confers with us through the little trap-door, and then we get out of the block and go round via Alexandra Gate and Sloane Street and arrive at Victoria Station with twelve minutes in hand. A friendly porter gets us two seats in the 5.35 for Brighton—lavatory carriage and only we two, and two men. Sun smiting on the carriage all the way down to Brighton, which we reach all safe.

Up to 2 Clarence Square; Mr G. gone to bed and from all accounts is very bad. It now comes on to thunder and rain very heavily.

The storm having abated, we make our way home to our old bed again, and the holiday of 1914 is over, and we shall have to buckle on our armour for the work of life next week.

Beddgelert

1915

Wednesday 23 June. England is at war—only four words, but what a terrible amount of tragedy they convey.

Last year, when we were at Ross-on-Wye on our 1914 holiday, not a breath of war was in the air.

With startling and dramatic suddenness, on 4 August 1914 we were compelled to declare war against Germany, who had declared war against France and shamefully violated the neutrality of Belgium.

Now such a titanic conflict is raging, the like of which the world has never seen—on one hand Germany and Austria and Turkey; against them the allied forces of Great Britain, France, Russia, Servia, Italy.

For over ten months now, we have lived in a world of war. The piping days of peace seem a faraway dream of the past. All over England are soldiers training, and we have raised an army of probably three million men.

Brighton has been full of soldiers. The Pavilion has been transformed into a hospital for wounded Indians. The Workhouse and York Place School have been acquired for the same purpose. For hospitals for our own soldiers, we have the New Grammar School and St Mark's School. Camps have sprung up all over England. Life is changed, and we all have the War on our minds.

Hitherto, I am thankful to say, England has not suffered depredations to any extent, except bombardment at Scarborough and Whitby, and occasional zeppelin air-raids on east coast, Southend and Ramsgate.

The Germans have developed a submarine warfare against our shipping, and the biggest blot on any nation's record she made by sinking the *Lusitania* off Ireland, when quite 1,400 innocent men, women and children met their death. The world was shocked by this senseless crime, and characterised it as an act of murder.

I, hitherto a peaceful citizen, was on 31 August 1914 sworn in as a special constable of the Brighton Borough Police, and am now Special Constable no. 111 of the A Division: and, in company of a colleague, patrol the streets three evenings in succession, and worry the citizens, principally about obscuring their lights.

Also I have become an amateur soldier, having enrolled early in September in the Home Protection Brigade, 1st Battalion Sussex, and have been drilling and route-marching two or three times a week ever since. We now have uniforms and look like soldiers, and in case of invasion shall expect to do our bit.

Well, that gives you some idea of the revolution in our daily life. Also we had a deep trouble 26 June 1914, when we lost Millie's father after a painful illness. So altogether we have had some gloom.

However, we have decided, all being well, to accept Tom's offer to go a motor tour on the first of July. Fanny has not been well, and we are hoping to build her up on this trip.

Wednesday 30 June. Tom kindly invited us to sleep at his home this night.

Thursday 1 July. Nice morning. Tom having got the car outside the house, we begin to run to and fro with luggage and luggage-covers (which Tom, Fanny and Millie made one evening last week), and wrestle with a collection of straps.

We are taking a luncheon-basket, containing among other utensils and comestibles a kettle full of water. Tom picked this up, turned it upside down, and spilt all the water down his clothes.

Goodbye to Mary and Emily, and then at 8.43 a.m. we start. In the distance we noticed a car outside Mr E.C. Baldwin's house, and Fanny said, 'Hullo, Baldwins starting on their holiday today too.'

Soon we were bowling along up Preston Road, and 'Matilda' (that is Tom's pet name for his car) was now 'in her stride', and seemed to enter into the spirit of the thing, and bounded along like a thing of life, slackening or quickening her pace as the exigencies of the road demanded. Tom provided me with a type-written programme of our route, with copious notes referring to the portion from Guildford to Reading, which I gather is a tricky bit, there being several rocks.

In the High Street of Guildford we see Baldwin's car, and Tom finds they are going to Reading also, so he hands our route sheet to young Baldwin to peruse.

'Oh!' he says, 'I can show you a much better route—you follow me.' So we tailed in behind them and away.

Now, our paper said *not* to take the road to Frimley—Baldwin immediately takes it. We followed, but finding we were getting all their dust, we decided to turn back and follow the directions on our paper. We certainly went a very circuitous route.

Now we began to meet military transport wagons, huge unwieldy vehicles, soldiers marching, soldiers riding and leading horses and mules, which gave us some concern, as some of the horses and mules were inclined to shy. However, we got through all right, except one transport, driven very recklessly, nearly cut us too fine and gave us a little turn.

Passing a policeman, Tom pulled up and told him, but the constable said he did not notice he was driving badly when he passed him.

Looking back, I could still see him pursuing his mad career and steering very erratically.

At Pangbourne, just after passing the village, we selected a grassy spot alongside the river-bank, unlimbered the luncheon-basket, spread out the rugs and had a lovely lunch.

It was a sweetly pretty scene, the glorious river sweeping by, the sun shining, the air pure, wild ducks scurrying over the water; we, nomads, revelling in the freedom of the broad highway. Anon another motor draws up behind us, and they lunch also.

After a rest we step up, and off we go again. I notice a quaint inn sign, the Beetle and Wedge. At Reading we find the Baldwins: they are just going to put up for lunch.

We pull up in Oxford, but feeling it would be silly to try and see colleges without we made a proper stay, Tom gathers up the reins again, and Matilda gees up, and we dash off to Woodstock.

We now drew rein and stopped, and unstrapped the luncheon-basket—lit the methylated spirit-lamp, boiled the water and made tea, which we drank out of four huge pots like beer-pots in a country inn: then heigho for Stratford-upon-Avon, where we proceeded to interview the proprietress of the Golden Lion Hotel. They were pleased to have us, so it was off luggage and round into their nice garage with Matilda, which as Tom says is 'some car'.

A welcome wash, and then decide to take a river trip on the petrol launch *George Washington* at sixpence a head—we four only. A large number of punts and canoes were about, and they seemed to resent our launch rather much.

We now sit beside the river and watch the antics of a dirty little girl, until we feel so sure that she will fall in, that we get up and stroll to the post office, which is closed. However, up a side entrance the girls find an open door, and enter, and enquire if a telegram addressed 'Garrett' has arrived.

'No,' says the man. He then shut the door.

There are several ways of shutting a door—he shut it as much as to say 'I'm d——d if anybody else comes worrying me again tonight.'

Back to a hard bed—now, we like a feather-bed. Mother was rather restless.

Friday 2 July. We could never have left Stratford-upon-Avon without paying a visit to Shakespeare's house, to render homage to the memory of the immortal Bard. It is a veritable treasure-house.

One point struck me, and that was the undoubted reality of all the things we saw. Here are actual deeds signed—the real early printed plays—the actual room in which Shakespeare was born—actual records from parish registers.

The attendants were most courteous, and spared no pains to explain everything we cared to look at, and Mrs Rose who presided upstairs was quite a *grande dame* in her manner, and exceedingly well versed in her subject. But gladly as we would have liked to linger, our skipper was anxious to be on the road, and we tore ourselves away.

We are now on the broad highway again, and I can conceive nothing more exhilarating—freedom, movement and sunshine, and Matilda has the legs of pretty nearly everything on the road. Hills have no terrors for us. Our skipper may bend down and move a handle to alter a gear, or he may not, it's all one to me. I and Mill sit side by side on a beautiful seat—no responsibilities or cares. We feel good as we fly over the bosom of this beautiful England of ours—dear England, a priceless gem set in the silver sea.

Anon we reach Bridgnorth, find a nice field and partake of a sumptuous lunch. Millie has a few qualms, as there are cows the other side of the field, but we manage to control her.

After a sleep we strap on our basket again. Tom turns the handle and starts the engine, and Fanny and I spring on the throttle to stop her racing, as we get into trouble if we don't stop her down smartly.

Away again, my lads, let her go, we are reeling off the miles—running by finger-posts, and then coming back to see if we are on the right road. Matilda never likes to slow down before we get to a finger-post. She disdains them. Then she begins to have her doubts—Tom does something with his foot—she stops—he touches a lever, she begins to go backward, and we show her the finger-post. Then we look at our route papers—'Yes, Much Wenlock is the next place.'

Matilda is listening, gives a satisfied purr, and springs off like a racehorse. Through Much Wenlock, Shrewsbury, Oswestry and Gobowen, where we take in two gallons of petrol, and the girls order tea at a nice little hotel. Tom walks into a lamp suspended from the ceiling, which makes a clatter—and when he tells the maid, she cheerfully replies: 'People are always doing that.'

Feeling refreshed by our tea, we shape our course for Llangollen, where we pull up at the Sun Garage and feed Matilda again with six gallons of petrol—what a thirst she must have.

After leaving Corwen it commenced to rain, so we put up the hood: but as we were now within forty miles of Beddgelert, and as Matilda thinks nothing of forty miles, it seemed wisest to push on. We shot by the Royal Hotel at Capel Curig, and then it rained so heavily that we nearly went back and put up there.

'No—it can't be much farther now—as well put up with it and finish the job.'

Now we are on a wild mountain road, and a heavy fog swept across our way, and Tom said: 'If this gets much worse, we shall have to stop—we don't know what these mountain mists are capable of.' It was a grand sight, in one of the wildest bits of Wales—mountains all round, wrapped in wraithlike scudding mist, and giving everything a ghostly appearance.

By and by we came to a bridge, and I said: 'I know that bridge—good—there's Beddgelert Post Office. . . . Straight on, and you'll run in the door of the hotel in a minute.'

In a torrent of rain we pull up outside the Royal Goat. 'Boots' is now busy unstrapping our luggage—the luncheon-basket spilling water all over the place—and Tom and I house Matilda in the garage. I think Fanny was glad we had finished the journey.

Saturday 3 July. Tom and I strolled down to the village and tried to buy a newspaper, but the local postmaster, who is the newsagent, was so busy sorting the letters that we had to give it up as a bad job.

Braving the elements we tramped to the Pont Aberglaslyn through sub-Alpine scenery. To us who dwell in Sussex, where the landscapes are universally 'soft', this type of scenery is a great change.

Crossing the bridge, we looked down the sheer side of the rocks at a native fishing in the running water. Our fisherman was not a millionaire, to judge by his overcoat, which was split up the back; perched on his rock, with a short pipe in his mouth, he diligently fished the water, but without success.

We rode shanks' pony back home and to luncheon; then, being finer, Matilda is brought out and away we go to Criccieth.

I suppose that more people have heard of Criccieth since Lloyd George came into the limelight than ever before. Of course we had to see the great little man's abode, and by questioning a friendly police constable, found out where it was.

Up a steep hill we went, and—leaving Tom in the car—Fanny, Mill and I went up a pretty lane till it came in sight: a very plain white house—not very large, but beautifully situated on the high cliff, and with a fine sea view and nice grounds. I ascertained from a telegraph boy that L.G. was not at home—Mrs L.G. and one son was.

We sauntered back, admiring the ferns growing in the chinks of the walls.

'You've been a long time,' said Tom.

'Yes,' I said. 'No wonder—Lloyd George wants you to go up and have a cup of tea.'

A smile crept into his eyes. 'Jump in,' he said. 'We must be getting back.'

Home to dinner. We had got to the fish, when I saw Tom and Fanny glance round, astonishment over their faces—then a voice in manly tones—'Hullo Tom.'

Of all the surprising things, who should it be but Mr and Mrs Lord Thompson of Brighton. Soon we were all shaking hands, and they were telling us how they came from Brighton that morning, and retailing the latest Brighton news. Mr Thompson made us laugh with his stories, of which he seems to have an inexhaustible store.

Sunday 4 July. Fanny and Mill attend divine service at the church, and Tom and I go to the garage and oil the motor. Tom gives me a lecture on different parts of the mechanism. Undoubtedly the engine is a very intricate and complicated piece of work, and in my opinion somewhat of a triumph of engineering skill—mark you, it is all in a very small compass, and it works at a very high rate of speed, and develops 12/16 horsepower, and, as proved Friday, propelled a car containing four people and some luggage, a heterogeneous collection of tools and spare parts, 168 miles, at an average rate of 20 miles per hour, without a hitch.

It shows what strides have been made in motor-designing since those days, not so many years back, when we in Brighton waited hours for the arrival of motor-cars from London, on a famous London to Brighton run; then quite a large percentage 'jacked up' and never reached the goal. Now fifty miles really is nothing—a sort of stroll round after tea.

The funny thing is that the motor-car of today, which we think such a notable advance, may in time be relegated to a museum, and our descendants will look at it with the same eyes that we of this generation regard stagecoaches. Such seems to have been the fate of most inventions.

There seems no limit to human progress at present. I am always expecting to hear of some discovery similar to the power of electricity, which I consider one of the most mysterious of natural forces we have chained for human use. There are probably many similar things not yet discovered which, if scientists wrest the secret from Mother Nature, may revolutionise all our ways of life.

But that is of the future, and I must return to my work of cleaning the glass screen on the motor, so that our skipper may have an unimpeded view when next he proudly steers his dear Matilda along strange roads and ways in gallant little Wales.

I am quite a novice on motors, and set about my little jobs thereon in fear and trembling, as I have an ever-present terror of upsetting or scratching something. This fits in well with my own moods, in things which are my *very own* at home. I always tell my children of these special things, that they are sacred. My books are sacred.

Having tested her all over, screwed up where unscrewed, and put her all ship-shape, we have a wash and get to luncheon—and then once more the welcome sound of 'All aboard the lugger' as Tom pulls Matilda up outside the hotel. A beautiful afternoon, and we pass Llyn Ddinas, surrounded by mountains.

Stopping above Llyn Ddinas, we get one of the most beautiful views conceivable—mountains and lake. I mentally photographed it, and can now shut my eyes and see it—a fayre scene.

We bear uphill till we reach a level place called Gorphwysfa, 'the resting-place', also called Pen-y-Pass. We rest and try to let Matilda cool, but she is too hot to cool down much, so we begin the descent of the celebrated Pass of Llanberis, the finest carriage mountain road in Wales. We are soon running alongside Llyn Peris, on the opposite shore of which are the immense Dinorwic slate-quarries. Piles of slate-refuse tower about a thousand feet high, their bases resting on the edge of the lake, and the reflection in the clear water is very fine.

We are now in more open country, and it is strange how much we miss the mountains. I am sure there is a fascination in mountains—something that draws you back to them again. I go on in business, day in day out, then when the summer comes, I say to Mill, 'The mountains are calling.' When I see them I think of the lines: 'Before the hills in order stood or earth received her frame.' How strong and immovable they are—generations of men come and go, battle, murder and sudden death, but the mountains are unmoved. Tom is disappointed, because he has a notion that they will 'skip like young rams'—but no, there is never a 'skip'. They stare, darkly and grimly.

But now we have reached Caernarvon, and pulling up we ask a few questions of a friendly inhabitant. He rolls the Welsh names off his tongue in such grand style that we are soon completely bewildered.

I noticed he wore the badge of the Caernarvon Volunteer Training Corps, so I said, 'I see you belong to the CVTC—I belong to the Sussex lot,' and showed him my badge. Raising his hat, he left us and continued his stroll.

We gazed at the castle exterior, and then a policeman informed us it was open on Sundays, so we paid our fourpence each for admission in our best courtly style. It is undoubtedly a fine castle, and with the exception of Alnwick in Northumberland is reputed to be the finest in Great Britain.

We soon secured a guide, the funniest little man you ever saw—a soldier, every one of his somewhat few inches—upright as a pint pot—stiff as a poker—his stride martial—his face Lloyd George's—his eyes blue, with a wicked twinkle in them. Oh! how he did talk. Hearing Tom was a little deaf, he kept close to him and rattled off his descriptions in a loud commanding manner. Hearing also that our ladies were not very good walkers, as a special privilege he allowed them to walk on the grass.

Tom cracked a few jokes with him, and our guide turned round and said: 'He wants to walk on the grass too, but I shan't let him.' Then 'Follow me ladies—stand here—do you understand me ladies—' all in a very brisk commanding way.

He was full of the wonderful doings in 1911, when the Prince of Wales was invested—it must have been a very great function. They pulled down several houses near the quay to make more space for the people.

Saying goodbye to our guide we got in the car, and the last we saw of him was his little blue-clad figure standing in the centre of the King's Gate, stiffly at attention, his right hand at the salute, motionless as a statue.

Now the streets are full of people and soldiers, and we have to creep slowly till we gain the road outside the town.

We pass Llanbelig old church, and Llyn Cwellyn—a fine lake—and now we are fairly in the mountains again, and Snowdon high up on our left. Finally rattle into Beddgelert exceedingly pleased with our ride.

Dinner claims our attention, and then we walk up to Moel Hebog ('the hill of the hawk'). Here we come across a waterfall which our hotel has diverted to the garage, where it rushes out over a sink and gives a copious supply of water. Retracing our steps we indulge in sundry shouts, as we have found one or two echoes, then cross a field to 'Gelert's grave'.

Now, the legend of Gelert is a very pretty one. Gelert was a hound presented to Llewellyn by King John. On a day, Llewellyn went 'a-hunting' and left Gelert at home in charge of his little child. On his master's return, the dog ran joyfully to meet him, but the Prince was dismayed to see he was covered in blood. Llewellyn rushed to the nursery, and found the child's cradle overturned and the ground stained with blood. Jumping to the conclusion that the greyhound had killed the child, he drew his sword and slew him. But on turning over the cradle, there was the child alive and unhurt, and by its side a large wolf, dead. Then remorse came to Llewellyn, and how deeply he repented of his hasty deed. He buried Gelert, and we are now going to see his tomb. A very pretty idea, but it appears to lack one great essential, *viz.* truth.

When we reached the spot, we were greatly disappointed—it was a poor sort of tomb. It was surrounded by barbed wire, and as we turned away, Tom caught his coat on it and tore a nasty little place.

Monday 5 July. We jump into the car and through very pretty lanes to Penrhyndeudraeth, where we pay one shilling and go over a bridge.

On the other side we see a range of buildings in a sad state of ruin through fire. We understand it was a powder factory, and is now guarded by soldiers, and it looked as though soldiers were carrying on the rebuilding. As we came on, an old soldier carrying a rifle with a fixed bayonet signalled to us to stop, and said: 'Where from?'

We replied, 'Beddgelert.'

The next question is, 'Where to?'

Answer: 'Harlech.'

'Go on.'

It seemed to me a senseless farce.

Harlech is a pretty little place, nearly a mile from the sandy beach, affording safe and pleasant bathing. On the land between the village and the sea is an eighteen-hole golf-course. 'As an old war-horse sniffs the battle from afar off,' so does Tom when he sees this course, and I fancy some day he will have to come and play golf on these links.

Tuesday 6 July. To the Snowdon Mountain Railway and board the train. It is a queer little railway. Every precaution has been taken to ensure safety, and the rate of progression is slow.

In our carriage is a frail-looking white-bearded gentleman. As we ascend, Tom consults his little aneroid to see the altitude, this old gentleman takes out his aneroid, and they compare notes. He says he has walked up Snowdon thirty times—four times this month.

He looked at Tom and me rather contemptuously, and seemed to insinuate that only cripples went up Snowdon by rail. I did not say anything, because after all there is a 'feather-bed soldiery feeling' in being pulled up instead of winning your way step by step.

In about seventy minutes we get out at a dilapidated, neglected station, and struggle up a further thirty or forty yards until we reach the hut on the summit. It is not a very large space to move about in, as the large stone cairn, the refreshment hut, and the bedrooms (for foolish people who desire to sleep up here) take up all the space.

I wonder how many people who do stop the night ever see a good sunrise next morning. More probably it is raining, or misty, or blowing so hard that it would blow your hair off. The huts were prepared for wind and gales, being tied down into the earth by strong steel-wire hawsers—but it all looked as though it wanted money laid out on it, and a few coats of paint.

We sent off a few postcards from a box in the refreshment-room, then entered the last train of the day. As we near the bottom, the rack and pinion say, 'Chuck it, chuck it, c-h-u-c-k i-t'—and then it begins to rain. Luckily we put Matilda's hood up before we started, so she is all snug, and we jump in and get away home.

Dress and dinner. At 8.30 Tom, Mr Thompson and I walk to Aberglaslyn Bridge, and Mr T. tells us tales—one of a grand jury. The foreman said, 'Gentlemen, all we have to do is to see whether there is a *prima facie* case.' Then up and spake one of the grand jury: 'What is a *prima facie* case?'

And the judge says, 'The best illustration I can give you of *prima facie* evidence would be, suppose you saw a man come out of a public house, wiping his mouth—that would be *prima facie* evidence that he had just had a drink there.' I call that rather good.

Then it began to rain, and we trotted home and settled in the porch for a chat. By and by, two or three natives who had been up to the hotel for a meeting came out. One was rather elevated—his face was very red, and actually shone. 'Ah, ladies and gentlemen,' says he, 'I hope you're enjoying yourselves. Awm doin chawmpion.'

I think he was afraid of the steps, so he turned round and went down backward. The last we heard of him, he was wishing us '*Aur revoire*' as he disappeared in the gloom.

Wednesday 7 July. Tom and I give the car a lick and a promise, and clean up the brass parts. Then have a wash, and join the other visitors.

We are getting friendly with Mr and Mrs Marshall and Miss Webster. Mr Marshall is a smart-looking man with a military moustache, and I should imagine is the proprietor of an iron-foundry in Falkirk. Mrs Marshall is dark and plump—unfortunately she slipped on some polished oil-cloth in her hall six months since, and limps about with the aid of a stick.

Miss Webster, their great friend, is a tall big-framed woman who improved on acquaintance—a sensible person who had had her share of trouble in life, but had 'made good' and was still cheerful.

Mrs Leam or Leem was staying here accompanied by her son, a young officer invalided home on twelve months' leave as a result of injury to his eyes by shrapnel. He wore dark-glasses, so I did not see his injuries, but we all felt very sorry for him. Mrs L.'s husband was I believe a colonel, and was expected home from Persia wounded.

So Mrs L., who was the possessor of a fine motor-car, had set out to find some quiet spot where she could take a house and nurse her menfolk back to health, and in the course of her wanderings came to the Royal Goat, Beddgelert, and put up.

In a day or two we heard she had taken a house on the other side of the river, and was busy receiving furniture and engaging servants. One evening there was great excitement as she had wires to say three servants she had engaged were turning up—two at Portmadoc and one at Caernarvon. So her chauffeur bustled off to Portmadoc with the big car, and the hotel people had to send their car to Caernarvon, and as the new house was not ready the chauffeur had to get them beds in Beddgelert.

Thursday 8 July. After breakfast we get Matilda out, and away to Betws-y-coed. We stop at the Swallow Falls and pay our money at the turnstile, and my verdict is that it is the best waterfall of its kind that I have seen.

Into the car again, and stopped outside the Fairy Glen; we walked up a pretty lane, meeting a dear old lady who is in charge and suggested to us that we might as well pay our twopence admission to her then, as she was going down to her cottage to get something.

It was very hot down in the bottom of the glen, so the two girls took off their shoes and stockings, and dangled their pretty little feet in the cool waters. Afterwards it was amusing to see them struggling to get their stockings on, and then take shelter behind a rock to do the finishing touches to their toilet.

We now toil up to the top again, and just outside the gate there is our dear old lady. We purchase a glass of fresh milk each, and the old lady shows the girls specimens of socks etc. that her aunt, an old lady over eighty, knits. Millie bought a pair of boy's long socks, suitable for cycling hose, and Fanny purchased a pair of baby's socks, and the old lady seemed genuinely pleased for her old aunt's sake.

Bidding her a tender farewell we left her, and she at once turned her attention to extracting twopences from a bevy of 'flappers'.

Who so happy as we—we will not think of war's alarms—we steadfastly set our minds to forget all troubles, and if a thought intrudes, we ruthlessly crush it. We are, as children say, 'tending—'tending that all is well in this best of worlds. Is this heartless, with so much sorrow all around? I think not—the bow cannot always be bent. We have lived in a nerve-racking time, and a respite is good.

But for all our 'tending, this hideous spectre of war is still ready to rear its head and gibber at us if we gave it the slightest encouragement. Our real state is as of a person under anaesthetic to relieve pain. We drug ourselves with mountains and scenery, instead of chloroform or ether, that is the only difference.

We now regain the road, and Matilda would, if she could, wag her tail and welcome us back—for these things, although man-made, do by their constant association with their owners acquire some far-off touch of 'soul'. We clamber into Matilda, and Tom 'turns her up', and Fanny throttles her down, until her engine beats with a gentle rhythm, and 'off we do agen'.

Now are we in absolutely wild country, and Tom keeps consulting his pocket aneroid—through Pont-y-pant, then through Dolwyddelan and Roman Bridge, and poor old 'Tilda' is boiling all over the place, and Tom looks at the old aneroid and says, 'We've come up nearly thirteen hundred feet, my friend.' I think his heart is sore for poor Matilda—a merciful man is merciful to his beast.

At Festiniog the claims of luncheon began to press, so we pulled up at a small hotel. I went in and asked the landlord if he could manage lunch for four.

I could see I had staggered him. He dived downstairs and up came his wife, a nice little brisk woman. 'Ah,' I said to myself, 'the grey mare is the best horse here.'

She was very sorry, but this year there was no demand for luncheons, so they had given up providing.

What could I do? Here was a nice little woman, genuinely sorry she could not feed us—here were rows of bottles—the good of the house had to be considered. 'Will you let me have a small Worthington?' I said.

Then the cork had to be drawn, and the foaming contents carefully poured into a glass, and it looked a picture. I raised it to my lips, intending to enjoy it—when outside the confounded electric hooter began to kick up a d——l of a noise.

I drank it up, said goodbye to my hostess and strolled outside.

'Come on old man, what a time you've been—can they do it?'

'No—they're awfully sorry, but they can't—better go on to the next place.'

On again till we reach Maentwrog, a very old village. By my halidame, here is a hotel—the Grapes—'LUNCHEON AND TEAS PROVIDED.' 'Eureka,' says I.

Fanny and I interviewed the 'ooman. My word, she was stiff—an angular female, past middle age, and my heart sank. She hadn't much in the house—some cold mutton. 'Yes, all right. For four, please.'

The mutton joint was a little the worse for wear, but it panned out, and we had a real good meal—some exceedingly nice tomato preserve, angular female's own make—some very nice eschalots.

We now borrow a leaky can from 'angular', and fill poor Matilda with water; she gulped it with a will, and a contented sigh escaped her as she ran out what she couldn't hold. 'Angular' says goodbye and we wave adieux.

All went well until we were within three miles of Pwllheli,* when a loud report rang out. 'Hullo,' says I, 'Germans dropping bombs, eh, what?'

Poor old Matilda, gone lame in her off hind-foot—tyre burst, by gum. To it, my lads.

First a pipe for me, and a cigarette for Tom. Then see us hurry—have you ever seen a firemen's competition? There you have us to the life—

*'Pwllheli' is a formidable word to a southerner, may I without being pedantic ask you to please pronounce it 'Poolth-helly' and it means 'the salt-water pit'—the way some people pronounce Welsh names sets my teeth on edge. (Author's note.)

busy fingers unstrapping refractory buckles—getting out tools, screwing on the new wheel, making all snug, in next to no time—what smartness! How proud the girls are of their husbands' activity. Jump in, slam the doors, and off again just as if nothing had happened.

Pwllheli a pretty little place—we make our way to the esplanade—six or seven dilapidated bathing-huts in a mournful row. 'You ought to have a bathe,' said Tom. 'We'll wait for you.'

'Well, I should like to, if you don't mind waiting.'

I found the office, and armed with the necessary equipment—bathing-ticket, costume and towels—I entered the dirty sand-strewn hut and hastily disrobed. Drawing on the costume, which was much too small, I waited a moment to admire my well knit manly frame, then went out and got Tom to button up the costume. Now, at last, plunge—beautiful. The best sea bathe I ever had away from home.

Limber up again, noticing on our way several of the most antique, ramshackle one-horse tram-cars I ever saw. I would not have credited that in any part of Great Britain, in this year of grace, there were such vehicles running. They ought to be put in a museum.

Threading our way out of town through a number of khaki-clad warriors, we got out on the King's highway, and reached home after eight o'clock. Dinner well started, so we go in without changing, and do fair execution. A crowded day of glorious life.

After dinner, up into the billiards room. Unfortunately the table was in play, and we had to wait. Mr Marshall rang for the waitress and ordered Scotches round. The waitress came, and said: 'Please, Mr Pullan says it's ten o'clock. Billiards have to stop at ten.'

It seemed foolish as applied to visitors staying in a hotel; however, we stopped at once, and put out the lights.

Friday 9 July. Set out to ascend Craig y Llan, and down the other side. I was impressed by Mrs Lord Thompson's gameness, on what to a lady must have been a trying walk—not one word of complaint all the way—be she scrambling down a huge rock, up to her waist in bracken, or over her boots in water. Why, half the women would have worried your life out of you, asking foolish questions as to when we were going to get to the road, or declaring she couldn't take another step.

On a good road again we came to a tiny village called Nantmor, and discovered a little general shop. What a heterogeneous stock-in-trade! What a blending of odours! How it was all crowded together! Bacon and provisions, tinned goods (very ancient), cheese, soap, sugar, tea, biscuits, stockings, blouses, haberdashery, etc. A nice young woman let us drink soda and milk as long as her stock held out, and then ginger-beer and milk. Then away, and now we are on our native heath.

Luncheon, and then Matilda comes into her own again; we scuttle down to Hughes Motor Works (telephone no. 32 Portmadoc), and stop outside while Tom gets them to take off the old burst tyre and put a new tyre on the car. They were nice chaps, but exceedingly dirty elfs, and I pitied poor old Tom as he saw them smashing on the new tyre—not the way we treat dear Matilda.

Fanny worked at some fancy work, and Millie wrote some postcards. I smoked and watched the men, and two Red Cross nurses nailed us for four flowers at sixpence each, for French Flag Day.

Saturday 10 July. Millie, Mrs Thompson and I walk over Pont Aberglaslyn, enter the woods, and up river—views grand. We hear someone shouting from the road, but can't see anyone. Then we hear singing, and the strains of 'Sussex by the Sea', and Mrs T. says, 'Oh! that's Jack come to meet us.' We reach home very pleased with our walk.

Tea was very acceptable—then a wash and change. Tom not just the thing, and does not shine at dinner.

Sunday 11 July. We pack with sadness, putting all except necessaries in our large green box, which Mr Pullan is going to send home by rail. The necessaries go into our portmanteau, being 'WANTED ON THE VOYAGE'. Now to pay the 'shot'.

Partings are never pleasant, and we had got into the picture at the Royal Goat. Still, this is childish—buck up, and play the man—you've had a darn good time.

The motion gradually revived us; we bustled on to dear old Harlech, and now we are on our old ground of 1910—a fleeting glimpse of Hendre Hall where we stayed, then over the bridge at Penmaenpool, and through narrow lanes till we draw rein alongside Tal-y-Llyn, unstrap luncheon-basket and have lunch. What a superb scene it is.

Away again to Abergynolwyn, a village of quarrymen, and then to Aberystwyth on the look-out for a hotel. Finally we pull up outside the Goderddan Arms and Lion Royal Hotel, and accost the 'Boots'.

'Boots' means us to stay there—I think he would have said 'yes' to any question if he thought we wanted him to. Tom and I run the car down into a fine garage in North Parade, then back to a good supper at eight o'clock. Fine tall waitresses, evidently specially selected for stature and looks. Then out for a walk.

On the front is the University College of Wales, erected in 1860-something, a conglomeration of almost every style of architecture. It has a frontage of over 400 feet, but I was not impressed; it looked tawdry and gingerbready. It was originally intended for a hotel, but after an expenditure of £80,000 the scheme collapsed and it became a 'white elephant'. In 1870 the building was purchased by a committee for college purposes for £10,000.

We dawdle up Pier Street, have drinks round, and go to our respective bedrooms. Poor old Mill in great distress—no night-dress in the 'wanted on the voyage' bag. Either she left it at Beddgelert, or packed it in the green box for Brighton.

Monday 12 July. Settle up the bill, and away—lovely views of the Vale of Rheidol on our left.

We are now in a very wild country, and see a little girl with a can of water, under an iron pipe at side of road, from which water was dropping into the can.

We wanted water for poor Matilda, so I jumped out. 'You'll let me have this can of water, my dear,' I said to the little girl, as my fingers closed on the handle.

I thought she didn't seem to jump at it, but she did not say 'nay', so I started pouring it in old Tilda's inside. While thus engaged, the others talked to the little girl and gave her twopence for the water.

I am horrified, when we are on our way again, when they tell me the poor kiddie said the water came so slowly today that she had waited an hour to fill her can. It was too cruel—whyever didn't she tell me before I so ruthlessly commandeered her hard-won water?

I was ashamed, but it was too late. I reflected that twopence was a lot of money to her, so laid that flattering unction to my soul—but it was too bad for all that.

At last we decide to pull up for lunch, and in selecting a spot, bump in a hole and do a little damage to the machine—I know we bent a brake-rod, and I fancy we broke a plate on one of the front springs.

We find a lovely field, and get to lunch, and away to Elan Valley to see great Birmingham Water-Supply Works. Presently we come to a gate, and a sentry stops us. 'Your driving licence,' he demands.

Terrible job to find it, but at last it is dragged out of one of the car pockets. 'All right, pass on.'

Away we go to the first dam, then another, and yet another. Here are sentries furnished by the Herefordshire Cadets, a smart lot of lads, and we decide to stop.

A work of this magnitude takes one's breath away. Look at the massive strength of the masonry, 104 feet thick at the base, holding back 2,000 million gallons of water; when heavy rains occur in the mountains ahead, it must be a grand sight. If one of these dams should burst, why, the waters would destroy everything for miles.

Tom has been here before, when he was ill some years ago. It is quite a show-place, and several cars and parties keep coming up.

As we think about returning, Fanny spies a boiling kettle in the cadets' guard-room. No sooner said than done—we get out our tea, and willing cadets scald it for us, and we are soon sipping out of our four old pots. Then off we go, through lovely wooded country until we reach Llandrindod Wells, where we put up at the Hotel Metropole—a much more pretentious place than I expected. At the front door, a long-handled dusting-brush, with a notice requesting visitors to dust their boots, gave me a slight shock. These people were evidently too good for this poor dirty old world.

Up an electric lift to our rooms—very nice. I was appalled to note the recklessness with which Millie, totally unaccustomed to lifts, was soon manipulating it herself. She cannot know the danger ever lurking around lifts.

Shave, and down into a very large dining-room. People a little stiff—not like our old Beddgelert Goat. Then a stroll—the town very clean, all the houses spick and span—a little air of smugness about the place I seemed to fancy, as though the people thought themselves rather superior.

Tuesday 13 July. Walk to the Pump Room, a very clean airy hall, with plenty of bench seats around the walls—in the centre an oval bar, at which from several different 'pulls' (like beer-pulls) the waters are dispensed by one male attendant in a holland uniform, and one smart female attendant. Four glasses of sulphur water Tom prescribes for us, and we retire to a seat.

When I raise the glass to my lips, I am nearly sick. A terrible smell assails my nostrils—a blend of rotten eggs and a country WC. However, it must be drunk, and Tom says: 'This is the Mecca of all true Welshmen.'

We sit and watch a constant stream of people, mostly elderly. With set faces they approach the bar, hand over a glass (for the *habitués* nearly all bring their own glasses), receive their water and walk into the grounds, sipping it. This routine they carry out religiously three times a day.

We struggled gallantly with our lot. Tom and Mill finished theirs—Fanny and I gave up ours half-way. Feeling the effects of the sulphur, Tom kindly piloted me to a range of about thirty-two WCs—very liberal providers, these Pump Room people.

Back to hotel garage and tune up the car, strap on the luggage, and start off at two o'clock. Arrive at Worcester all well, and as Tom is doubtful about our money lasting, he decides to wire to Burt for £10.

To the Star Hotel in the main street—rather noisy, as there were trams constantly running, and a railway bridge just above. We get rooms 30 and 31, and are soon operating the electric Otis lift.

Wash and down to dinner in a quaintly shaped room which puts me in mind of a ship's cabin. The head waiter anticipates our every want.

They seem rather slack, and there is no doubt this War is being felt very much by hotels.

Wednesday 14 July. To the post office, where Tom draws the £10 Burt has kindly despatched, and the man hands him Burt's little message: 'You appear to be going strong—write safe receipt—Burt.' Back to hotel and settle up.

As Tom has got the £10, I pay the account by my cheque, just to prove that they will take it. Quite simple—'Here is my home address'—then I show my 'special constable' warrant. 'This will prove my *bona fides*—that will be all right?' And the thing is done.

Peerless and Son's cheque is practically like a bank-note, and will generally pass all over England.

At noon off we go to Droitwich, as I have always understood the houses were falling out of upright in consequence of the salt-brine being pumped out of the earth. We got there and ran around—never a house that struck me much. True, there was the Crooked House Restaurant, but that was nothing. Disappointed, we turn away to Evesham for lunch at the Northwick Hotel.

Away again, and occasional showers, so we put the hood up and down at intervals, and succeed in pinching Tom's finger. It is supposed to be a one-man hood, but it is not exactly easy for two men to put up.

We ease up slowly through Broadway, probably the prettiest village in England. Every house has been built to harmonise with the old cottages, and the tone of the place is charming. I understand wealthy people have taken the place up, and have houses and cottages built. It certainly deserved all that Tom and Fanny had said in its favour.

Running through Oxford, a 'bus splashes mud in Millie's eye, which makes her squeak. We arrive at Henley in a deluge of rain, and put up at the Catherine Wheel Hotel.

Several officers here; one from Brighton, going to Scotland on a small car, put up here for the night because of the rain. A major at the top table has a most dreadful cough.

Thursday 15 July. Settle the bill, where I work off another cheque. Off through Maidenhead, very pretty, then to Windsor, where we meet soldiers going up to change castle guard.

On through lovely country to Woking, then to Crawley, and Tom calls at one or two of his jobs. Mr Ockenden, one of the builders, presents Fanny with a bonnie lot of roses—also does he surprise Tom by a specimen of a lead water-pipe, gnawed through by rats. Away again past a military camp, then through Balcombe Forest to Hassocks—glimpse of the Home Protection Brigade Camp as we fly past—and Tom runs us up to 12 St James's Avenue, where we find all well. We regretfully say goodbye, and the 1915 holiday is over.

As we lie down in our own bed, we feel deeply thankful to the giver of all good, who has watched over and kept us in our wandering, and also those we left behind. And now we must think of taking up our daily life again—goodbye.

Bude

1916

Sunday 25 June. It is a year since I last penned lines in a similar book to this. What a year! We have lived day by day obsessed by one thing—WAR.

Every placard on the street is something about the War.

Soldiers everywhere—wounded soldiers, poor creatures without limbs, jar on one at every turn. Sensation after sensation comes on us every day. I wonder if I can recollect all the things that have assailed us—submarine warfare waged by Germany in a most barbarous manner—zeppelin raids on east coast of England, London, and once or so on the Midlands. Brighton has hitherto escaped, but we have had several 'alarums and excursions'.

Military service bills—military compulsion—Derby recruiting schemes—income tax raised to five shillings in the pound—war loans—Exchequer bonds—military tribunals—losses of ships—Gallipoli expedition—Verdun—rebellion in Ireland by the Sinn Feiners—women tram- and 'bus-conductors, ticket-collectors on railways, porters, postmen, milkmen and munition workers—paper money—death of Lord Kitchener, blown up on HMS *Hampshire*—suspension of bank holiday at Whitsuntide—early closing of public houses—no treating in many areas—forms for employers employing men between 18 and 41 years of age—trade union rules in many cases overridden—dilution of skilled labour—great advance made by Russia—naval battle in the North Sea, where we lose many gallant men and ships, but inflict crushing losses on the enemy—oh dear! What a revolution for dear old England. The contemptible little British Army, as the enemy dubbed Lord French's command at Mons, is now a great army of at least five million, and I fancy we have surprised the world by our efforts.

Munitions we now manufacture on a colossal scale. We still rule the sea. Another social revolution for conservative England is the adoption of 'British Summer Time'—advocated for many years by the late Mr W. Willett, a London builder and contractor, under the nomenclature of 'daylight saving', it was once or twice debated on in Parliament within the last few years, and a Daylight Saving Bill was introduced, only to be defeated by ignorant opposition. But war is a stern master, and under its influence the Government triumphantly carry a measure on the lines advocated by the late Mr Willett.

Accordingly at 2 a.m. on 21 May all clocks were advanced one hour, with the result that we now have an extra hour of daylight in the evening—one of the greatest boons we ever had. The saving in artificial lighting is incredible.

On 25 January our eldest son Cuthbert enlisted in the Inns of Court OTC, trained in London for a few months, and then went into camp at Berkhamsted, Herts, where he is at present. Reggie attested on 5 June, and is transferred thereby to the Reserve.

And yet, notwithstanding all the 'slings and arrows of outrageous fortune', with the summer has come a desire to be off again on the broad highway—to leave the noise and bustle of the town and market-place, to be free once more for a short time in the open air, under the wide canopy of heaven, away from houses, to see the everlasting hills again, to pass through sleepy villages where hurry and bustle are not known, and to forget if possible, for a time at least, that the nations of Europe have gone mad, and are cutting each other's throats.

A mad world my masters—men, bred, born and reared, with who shall say how much care and trouble, and in many cases with self-denial and privation by parents, at the behest of one man blinded with ambition and the lust of power, hurled to death like sheep driven to slaughter, or maimed for life, or health and strength broken by the rigours of the campaign.

But one cannot dwell on these horrible things. Accordingly to Tom we go, and together knock up a programme for a tour with him and Fanny on our old friend Matilda. And now I am waiting to see whether we shall be able to start on Saturday afternoon next, as provisionally arranged. The future lies on the knees of the gods—what will it bring us?

Friday 30 June. It brings this. Tom was anxious about an appeal he had lodged for Howell, and I was in the same state about Scrase. Tom was represented by Mr Cane, I by Mr Cushman. Result: Howell, six months' exemption—Scrase, exemption conditional on his remaining in our employment, as his is an exempted occupation. This gave both our minds relief, and we now felt quite free to start tomorrow.

Saturday 1 July. At 3.30 p.m., Tom and Fanny hove in sight on Matilda. We soon had our luggage aboard and away we went. A very high wind, and cold.

Along the front we bowled, and we were just beginning to realise that we had actually started on the 1916 holiday when we heard a loud report, and found we had badly burst a near-side hind tyre.

Out we jumped, and soon had a new wheel and tyre in place, and off we went again. On to Havant, and Millie and I began to note the old spots we grew to love so well when we used to rail to Havant and cycle on to Lyndhurst.

On to the Woolston–Itchen ferry, and I have never seen it so crowded. Ahead of us was another motor, also packed with people, children and perambulators. On the opposite shore Matilda picked her way daintily over the dirt, and we swung into High Street and pulled up while Tom and I went along East Street, Southampton, to inspect a threepenny and sixpenny bazaar, carried on by a firm named Woolworth, and I understand Tom has something to do for someone who is letting them a place at Worthing.

On again until we reach the New Forest, and eventually pull up outside the Fox and Hounds Hotel, Lyndhurst. Mr Ings welcomes us, and Baby—now a strapping young woman—helps us down with our luggage.

We had arranged for a supper, and a right royal one they gave us—salmon (very fine), lamb, strawberries and cream, cheese etc. Then a stroll to the Knoll, where we sit and watch soldiers acting the fool with a football. As the soldiers and a telegraph boy or two kicked the football, two dogs ran after it: one, a black terrier, being especially keen on it, and I have never seen a dog enjoying himself more.

Presently a soldier gave the ball a tremendous kick. Little black dog was looking the other way—on came the ball and bowled him over. He picked himself up, gave one sad look, and solemnly marched home.

Close to the Knoll was a large camp, used as a grenade school, and here the soldiers come for their grenade course of about a fortnight. When they are practising grenade-throwing, the noise of the explosions is terrifying.

Fanny and I stroll over and enter the camp, surprised not to be challenged: but deeming it wiser to let well alone, we pave our way to Fox and Hounds, and have a chat with Mrs Ings. She gives us a very bad account of some of the officers who pass through the grenade school, who have victimised several people by cheques which are returned marked 'R/D' or 'No a/c' etc., until, taught by experience, the gentle natives of Lyndhurst have now adopted the 'pay before you have it' line with them. Officers' cheques are out of favour at Lyndhurst just now.

Sunday 2 July. Awake to find the world sunny and bright, the air sweet and fresh. We gather for breakfast—haddock with poached eggs, very nice indeed. Our appetite assuaged, we gather on the verandah, and buy an *Observer*, and are rather pleased with the favourable war news.

Then to church. As there was no sermon, we got out earlier than expected and went for a stroll. Up to the green, near the pretty thatched cottages, where some years ago Burt would persist in standing when one of our party was photographing. Thereafter we lounge on the verandah and watch the men; one, very stout, is lying on the ground under a Royal Blue Bournemouth motor char-à-banc which has jacked up and refuses to be coaxed into going.

Now with a dash and a rattle, a fussy little two-seater draws up, driven by an officer or military doctor of youthful appearance, accompanied by a stylish young lady—on their honeymoon, said the girls. We saw young officer go and talk to our fat motor driver, who had emerged from under his char-à-banc, and was gazing disconsolately into the engine. As they come nearer, I hear young officer say, 'Look heah, I've been to the War—look at my hand—surely you can do this for ME.'

Fat driver looked into the innards of the little car, pointed out to him that engines and moving parts required oil, and proceeded to pour oil into sundry obscure parts. He then explained that there were three speeds, actuated by levers etc., which he pointed out. Things were now put back on the car, the lady-friend got in, fat driver gave young officer a few parting instructions, to which in a very airy way he responded 'Right-ho,' and away he went for Bournemouth. Whether he ever reached that salubrious town is a matter of doubt.

Monday 3 July. I pay the bill while Tom talks to fat driver (who has been tinkering with char-à-banc till late last night and from very early this morning, and is about as far off as ever). Having now limbered up our goods and chattels, Tom grasps the reins and Matilda canters away. We turn off for Fordingbridge, and soon pull up in consequence of deep water right across the road. We three got out and went over a little plank bridge, and Tom put Matilda through all right.

It was Tom's intention to skirt the city of Salisbury, and just after we had had a splendid view of the graceful spire of the cathedral, we came on quite a crowd, and found a disabled aeroplane resting on the ground. Engine trouble, someone in the crowd told us, had forced them to come down. I don't know whether it was an English or French 'plane, for I noticed the tank was painted red, white and blue, so it may have belonged to some of our Gallic friends—'*Vive la France*.' Poor France, how great has been her sacrifice in this wicked war.

We are now in a very lonely part of the world, and suddenly come on a cart laden with hay, accompanied by a large clumsy dog. Tom brought Matilda to 'dead slow', but the silly old dog blundered under our hind wheel. He only yelped once, so I know he was not really hurt.

On again, until we pull up at a desolate inn called the Ship. The landlady came forward and eagerly asked us for news of the War—I could see that news percolated slowly to this district, and she was pleased when we told her the news of the British advance.

We at last reach Exeter in a heavy downpour. The roads were drenched and muddy. I noticed several special constables on duty in the streets, although it was only the afternoon, so evidently they do day duty.

We decided to put up at the Bude Hotel (Family and Commercial), Paris Street. The girls go and select rooms, while Tom and I go with Matilda to Parker's, a badly constructed garage. The roof was supported on a number of iron columns, which made it inconvenient to get a car into the lock-ups at the side, and a false move might have brought the whole roof down.

Tonight, after a day or two on the open road, away from everything and everybody, the trams, the streets, the noise and the people grate on me a little.

Notices in bedroom to be careful over electric lights under Defence of the Realm regulations.

Tuesday 4 July. We pay the bill and point Matilda's nose for Tedburn St Mary. The road is notoriously bad, and always under repair. At 10.50 we were held up by a burst in off-side hind tyre.

The road now improved and we bowled along to Okehampton, where we found a motor engineer's, Day & Sons.

Tom made enquiries for a new Michelin cover. I don't think he thought for a moment they would have it—115/105 mm, I believe he said. Yes, they said they had one, and later produced a new inner tube, and proceeded to instal it on the spare wheel. Tom paid their bill, and away we went for Hatherleigh.

I don't suppose it entered our heads that we should ever see Day's again. How true it is, 'We know not what a day or an hour may bring forth.'

We drew out of Okehampton, and began in joyous mood to scan the road for a suitable spot for our wayside luncheon. Luck favoured us, and we pulled up at a splendid place: a disused wayside pump in a stone basin. Behind the pump was a wooden seat, roofed in and supported on wooden posts, quite snug. We enjoyed our lunch as much as any we had had. In due course we limbered up, and like giants refreshed drove our way westward.

About 2.30 p.m. a startling change came over the spirit of our dream—Matilda stopped. The engine had died out. What could it mean?

Tom jumped out and wound up the engine. Matilda did not respond.

Tell it not in Askelon, publish it not in Gath, lest mine enemies have me in derision—Matilda, heroine of a thousand runs, who has toiled up terrible Welsh passes where the foot of a motor seldom treads, has jibbed.

Tom proceeded to do everything—taking out this, trying that, and ever and anon giving the starting-handle a wind. Each time the cheque was returned marked 'No a/c' or 'R/D'.

I suppose we had been stranded nearly an hour when a large coal motor-lorry passed by, and Tom sang out to the driver.

He was a nice young fellow, and appeared to know all about motors. 'Can you wind?' said Tom. Yes, he could, and he proceeded to wind until he had to pause for breath. No effects.

For about an hour and a half did that young man do all he could, until Tom said: 'This is very good of you, but you'll want to be getting on.'

'I'm my own master,' he said. 'Most of our men have been called up'—and at it he went again. No go.

The young man, whose name was Gunn, then said, 'Look here, I must deliver my coal at Hatherleigh. Then I'll come back, and if she won't go I shall tow you into Okehampton.' So off he went.

Tom seemed to think that the petrol was the seat of the trouble, and he and I decided to walk into Hatherleigh, see if we could empty out the tank, put in a two-gallon lot of good petrol Tom carries, and see if she will start.

We found Gunn delivering his coal at the Bridge Inn. He fell in with our scheme, and borrowed the can from the landlord. Being very dirty after unloading the coal, Gunn retired to wash, and on his return was bleeding profusely from a wound on his nose caused by a motor-bicycle accident, which his vigorous washing had reopened.

Regaining Matilda we empty petrol, put in Tom's canful and try again—dead!

Gunn now borrowed a chain. We turned Matilda round and hitched on the chains, which I noticed were very old and poor; the girls got up in the lorry and squatted down among the coal-sacks, and Gunn's man Jack blundered up with them. Gunn's motor was decidedly asthmatical, but off we went, puffing and blowing.

We had not proceeded far when I heard Jack and the girls shout out, and found the tow-chain had parted company. Gunn backed a bit, and Jack kiddled the broken links up with a piece of wood he cut from the hedge.

Off again, the road very hilly. Gunn's old kettle boiled away merrily, while I, under Gunn's directions, pumped away on the compression-pump and watched the cap on the radiator bob about with the escaping steam.

However, we reach Okehampton safe and sound. Having stowed Matilda at Day's, we go to Plume of Feathers Hotel, and have a welcome wash and supper.

We now go for a little stroll, and find Day's shut up, so meander around, and it was a relief and cheerful to see the lights unobscured. A small cinema was quite a blaze of light outside.

Wednesday 5 July. To the premises of Messrs S.P. Gunn & Sons, Mineral

Water Manufacturers, Coal, Coke and Wood Merchants. Young Gunn was as bright and energetic as ever, showed us the mineral water plant, his motor-bicycle etc., and then we came to business. Tom makes him a little speech, saying how much we thank him for all he did for us yesterday, and winds up with a request to know how much we are to pay.

'Ask Father,' is young Gunn's reply.

I gravitate to Day's, and see that they have just got Matilda's entrails in going order. Tom was dubious, but they put in all the red petrol again, saying, 'She's all right now sir,' and we find Gunn senior and pay his account. At about three o'clock, off we went. I could see Tom was ill at ease, but I thought: 'That'll soon wear off.'

Our way out brought us to a steep hill. About half-way up, Matilda jibbed and stopped. 'There you are,' says Tom, 'I knew it. These motor fellows are all alike, I tell you. We must take her back.' So we let her run down backward, and crawl back to Day's.

Little engineer is astounded—'But she went beautifully this morning. I'll come back with you.' So off we go, engineer riding on the footboard. Deuce take it, with extra weight up she goes, and a steep hill too.

'She'll go up this time you know,' says little engineer, a ring of triumph in his voice. He hopped off at the top. 'You won't have any more trouble—goodbye.'

Away we went, Tom on the *qui vive*, straining to catch the sound of the engine. He said, 'My only chance is to drive her as hard as I can. If I stop, I shall be done.'

I was just getting lulled into a sense of security, when we came on a woman driving a cow and a calf, and a man with two or three bullocks. Obliged to pull up dead slow—then, by my halidame, she stopped. Consternation in the camp. 'You b——h,' says Tom.

A large motor-car drew up, and the old gentleman in it said could he do anything for us. 'He's very deaf,' said the chauffeur. 'You must speak up.'

We told the old gentleman how we were fixed.

'Well,' he said, 'there is an inn at Brandis Corner—they might put you up. I'm sorry I can't do anything more. Good afternoon,' and away he skimmed.

We resume our gazing at Matilda's private parts, Tom plugging away at this or that contraption, but never a quiver, never any necessity to spring like mad and throttle down. We now held a council of war, and it was decided that I should walk to the inn and see what could be done.

Off I went, and was soon larding the lean earth with good creamy perspiration. After a while I saw a house, so I rang the bell. A neat maid answered.

'Sorry to trouble you, but could I telephone from here?'

'No sir.'

'Ah, do you know if I can telephone from the village?'

'No, I don't think so.'

'Thanks very much—good afternoon.' And I resumed my march.

My spirits rose when I reached Brandis Corner, for there, tucked away, was a 'duck' of a little post office—quite a new-looking place, about the size of a large chicken-house. What ho! says I—here I can telephone no doubt. No, it was all locked up. I kicked and cuffed the door, but no one was within, so I made my way to the inn.

A sweet young maid received me. 'The only thing would be to go to Dunsland Cross railway station, and telegraph.' So to Dunsland Cross I wended my way, feeling very sorry I had omitted to take off my woollen sweater before I started.

On arrival I saw the station-master, and wired at 5.15 p.m.: 'Days Garage Okehampton Sunbeam engine stopped mile short Brandis Corner send car and engineer help. Garrett.'

Back to the Bickford Arms at Brandis Corner. Could they put us up for the night? No. Were there any shops where I could buy some food? No. 'Could *you* let me have something?'

She said I could have a few biscuits, so I bought all she could spare, about four pennyworth, and walked back.

The girls had taken refuge in knitting. I told them how far I had been, what I had done, and displayed the biscuits in triumph. I think there was a kind of what-are-those-among-so-many feeling in their looks, but they were too courteous to say anything.

We debated what we were to do when night fell. As we had heard that a farmer lived up the road, the universal opinion was that the farmer must soon see us, come out and interview us, fall on our necks, and finally march us all up to the farm and give us a right royal spread, and in all probability press us to stay the night. Then began a weary wait.

Soon after 7.30 we heard the welcome sound of a motor-car, and up dashed a Ford, with our own little engineer and a lad with him. He and the lad wound and wound—no go.

He then put in four new Bluemel sparking-plugs, wound again and hurt his hand. He had until now been very cheerful and cool, but he looked very sour as he held his hand, and swore under his breath.

And now, from the road leading up to this wonderful farm, came slowly an old farm-hand. He stopped, and Tom plied him with questions.

Was the farmer at home? No: he and his daughter had gone to Holsworthy Market. Would he be coming home soon? Yes, he would. Was he driving? Yes. Would he, do you think, let us put the car inside his gate for the night? Yes, he thought he would.

After the farm-labourer had plodded off on his homeward way, we espied a man and a young woman in a horse and trap. By gum—it's our farmer! Tom and I rush up just as he gets to the gate.

Tom puts the case to him, and before he had said many words in reply, I saw the royal spread vanish. The old boy hated motors. 'Osses, now, would have been different.

I whispered to Tom to ask whether he had any empty petrol cans—and then the old boy stroked me with his whip, and said, 'What's he got to say?'

I asked him about the tins. 'No, never had such a thing.'

His pretty daughter told him she had a washing-tub, galvanised iron. Pretty daughter I could see was a friend of ours, but afraid of the old man.

Mr Wonnacott, which we gather is our old farmer's name, gave us permission to run the motor inside his gate if necessary, gave his horse the head, and bowled away up the road.

Our engineer was getting despondent. 'Look here, sir,' said he. 'Something had better be done about the ladies being put up for the night. I had better run them into Hatherleigh on my Ford—then I'll take you two gentlemen and the luggage.' So away they went.

Time seemed to go very slowly, and the consumption of tobacco went on at an alarming rate.

At last he dashed up again and commenced to take the carburettor to pieces. Ultimately he took the magneto right off. Then we pushed Matilda fifty yards up the hill, and manœuvred her into a field. Then away we go, at twenty minutes to eleven o'clock.

The old Ford seemed very latchety, and our electric lights were continually going out, necessitating the engineer getting down and playing with them. Anon, when our lights happened to be burning nicely, we met a policeman, and engineer sang out a cheery 'good night'. Policeman I thought seemed rather gruff.

Hatherleigh was like a city of the dead. We pulled up outside an inn, and were met by the girls and landlady. Lugged in the luggage, blundering in the dark, and went upstairs.

Soon after, looking out, I see two glowing points emanating from the cigarettes of engineer and boy, and they clamber into their Ford, promising to telephone us tomorrow morning at the chemist's shop next door.

And now, with an air of mystery, and in low tones, the girls tell us they don't relish their quarters. They hint it looks none too clean, and tried to get out of it after engineer left them. The landlady had nothing to eat in the house, and to mend matters it was early-closing day. However, landlady soon appears with two fried mutton chops, and two boiled eggs for Tom and me; we take our seats and fall to. Paraffin lamp sheds a dim light, and it is all a little ghostly and unreal.

I find we are stopping at the London Hotel, and I daresay in the old coaching and posting days it was a prosperous establishment. But now, '*ichabod*', it has fallen on evil days, and I should say not making a fortune. The girls had made me a bit creepy, but the landlady seemed quite a decent body, and evidently doing her best.

Tom and I promised to see to the lamp and windows for her, and seated ourselves around the open window. The church clock chimed out the midnight hour. It was very dark, but the air was beautiful.

Then with lighted candles we crept away, carefully avoiding pitfalls in the shape of odd stairs, which I imagine the builder had introduced purposely to trip up the unwary. Spent a restless night, and I heard the church clock chime three.

Thursday 6 July. Breakfast very good—well done, London Hotel—then to chemist next door and telephone Day's.

'Hullo—oh, you have found the trouble—the armature is burnt out—you will have to send it away to be rewound. Well, we want to get to Bude. Send a car for us, and put us on rail at Dunsland Cross. We shall expect you.' I sat down to read *The Sign of Four* by Conan Doyle, and a feeling of stagnation settled over the party.

Suddenly we all spring into life. A Mr Johns, who owns a Ford car, comes to say that he can take the girls and the luggage to Halwill Station. The girls agreed to go to Bude and select a hotel, and leave word with the station-master where they had put up.

The feverish activity of their departure over, I got on to *The Sign of Four* again. Then out, and gaze anxiously on road to Okehampton—hullo! Here they are in a Darracq, our little engineer as cheery as ever. He seemed very disappointed when we said the ladies had gone on.

We settled our bill and at 5.50 away we went, Mr Day driving a shade recklessly, but quite serene. He promised to return to Matilda, put her in a shed, strip off all her movable accessories and spare parts and the petrol, and convey it to Okehampton. As soon as he gets the armature back, he will communicate with us at Bude.

At Dunsland Cross, Day shot us out at the station in plenty of time to catch the last train. The station-master informed us that she had been late every night lately, but at last we got away. At Holsworthy a Jack Tar entered our compartment—what men these British sailors are. This one looked full of reliance; one would like to have him at one's side in a hot corner.

At Bude we sought in vain for the station-master. Looking in the parcels office I saw a rush-basket, and it flashed over me: 'Good heavens! why that's our rush-basket, I left it in the train.' Having found a porter, I ask where the station-master is, as he was to have a message for us from two ladies, where we were to go.

He said: 'Well, the station-master wouldn't know, he's been away for a holiday and came in on same train as you. We've had a relief all week.'

'Well, where is *he*?'

'Oh, he's gone off by the other train.'

I began to imagine Tom and myself wandering around Bude, knocking at every boarding-house door, and saying: 'Sorry to trouble you, but have two ladies put up here, who were expecting two husbands? We are the two husbands, please.' What a prospect for two men of our rank.

This sad outlook was suddenly changed by the porter, who espied a piece of paper beside our rush-basket. 'Is this what you two gentlemen are looking for?'

We clutched at it eagerly:

> Messrs Garrett and Peerless—We are at Erdiston Boarding-House, Summerleaze. A.S.P.

Eureka! 'Where is this place, porter?'

'It's on top of the hill,' he said—and 'Thank you, gentlemen,' as we deftly slipped a little *douceur* into his willing palm. So off we marched; 400 yards brought us to the bridge, we turned to the right, and then 'There they are!' said Tom, and out of a gate rushed the girls, wagging their tails with pleasure to see us.

'I hope you'll like the place,' says Fanny. 'It's not very dear at six-and-sixpence a day. I got the terms first, and then told them our motor was broken down.' Artful little cat—saved us 1*s* 6*d* a day each.

Millie conducts me to our bedroom, and I saw at once that they had picked the right place. 'This is a most healthful spot,' said I. 'I think we shall like it.'

Friday 7 July. Tom and I took the train to Dunsland Cross, and padded the hoof up to Brandis Corner. 'I'll bet you Day hasn't got her up in the shed,' said Tom. 'You don't know these motor people. I've had fifteen years of them, and you can't trust them.'

'All right,' said I. 'Wait and see, as old Asquith said.'

As we came into sight of the shed at the Bickford Arms, there she was—not a scratch, and they had shipped everything movable as arranged. I felt more comfortable, for I did not like leaving Matilda about the country in fields; it went against my ideas of property. I like my property under lock and key.

We now adjourned to the bar of the Bickford Arms and interviewed Mrs Munday, a very nice bright woman. 'Oh yes, it'll be quite safe there—no children to interfere with it—only mine, and I have told them not to go near it.'

We chatted, and I was startled when she told me she was a London woman. The difference between London and this out-of-the-world spot was so great that I could hardly conceive anyone bearing such a transplanting.

'My word,' said I. 'What a change. Whatever did you think when you first came here? Didn't you sit down and have a good cry?'

'No,' she said, 'but it was a long time before I would get out of the car when I first drove here with my husband three years ago. I thought I never should stand it, but we've got used to it. We came because our children were never well in London, and they're strong enough now.'

We find this house is owned by the People's Refreshment House Association Ltd, Broadway Chambers, Westminster, managed on reformed lines, and if ever you see a pub anywhere with the letters PRHA outside, don't hesitate—go in. Mrs Munday gave us a list of their inns.

Tom and I now trolled down to Dunsland Cross Station to catch the 4.36. Station-master now begins to know us, and says: 'She'll be late again, gentlemen.'

She was, and it was 5.14 before she ran in.

Saturday 8 July. At ten o'clock we parade outside the motor char-à-banc proprietor's house.

To what base uses we may descend, Horatio! A few days ago Tom paddled his own canoe on the road—in other words, drove his own motor-car. And today how do we ride? In a public char-à-banc, my masters.

This vehicle now draws up alongside us, and there is this saving clause in our humiliation, it is a new car and without doubt a really good one—enamelled a soft grey, nicely padded and upholstered in good leather, electro fittings, and quite a spanking turn-out.

A wounded Canadian soldier of Strathcona's Horse was also on the car, and I understand they let him go these trips as often as they can. He was a very nice fellow, not bad-looking, although he seemed in a shaky nervous state. We got rather friendly with him.

Our driver was a bright-eyed, plump little fellow, good and careful. He had been a horse-driver on these trips for many years, and there is no doubt if men of his experience take up motor-driving, they make the best chauffeurs.

We began to get fine views of the sea, and presently we pulled up and stopped at Clovelly. I had never been here before, although I once passed it in a steamer. It has a world-wide reputation for quaintness and beauty: a narrow road paved with stone cobbles, descending steeply towards the sea.

I suggest to Tom that I had better wait for Mill, who is behind with

Fanny, but he says, 'No, come on my little man, she can manage all right,' so we continue our descent. On each side are bright whitewashed cottages and small shops, many clothed with myrtles, fuchsias and roses, giving quite a continental air to the place.

We had not proceeded far before Mill frantically waved me to come back, and requested to know what I meant by leaving her to come down such a place alone. In imitation of Adam, who excused himself by saying 'It was the woman thou gavest me' etc., I said: 'I told Tom we'd better wait for you—but I'm here now. Gently does it—now down the next little step—quite easy, isn't it.'

'No it isn't,' says Mum.

So like cats on hot bricks we continue the descent, until we see a large inn: 'LUNCHEONS.'

'The very ticket,' said I, and entering we find ourselves in a fine dining-room—distempered walls and old oak beams. Two or three smart waitresses flitting about, and they looked very nice in their black dresses and snow-white aprons, cuffs and caps—clean and bright—a sight for sore eyes.

I suppose 150 years ago Tom and I would have roystered in and kissed one or two of the wenches, but in these more prosaic days of the twentieth century we sit down meekly and peruse the menu.

By my faith, troth, and maidenhead, there is lobster salad. 'Lobster salad for four if you please.' It was a tip-top lunch in every way.

Having paid our bill, we continue our descent until we reach the sea. Here are a few longshoremen lopping about—also two ancient donkeys waiting for customers. They spend their lives carrying people and goods up and down the precipitous street, and they seem very solemn over it. Then back and off we go again, and after a delightful drive pull up for our Cornish tea. We invite Strathcona, and are merry, and chatter and laugh.

Strathcona did not say much, and his nerves seemed shattered. I was afraid he was trying to swallow his knife, as several inches of the blade disappeared in his mouth. Still, he was a very nice chap, quiet and unassuming—nice face and eyes, but a kind of pinched look that told you he was far from well.

When I went up to the woman to pay, I said, 'How much each? There are five of us.'

'One shilling each, sir,' she said.

Just then the old lady who sat in front of us on the char-à-banc said, 'My husband has paid for the soldier.'

The devil he has, said I to myself. 'Has he? We invited him to tea, you know.'

'Oh, he likes to do it,' said she.

So to the woman of the cottage I said, 'Very well then, that's four I have to pay for. Good afternoon.' I raised my hat and made my way out.

Away and away, until we reach Bude. On arriving in the dining-room we find we are somewhat circumscribed for room, and Beatrice, the fresh-coloured auburn-haired waitress, is continually butting my arm with her hips as she squeezes by with different viands.

Sunday 9 July. We adjourn to the sands, charter four deckchairs, and watch the people bobbing in the surf. It was a real laze.

Lunch, and then go for a long walk to a bathing-pool called Sir Thomas Acland's Pit and watch the pleasure-boats. Several longshoremen lean airily about, and we see our Canadian soldier talking to some of them, and give him a nod.

After supper we parade on the lawn and watch a gorgeous sunset. As the light varied, one could fancy all sorts of strange shapes in the sky—not a new thing, for we all know how Hamlet says to Polonius, 'Do you see yonder cloud, that's almost in the shape of a camel?' And poor old Polonius (whom I am always sorry to see killed off so soon) replies: 'By the mass, and 'tis like a camel indeed.' 'Or like a whale?' Polonius: '*Very like* a whale'—and so with us, we fancy we could see zeppelins, flaming castles, lakes of fire etc., until the glory dies down.

Monday 10 July. Get on our grey motor char-à-banc and start off through lovely country. We pull up at Boscastle and have a drink in a primitive club; two or three ancient *habitués* in the bar appear to have a salty appearance, as though they were toilers of the deep.

At 12.30 we resume our journey and arrive at Tintagel, a long straggling village with some exceedingly old houses. As we are nothing unless we keep eating, we file into the coffee-room of Fry's Hotel—a very comfortable temperance hotel—and they gave us a really good luncheon.

We then walked down towards the sea. On our left towered the ruins of King Arthur's castle, which I could see with my field-glasses. It looked a terrible tug up to it, and I decided to 'take it as read'. Millie fell to knitting furiously, and I scanned the horizon and picked out several ships.

Back in the village street we see Canadian soldier gazing in a little fancy articles shop. He says he wants to buy a little present, and will follow us directly.

We order five teas at Fry's, and soon fall to. Anon, Canadian comes in through the window and gets to work—I am pleased to see that if everything else fails him, he will only require a little practice to become an expert knife-swallower; as an amateur, he can now put more knife-blade in his mouth than anyone I ever saw.

During tea, he proudly produced a tawdry little purse that he had bought to present to a girl in London. It was, as Tom and I agreed afterwards, really pathetic to see a decent chap, as he undoubtedly was, so genuinely proud and pleased at such a tinselly gingerbready article.

Soon afterwards our char-à-banc turns up, and away we go for Bude and dinner. After, we stroll on downland to Maer, sit on a covered seat and watch sunset—rather poor. Fanny sits in a hole in turf and looks very quaint knitting.

Tuesday 11 July. Grey morning. At breakfast everyone appears very red in the face, burnt by the wind and sun yesterday.

Mill and I to post office and find a letter from Burt, in jocular vein, casting insinuations on Matilda's chastity. We go to Wonnacott's Dairy and send off several lots of clotted cream, then hot-foot to station and take train to Holsworthy because we have heard there is a Cornish fair being held. On arrival we find the main street crowded with people, and the square blocked with stalls, hoop-la stands, Bunty-pulls-the-strings, and a gigantic roundabout dubbed a scenic railway.

Tom suddenly conceives the brilliant idea of writing to the Sunbeam works to see if they could send a new armature, and dashes off into the post office. We meander round the sideshows, then away by the church and see the horses and hundreds of farmers, gypsies and horsey-looking individuals. We said we are sure to see our farmer here, and we had not been there long before we spotted him.

Then home to dinner; rather deserted this evening as many of our visitors have gone over by motors to Holsworthy Fair. It was suggested we should do so, but I expected it would be very rough at night, and I have no penchant for drunken gypsies and drovers and street-fights. From what I heard later, I think we were wise.

Wednesday 12 July. Dire consternation in our camp—letter from Day saying 'No armature received'. It is lost in the post.

We sat down by the rivers of Bude and wept, when we remembered thee, oh Matilda, and thy armature. But each sling and arrow only makes us sterner and stronger: Tom and I are men of action.

Clearly the first thing is to talk to Day; therefore to the post office we go, and get through to him on the telephone. 'Yes, the armature is lost—postal service is very irregular now, you know.'

'Well, we wrote the Sunbeam people yesterday, and they may send a new armature on to you. We'll ring you up again if we hear anything.'

Back to lunch, and then—hurrah! A telegram from the Sunbeam Company: 'Posting new armature today.' You should have seen us slip hot-foot to post office with our joyful news—then back, and partake of tea in the lounge.

I think this is a good opportunity to enumerate the other visitors staying at Erdiston, viz.:

An old gentleman (very reserved).—

Two ladies with him (one bears a striking resemblance to what Lily will be if she is spared to reach this lady's age—in certain positions I could see Lily just as plain as can be).—

One gentleman (probably an officer who has been wounded, evidently in a weak and shaky state).—

A young lieutenant (with above, might be a younger brother).—

His sister (no doubt a nurse at military hospital, Exeter).—

Mummy (a rather Jewessy bold-eyed woman, has a fine leg, and a pretty taste in white stockings).—

Two children (Mummy's little girls).—

Uncle (Mother's brother-in-law, a tall large-framed man).—

A young man and his wife and little girl (very decent people).—

A young military doctor and his wife (man appears to ape being old—wife looks frivolous but improves on acquaintance).—

A young lieutenant (wounded and sight partially injured, head probably a little queer, affecting his memory—when being brought home, ship torpedoed or mined and he in the sea, additional shock).—

An old lady and her daughter (daughter very dark hair).—

Two ladies (I believe maidens).—

Dr and Mrs Payne (wife spoilt by trying to be too youthful).—

Mr Waters (a colonial soldier, slightly wounded in the hand—fine-built chap—quite a good sort).—

His sister (a very nice quiet girl—their fondness for each other is beautiful to see—has a splendid voice when singing—niece of proprietress).—

An old gentleman and his wife (old chap, rather reserved and not over-well—the good lady rather talkative).—

Mummy's husband (turns up at weekend, great likeness to Uncle).

I believe that is a fair *résumé* of the people, and includes all the most important—a few who came and went not included.

After tea, all out on the sands. Tom and I play football with a large piece of cork.

Thursday 13 July. Dull and cloudy—I sit in lounge and read *A Girl of the Limberlost* (a sequel to *Freckles*), oblivious to my surroundings. Tom by now feeling neglected and pining for my society, so we go out and take the ferry-boat to the Breakwater. Later we explore what we call 'Tom's little beach', as he discovered it.

Friday 14 July. As the clock strikes nine, we enter the post office and telephone to Day's. 'Yes, the new armature has arrived from the Sunbeam Company.' Tom and I are to meet Day at Brandis Corner, and bring Matilda home to Bude. It made one feel like singing the *Nunc dimittis*.

I proceed to the sands and enter a bathing-tent—quite a natty little affair with slate batten frames, covered with striped canvas. Sir Thomas' Pit was not at all a bad place for a dip, except that it required a few hours of direct sunshine on it.

Having had enough, I went to rejoin my companions on the Breakwater. On approaching the river I found the tide was rising: but a very ancient aborigine had run over a little portable bridge, a cute affair which at certain stages of the tide he fixes up. On the frail bridge I boldly stepped, to be hailed by the ancient one: 'One penny toll, sir, please.' I can find no remedy for this consumption of the purse.

On rejoining the others I began to watch the fun. There were three or four gentlemen, among whom was Dr Payne, who were anxiously waiting to undress and bathe, but their operations were seriously impeded by the presence of sundry females who absolutely refused to budge.

Back and to lunch: then Tom and I catch 1.48 for Dunsland Cross and tramp away for Brandis Corner. Poor Tom still pessimistic: 'They won't turn up, my boy,' says he, 'you'll see.'

As we turn into the main road we meet a motor-car which pulls up. 'Good afternoon, gentlemen, thought I'd run up and fetch you. My man is putting on the magneto'—and in a brace of shakes we pulled up at Brandis Corner.

Matilda had been backed partly out, and our little engineer was tinkering away as happy as a king. 'You'll be all right now, sir,' he said to Tom. 'We've brought all the things back.'

The last screw is put in, and there is a tense moment as the little engineer goes round to the starting-handle—one, two, three—the engine springs into life, and once more we hear the welcome rhythm.

'How about your bill?' says Tom. Day produced it with alacrity.

It did not err on the side of being too little; in fact there is no doubt that it was laid on fairly heavy. However, Tom paid up, and away we went. Congratulations from everybody on Matilda's recovery.

After tea most of them come outside and have a smell round Matilda. Great excitement, an airship is in view—telescopes and field-glasses spring up like mushrooms, and everybody is gazing skyward, until the airship fades away over the sea. Tom then proceeds to oil up old Matilda, and being so pleased he gives her too much, which she resents, and steadily ejects oil into a newspaper funnel arrangement Tom has made. The flow of oil having slackened, Tom carefully picks up the funnel arrangement, takes it across the road and throws it over a fence.

Dinner, then all four over grand downs and home. Here we find excitement over non-appearance of the boy officer I mentioned as having his sight slightly injured, and head a little queer. He did not come home to lunch or dinner, and they are beginning to feel anxious.

The last person who recollects seeing him is Dr Payne, who met him on the Breakwater this morning, and the boy spoke to him, as he could not quite see what the towel was that the doctor was carrying on his stick. Visions of the poor lad falling over the cliffs, or wandering about the country losing his memory, began to crowd into our minds; search-parties and police began to be talked about.

As the excitement was growing, somebody came with the welcome news that it was all right—he had just come back.

Saturday 15 July. The shadow of departure is on us. After breakfast Tom gets Matilda, and I settle the bill. Then, as I understand that Hicks & Company are inclined to mess about over allowing for a penny each on bottles returned, which they have made me pay, as a matter of principle I run down to Hicks' shop and draw 1*s* 10*d* for 22 bottles, and return in triumph. Having settled everything, away we go, and reach Exeter at 1.3 p.m. Draw up at general post office to find that it closed at one o'clock.

Of all the idiotic things I ever heard of, this takes the palm—to close a head post office in an important city from one to two o'clock, under the pretence that we are at war, is too silly for words. As I say to Tom, when this war is over we're going to have a job to get our rights back again. There'll be a revolution if they don't look out.

We shaped a course for Salisbury, and ran into a huge camp or camps. Thousands of soldiers were about. We drew up, and I asked some soldiers the name of the place. As far as I could understand, they said it was Sutton Mandeville and Fovant camps.

Behind the camps was a range of hills, and we were attracted by a series of regimental crests on the side of these hills, most beautifully executed in white chalk. They varied considerably in size, and it was difficult to judge their dimensions, but some must have been a job to execute. They were works of art, and produced a fine effect, and I imagine will be preserved as a memento of the Great War.

As we ran into Salisbury—crowded with soldiers, people and traffic—it began to be a question of deciding where we should lay for the night. Tom was half-inclined to pull up and stay. I, on the other hand, after the glorious freedom of the King's highway, felt stifled and penned in, and I was rejoiced when Fanny said: 'No, don't let's stop here—let us get out into the country.'

'You'd like to go on to Lyndhurst, I know,' said Tom. 'All right, Lyndhurst it shall be.'

I do not think I have ever enjoyed the New Forest more than I did that evening. The weather was perfect, the roads good, scarcely a soul about, and we practically had the world to ourselves.

Presently we drew in by Emery Down, rattled into Lyndhurst, and drew up outside the Fox and Hounds after a run of 163 miles—a splendid journey and not a hitch.

Sunday 16 July. To Beaulieu—a beautiful ride, and when we pulled up near the lake, Tom had a nice little play with his favourite accessory, pumping up the tyres with a drive off the electricity. A fascinating pastime—just couple it up and see it do the work for you—a perfect labour-saver.

Having completed the tyres, Tom and I are soon deeply interested in a little boat to which is affixed at the stern the dinkiest little motor arrangement you ever saw, with a sweet little propellor and a dear little petrol barrel tank—all very neat, and you could fix it on to any boat in a few minutes.

Two gentlemen (one of whom we took to be Lord Montagu) got aboard, and then a footman came along, staggering under a large luncheon-basket, then two ladies arrived and embarked, and away they went, gracefully sweeping over the water.

While the gentleman whom we took to be Lord Montagu was waiting in the boat for the luncheon-basket, Tom had a chat with him, asking several questions about the little motor arrangement.

We now dawdle back to the car, and start on the last lap of our journey. Pull up at Balls Hut for tea—rather a poor show—then on again over Ham Bridge at Worthing, over Norfolk Bridge, Shoreham, and presently pull up outside 12 St James's Avenue—pleased to find everything in order and all well.

So 1916 holiday days are over, and tomorrow we shall have to face the realities of life which we have for the last fortnight evaded. It has been a very pleasant change for us all.

The New Forest

1917

Wednesday 23 May. Today I wrote to Superintendent A.O. Jennings of the Brighton Force of Special Constables, saying I was wishing to be out of Brighton from 26 May to 11 June. Tom and I had arranged to visit Dartmoor, but we live now in an age of restrictions and regulations.

It used to be a proud boast of every Briton that we lived in a free country—'God save the mark' is a sweet oath savouring of Shakespearean times. I say it is free no more. At every turn we run against some restriction under the Defence of the Realm Act.

Under the Military Service Act, they take our sons and assistants until business becomes almost impossible to carry on.

They take away our beer, the blessed birthright of every free-born Briton. You must not buy more than a cut of lead. You must not carry out any building job over £500. You can only sell one per cent per month of your stock of imported soft woods, except for Government work, and then you have to fill up forms and get certificates. You have to close at eight o'clock on weekdays, and nine o'clock on Saturdays. Railway fares are advanced 50 per cent, and train services curtailed and restricted. They strip the land of labour, and then tell you to grow more food. One day they say you must have meatless days, and then they tell you to eat more meat and less bread. Potatoes and sugar are difficult to get. The cost of living steadily rises. Entertainments are increasingly taxed. Tobacco, that boon of mankind, has a further tax clapped on it, until a decent tobacco is ninepence per ounce. Oats that used to be 21 shillings per quarter are now 66 or 67 shillings. Zinc, that was formerly *27s 6d* per hundredweight, is today £6. Petrol is only obtainable under a system of licences.

There are a hundred and one other galling little pin-pricky things that get on one's nerves, but up till now the people bear them wonderfully well, playing the game as I never expected they would, for we are still at war.

Well, after several palavers with Tom, we decided that we had better not risk going so far as Dartmoor this year, but go to Lyndhurst instead. Tom had gone so far as to send his petrol licence to Exeter, to Parker's Garage, to arrange for them to supply his petrol, and after an unconscionable delay they returned it, saying there was a fresh order out, stopping all supplies of petrol in that area: so Lyndhurst we said it must be.

No sooner had this got bruited about, than Grandma Garrett said she should so like to come with us. It seemed a little awkward, because Tom had been imploring us to cut the weight down on the car, as extra weight makes all the difference to the tyres; however, we wrote Ings to see if he could give us the extra accommodation, and duly received his telegram: 'Room reserved as requested for lady.'

Saturday 26 May. At 2.45 p.m. Tom drew up in his motor-car outside 12 St James's Avenue. Then with Tom and I in front, in all the pride of our manly beauty, and Fanny, Grandma and Millie in the back, in all the pride of their womanly grace and charm, in brilliant sunshine I saw Tom stiffen and take hold of the steering-wheel, and Matilda sprang off like a hound from the leash.

I was soon disbursing the toll at Shoreham Bridge, and we ran on through glorious country until Tom drew rein at Fareham, and we trooped into a confectioner's for tea. We were at once up against some regulation about not having more than two ounces each of bread and butter or cakes, and the young lady solemnly weighed each portion. It seemed farcical.

Then we resumed our journey, and it was pleasant to note places we had often passed in years gone by, when we had fewer cares and responsibilities, and no war on our nerves. Tom kept remarking that we seemed to be the only motor on the road. However, I had no qualms, for I knew that we all deserved a change.

We drave steadily westward, like Drake, and in due course came to our old friend the floating bridge at Itchen and Woolsten. We crawled on, and a feeling of revulsion sat in with me at the proximity of so many people—I intensely disliked them all, and longed to get out again on the broad highway.

At Totton level-crossing an ass in a fussy little car actually cut in on our left side, and cleared us by a hair's breadth. 'Blasted idiot,' I said to myself. It is inexplicable that anyone could be so discourteous as to deliberately violate the rudimentary rules of the road in such a manner. I have ridden on public highways for nearly forty years now, and I don't think I have ever cut in on the wrong side of anyone.

I am told that once I turned out too quickly for a motor that was behind me, and gave the occupants a shock, but at the time I was as innocent as a babe and never dreamed of anyone being near my behind. That only shows how careful users of the road should be.

We soon reached the grand road leading to Lyndhurst. It was as beautiful as the first time I cycled on it. In our family, I claim to have discovered the New Forest, and it has gained a considerable hold on my

affections. We drew up outside the Fox and Hounds at seven o'clock, and Tom and I took Matilda down to Haynes' Garage. On inspecting the speedometer we find the trip, Brighton to Lyndhurst, is registered $73\frac{3}{10}$ miles.

This speedometer is the cutest little box of tricks—it has a trip register on its dial, which you set at 000 when you start, and it registers by tenths of a mile all the while you are moving. It is quite fascinating to watch the little jigger silently slipping different figures into the ◯◯◯ —then ◯◯(1⁄10) until it gets to ◯◯(9⁄10), then ◯①◯—but the screaming time is when it gets to a combination like this:

meaning $29\frac{9}{10}$ miles as you proceed; there is suddenly a terrible commotion amongst the sliding figures, until it stands:

③⓪◯

It is absolutely clever and very interesting.

We soon saw Mr Haynes, and it was funny to see him trying to pretend he knew us, when it was quite apparent that he could not recall us at all. He seemed rather sore about the restrictions under which he now has to carry on, and pointed out his daughter, who now has to help him by driving a motor. She was a bright, nice-looking girl, and we were soon on good terms.

Then up into the familiar old dining-room, and out for a stroll. Rather put out to see so many soldiers under the influence of drink, so turn back. Sit in our little room and look out on the street, which seems rather busy. Millie restless all night, and I am told there was thunder and lightning.

Sunday 27 May. Adjourn to bathroom and draw some hot water. I discover three beetles in the bath, and persuade two of them to go to kingdom come; one, a rather acute fellow, effected his escape. Reflecting that I have bagged 66.6 per cent of the enemy, I return in triumph.

Mrs G. and Fanny, like good Christian people, set out for divine worship. We lounge, and at twelve o'clock purchase *Lloyd's News* and the *Sunday Herald* from a diminutive boy enveloped in a sack—raining heavily. I then telephone to Gladys and Reggie, and discuss his visiting us at Lyndhurst.

Tea in drawing-room: then Tom and I walk out on the Beaulieu Road, and pass the Trench Mortar School, and into the woods, where a large quantity of trees have been felled.

Monday 28 May. On muddy roads we walk up to Emery Down, and then on the Ringwood Road; a number of War Department wagons transporting pit-props, which we notice are chained, and an aborigine in a cart tells us there has been a fire in the forest.

Coming back, we call in the New Forest Inn and order some cyder. They bring us a pint each, which is rather above and beyond our capacity. Tom has to cry hold, enough, and to my regret, leaves some of his.

Lunch, then a rest in the drawing-room. Deeply regret to hear one of the daughters of the local chemist set her blouse on fire in the shop during the morning, and is terribly injured. Several doctors are now attending her, and neighbours appear to be doing all they can.

Laze until the maid appears with welcome tea. We watch a great number of holiday-makers outside our window, who arrive in motors, on bicycles and on foot. Then suddenly the heavens darken and the sky is rent asunder by lightning, and the thunder roars, and the people in the street run helter-skelter for shelter.

Thank goodness it is not of long duration, and we all five sally forth and meander on to the grassy common to a wooden seat. It is wet and dirty for the feet when we are seated, so we collect all and sundry of old tin-cans, pots, kettles etc., and use them for foot-rests, which looks rather comical, but prevents our feet getting wet, although it is a work of art to keep the old tins balanced.

Stroll back to dinner, during which excellent meal I notice a mouse once or twice scamper out from under the sideboard. After dinner we sit at our drawing-room window, on a level with the street, and see with sorrow that several doctors are still at the chemist's, where their cars have been awaiting them several hours.

We were interested in a very youthful soldier who constantly passed and repassed up and down the street in a very aimless manner. He did not appear to have a friend in the world, and was a little the worse for drink, and looked very miserable and solemn. How many times that boy passed up and down I should not like to say.

As a rival attraction there was a funny little sailor who also perambulated the street in a very jerky manner. At regular intervals a military picket slowly and solemnly marched up and down.

The people gradually get fewer, and we decide to say good night. Millie is very restless, and at 4 a.m. rouses me and says she is sure there is a mouse running about the room—I flash on my electric pocket-lamp, and sure enough there is a mouse by the skirting.

As I am not paid to kill mice in the middle of the night, I condole with Millie on this discovery, and resume my sleep.

Tuesday 29 May. The maid tells us the poor girl who was burnt died about four o'clock in the morning.

Then a beautiful walk to Emery Down and entered the New Forest Inn. The landlord appeared on the scene today and did not favourably impress me. I was unable to make up my mind whether he was mad or not: in appearance he was ghoulish and hawk-like, and seemed to ramble in his talk. He had some wonderful tale of some priceless art treasures he could show us, and seemed to particularly want us to come up by night, about nine o'clock, and he was then to show us such marvellous things and also show us the forest by night.

He muddled on about the old inn having originally been a caravan left by the French, and pointed out several antiques in the walls. We had quite a difficulty to shake ourselves free, and at last nothing would do but we must go through the house and back to Lyndhurst through the forest. He volunteered the statement that he never walked on 'blasted roads' if he could walk in the forest.

He piloted us to the back of his premises and away we went, and through the trees caught a glimpse of a tent occupied by a young man whom Tom and I saw in the inn yesterday. He was then wearing the silver badge for services rendered, and we gathered he was now camping out in the forest.

As I anticipated, in about three minutes we were through the old ass's woods and on the road again, and soon after we entered Lyndhurst and sat down to a good lunch. Then Tom got up Matilda, and heigho away we went for Brockenhurst. Today we were riding by the map, and it was interesting to measure the distance roughly on the map, keep an eye on the speedometer, and when it had registered about the mileage, be on the *qui vive* to turn off on crossroads etc.

According to the map we had to cross the railway three times, and we eagerly counted each crossing, and felt we were prospecting the route very cleverly. By and by we reached the Christchurch and Bournemouth road, a fine surfaced road, and ran on down to Hinton Admiral and stopped at the Cat and Fiddle, a very old inn supposed to be 600 years old. We about ship and turned her nose homeward.

Dinner, and then watch brilliant lightning and listen to some heavy peals of thunder. Try to telephone to Brighton but it is a fiasco.

In the middle of the night I am roused by a smart clicking noise in the bedroom, and Millie says, 'What is that?'

I reply, 'That is the mouse-trap—we have caught one of your friends.' Then, as I am not paid to get out of bed to unload mouse-traps, I turn over and go to sleep.

Wednesday 30 May. The post has brought a postcard saying Dottie and Beattie expect to arrive this afternoon.

Suddenly we hear a motor, and rushing to the window, are very glad to see Dottie and Beattie outside. We give them a hearty welcome and some tea. We are quite a large party and very jolly.

All early to bed. Millie beginning to heartily detest our bedroom and the little mousy visitants.

Thursday 31 May. After breakfast, we feel that as we are the proprietors of the New Forest, we must do the honours and show some of its beauties to our new arrivals: so we steer across to Emery Down and Beaulieu Abbey, and then tally-ho for Lymington through beautiful moor country.

In the evening we stroll to the camp near the Bench, and Dottie gives us many interesting details of her YMCA work in the military camp at Larkhill near Salisbury.

In consequence of the mice, Mrs Ings has shifted Mill and me into her bedroom, and Mr and Mrs Ings have shifted into our late room. Mother has a really restful night.

Friday 1 June. Marched out to that quaint dear old inn at Minstead called the Trusty Servant, and on to the Rufus Stone. Then we pulled up at the Compton Arms Hotel, Stoney Cross. The door was locked, so I rang the bell, and when the landlord unlatched the door I proffered a request for some refreshments.

He took out his watch to make sure it was twelve o'clock (as a matter of fact it was well over that hour, or I should not have requested admission), and apologising for his untidy appearance, he ushered us in and soon reappeared with biscuits, cheese and liquids.

I did not consider that he welcomed us with any show of effusion, and I understood him to say he thought when we rang that it was the postman, or he would not have come to the door without a coat; but after he had served us, and got into his coat, he seemed to regain his self-esteem, and came back into our room looking a typical British boniface, and turned out quite a nice old boy. He was soon telling us how many years he had been there and what a large number of distinguished visitors he had had.

It appeared that when Sir William Vernon Harcourt was building Malwood Lodge he lived for a long time at the Compton Arms. He had also had the Crown Prince of Germany and his suite as guests; two bishops had stayed there at the same time.

He then went and fetched his visitors' books and we were astonished to see the large number of titled and distinguished people who had stayed there. As an autograph book it would in years to come be of considerable value. It contained a pen-and-ink sketch by the Crown Prince of the Huns.

Saying adieu to our friendly landlord, whose name was Beech, we strike the main road and in due course reach Lyndhurst. We hear that while we were gone, the funeral rites of the poor young lady who was burnt were carried out. God rest her soul.

Great excitement, there is a telegram from Reggie to say he will arrive at Southampton at 7 p.m. So Tom, Grandma, Millie and I on Matilda to meet him.

Now in all the affairs of human life there is a strange kind of cussedness, which I have seen exemplified a thousand times. For instance, you shall meet a man every morning on your way to business, and never want to speak to him, till one morning it is important you should see him, and then sure you fail to meet him. Today this cussedness was triumphant, for there are two stations at Southampton, and of course we go through most difficult traffic to one station, only to find we have to go back to the one we passed.

However, we pulled up outside Southampton West, and there was Reggie on a seat, like Patience on a monument. I hailed him, led him in triumph to the car, and lit my pipe while the others fell on his neck and kissed him.

Poor little brute had been waiting over an hour. However, Reggie was obviously pleased to be in the New Forest again, and it certainly is a pretty run from Southampton to Lyndhurst.

All went well till we got to the level-crossing at Lyndhurst Road. A goods train was shunting, and how many times that doggone engine shuffled and dealt those trucks I should not like to say; we began to know the different trucks as they passed and repassed. I began to see us stuck there for all time, haunted by puffing engines and creaking goods-trucks.

When at last the gates swung open, Tom coaxed Matilda to life again and we bounded off. Oh the mad joy of it, bounding along full of strength and power, able by a deft turn of the wheel to swing right or left, and still irresistibly forging our course.

We had been hung up so long that we were very late for dinner. When we were all assembled at this important function, with Signals (Reggie) as vice-chairman facing Uncle Tom, we were a merry party. But oh dear! what a tale of woe the girls had to tell us.

B. and Dot and Fanny had set out in B.'s car to Boldrewood, but the heavy motor-lorries drawing timber had so cut up the road that it became impassable; then they had to walk—then it came on to rain—then they got separated and lost each other. I don't think they really carried the car, but they evidently had a rotten time.

Saturday 2 June. To breakfast; afterward Tom telephones to Howell. Things do not appear to be working smoothly in Tom's absence, some nonsense about hot-water pipes showing in rooms, and Tom says, 'Tell them to take them down and chase them in the walls.'

B. gets her car up, and she and Dot set off for Christchurch, and we follow in Tom's car. Soon we lose sight of them. At Hinton Admiral we lounge about and wait, hoping Dot and B. will turn up—but no, never a ghost of a sign of them.

I thought it was a peculiar way of going out in cars together, never to see each other again, but I calculated that there was something I didn't understand, being a tyro in all matters appertaining to motors, so I smoked my pipe and enjoyed the motion and the occasional scraps of converse as we bowled along.

Home to lunch, and then most awful alarums and excursions, as our old friend Shakespeare puts it: fifty-five wounded soldiers arrive on an outing for tea at our hotel. Mill, Fanny and Dot help to cut bread and butter for them. Reggie and I down to Haynes' Garage to see Tom and Beattie oiling up their motors.

It was quite delightful to see B. getting gloriously dirty and oily over it, and I could not help thinking how things have changed and how women have broadened in their views and actions—why, my dear sir, when I was a boy, do you think a woman would have got gloriously grubby and dirty oiling anything? Certainly not.

Back to tea. As we peep in at the wounded soldiers in our dining-room clouded with smoke, and listen to a song or two, they espy Reggie and nothing will do but Jack Tar must go in, and they give him a great ovation. They clamour for 'Jack' to give them a song, but Reggie says his throat is bad, and I think makes a little speech and effects his escape. Later I hear the gentleman who is host and the donor of the outing pressed a big cigar on to Rennie.

Descending to our little drawing-room, we watch the wounded warriors and nurses take their seats in two large char-à-bancs, and move off. The cheering and hat- and handkerchief-waving is stupendous.

Sunday 3 June. Dot and B. go off to chapel; Tom, Reggie and I stroll into the forest, well away from everything and everybody. A fine walk.

Monday 4 June. Telegram from Maisie to say 'Unto us a child is born': Tom and Fanny are now grandfather and grandmother. What a whirligig is time.

About ten o'clock Dot and B. set off in their car, and we follow on Matilda. We make for Cadnam, and get into traffic of a large camp which we have to pass—then we reach Romsey, a very pretty ancient town. The fair maidens from the 'West Countree' were now anxious to get on the road for home, so we wished them an affectionate farewell.

Banishing our regrets, we go with Tom to buy a few collars. It is sad to relate that later Tom finds the collars he bought were not the size he distinctly ordered, and I am very sorry a trader should indulge in such a nefarious practice. In trade, I always hold, the seller should be punctilious in dealing honestly with the buyer. That is the only sure basis on which to build up a business.

We now turn our backs on Romsey, and I ask Tom if he would mind going back through Totton, as I wish to call at a timber-yard there and see if I can do any business. Cheerfully he says, 'Right my son,' and away we go through lovely lanes. Rather too narrow for a motor really, and we get hung up behind some of Strong's great drays. However, the burly car-men were good chaps, and soon drew in the side. Matilda picked her way by, and found Rose and Andrews' yard.

Eventually I got hold of Mr Andrews, and found him a good old sort, but full of woes over shortage of labour—orders months behind—timber lying out two years and quite unable to cart it in—machines standing idle because no one to work them—and it was quite useless to get him to undertake any orders from me.

So we shook hands and parted, and I rejoined Tom, who I was afraid must be getting tired of waiting, as old Mr Andrews had a way of sitting down to rest on a tree at every opportunity. Limbering up, we were soon on our old road to Lyndhurst. Put Matilda in the garage and went up to lunch.

I might mention that the hotel telephone is in our sitting-room, and I often answer it and get someone in the house to come and take the message. This afternoon a ring came and I found it was for 'Baby', as we still call Miss Ings. It was really pitiful to hear her replying; she was evidently speaking to a man who was sweet on her, and very jealous, and the pathos in her voice was tragical. She was like a tragedy queen and well fitted for the part. The break in her voice was really touching.

After tea we dispose our carcasses in or about Matilda and off we go on the beautiful Bournemouth Road to the noted King and Queen Oaks.

Oh, what a shock when we reach them—do my eyes deceive me? Is it some nightmare, some disordered figment of the brain? Alas and alack it is too true—that noble oak, the Queen, has been blown down and lies on the ground, dead. I felt really saddened to see that fine old tree demolished after all the years it had reared its enormous limbs aloft. The widowed King still bravely holds his own.

Some distance away is a little oak, with a tablet to tell us that this tree was planted in 1902 as a memorial of the coronation of King Edward VII. Poor Edward VII, you were a good king and we were sorry to lose you. On the right of this is another enclosed tree planted in 1911 to commemorate the coronation of George V, whom God preserve.

I was sorry to see that the trees stood a good chance of being strangled by the gross undergrowth of brambles, and if I lived there I should very soon get a swop-hook and give the trees more room.

Tuesday 5 June. Laze till lunch-time, then the shadow of Reggie's impending departure comes over us. But we put a good face on it, and away we go and draw up at Southampton West Station half an hour too early. Well, we say, the boy has enjoyed the few days' change, and it has done him good. Back, and sit in our sitting-room.

There is excitement in the air tonight in respect of the return from the Front of a soldier who has been two years and four months in France, husband to a woman who helps in the hotel. Information has come to hand that he was seen and spoken to at Lyndhurst Road Station this afternoon, but he has not yet arrived at Lyndhurst. His wife has been down on the 'bus to Lyndhurst Road, but he is not to be seen. She is now inclined to get hysterical.

There are many solutions and rumours. Personally I am inclined to believe that he was not seen at Lyndhurst Road. Mrs Ings says, oh yes, the lady who told her was the wife of a colonel who knows him well—saw him, aye shook hands with him. The plot thickens, and it seems that the problem is insoluble. Where the d——l can he be?

Suddenly, quite late in the evening, we see a soldier and a woman arm in arm come up the street—is it the missing one? Oh how high excitement runs now. They turn in to Fox and Hounds—it is he! Excursions and alarums—Mr and Mrs Ings and the soldier are soon closeted in Mr Ings' little room and I believe refreshments were provided. They were still there when we went to bed.

Wednesday 6 June. Off on the car to Ringwood—crowded with farmers' light carts—then pull up at Wimborne Minster, where we are taken in hand by rather a superior fellow. I was deeply interested in the orrery clock, a most cute ingenious box of tricks.

After passing through Wareham we come to a large new munition factory, and now set Matilda's bow for our goal, Lulworth Cove. We find one road closed in consequence of a military camp; no matter, we turn to the right and get there just the same.

To the Cove Hotel and sit down to lunch—not over-grand, and not served prodigally—then stroll down to the sea. A quantity of soldiers come down and go off in rowing-boats; others bathe in the sea, and it is a lovely scene.

Tom and I toil up to the coastguard station, and Tom informs me when they stayed in the village they used to come up here every night to bring the man his beer. Back to the girls and lie on the grass.

Thinking what a pretty little bay it is, I make a rough sketch of it for my book, and compose myself for a nap. I hear Fanny and Mill say something about the signalling up at the coastguard station to someone on the shore—too sleepy to take much notice.

I am aroused by a voice saying, 'Excuse me, but I think you have been sketching.'

I peer at a man standing in front of me, and notice he is a soldier, and has the rank of sergeant. 'Yes,' I said, 'I did make a rough sketch. What's the trouble?'

'Sketching is not allowed,' he said. 'You had better give it to me.' I produced my little notebook, tore out the leaf and handed the poor little sketch to him. I was sorry it was so badly done but I had only just roughed it in, meaning to amplify it at my leisure. He said, 'Would you mind writing your name and address on the back?'

'With pleasure,' I said. 'And here's my card.'

'Oh, Brighton,' he said. 'I should have thought you would have known sketching was not allowed at seaside places.'

'To tell you the truth I never thought about it. It has always been my habit to make little sketches in my book when I am away.'

Tom said, 'My friend is a special constable. See his badge.'

'Yes,' he said. 'It was the badge—that's how we knew which of you it was.'

Tom said, 'I suppose that's what all that signalling was about, then.'

'Yes—they signalled to me that someone was sketching. I'm answerable for this part of coast. Good day.'

Well, what a blessing to think we have such vigilant coast-watchers. We decided to pull out for home.

Thursday 7 June. A lovely morning—we were as merry as grigs, and no premonition of evil.

After breakfast we telephoned through to Howell—still trouble with those blasted hot-water pipes. Tom suddenly seemed to feel that he must get home at once and set things right.

We never dreamed at breakfast this morning that ere tea-time we should be on our way back to Brighton. Ah well—away we went about two o'clock, and Matilda ran like velvet, and in due course we pulled up at Tom's job, 14 Third Avenue, Hove. Tom and I run over the house. I feel it is quite right for Tom to have come home, as I fancy the job wants a directing hand.

Well, we have had a pleasant jaunt, and we must now settle down again until next time, when we hope the nightmare of war may have passed, and the world become sane again.

Lynton

1918

The fourth year of the War, and we stunned and strained by the loss of our dear son Cuthbert.

It is somewhat hastily arranged that Tom, Fanny, Millie and I shall snatch a change at Lynton. We fix it all up at Cook's.

Saturday 8 June. To Brighton Station. Tom and Fanny arrive soon after, and we take our seats with quite half an hour to spare, which we considered wise, as trains being now considerably curtailed are generally overcrowded. Brighton has been invaded by a large number of London people, who have come to escape 'air-raids', and journey daily to town, thus putting a severe strain on the carrying capacity of the London, Brighton & South Coast Railway

Arriving at Victoria we chartered a 'growler' and ambled off. When we drew up at Waterloo I was amazed to see what a poor specimen of a horse we had been sitting behind—he looked a bag of bones. A porter collected our luggage and told us the train started from no. 7 platform, and very soon a large number of people began to form up outside the gate.

Suddenly the train, looking like a long serpent, began to back in alongside our platform. An electrical thrill seemed to run through the waiting crowd.

The porter shepherded us in, and a lad with an artificial arm got in too. Then the porter asked Millie to let him slide a suitcase under the seat. She jumped up, her eye came in contact with a trunk Tom was lifting, and hey presto, poor old Mum was crocked. She didn't know whether to laugh or cry, and said so. I advised her to cry.

Much to my surprise an attendant now struggled along the corridor, littered with luggage and passengers, to enquire if anyone required luncheon. I had been given to understand that luncheon on trains had been abolished.

I found my left-hand neighbour a most pleasant man, grey-haired but with a young laugh and a tender manner to his wife and daughter, which was refreshing. The poor lad with the artificial arm (and Fanny said shrapnel in the lungs) was a pathetic tragedy, and yet he was so bright and brave.

Oh! how damnable are the effects of this wicked War. It makes my blood boil to see these wrecks, in the first flush of youth, maimed for life—and all for what? For the lust for power of one man, or a few men, who for their own selfish ends did not hesitate to plunge Europe into this maelstrom of horror and suffering.

Poor Mill's eye was now running at a furious rate. A brandy-and-soda sparkled the little woman up a little—only when she laughed, when a bag fell down on my grey-haired friend and knocked off his hat and *pince-nez*, it hurt her so, she had to tell him not to make her laugh again.

Through very pretty country we ambled on. I was much struck at the amount of yellow kilk in the fields. It seemed to me that the land was not being kept clean—lack of labour.

About 4.30 we arrive at Barnstaple, dash across the platform, and enter a carriage of the toy railway. At Lynton the Valley of Rocks Hotel man puts us in a landau, and at last we pull up at the hotel. Here we immediately enquire for a doctor. They telephone for one, and soon the doctor arrives. He is a sporting old boy, very deaf. He examines the injured eye, holds up one finger, then two, and tests the field of vision.

The surface of the eye is reported bruised—he hopes the sight is not injured—tells me to procure a dropper, i.e. an instrument like a fountain-pen filler, with which I am to flush the eye out with a lotion which he will send.

Poor old darling has a little outburst of crying, and I feel very sorry for her, but keep a stiff upper lip, and make as light of it as possible. We are pretty sorry for Tom, as he is worrying over the eye incident.

Thank the Lord, Mill soon falls soundly asleep. Nothing could be better: sleep is nature's own restorer. During the last few years in Brighton, pacing the streets in the darkness of night (as a special constable), I have often thought on sleep, and wondered whether the occupants of the houses I and others have guarded ever give a thought to those who pace their lonely beats.

We owe much to the police. The inspectors of the regular police know everybody and everything in a town—on their rounds, every sense is on the alert—they will stand still and sniff, if they fancy they scent a smell of fire, and never move on until they are satisfied. Think what that alone means to the unconscious sleeper of a town or city, and don't indulge in cheap sneers at the expense of the police.

Sunday 9 June. Roused at 4 a.m. Mill's eye a bit blurred. At 11.30 the doctor arrived and said, 'I am going to drop something into your eye. Tomorrow the sight will be more blurred, but really it will be doing it good.' He then skilfully dropped in two drops and departed.

The weather now being better, Tom and I go out and walk to Lynmouth. We cross two bridges and pull up to watch anglers. A boy had caught four quite decent eels. I am not a fisherman, but it must be a soothing occupation for leisure hours, and sometimes I am half-inclined to give it a trial.

Monday 10 June. Wake up, and our first thought is that this would have been our dear old Cuthbert's birthday. Poor son—it makes one feel rebellious against Fate.

Breakfast, then Tom, Fan and I descend to Lynmouth and enter the grounds of Myrtleberry, a little refreshment place surrounded by large gardens. The proprietor, Mr W.G. Attree, soon pounced on us, and after we had ordered some strawberries and cream, hauled us off indoors to look at photos etc. of his five sons who were serving in the Army. He had many little curios and souvenirs, but his especial delight seemed to be a dinner-gong, made by one of the said sons from a German shell—rather ingenious and quite well made, but Mr Attree rather palls on me. I recollect him last time I was here.

With difficulty we shake Mr A. off, and then heigho for Lynton, a little late for luncheon, but enjoy it all the same. Mill's eye much better.

Invigorated and refreshed, we go out and turn into the private drive leading to the late Sir George Newnes' house on Hollerday Hill. Tom is somewhat nervous, because it is private grounds, and he has as holy a horror of trespassing as any man I know.

Sir George Newnes certainly chose a sweet spot on which to erect his house, which unfortunately has been damaged by fire, and all the roof appears to be gone. I have heard rumours that this fire was the work of suffragettes: if so, it was a shameful act. I hate destruction; it is so difficult to build, and so easy for some misguided lunatic to destroy.

Arriving at the summit the play of light and shadow was very fine, and the air exhilarating. Who could imagine that only a few miles over the water, Death and Destruction stalked supreme, and Humanity groaned under every hideous device pressed into the service of modern warfare.

Tuesday 11 June. Tom and I go off on our own, and take a long walk to Woody Bay—absolutely deserted. It is like fairyland, and we, staid respectable middle-aged men, paddle in the sea like a couple of children. Then we inelegantly regain the spot where we had deposited our boots and socks; I make a pathway by laying down two large pieces of seaweed, step on one, lay another ahead, and so on.

Our handkerchiefs were inadequate to dry our feet, but 'King Sol' lent his aid. A few straggling people now stroll into our ken, and the spell of fairyland is broken. A farmer on a horse pulled up and said: 'Have you gentlemen seen a glove on the road? I've lost one—a new pair too.'

At the end of our journey we go down a terrible hill and reach the hotel. Our girls quite thought we were lost forever. A wash, then watch lawn tennis and get my hair cut. Dinner at 7.30 p.m.; Tom punishes the asparagus terribly.

Wednesday 12 June. Mill and I go across the road to Dr Edwards. He tests her power of vision by holding up little articles and enquiring what they are; then taking a magnifying glass he has another good look at the optic, and at last seems to decide that Millie has had a lucky escape, and that he can now safely relinquish the case.

Having ascertained that his fees are two guineas, and having placed the amount near his hand on the table, we rush hot-foot to our char-à-banc and away to Hunter's Inn—a really grand drive. Two of our fellow passengers give Tom and me a potato cake each, quite a new thing to me, and really very nice.

Back and sit in lounge, which we call the refrigerarium, as the people are all like icicles, they are so cold and stiff and solemn.

Thursday 13 June. Tom and I go down to Lynmouth to find Glen Lyn, which I visited when last here, and have vivid recollections of its singular sylvan beauty.

The gateway is closed, and on enquiry from a native I find the estate has been sold and the glen closed to the public. D——n. We therefore make our way to the sea-front.

Just below the wall of an esplanade is a ship's boat painted a dull slaty colour. Several people go and look at it with interest, and we also notice a man who has the appearance of a Customs officer, and who writes on it with a piece of chalk.

On arriving at the boat we find it has been shipwrecked and has a nasty gash one side, evidently caused by striking on a rock, and the iron plates have been much bent and battered. It is inscribed 'SS *West Point*, 23 persons'. We also find that our naval friend the chalk-writer has written on her outside: 'Boys are not to play with this boat.'

We thought it was as weak a thing as we had ever seen, and as a deterrent to boys worse than useless. A big stick wielded by a strong man is the best deterrent to small boys.

After an early lunch, Tom, Fanny and I start off to the village of Countisbury, a quaint little place. Here are cottages and farm buildings cheek by jowl in the little main street. Several of the cottages have that distinguishing Devonshire mark of the chimney built on to the outside wall.

I was rather struck by a farm-labourer wearing spectacles, which I do not believe I have ever seen before.

At the Blue Boar Inn the landlady served us with some excellent boiled eggs. Glancing through the visitors' book, I notice they have had a large number staying in the past, and all seem to have been wonderfully well treated, according to the tenor of their observations.

We regain our hotel about six o'clock and see our old Mill again. Dinner and bridge: but it is a restless game, as people keep leaving the door open, which keeps us busy shutting it, as the air is cold. The tense way in which we watch to see whether they will shut the door is grotesque.

Friday 14 June. Breakfast, and then out and buy butter etc. The hotel has cut us simply too short of butter, and we feel triumphant that we have secured some. Now we will wallow in butter for the remainder of our stay.

Saturday 15 June. Scramble on a char-à-banc and away we go down the hill to Lynmouth. Here a trace-horse hooks on to us, and the driver requests as many as possible to get down and walk, which we do, all except Millie who remains in triumph.

We now toil up Countisbury Hill on foot, quite a crowd of us, for beside our char-à-banc there is the regular daily char-à-banc also.

The boy on the trace-horse is a sullen individual, and I do not think there is much love lost between him and our driver. Our driver is quite a respectable decent man; his son, a young lad, acts as conductor. At Countisbury we drop our trace-horse, and I was not sorry to see him go back.

Our driver keeps talking to his horses. 'Charley!'—'Now then altogether'—'Now then mare, sweet, sweet'—'Now then Charley.' At Yearnor Moor Stables first char-à-banc changes horses, and as we have to go through without a change our driver feels this is a grievance.

The little boy puts the skid-shoe on the wheel going down a hill, and when we get to the top of Porlock Hill he gets down to put it on again, and lo and behold the skid-shoe is not there—the little goat evidently did not hang it on the hook securely. Driver sends him back for it, and we wait and wait. Then driver asks me to stand at the horses' heads while he goes back to find the boy.

At last we espy them coming back toward us, and glory be, they have found the skid—'Over three quarters of a mile back, it were.' We get aboard again and off we go, with care negotiating Porlock Hill—very steep and dangerous, and I imagine there are not many worse hills in England. The views are superb.

At the Ship Inn, Porlock, a quaint old hostelry, we pull up and I imbibe a small Bass. Off again through much tamer country.

At Minehead we meander down to the sea-front and unpack the hotel lunch. Oh my giddy aunt, there were sandwiches, and nothing but a smear of bloater paste between the bread, and precious little butter. A perfect swindle.

At 2.25 our char-à-banc is ready, and we climb on. And now all is bustle and excitement as two motor-'buses run close to us; then the London train steams in and disgorges a large crowd of people. It is a lovely scene, and the motors go off with people lying on the roof with the luggage. Then we set off and rattle into Porlock.

Ahead of us now is Porlock Hill, and our driver intimates that he expects us all to walk up. This is very disquieting news, but Tom insists on the driver allowing Millie to ride up. Tom, Fanny and I slowly commence to climb.

It is a terrible hill in truth, as it rises a thousand feet a mile, and it makes us puff as we near the top: then we sit down and rest, and soon catch sight of our team struggling up with old Mum sitting in silent majesty.

Sunday 16 June. All four along the cliff walk and into the Valley of the Rocks. Back to dinner—very bad indeed, both in quantity and service. I fancy there is trouble behind the scenes.

Lounge in porch, and fancy we keep hearing the reports of heavy guns.

Monday 17 June. To Lynmouth: sit on the quay and watch the loading of pit-props into a sailing vessel, which operation proceeds in a very leisurely fashion. We also watch three or four men fashioning a yard-arm from a piece of timber, and progress is so slow that it makes my blood boil.

After a lazy morning we partake of lunch, then walk up Summerhouse Hill. We can just see the railway station, and soon we espy the little train winding its fussy jerky way up.

When we reach the main road, all is life and bustle as the vehicles tear along from the station. One motor-car belonging to our hotel gave us quite a turn as it tore madly along the road, and suddenly swerved across the road on to the wrong side to pass a vehicle coming the other way. It was a reckless bit of driving, and would have led to an accident, sure, if the approaching vehicle had been in the hands of a stranger to these parts.

Tuesday 18 June. Rain. The hotel visitors lounge about and make the best of a bad job. A stout man and Jimmy (the young fellow who has lost an arm) and I adjourn to Globe Hotel and have a few Guinness. Then to Tom's room and gorge strawberries.

Wednesday 19 June. Thank goodness it is finer, so we go to Tom Jones' coach office for ride to Doone Valley, and off through very pretty country—dragonflies sporting over the water, and fish leaping. At 3.30

we head for home—a narrow road, and when we meet a motor-trolley, we are at an *impasse*.

We all had to get out, and there was a great amount of juggling with our horses, as the motor had a rotten engine and could not go back, and was hardly strong enough to go forward, but at last we did scraze by, and in due course our charioteer deposited us at the gates of the cliff railway.

Dinner, then adjourn to Tom's bedroom, and Tom makes tea. This is really a most entertaining sight, as the tommy-cooker on which he heats the water is not very strong, and there are innumerable excursions and false alarms about its boiling, which really seems impossible, but at last steam is emitted, and the tea is brewed and consumed with great zest in a scratch collection of drinking-vessels—all very jolly and bohemian.

Thursday 20 June. Tom and I walked by Myrtleberry to the quaintest little village I ever saw, yclept Bridge Ball, and then on the road to Simonsbath. When we got on Exmoor we began to spread ourselves, and felt like giants. We then enquired of an aborigine who was loading peat in a cart, and elicited from him that Simonsbath was about four miles farther on.

We held a council of war—shall we push on to Simonsbath? The want of a proper system of commissariat, on which Tom held strong views, eventually decided us to turn back and steer for Brendon. As we progressed, the pangs of hunger got hold of him and he began to speculate on what escaped German prisoners found to eat, and whether it would be possible for us to eat grass like Nebuchadnezzar. However, at last we drew up at the Rockford Inn, Brendon, and got some bacon and eggs, and Tom began to expand every minute.

Leaving our welcome hostelry it began to rain, and Tom appeared to think we were lost. A little farther we met a most comely wench, and of course I could not get Tom past her; he was soon in conversation and asking her the way. 'Yes,' she said, 'you should have gone through the farm, and then you would have seen the path.'

Saying goodbye we resume our walk, and I am able at last to show Tom a signpost with LYNTON on it. We plugged on slowly, and ultimately arrived at our hotel quite ready for dinner when the gong announced it.

Friday 21 June. To my bankers Messrs Lloyds, where I do change me two £1 Treasury notes into silver. Then to my coach office, to engage a pair-horse landau and drive to Simonsbath as a private party of four.

At 11.25 our landau, a nice-looking two-horse equipage, draws up outside hotel, and we stow ourselves in. But alack-a-day, we had not proceeded far when it began to rain, it was no good blinking the fact, so we asked our coachman to close up the roof. Out on Exmoor it rained in torrents, and the view was cut off by heavy mists. It was absolutely bleak, miles from anywhere and not a soul in sight.

When we finally reached Simonsbath the rain still fell in torrents, so we sat in the landau and ate our lunch. The coachman was I believe genuinely sorry on our account that it had turned out so terribly wet.

Tom, Fanny and I essayed several little runs round the village, but it was really 'no catch'. The rain slopped off the trees, and the mud was chronic—but they saw enough to see that if the sun had been shining and it had been dry underfoot, it would have been a most sweetly pretty little village. Meanwhile Millie sat in the landau and knitted.

Then we go into the Exford Hotel and order four cups of tea, and I glance at the other occupants of the room, all people who came on char-à-bancs, and have been exposed to the rain coming, and now look very dejected at the prospect of the ride back.

At 3.20 we start off: a long drag out of Simonsbath, and when we get on the moor, the rain and wind are heavy and strong—poor old coachman. He is a good sort, and tells us he lets apartments to visitors, so on the chance that at some future time it might be useful to know, I take his name and address: Mr W. Baker, 7 Park Gardens, Lynton.

Saturday 22 June. Finish packing. At 7.45 a.m. in hotel motor to station, and off down to Barnstaple. Such a nice-looking naval officer opposite to me in the carriage; it's funny but we do all love Jack.

At Barnstaple we go off on an earlier train than we intended. Change again at Exeter and arrive in good safety at Waterloo Station, where we secure an old 'growler'.

At Victoria Station, Tom and I studied the train-time indicators, those most plain and useful contrivances which now seem to be almost universally provided at railway stations, and which are in my opinion great boons to travellers. Then in a crowded train, and reach old Brighton without mishap.

It is a queer feeling to drive again into one's native town, after even so short an absence, to know every shop, house and street, when for a fortnight you have been where you know no one, and where every street is new to you, and not a scene dulled by familiarity. First we proceed to 109a King's Road, and say farewell to our *companions de voyage*, and then make for 12 St James's Avenue.

It is gratifying to find that all has been well during our absence, and we feel thankful that we have been protected and guided in our wanderings, and brought back home safe and ready to enact our parts in that great drama called Life.

Au revoir.

Yorkshire

1919

July. A great weight has been lifted from the world by the signing of peace, and the ending of the Great War.

Tom, Fanny, Millie and I held several committee meetings anent the first peace holiday since 1914, and decided to go to Crescent House, carried on by a Miss Bradley at Ilkley, provided she could get garage accommodation. It was also decided to start at 4 a.m. on Saturday 5 July so that we could get to London early and escape the heaviest part of the traffic.

Friday 4 July. Reggie met Uncle Tom at the yard, 47 Middle Street, and assisted in putting in Matilda (the motor) for the night, and enveloping her in tarpaulins and sacks, and handed our best 'alarum clock' to Uncle Tom, to ensure his being awakened next morning.

Saturday 5 July. I arose at 2.20 and called round at the market, where I found carts and vans and men beginning the business of the day. At the yard I divested Matilda of her sacks and tarpaulins, and at 4.5 a.m. went out and saw Tom and Fanny coming along.

We strap on the luggage and commence our journey—Preston, Clayton Hill, St John's Common, Burgess Hill, Cuckfield. At intervals now we meet a shepherd or agricultural labourer going to work.

We run into Redhill about six o'clock, and now meet many men going to work, but all seem rather sleepy. Nearing the metropolitan area we begin to meet workmen's trams, and then it begins to rain and we have to put up the hood.

On through ever-increasing traffic and trams, over Westminster Bridge and up Whitehall, raining pitilessly, and the hood developing leaks, especially on poor Fanny. Up by British Museum, turn left, and to Finchley.

One poor wretch (sheltering under a tree), of whom we asked if we were on the right road, said he didn't know, as he only arrived in London at five o'clock that morning, and I could not help pitying him in having such a watery introduction to the greatest city in the world—how pitiless it can be to the stranger within its gates. 'The devil take the hindmost' is the rule in the busy city.

On we run through Barnet, Potters Bar and Welwyn, very pretty indeed. We make a detour to Letchworth, the Garden City, which we much admire—clean, well laid-out, the majority of the houses well designed, all detached, and undoubtedly a model village. Regaining the main road we pull up in Royston and have a drink. The landlord bewails his lack of spirits, and seems in a very pessimistic humour, albeit I would wager he had had more to drink that morning than I.

We reached Cambridge about three o'clock, and put up at the Bull Hotel in Trumpington Street. The car was in a wet and dishevelled state, so Tom gave her a good hosing and chamois-leathered her over, and tickled the drum brake which has a nasty little way of hanging up. Then venture out to the market-place, and Fanny—with a pertinacity that is really admirable—goes into hundreds of shops in quest of some special knitting-needles for Millie.

Back to a good dinner, and we think the Bull is going to be all right.

Sunday 6 July. Dull but fine. Strange to see dons and undergrads in the streets in cap and gown.

After breakfast to King's College Chapel. The service was in recognition of the Peace; the music and singing were superb, one treble and one tenor perhaps the best voices I have ever heard—special psalms and prayers for the occasion.

Looking round on the young undergrads—nice clean healthy-looking English animals, with all their futures before them—I could not help speculating on what those futures might be. Surely here we have, in embryo, bishops, renowned clergy, great and popular surgeons, barristers, judges perhaps, politicians, great engineers, civil servants etc. It is strange to look at their fresh young faces now, and to know that in time they shall be bent, wrinkled, and similar to the old clergyman who conducts the service today. Some of course will fail in life's battle, and become sad specimens of derelict humanity.

At the conclusion of the service we file out to the river. I could not help thinking how a fellow who had been a King's man, in after years stewing in some wretched outpost of our Empire, must at times see this fair scene in his mind's eye and yearn for it again.

We enter the Great Gate of Trinity College, and try the echo which I remembered from my former visit, then into the noble chapel. Here we are saddened to see the long lists of Trinity men who have perished in the Great War just concluded.

Back to our hotel to luncheon—quite good—then all on car to Newmarket. Here is a hospital parade, an enormous crowd, banners etc., police marshalling. We have to pull up and wait, and then a police inspector comes and intimates that our room will be more desirable than our company. So Tom gets the engine running, and hoot-toot-tooting at a most alarming rate Matilda picks her way through a rotten crowd, back to Cambridge.

Monday 7 July. Away we go to Peterborough and then Stamford, looking for a suitable place for luncheon. We slip by place after place: however at last we sight a stone on the roadside, and pull up at once. It serves as a table and seat for Millie.

This is always our chief consideration in selecting a spot—is there anywhere Millie can sit? She does not shine sitting on Mother Earth, it being a bit of an undertaking to get her down and somewhat worse to get her up again.

We have a tip-top lunch, then limber up again. We are now 86 miles from York, and Matilda settles down to work in earnest. It is amazing to see how we decrease the distance as milestone after milestone rushes by. We reach York about 8.15 p.m., turn down Coney Street and find the Swan Hotel. Our room is heavily furnished: the bed old mahogany, with hangings at the head.

Then all to York Minster, a noble pile. Restoration is almost always going on, and there is a great scaffolding which looks weatherbeaten and has evidently been up many years; I should say the work is stopped for the present.

The peacefulness of the Deanery Gardens was like a soothing balm to one's senses. Having made the circuit, we retrace our steps to hotel through a rough-looking lot of people.

Tuesday 8 July. Tom and I out; buy some gloves for Tom to drive in.

Two exquisite objects arrest our attention—heralds decked out in gorgeous array, marching along with an importance and dignity that is irresistibly comical—they certainly think they are the two pillars of State that hold up the whole fabric of the British Constitution.

We decide that they are on their way to sound a fanfare as the judge drives up to the Assize Court. We follow them to York Castle and enter its precincts.

In a few minutes a carriage arrives. Officials line the steps, and as the judge steps from the carriage, the trumpeters blare out a loud blast. With solemn dignity His Lordship the judge and the officials march into court and the little ceremony is ended. This perpetuation of old-world ceremonial may dignify the law in the eyes of the masses, though it is open to argument in these days. It certainly does not hurt us.

Tom seemed inclined to go into the court, but I felt we had little interest in Yorkshire criminals, and I have cooled my heels in assize courts at Lewes until I felt weary and disgusted at the waste of time. So we turned back to the magnet of all travellers to York, the Minster, and began our tour round, our guide describing everything with a most courtly air.

Internally, its size and height make it the most imposing of our cathedrals. In the east window the stained glass dates from 1405, and comprises two hundred subjects from the Old Testament, Revelations etc.

In these days of the twentieth century, when labour seems to have a most exaggerated idea of its monetary value, it may not be out of place to record that John Thornton who made this window received a wage of four shillings a week, £5 at the end of each year and £10 extra on the completion, in all about £55. I know I shall be told money was worth much more in AD 1405; even so, £55 for three years' work, wherein you express your soul in beautiful handicraft, does not seem to err on the side of generous treatment.

What say you trade unionists and knights of labour?—poor down-trodden wretches, who on munition work recently have only been picking up a paltry £7 or so a week.

We part with our guide cordially, and enquire the way to the Shambles. We find it is a narrow lane with most ancient houses and shops which appear to be drunk, for most are leaning out of the horizontal. Several are not occupied; I imagine they are not fit to live in. Originally it was the butchers' quarter; it is interesting on account of its age, but very squalid.

Then all to lunch—say goodbye to our buxom landlady, get Matilda out and do not pull rein till we reach Knaresborough. The view from the bridge over the River Nidd is charming—much boating was going on.

We rattled on to Harrogate, a fashionable place: good shops, crowds of people, everything flourishing. We notice a number of people limping along, evidently rheumatic patients; numerous baths, kursaals, municipal orchestras etc., in fact everything that constitutes the modern inland watering-place or spa. How many medicinal springs it has I won't say, their name is legion, and I daresay if demand should arise for some new special spring, by hook or by crook the Harrogaterians will produce it.

We now steered for Otley, on a bit of road that required a considerable amount of skill in driving. It was practically deserted moorland, perhaps the best bit of moor we did at all—the hills were terrific, the bends hazardous—in fact not a road suited for horse or motor traffic, and I think it is universally shunned by local people. But in due course we reached Ilkley and pulled up at Crescent House.

I can see it is a healthy spot up here, and fine air, but the other visitors are a funny collection—one old gentleman who looks fairly disagreeable, one middle-aged man who looks supremely miserable, one very old widow, and the remainder look like angular old maids—rather a depressing lot.

The middle-aged man meets me on the landing and desires me to put out the gas on the landing when I have done with it, which I promise to do.

Wednesday 9 July. We gather in the drawing-room—all the ancient crocks are there in high feather—then out on to moor and climb to top of a craggy hill, very fine indeed. Coming back we go into the old Roman Baths, paying twopence each for the privilege. Funny little place—two small stone baths let into the earth, and a number of pennies in the bottom of the water which I do not understand in the least.

Then up to the band. The performers a most odd-looking lot—not in uniform—like a collection of Methodist parsons out of work. The conductor is a sketch, and his bow when the audience applaud is grotesque. The girl who collects the money for the seats is a shriek—thick-set, stumpy and awkward, but somehow I think she gets the twopences and few escape her Argus eye.

We spend a pleasant evening in the open air, except that a sadness creeps over when two or three nurses come up with some blinded and wounded soldiers. Poor fellows, they seem to try and be cheerful but it is a cruel sight and gets on my nerves. Damn the War, I say to myself.

It is good to see how carefully the nurses look after their charges and feed them with cherries or help them to light cigarettes or pipes, but their poor glazed eyes give me the creeps, and to see them try to strike matches is pathetic—as are the actions of one poor chap, blind and probably legless, who is in an invalid chair covered in blankets, and beats time to the music.

What a terrible thing it is. A few years back here were strong healthy men full of life and strength and vigorous manhood—now helpless lumps of clay, God's sun and light gone from them for ever, and dependent on others for every little act. Oh bitter honour—and this is the twentieth century, and Europe is supposed to be a Christian state.

Thursday 10 July. Oil up engine of car, and away through pretty country to Bolton Abbey. Here are several motors, and Matilda is placed among them in spaces for leaving motors—motor-stands, let us call them.

Having explored the abbey we continue to Lofthouse, the terminus of the Nidd Vale Light Railway. Middlesmoor, which is one of the places we wrote to for a hotel, is only about a mile from Lofthouse, so to Middlesmoor we set a course.

The road was none too good and rather hilly, and Matilda turned sulky, so we all got out.

I think the majority of the party began to take an intense dislike to Middlesmoor, but having come thus far I knew it was my bounden duty to toil up and view the Crown Hotel kept by Mr J.T. Carling who had written me what I considered a very nice letter, and although I have never seen him I have an idea that I should get on well with him, and I still have a soft feeling for Middlesmoor.

I found the Crown Hotel all right, a thousand feet above sea-level, and the views of mountain and valley magnificent—the air pure and bracing—the village old and tiny. I saw several nice ladies and a dear old clergyman having tea outside the hotel.

Back through Harrogate, Matilda's engine dies out—every drop of petrol used up, so no wonder she objected to the hill to Middlesmoor. The reserve can of petrol poured into her stomach sets everything right again, and we reach Ilkley in good safety about seven o'clock.

Friday 11 July. A man and his wife have arrived from Leeds, and are quite nice people. I call him the 'Human Being', as he is such a contrast to the collection of typical boarding-house antiques and oddities we found here. He is a keen shrewd man with a merry twinkle in his eye, and we discuss the topics of the day.

We are jubilant at dinner this evening, as Fanny has after infinite labour succeeded in getting us some butter on our table for the first time. Until this most happy event, we have writhed under Margarine, which is all the management seem to be able to provide. Is it any wonder that we are light-hearted tonight?

After dinner we adjourn to our bedroom and essay to play Royal Auction bridge. But Tom and I had not reckoned on the fact that our amiable friend who holds sway over the band near our house had willed it that this evening should be devoted to jazz music. No sooner had we commenced than both girls began swaying to the strains of the music, giggling and generally fooling about until I believe they were almost hysterical.

Tom began to get more restless every minute, which I think made the little cats worse. But it's a long lane without a turning, and presently with one accord we all four spring to our feet and stand at attention as the notes of 'God save the King' smite our ears. Then we are able to settle down and have a proper game.

Saturday 12 July. Steer our way to the ancient city of Ripon. We run through its narrow streets to the market-place, a fine open square. On top of the market-cross is a wakeman's horn adapted as a weathercock. There is a significance in this, because here they still keep up a most ancient custom of sounding a horn at nine o'clock every evening, blowing three blasts at the market-cross and three in front of the residence of the mayor. These old customs are very refreshing in these hurrying feverish bustling days and I should be loath to see them fall into desuetude.

I got an impression that Ripon was perhaps a little decayed.

Next we shape a course for Fountains Abbey. We drive up to an entrance, and a gentleman comes out of the lodge, and intimates that he would now relieve us of sixpence for the motor having come up to the gate. It seems playing the game rather low-down; however, I suppose the owners of these places are not very rich, and sixpence is sixpence to them.

We enter the grounds, and are charmed. Here is the finest ruin that I have yet seen—it is a feast. Several fine plans of the site were hung up in different parts, and added greatly to the interest of what you saw.

Leaving here thoroughly satisfied, we now worked down to Ripley; this charming little village is practically one broad street prettily shaded with trees. Soon after we left it rained in torrents, and we pulled up at the side of the road and the water dripped on Fanny terribly, so we laid a piece of macintosh I had in my pocket, and made a depression in it and caught the droppings and emptied them out at intervals.

Sunday 13 July. Tom and I over to the garage—car repairs and oiling until 12.30. Then Tom, Fanny and I walk on the moor until we reach the so-called Cow and Calf Rocks.

Whyever these rocks were christened 'Cow and Calf' I am at a loss to understand. Even the guide-book says, 'The rocks have not the slightest resemblance to the animals whose names they bear'—and that is a pretty admission for a guide-book to make, as their general mission in life is to puff up everything, and have you believe that the district they are dealing with is the most charming in the whole world. However, these two rocks are certainly enormous pieces.

In the side of the 'Calf' little cavities have been cut, just large enough to insert one's foot, and as it seems to be a custom to climb up I thought I would essay the performance.

It was exceedingly sheer, and one had to cling on with one's nails, and the wind whipped viciously around as if wishing to sweep one off. I do not recommend it to the elderly, or infirm people, or anyone prone to giddiness.

Monday 14 July. Off to Bolton Abbey again; a number of children are having a school treat here. Of course they must swarm on the stepping-stones, and the reflections of their legs and bodies upside-down in the river were quite pretty as they scrambled to and fro.

To Ilkley and luncheon, then have a charming walk in search of Middleton Lodge, an Elizabethan mansion we can see from our dining-room window. We got quite close but failed to get in the grounds.

Dinner, and then go up to the band. A dog howls horribly when the music gets on his nerves. Once the conductor expresses a wish that he had his gun with him.

Tuesday 15 July. Settle account, and away in glorious weather through Skipton, Hellifield, Settle—then pass a quaint sign, the Naked Man Hotel. Look for the Naked Woman in vain.

Turn off to inspect Ingleton and the Ingleborough Hotel, kept by one Albert Yates. This is one of the places we might have stayed at, so we feel glad to have seen it. The hotel struck me as a very slow and sleepy place.

When we get to a bridge which I think is Levens, I go and interview a lady motorist who is standing beside her little car, and she says, 'Yes—this is Levens Bridge.' As pleasant a lady as ever I did meet; I could have made a fuller acquaintance with her, but I had to hasten back and report to the captain of the ship, who gets restless when the craft is hove to for a minute.

Away we go through beautiful country to Windermere. In the Lakeside Hotel we interviewed a very nice lady manageress; she juggled a bit with the books but finally decided to put us up—for which relief much thanks. We had a grand view of the lake and hills.

Wednesday 16 July. We all troop aboard SS *Tern* and away up the lake. Dash off at Ambleside and are soon besieged by dozens of char-à-bancs. We decide on the Langdale Pikes drive, and off we go. The only thing wrong is the pest of flies, hundreds of whom swarm round us and our poor horses.

By Elterwater Tarn a crew of children follow us, crying: 'Heep! Heep!! Harraa!!!' A lady in the back seat, who seemed to know the district extremely well, said: 'They mean "hip hip hurrah".'

By Grasmere and Ambleside—dash on board SS *Swan*—a lovely run down the lake, and to dinner. At nine o'clock, out in a boat; Millie will not come tonight.

What an evening it was—Tom and I pulling pairs each—Fanny sitting on cushions in the stern like some eastern *houri* on a divan. Surely there is no trouble or care in the world, or is this a blissful dream? Then I suppose the devil, thinking we were too happy, decided to take a hand in the game; so a suggestion came into my head and I said, 'Let us ship one scull and pull one each, instead of pairs.'

We proceeded to carry out this manœuvre, and in unshipping one of his sculls, Tom dragged his gun-metal rowlock out into the water. It seemed to remain poised in the air for the thousandth part of a second—then I saw it gradually sink until it was lost to view.

Oh dear! A moment before, peace and serenity—now everything's wrong. Why did I want to have anything different? And Mephistopheles laughed, and said: 'I can't have people so happy as they were, it would never do.'

The boatman was very nice about the lost rowlock. 'Don't let it upset you. . . . I'm never upset myself,' he said, 'without somebody hits me.'

Thursday 17 July. Take an affectionate farewell of the hotel manageress, and away we go to Levens Bridge. I look for my charming lady-friend, but woe is me, she is not there. On to Lancaster—a fine town and a grand town hall—several large motor char-à-bancs crowded with men standing about in the streets, and when we ask our way they all seem to want to direct us.

Away to Garstang—very dirty place. Out into country again and pull up at the Roebuck Inn at Myrsechough; I believe that is the name but it was very difficult to catch it. The landlady was a most jolly woman, fat as a mole, and a beautiful skin. On again through Preston—another dirty hole—then to Longton and finally to Southport. We spot the Sandringham Private Hotel on the front and succeed in getting rooms, then Tom and I walk on the front.

Here is such a sight as would be difficult to match: water-chutes, roundabouts, swing-boats, lighthouse mat-chute, and divers other shows—a conglomeration of side-shows like a glorified White City—just a little low tone it appears to me.

Then we go over a wild rough waste of sand to the sea and watch Sopwith aeroplane flights, fast and furious. I feel strongly I ought to go up, but £1 1*s* 0*d* for a few minutes seems too much money. So we go up to a park which is brilliantly illuminated with coloured electric lights and a fine band discoursing sweet music. A lovely night.

Friday 18 July. We pay hotel account and get away. At one turning we ask a venerable bearded cabman best way out. He came over and leaned on the side of the car and said, 'Straight oop to chapel, toorn left, then right.' Tom asks where then. 'Aah—then you moost aisk soombodye else.'

We soon get out on the open road again, through Holmes Chapel—have good refreshments in a quaint old inn kept by an ancient dame—pass an inn with a peculiar sign, the Legs of Man, then through Newcastle, Stoke, Stone, Wolseley and Rugeley.

Just as we enter Lichfield, bang goes a tyre. Here were crowds of people watching the putting up of decorations for tomorrow's Peace Celebrations. We hop out and put on a new wheel, limber up and get away again—to Canwell, Wishaw, Coleshill, Stonebridge. We had some idea of putting up here for the night, but there was the pressing trouble of the purchase of a new tyre. Tom entered into conversation with an AA man who was on point duty, and he strongly advised going on to Coventry where he said we were sure to get a tyre.

When we entered Coventry we at once got tangled up with crowds of people, trams etc., a holy muddle and very annoying to us free rovers on the King's broad highway. The crowds were in the streets, beginning the Peace Celebrations. We pulled up in Hertford Street and I went across the road to the King's Head Hotel. 'Yes, if you are going off early we can put you up, but we have a busy day tomorrow.'

Job to cross the street—people like rabbits all over the road—quite a conjure. Serene at last in a large old garage packed with cars. A good dinner, then try to find a shop selling tyres; all shut up, and the garage man says that to buy a new tyre in Coventry is like trying to borrow money. It does not look very promising.

Presently a tram-car came along, beautifully decorated and studded with electric lights—a fine sight. We feel Peace Demonstrations are beginning. Bands of hobble-de-hoys are now parading, singing uproariously. Back to hotel and find the girls in our bedroom overlooking the street, and we get a view of the singing crowds. The uproar goes on until about twelve o'clock.

Saturday 19 July. Bustle about to get off, as all streets will soon be closed for traffic. Tom announces he has left his stick at Southport, and Fanny has left her *pince-nez* under her pillow at same hotel.

Away through a number of people, but not nearly so dense as last night. Pass processions in fancy dresses. Clear of the town we head for Kenilworth, a sweet little place.

Try to get new tyre at Eykyns Garage—closed. D——n. Then thanks be, Mr Eykyns—a young man recently demobbed—comes on the scene.'Oh yes, got some in yesterday. How many do you want?'

I thought it would be a quick job, but it was nearly an hour and a half before we were able to limber up again. Away again to Warwick, a grand old place—unfortunately castle closed, but we had a great treat in going over the Leycester Hospital, a foundation for twelve old soldiers, dating from 1571. A fine old chap showed us round, frequently telling us that the place was given by the Earl of Leicester, the favourite of Queen Elizabeth. I would say it is the most interesting old place I have ever visited.

Off to Stratford-upon-Avon (crowds of people) and on to Shottery, Shipston-on-Stour, Woodstock (wet), Oxford (very wet)—lot of children in fancy dresses—Abingdon, Ilsley (wet), and Newbury (damp). Here we try the Chequers—never saw such a slow lot in my life. Could they put us up? Girl would see.

I waited and waited. Then Fanny came to see whether I was lost. We waited. Decided to turn it up and try somewhere else—just then the manageress appeared. She was a businesswoman, and we soon fixed up. Manageress explained that they were all at sixes and sevens over the Peace Demonstrations—obliged to let the maids go out.

A cold supper, then all four dash up in the middle of our meal to see a procession go by—fancy dresses, decorated wagons and trolleys representing tableaux.

Complete our supper, and then to the Market Square—the whole place full to overflowing with people, small bonfires, fireworks galore, the town band playing, and hundreds of couples dancing in a space kept for them by the police. A noisy, rollicking, lively, exhilarating scene. It was very dirty underfoot, and drizzling, but it was a good-humoured honest enjoyable crowd and gave one somewhat of an idea of the simple outdoor pleasures of the old days when England was dubbed 'Merrie England'.

We were very hot in our coats, and it was tiring standing about so long, so Millie and I retired to a doorway and leaned against it for a rest. We had not been long entrenched in our position when the door was suddenly opened and we staggered back on to two young men—laughter and apologies—settled down again, propping each other up, and then the door was opened again by two women, and we staggered back again.

Sunday 20 July. Pay up and say goodbye. On to Whitchurch, Sutton Scotney and Winchester, then pull up at Stedham and invade Lintott's timber-yard. We settled down in a very nice sawpit, and the spirit-kettle was lit, and water for our tea began to heat. We seemed to be the cynosure of the eyes of every boy in the village who evidently made the yard their happy hunting-ground on Sundays. One boy informed me that he was a grandson of Lintott.

Later I saw a lame man limp along, and found he was Lintott's son, so I was one degree of consanguinity nearer to my quest. I said, 'I should like to see your father now I am here.'

Old Lintott arrived on the scene, and after a deadly slow negotiation I bought a few oak planks and cleft oak laths.

Gathering up our goods and chattels we limber up and away to Brighton. Then at 6.45 p.m. comes that saddest part of a holiday, when we have to say goodbye to Tom and Fanny.

We have covered 1,030 miles, and once more we have to render thanks to One who has guided and guarded us out and home. We enter our mansion and close the door, and the 1919 holiday is over.

Bath

1920

Saturday 5 June. On the 5th day of June, two human atoms arose from their bed at 12 St James's Avenue, Brighton, breakfasted, and awaited the advent of a taxi-cab. At 9.30 a.m. this taxi drew up, impelled by some unseen power.

One of the atoms is a wife, a mother—but sad to relate she has a limp arising from a rheumatic affliction in the hip. She is fairly plump, very pretty, and a most adorable woman, has been married nearly twenty-nine years, and except for the rheumatic hip, is as sound as when she was a girl of twenty.

Now it is a funny thing in life that half the people in the world know exactly what the other half ought to do to be cured of anything, and these wise people keep saying to this adorable lady, 'You ought to go Bath,' or 'My dear, whyever don't you go to Bath' etc. *ad nauseam*. Bath became an obsession—so as you may have gathered, the objective of the pilgrimage is Bath.

The other atom is one of those unconsidered trifles, a husband.

I wonder whether there is any period when a husband is of any importance. Even now, I feel with bitter resentment the ignoring by nurse and doctor of a husband during his wife's confinement. He may eat his heart out with anxiety, and no one throws him a kind word—he is hustled out of the way, and has to crave admission to his own bedroom to see his own wife. Later, should illness come to a wife, doctors and nurses calmly cut and carve at their own sweet will, all claims of a husband simply ignored—and he, poor devil, is left desolate, to come home to a house which is empty, dark and gloomy. They are greatly blessed in this life who do not have to have recourse to doctors.

Years ago a husband, if he had a business, at least had one sphere in which he could be of some importance, but even this small satisfaction has gone since 1914, for now a man in business is not really a master—his authority is a shadow. The men are now the masters. And so this world, which was to be made fit for heroes to live in, goes on, and the businessman sees that labour and politicians between them are doing their best to ruin trade and destroy civilisation.

*　　*　　*

The taxi arrived at Brighton Station, and soon we started. At Victoria we secured a four-wheeler—I like to encourage the poor old horse-cabman now, as their business is gradually being taken over by motor-cabs. It is a world of change, and nothing ever stands still.

We feel very happy together jogging along the highway. Passing Hyde Park we see large crowds, soldiers, mounted batteries and police—ah! the celebration of the King's birthday. God save the King. There may be other forms of government, but a limited monarchy is the safest and best form for England—or shall I say Great Britain because the Scots hate to hear one say England.

We arrive at Paddington Station and get a rather poor lunch in an Express Dairy Company. I manage to secure a bottle of stout in a noisy pub, stroll back into station and sit down. There is plenty to see, an ever-changing crowd, all intent on something, and we feel we are seeing life.

At 2.45 we start—seven in our compartment and all quite nice people, at least the other five were.

Near Burnham Beeches we were appalled to see a dump of government motors, thousands of them out in the open and spoilt or rapidly spoiling—the cruel waste of it makes one feel ill and we taxpayers have to foot the bill. Surely something must be done to check the awful expenditure before we are strangled by taxation.

We stop at Reading, Newbury, Hungerford—get splendid view of the White Horse cut in the hill at Westbury—stop at Devizes, Holt Junction and Bradford-on-Avon, and reach Bath at 5.30 p.m. We squeeze into the hotel 'bus, which is ancient and like a hat-box on wheels, and draw up outside Christopher Hotel—evidently an old hostelry. Then I telephone to Dr Cave, 16 The Circus, Bath, to make an appointment for Millie. The earliest he will see her is 2.20 p.m. next Tuesday.

To me it seemed rather autocratic, and I was inclined to shut off the 'phone and try some other doctor, as it seemed a wicked waste of valuable time between Saturday and Tuesday afternoon. However, Dearest seemed to fancy seeing Dr Cave, so I told the girl to book the appointment for 2.20 on Tuesday.

Sunday 6 June. We walk to the Circus, where Dr Cave resides, as I always believe in reconnoitring the ground. I should imagine that the Circus is the Harley Street of Bath.

Dinner at 1.30, then get on the tram to Bathford, right out in the country. We sit on a seat and watch tram after tram come up, filled with people, for Bathford is evidently a favourite Sunday evening jaunt.

The majority of the people make their way to the Crown Inn which is choked inside and outside with customers, and it must be a little goldmine.

Monday 7 June. Early tea in bed at 7.30—very punctual, which pleases me. Like a giant refreshed, I then sally forth and get me *Ye Dailie Maille* and also do buy some of a noxious weed called tobacco of the which I do smoke and feel at peace with the world.

The Duchess of St James's Avenue and I do then go out into the streets together, and I cannot but think that the people must be pleased to see so comely-looking a pair. First we go to the Grand Pump Room, and here is a sedate lot of people, mostly halt and lame, industriously sipping warm water out of glasses with handles, each glass containing 12 ounces as testified by the marks thereon inscribed, and it strikes one almost like being in a church, all being so solemn.

In the centre, a damsel with black hair presides over a fountain from which the water steaming hot flows into glasses placed around it. We are agreeably surprised to find it quite palatable, and being warm it seems to lie lighter in our interiors.

We were a little shy of spa waters after our never-to-be-forgotten experience of the waters at Llandrindod Wells, which is the most noxious compound on this earth.

Then to Boots in Union Street, and to Amelia's great joy she finds a 'lift', and as it says 'PRESS THE BELL' we press it, and get no effects. Then we again press the bell like h—ll (this is poetry not profanity); still no effect, so as we are now beginning to attract attention, the shop people begin to bestir themselves and dig up a little maiden who whisks us up to the next floor, and we make our way to the lending-library counter, and Mrs Peerless is duly enrolled as a member for two weeks at an expenditure of 1*s* 4*d.* She has thoughtfully prepared a list of books and is soon furnished with one called *Yellow English* which we bear away triumphantly.

Out and through an arcade called the Corridor, and the little woman expressing a desire for an ice, we go into a confectioner's and order two. Not bad but a little 'sloppy', not quite frozen enough.

Then to the Institution Gardens, where we sit and listen to the band of the Royal Inniskilling Fusiliers conducted by Mr Griggs. This band has a little drummer-boy whose chief duty seems to be leading about a huge hound much larger than the boy. These grounds are very pretty, somewhat like our Pavilion grounds, and here is the inevitable hot-water fountain and visitors sipping the waters.

At 2.30 we try to get a char-à-banc to Castle Combe. The first car goes off with one vacant seat, and eight of us are left on the pavement, and the man in charge says, 'As there are only eight, the other char-à-banc cannot go.' We disperse moodily, and get on a tram to Weston.

We find Weston a rather poor old place, quite one-eyed, and the population seemed to be of children: there were myriads of these, and I believe we saw three or four adults only. Catching the next tram back, we walked to Milsom Street and had tea at Fortt's—a tip-top place crowded with people, and a small orchestra discourses dreamy music.

When we go out again we see several motor-cars waiting outside, and as we now scrutinise every light car we see, we poke about among these and get into conversation with a chauffeur in charge of a 11.9 Bean, and gather from him that the Bean is a good reliable car.

Back to write letters, then to bed, after studying the fire-escape which reposes in swathing-cloths beneath our toilet table; hope we shan't have to use the durn thing, or I shall have a busy time stowing all the people into the canvas shoot, and our room will be a regular highway, as just outside our door is a tablet 'TO NO. 17 AND FIRE-ESCAPE'.

Tuesday 8 June. To the Grand Pump Room; read *The Car* and imbibe two glasses warm water. Then pay sixpence each and go into the Roman Bath, a fine relic of the past, and many most interesting things in what they call the museum. Poor old Mum's stomach turning over with nervousness about the approaching medical interview.

Our appointment is for 2.20, and at 2.21 we are ushered into the 'Presence'.

The 'Presence' proves to be not at all formidable—I might say rather a 'scrubby' man—but he turns out a real good sort, and in a short space of time I am convinced he knows his job, and I feel confidence in him, and am sure with further intercourse we should become great friends.

He questioned Millie closely, made her walk about the room, requested her to lie on the sofa and twisted her legs about in divers directions and then sat down and wrote out two prescriptions.

> Mrs Peerless
> Deep baths at 100° for 20 minutes and wet douche to right hip for last 7 minutes at 110°
> Pack 15 minutes
> Cooling room 20 minutes, home and lie down for an hour
> Bath 3 days a week
> Drink 12 ozs Bath mineral water 3 times a day about 11–12 and 5.30
> June 8 1920
> E.J. Cave MD

After a little further conversation, I say: 'What is your fee, please, Doctor?'

He says: 'Oh, do you want to pay now?'

'Well, you don't know me, and short reckonings make long friends.'

'Two guineas,' he said, 'and after this I'll see you for a guinea.'

The money passed from me to him, and shaking hands we departed, and I think he watched us as we crossed the Circus.

Before we left, he gave us his card and promised to send a masseuse.

We walk to Broad Street, and see some boot-trees in a shop kept by one called Payne. Millie goes in, but the young lady says Mr Payne is out, and she hardly likes to sell them, as they are in a pair of boots at the window and they are very short of them.

Home to dinner, then via Pulteney Street (a fine wide street, with large decaying houses) to Sydney Gardens. Here we sit and watch dancing on the lawn to the band of the Royal Inniskilling Fusiliers.

We quite enjoyed looking at so many people enjoying themselves in a rational way, and soon began to recognise the dancers as they drifted round. Had I some young ladies with me whom I know, I fancy we should also have disported on the light fantastic toe.

Wednesday 9 June. Out with Millie and leave her about 9.45 at Queen's Bath. Then I walk to Midland Railway goods station and spy out for Windebank's timber-merchant's yard—much farther than I anticipated, so I retrace my steps and meet Mill at 11.15. She is really pleased with the deep bath with extra douche—I think she rather dreaded it, so it is a great relief.

We take the waters and then creep out of the solemn funereal atmosphere of the Pump Room, and fix up a char-à-banc ride. Off we go in a 22-seater into rather plain country, but it improved as we neared Wells.

We pulled up in a large square outside cathedral grounds among a quite enormous number of char-à-bancs and motors which were packed in a seemingly inextricable mass. One end of this square was flanked by the courts wherein the assizes or sessions were evidently being held.

I just had a look round, and someone soon asked me whether the gypsy case was over. I said I knew nothing about gypsies or cases; I fancy it was rather a serious affair though.

To a tea-room—I think the slowest place I ever struck—then I to the abbey, and Mill to the char-à-banc. The abbey is certainly a noble pile, and the west front is a magnificent piece of sculptured work. To me it seems that there is almost too much carving and sculptury, and that something a little less ornate or flamboyant would strike a more dignified note, but then I am perhaps rather a plain-minded man, not over-given to think too highly of trappings and fal-lals.

Glancing at my watch, I hasten back to our char-à-banc in the square. The trial is evidently not yet concluded, and I notice some of the gypsy prisoners' female relatives waiting anxiously for the verdict, and several of the tradespeople keep coming up to see how affairs are progressing.

At 5.15 p.m. we started for home through Radstock. We were rather interested in one of our passengers, not at all an old man, who was quite crippled by rheumatism or some kindred disorder, and we were very pleased to see how a young man with him, whom we took to be his son, did everything in his power to help him. On arrival at New Bond Street, a Bath chair was waiting for our passenger, into which his son dutifully assisted him, and away they went.

Thursday 10 June. To Pump Room and drink waters, then to Colmer's, a large outfitter's establishment, and purchase six collars and two pairs of socks.

Stroll up Milsom Street, criticising every motor-car we see, and there are quite a large number outside the shops while their owners are shopping. Then back to hotel, and I leave Millie to be massaged by Miss Ewbank.

I out for a long walk to Forester Road and see the boating-station: river very pretty, and a few people boating. Back across bridge, for which they have the audacity to charge me a halfpenny—that is how we are imposed and trampled on in this country.

Home just after six o'clock, dress and dine. Then off we go to a picture-palace, and find it not at all bad.

Friday 11 June. Early tea, punctual as usual; quite a desirable feature of this hotel is the punctuality of the arrival of early-morning tea in bedroom, and also that the hot water is really hot. In many hotels the water is a sickly lukewarm. I do like hot water with a sting in it. Should it be too hot I can reduce its temperature, but if it is too cold you are impotent to remedy it.

I hate that impotent feeling about anything: it makes me feel cold inside. To be happy I must be up and doing.

I go out later to baths for *Aix douche* and *massage double*, leaving Millie telephoning to Wises at Bristol. I am received by an attendant and requested to sit in the waiting-room, a nice place packed with easy lounge-chairs, settees, small tables, and well supplied with papers, illustrated periodicals etc.

The attendant then looks at my ticket, ushers me into a little dressing-room and leaves me to doff my clothes. In due time he comes back to say, 'Quite ready for you, sir, please follow me,' and I follow him to a large bathroom, the floor and walls of which are tiled. Here is another attendant. They sit me on a kind of stool, and then one attendant stands in front of me and one at the back. They each hold a hose under the left arm, from the nozzle of which issues a stream of hot water which is directed on to my body, and where the water touches me, they massage—a most agreeable sensation, and I was quite sorry when the operation was finished.

One attendant now departed, and I was directed to a corner of the room and douched with warm water gradually cooled to cold. Then I was lightly dried, covered with towels and taken to my dressing-room. I donned my clothes feeling very nice all over.

Make my way to the Pump Room and meet Millie. She says Dottie has arranged to send Alan's car for us.

At 2.15 the car, a nice little Rover, draws up. Mill and I are placed in the two back seats, Beattie takes the wheel, and their chauffeur (Dyke) sits beside her and gives his moral support. Slight rain, and we have to put up hood. At Brislington they receive us with open arms—Dottie and Alan, and two lady visitors, Mrs and Miss Carwardine.

A welcome cup of tea, then four of us play a game I have never seen before, called Bumblepuppy. A pole is erected in the ground, and at the top a rope is fixed, reaching to within about 18 inches of the ground. At the ground end an old glove holding a ball within it is firmly attached.

Each player is furnished with an old tennis-racquet. Two players *vis-à-vis* play against the other two. The game is to wind the rope round the pole so that your opponents cannot hit it free. It is not at all a bad game.

Unfortunately after one mighty swipe, Miss Carwardine got a blow on the eye, which brought tears, and she had to be hurried off and have it bathed.

We play until our arms ache, then Dottie suggests that Dyke should get out the car and drive us round the old spots at Clifton that Millie knew in her girlhood, and ultimately deposit us at the railway station. Dottie is a capable guide, and very proud of Bristol. It is certainly a busy city and shows every evidence of prosperity.

Saturday 12 June. After breakfast it begins to rain. I moon about all morning, and as a last resource take shelter in the Pump Room which is as deadly lively as possible. Then to Boots the Chemists to ask what time they close this evening, as we want to change the book *Doggie*. We are informed they close at eight o'clock.

Back to dinner; raining as we go, Millie skipping bits of *Doggie* to finish it. At 17 minutes to eight I hasten to Boots—all shut at back entrance, dash round to front only to find it if anything more securely closed—back to hotel and report, and we lift up our voices and weep when we remember that they definitely told us eight o'clock.

Sunday 13 June. Out to the abbey to morning prayer; too much echo to hear anything clearly. Then purchase two tickets for motor char-à-banc drive to Bratton.

A good tea at the Duke Hotel on the lawn. After tea, two ladies in front of us on char-à-banc suggest changing seats with us as they have heard Millie complaining that the leg-room is rather restricted.

We thank them, and now sit beside the driver. Much more room for the feet, but the heat from the engine makes itself very apparent and I begin to think this had something to do with our kind ladies offering to give up the front seat.

Monday 14 June. To Boots; change book and buy some soap. Soap is a very necessary commodity in modern life, and I am never happier than when bathing and washing. Then to Pump Room, and two glasses of water each.

Fancy me drinking two glasses of water at a sitting, but when you are in Bath you must do as Bath does. It strikes me it is rather 'like a chip in porridge', as they say in Sussex—not much good and not much harm.

Then to a seat on North Parade and get into conversation with a jolly old boy, a farmer of 3,000 acres—very entertaining but perhaps a little purse-proud in his talk, which always so spoils a man. Your self-made man will always obtrude his money into his conversation. It is a pity because a man who in business has handled money all his life would never dream of letting it dominate his utterances.

At the same time all honour to the self-made man I give, because it represents work, application and self-denial, and it requires a soundly balanced character to get the happy medium between the spendthrift and the miser.

Lunch, and then to the Baths. The attendant conducts me to the deep bath: you enter the water by a flight of stone steps and are then just up to the chin in hot water. The attendant then hands you a hose attached to a hydrant and turns on the water. This rushes from the end of the hose at a great force, more than you can conveniently bear. However, by keeping it away a little distance you can get it to the force you think most advisable and it is then quite enjoyable. The attendant warned me not to let it strike over the heart, and he is quite right. I think it would be dangerous and very harmful.

After seven minutes, the attendant reappears and conducts me to my dressing-room and deftly envelops me in numerous hot towels (and they were really hot, I warrant you). I then lie on the sofa in this 'hot pack' for fifteen minutes; it is burning hot and I perspire profusely. The attendant then comes in to say the fifteen minutes is up, and hands me more dry towels, and between us we mop up the body. Then dress, and meet Millie in the cooling-room; we ought to go home and lie down, but instead we go to the Café Theobald and have tea.

Tuesday 15 June. Breakfast alone, then I go out to Windebank's timber-yard. They have a nice stock of sawn mahogany, but their prices are too steep.

53 3/8	Honduras	they ask		
52 1/2	do	2/- ft super		
3 3/4″	—	2/- — —		
1″	—	2/6 — —		
3″ + 4 3/4″		2/6 as 1″		
1″	figd Amn Oak	10″ + up	2/6	ft super
5/8″	Satin Walnut	13″ + up	1/2	— —
1″	do Prime	6″ + up	1/4	— —
3/4″	do do	6″ + up	1/3	— —
3/4″	Satin Walnut	12″ + up	1/4	ft super
1/2″	Medm Sat. Walt	4″ + up	8 1/2	— —

Get my hair cut at W.F. Napthen, 15 Westgate Street, and hurry back to our bedroom. Find Miss Ewbank busy massaging Mill—also find Gladys has sent Millie's dress and Cuthbert's watch by post. As the cap of the winding-stem of the watch is broken, I take it to a Mr Scrine, a working watchmaker at 7a York Street.

Mill and I to lunch, then book two seats on motor-coach for Castle Combe. Out by Bathford, and then all uphill with very fine views; gear-changing very noisy.

At Castle Combe, a most charming village, we have tea in the front garden of a cottage—quite a success. Then into an enormous church, where a woman pounces on us and volubly explains everything, and we get away one shilling poorer.

Off again in motor; weather very threatening. Some lightning, and we expect to get torrents of rain every minute, but we keep escaping it. We find roads running with water, so we only escape it by a matter of minutes, but reach home quite dry.

Dinner and then to a cinema, *Jane Goes A-Wooing* and *Lady Hamilton and Nelson,* quite good pictures. Late to bed as Millie darning combinations.

Wednesday 16 June. Take a tram to Glasshouse and then change into the motor-'bus to Frome—very pretty country. Get tea at an adjacent confectioner's, leaving our coats on the seats we have occupied on the 'bus, as it is market-day, and quite a lot of people—farmers and their wives or someone else's wives—anxious to get the 'bus.

Back and secure our seats; lot of passengers have to stand. One, a nice-looking middle-aged farmer, has been imbibing fairly freely; he is very talkative and everybody laughs, especially the women to whom he is very polite, and I fancy he was a d——l among the women. Anyway he had a wicked twinkle in his eye, and the women seemed to cotton to him a lot, especially when he addressed them in a half-whisper in their ears.

We stop at Norton St Philip, an ancient village. The George Inn is an old-world dream of a building, and I should like to have seen the interior.

Home at 6.45; dinner at seven. Then to Bath Theatre, a frowsy building that certainly wants redecorating and reupholstering: it looks as if money is not too plentiful in the theatre exchequer. The audience too is a queer-looking lot. *Mice and Men*—rather a queer show. Very provincial. During the play a most awful rainstorm came on, and the rain actually poured on the stage in bucketfuls, so I judge the roof is in as bad a state as the interior.

It certainly was rather weak to see a place that pretends to have been a great playhouse in the palmy days of Bath, when it was the fashionable rendezvous of all the bucks and fine ladies, fallen so low as to have such a leaky roof.

Thursday 17 June. For several days I have been rather dreading leaving Queenie here alone, so I at last make up my mind to stay another week with her. To Pump Room, then Mill and I catch the train to Bristol, and up to Clifton Down. Sit and gaze at the suspension bridge and the mud of the river far below. A young man is also sitting on our seat, an engineer from the north of England, on business in Bristol. Having finished for the day, he thought he would come up and explore the beauties of Clifton.

The weather suddenly took a decided turn for the worse; lightning flashed and thunder pealed, and we three squeezed up under the shelter of the tree and waited. After 1¾ hours we decided that our afternoon was entirely spoiled, and braving a very heavy rain we hurriedly walked to the cliff railway station, descended and got into a tram.

Quite comfortable when we started, but at a halt the car was invaded by an enormous crowd of male and female factory-hands of a very loud and boisterous type who blanketed us and dominated the whole car and seemed to glory in making the original passengers as uncomfortable as possible. The car soon began to be rather smelly.

Getting off the tram, we go along Burlington Road and look at no. 21, and Millie expatiates on the days of her youth when on holiday at Bristol, when she and Fanny appear to have been irresponsible young ladies hiring tricycles and eating ices and generally setting the village on fire and eluding the rather narrow surveillance of their elders.

Leaving Burlington Road we get on the top of a tram and have a nice ride to Westbury-on-Trym, where we stop near a war memorial in course of erection.

Friday 18 June. Great joy as we both go down and breakfast together—I hate breakfasting alone. Up to bedroom, and Mill has a washing bout of gloves and stockings in Lux (wonderful stuff, Lux).

Letters—one from Jack Port *re* his Horstmann car. I go to James Street workshops, on premises built for a skating-rink; I get a catalogue of their motor-cars, and elicit that they could not give me delivery of one under four months.

Wend my way back to Pump Room and wait for Mill to come out from her bath. Then to Norton St Philip Dairy in Bridge Street and send off six clotted creams to the following, viz. Messrs Peerless, 12 St James's Avenue, T.G., B.D.G., Uncle Sam, J.M.P., C.M.P. We indulge in two strawberry ices, very prime, and buy a quarter of a pound of beautiful butter for tenpence.

Then luncheon, and get a 'bus to Lansdown and the battlefields, and gaze at a monument to Sir Somebody and Battle of Lansdown, Cromwell etc., 1643 or 1645.

Saturday 19 June. Walk up Lyncombe Hill to Beechen Cliff: a really superb view. Back, and Millie gets up for lunch.

Then to the Old Tea Parlour, Margaret Buildings off Brock Street—most quaint place and full of antiques. The proprietress is a kind of faded Dresden china gentlewoman, probably a duchess in disguise; most excellent home-made bread. Unfortunately it is saccharine instead of sugar for our tea, and we have forgotten to bring our little tin box of sugar which in these troublous times we cart about with us.

Dinner in due course, and then sit at window and watch the people and the troubles of a man, evidently a beanfeaster, much the worse for drink.

Sunday 20 June. At twelve o'clock in pouring rain to Pump Room and have three glasses each of water, which shows that we are industrious persevering people who do honestly try to do our duty by these medicated waters.

Out and take tram and motor-'bus for Radstock and back. The 'bus is a ramshackle bone-shaker.

Monday 21 June. Oh dear! It is the longest day. Directly you have reached the longest day, it does seem so soon that the days take in, and I do love the light evenings under Summer Time.

Char-à-banc ride to Cheddar via Mendip. We drew up at Gough's Cave and soon were exploring it—a splendid cave on which a large amount of money has been spent to make it easy for visitors. The pathways are well laid and the electric-lighting arrangements admirable, and I have no doubt that, provided one was prepared to lay out the capital, its ramifications could be greatly extended and further beauties of the underworld revealed. Gough will probably rest on his laurels, but I always feel in these places that if they belonged to me I should never rest. I have the same feeling about excavation work on buried cities in Egypt, Palestine, Italy etc.

On again via Radstock and notice quite a number of coal-mines—I had no idea that there were coal-mines so far south.

We reach the Guildhall at nine o'clock after a splendid drive. Upstairs to no. 17. A man tries to open our door; I tell Mill I suppose she forgot to tell him I was staying on.

Tuesday 22 June. I walk to Horstmann's Motor Works and see works manager *re* Jack Port's gear-box. It is sad and sorry work to get a move on motor mechanics.

Wend my way to the Royal Swimming Baths and have a swim—very nice indeed but the water is too warm, and rather enervating in its effects on the system—not that bracing tonic that one gets from sea-bathing. Many people say they cannot stand sea-bathing, it makes them tired and languid. If these would undress quickly, run into the sea, swim out fifty yards, turn round, come straight ashore, rub down briskly and walk home, I think they would have a different tale to tell.

Lunch 1.15. Consternation as the chambermaid on our landing left this morning and the waitress leaves after lunch. I suppose it is a sign of the times—all servants or employees seem to be restless these days, and it is difficult to fit them out for long.

After lunch we walk to Dr Cave's. Millie is put on the couch and has her legs twisted about. She is to do leg exercises every morning and walk a mile on the flat every day. When she explains to Dr Cave that she has what she calls 'fidgets', he gives us a prescription for some tablets.

To Victoria Park and listen to the strains of the Argyll and Sutherland

Highlanders Band. Then home to dinner. They have dug up a new waiter from somewhere. He appears willing, but everything is painfully fresh to him.

Wednesday 23 June. Millie breakfasts in bed. I down to breakfast—our butter (which we keep on our table) gone, and I have to make the new waiter find it. I don't think he will lose it again. Miss Ewbank arrives to massage at nine o'clock.

Leave the sleeping-tablet prescription at Tylee and Cooper's, 7 Bridge Street, then to Messrs S. & A. Fuller's, Kingsmead Street, to see the Hillman motor-car, but they have not got one in stock. They show us several second-hand cars: 9.5 1913 Standard £350, £65 extra for a dynamo etc.; 12 Rover four-seater, electric lamps, dynamo etc., £635, self-starter £20 extra. The cheapest thing for the money seemed to be a new Ford Sedan, £435.

To Grand Pump Room and book a bath for Friday, as on Thursday they are going to close everything for the staff outing. Then on a char-à-banc to Frenchay Tea Gardens, Cleve. Pass a very large place, Carson's Chocolate Works; they appear to employ a large number of hands.

On our homeward journey the motor seemed in a dreadful state; the gear-changing was awful. Home and telephone to Beattie. It is arranged that she will come over in the car and fetch us tomorrow at twelve o'clock. Millie takes bromide and aspirin tablet and gets a good night.

Thursday 24 June. To Brislington, Beattie driving very nicely. She does the hostess charmingly. At 1.30 we go in to dinner; then Margery and Freda, looking very fresh, start playing tennis. Alan changes into flannels and rather surprises me by his activity, being rather a heavy weight for such a strenuous game. He was very nimble, but it made him perspire pretty freely.

Friday 25 June. Mill gets up at 11.15; out and deposit her at baths for her wet douche. I go to the tepid swimming-baths and have a swim for tenpence, then drink the waters while waiting for Millie to appear, which she does feeling very limp indeed.

We make our way to Fortt's and have a real good tea, and Mill bucks up a bit. Dinner, then upstairs to get on with the most unpleasant holiday task, packing. Revive our flagging energies with our usual Scotch-and-sodas.

Saturday 26 June. Take Mill to deep bath and wet douche at 10.30, then we go and have two ices at Theobald's.

Leave Bath at 2.35, late; arrive Paddington; taxi to Victoria. Engine dies out on the way but the driver gets it running again. At Victoria catch the 5.35 to Brighton, and charter a horse-cab home.

So now it's all over, and we have to see what Bath treatment has done for our little lady. We have true reasons for thankfulness anyway, that we have gone out and returned without a mishap of any kind, and for this guidance and protection we desire to be deeply grateful.

Goodbye.

Henry H Peerless

Epilogue

Towards the end of 1920, shortly after returning home from Bath, Henry Peerless bought a two-seater Bean motor-car and at the age of 53 learnt to drive for the first time. It may have been this, as much as Millie's increasing disability, which put an end to his almost unbroken thirty-year tradition of escaping each year for 'a brief jolly change'.

Together with his wife, Henry Peerless spent the next few years sedately making day-trips around the Brighton area, and spending occasional weekends in nearby Fittleworth where Tom Garrett owned a holiday bungalow. He may sometimes have ventured further afield, but no longer did he feel that his journeys were worth recording in a diary. Travel had ceased to be an adventure.

Henry Peerless remained active until his early sixties, when he suffered a stroke; and on 8 September 1930 he died at his home in St James's Avenue, Brighton. His coffin was taken in a horse-drawn hearse to the Extra-Mural Cemetery, where his wife Millie was laid to rest beside him eight years later.

In his will, Henry Peerless left his mahogany bureau bookcase and its contents—including his diaries—to his eldest surviving son, Reginald. After Reginald's death in February 1972, the diaries were passed on to his only son, James. However, when James Peerless fell incurably ill, his wife was quick to seek a divorce and to sell off anything which might have some kind of market value. The 27 volumes of Henry Peerless's diary eventually found their way to a dealer in Cheltenham, from whom I bought them—sight unseen—in November 1998.

Before receiving the cardboard box containing the diaries, I had dismissed any thought that they might be worth publishing: but within minutes of opening the box I had changed my mind. Within an hour I had decided to bring them to publication.

Over the next four years, while I worked on the manuscripts, I travelled to many of the places mentioned in the diaries and contacted dozens of local archivists and historians; and by a series of coincidences it was one of these correspondents—Christopher Whittick of the East Sussex Record Office—who managed to put me in touch with the last surviving members of the family who still remembered Henry Peerless. Both Robert Peerless and Mrs Marjorie Fox had known of the existence of the diaries, but believed that they had been lost or destroyed. I am glad to have been able to prove them wrong; and it is to them that I dedicate this book.

EDWARD FENTON
March 2003

Notes

1891

p.1, line 2, 'a fierce fusillade of old boots . . .' Henry Heathfield Peerless and Amelia Sarah Garrett had got married at Brighton's oldest building, St Nicholas's Church, earlier that day. The ancient custom of throwing boots at newly-weds was especially popular in the late 19th century; an 1871 engraving in the *Illustrated London News* shows Princess Louise and her new husband the Marquess of Lorne being showered with slippers as they drove from St George's Chapel, Windsor.

p.2, lines 33–4, 'cut all over with names of visitors . . .' The Mannerings were friends of the Peerless family; see also pp.40–1.

p.2, lines 37–8, 'a grocer's establishment named Garrett . . .' Garrett was Millie's maiden name (see above).

p.3, line 22, 'our gigantic national shipbuilding-yard . . .' Shipbuilding was one of Britain's most important industries at this time, and in the early 1890s the tonnage of new ships reached record levels. (See R.C.K. Ensor, *England 1870–1914*, p.278.)

p.3, lines 24–5, 'the Calliope *man-of-war . . . was exceedingly notorious . . .'* HHP clearly means 'notable'. On 6 April 1889, *The Times* published the text of a telegram from Sydney, New South Wales: 'HMS *Calliope* arrived here from Apia, Samoa, bringing full confirmation of a terrible and destructive hurricane last month, and particulars of her own wonderful escape from the fate which befell the American and German men-of-war. . . . She did not . . . lose a single man [owing to the] splendid manner in which she was navigated.'

1892

p.4, line 10, 'our dear old home . . .' The Peerlesses were then living at 20 Hanover Crescent, Brighton.

p.4, line 15, 'I prefer short-coats myself . . .' Short-coating was an important event in a child's life: the occasion when the long robes of babyhood were replaced by ankle-length skirted garments, which were easier to crawl around in.

p.4, lines 23–4, 'I purchased dear old Ally Sloper's Half Holiday *and* Sala's Journal *. . .'* These were two middlebrow magazines of the day. The former was named after the world's first comic-strip character. The founder of the latter, George Augustus Sala (1828–95), was one of the most famous and prolific journalists of the Victorian era: but his *Journal* was a disastrous failure, collapsing with huge losses in 1894, after just two years of publication. Sala died in Brighton shortly afterwards.

p.5, line 3, 'Mill is writing to Fanny . . .' Fanny Garrett (née Wise) was a childhood friend of Millie's, and had married Millie's brother Tom in 1889.

p.5, line 14, 'John—where's Beageley? . . .' John Moon Peerless (1874–1948), HHP's younger brother, worked with him at the timber-yard at 47 Middle Street, Brighton; Beageley and Ned were employees. HHP is reflecting on their early-evening routine at work.

p.5, line 16, 'I must write to Kate . . .' Kate Elizabeth Peerless (1875–1959) was one of HHP's younger sisters. She later married F.O. Miller, a photographer at Haywards Heath.

p.5, lines 22–3, 'I have been writing several letters . . .' 'The Governor' was HHP's father, David John Peerless (1835–1903). Charley Feldwicke was married to HHP's older sister Minnie (1861–1914); he was the father of HHP's niece Hilda (see p.7), and had been best man at his wedding. He owned a furniture shop in West Street, Brighton.

p.5, line 37, 'dream I am living in Duke Street . . .' HHP had grown up at 32 Duke Street, Brighton; Dukes Passage is a narrow alleyway running alongside his former home.

p.7, line 10, 'we stop and see Sanger's Circus . . .' George Sanger came from a family of showmen; the kangaroos and lions had been used in his most ambitious show, on the theme of *Gulliver's Travels.* Although Sanger was unusual for preferring to train his animals by kindness rather than intimidation, and was also known to be generous to his workers, in 1911 he was shot dead at his home in Finchley by one of his employees.

p.7, lines 19–20, 'we in Brighton are so used to seeing the firemen . . .' The headquarters of the Brighton Volunteer Fire Brigade were just a few doors away from HHP's childhood home in Duke Street.

p.7, line 28, 'Poor sewage-farm, it must be all burnt down . . .' 'A stack fire occurred at North Sewage Farm on Sunday morning last, resulting in almost total destruction of a large stack of about sixty tons. . . . Mr Fairburn, the bailiff, at once despatched a messenger to the police station, the officer in charge immediately ringing up the Volunteers, who soon repaired to the scene of the conflagration. The constable did not call the Borough Brigade as soon as he might have done, because the fire was outside the borough radius . . . just as though they would let the burgesses' property burn without endeavouring to put it out.' (*Tunbridge Wells Advertiser*, 19 August 1892.)

1893

p.8, line 29, 'through the Bois de Boulogne we bowl along . . .' Edouard Manet's niece Julie also described the Bois de Boulogne in her diary that summer. On 9 September 1893, she wrote: 'We came back through the Bois where there were newly-weds everywhere, which was most amusing. All these rather ordinary people seemed to be thrilled to bits to be in a carriage in the Bois de Boulogne for the one and only time in their lives.' (Rosalind de Boland Roberts and Jane Roberts, eds, *Growing up with the Impressionists: The Diary of Julie Manet*; London: Sotheby's Publications, 1987, p.38.)

p.9, line 11, 'mutilated by the Communists . . .' i.e. members of the Paris Commune, who had briefly taken control of the city following France's humiliating defeat in the Franco-Prussian War of 1870–71.

p.9, lines 28–9, 'a looking-glass where you cannot see your own eyes . . .' An optical illusion created by the joining together of separate mirrors at eye-level.

p.9, line 34, 'to La Morgue . . .' The Morgue was situated on the Ile de la Cité, just behind the cathedral of Notre-Dame, and dead bodies which had been found either in the Seine or on the streets of Paris were taken there for identification. The corpses were placed under glass, on sloping slabs of marble, and members of the public were allowed in to look for missing friends or relatives: although many, like the Peerlesses and the great actress Sarah Bernhardt, came simply to gawp. About 300 corpses were exposed in the Morgue every year, and those which remained unclaimed after three days were buried at public expense.

p.9, line 37, 'succeed in getting numéros *for an omnibus . . .'* A *numéro d'ordre*, a numbered queue ticket, established one's position in the bus queue.

p.11, lines 12–13, 'One subject called "Le nid" *attracts our attention . . .'* This sculpture by Aristide Croisy—dominated by a huge marble armchair on which the children are sitting—had first been exhibited in 1882. (*Musée National du Luxembourg: Catalogue Illustré*, p.187; Paris: Librairies–Imprimeries Réunies, 1890.)

p.11, lines 17–18, 'some to my mind were simply daubs . . .' The Palais Luxembourg contained the work of modern artists, but not exclusively of living ones. The 'daubs' seen by HHP in 1893 would have included paintings by Courbet, Tissot, Millet, Sargent, Burne-Jones and the diarist Marie Bashkirtseff, as well as James McNeill Whistler's famous portrait of his mother. (See Léonce Bénédite, ed., *Musée National du Luxembourg: Peintures, Sculptures, Dessins.* Paris: Librairies–Imprimeries Réunies, 1893.)

p.12, line 37, 'At Brighton we descry Mr T. Garrett . . .' Thomas Garrett (1839–1914) was Millie's father.

1894

p.13, lines 18–19, 'the street where our house is situated . . .' The entry for 9 August identifies this as St Ann's Road, at the foot of the hills; see also pp.16 (*illus.*) and 179.

p.15, line 7, 'merciful man is merciful to his beast . . .' cf. Proverbs 12:10, 'A righteous man regardeth the life of his beast.'

p.16, line 23, 'imbued with a Mark Tapley spirit . . .' Mark Tapley, a character in *Martin Chuzzlewit*, welcomed physical discomfort as it enabled him 'to take credit in being jolly'.

p.16, line 28, 'The fifth of November at Lewes . . .' For Lewes and its bonfire-night rituals, still noted for their elaborateness and mock anti-Catholic ferocity, see Rob Stepney, 'Flaming good night out'; *Observer*, 31 Oct. 1999.

p.17, line 23, 'passed the kitchen-garden of the late Jenny Lind . . .' The great soprano Jenny Lind (1820–1887) had bought Wynds Point on the Malvern Hills in 1883. (See also Roger Hall-Jones, *Jenny Lind, 'The Swedish Nightingale', at Malvern*; Malvern: First Paige, 1992.)

p.17, line 25, 'Tom and Fanny are here . . .' Tom and Fanny Garrett were Millie's brother and sister-in-law; Dottie Wise (see line 32) was Fanny's sister.

p.18, line 19, 'The verger starts us . . .' It is tempting to speculate that this was the same verger who so irritated the author and schoolmaster A.C. Benson in Gloucester Cathedral on 18 April 1904. 'We went round with an old, very pompous and tiresome verger, who had got his lesson by heart, and could answer no questions outside of it,' Benson wrote. 'I don't want to be taken round and *lectured.* I want to wander about, ask questions, and be just shown interesting things if I fail to notice them for myself.' (David Newsome, ed., *Edwardian Excursions: From the Diaries of A.C. Benson, 1898–1904*, p.134.)

p.19, lines 7–8, 'Cuthbert . . . has been smoking with me . . .' It is unclear whether Cuthbert was actually smoking tobacco in his pipe. In the 17th and 18th centuries, many people had regarded smoking as harmless and even beneficial for even the youngest children; the diarist Nicholas Blundell recorded seeing 'a boy not four years of age, smoake a good part of a Pipe of Tobacco . . . and when I asked him whether he would rather have a Pipe of Tobacco or a butter Kake he answered Tobacco' (see Margaret Blundell, *A Lancashire Squire: The Life of Nicholas Blundell of Crosby, 1669–1737*; Charlbury: Day Books, 2002). By Victorian times, attitudes were certainly changing; but when the Student Christian Movement spoke out against juvenile smoking at the turn of the 20th century, it stated that the principal danger came from cheap Virginian cigarettes, and recommended that boys should smoke pipes instead. (See Matthew Hilton, *Smoking in British Popular Culture 1800–2000*; Manchester: Manchester University Press, 2000, p.165.)

p.19, lines 10–11, 'Uncle Heathfield at Lewes . . .' HHP's uncle Thomas Heathfield lived at 7 Lansdowne Place, Lewes.

p.19, line 23, 'At Reading we passed Huntley & Palmer's large biscuit factory . . .' Referring to the 'folly' of those towns which had refused to let the Great Western Railway build stations there, the diarist H.C. Beeching wrote that 'Reading had more foresight, and in the half-century has more than trebled its population.' But he admitted that the railway could be a mixed blessing, and described Reading as 'like a strong ass crouching down between the two burdens of Sutton's seeds and Palmer's biscuits.' (*Pages From a Private Diary*; London: Smith, Elder, 1898, pp.52–3.)

1895

p.20, lines 12–13, 'deposited little Cuthbert at Queen Square . . .' This was the Brighton home of HHP's parents-in-law, Thomas and Harriett Garrett.

p.20, line 13, 'in Ellen Freeman's charge . . .' Ellen Freeman was the daughter of Martha and Frederick ('Uncle Fred') Freeman, of Goose Green, Warnham, and the sister of Alice and Fred. The Freemans remained great friends of the Peerless family; HHP's daughter Gladys was to strike up a close friendship with Fred Freeman, and Alice Freeman was one of the witnesses of HHP's last will and testament in 1929.

p.21, line 13, 'Next come . . . cabinet puddings . . .' A dessert made with fruit and custard on a base of sponge or bread.

p.22, line 1, 'JOHN BATCHELOR, THE FRIEND OF FREEDOM . . .' John Batchelor (1820–1883) was a local Liberal politician who broke the long-established Tory grip on Cardiff City Council. The decision to erect a statue to him was extremely controversial, and in 1886 the *Western Mail* published an alternative inscription, calling Batchelor 'A Traitor to the Crown' and 'A Panderer to the Multitude'. In a test case, the paper's editor was tried for libel and acquitted by Mr Justice Stephen, who made the landmark judgment that the laws of libel do not apply to the dead. (Information supplied by Paul Keenor, Local Studies Department, Cardiff Central Library.)

p.24, lines 39–40, 'that's Mr Wise's shop, and there's Alan . . .' Alan Wise was Fanny Garrett's brother; Annie, Dottie and Beattie were her sisters.

p.25, line 19, 'Time was made for slaves . . .' See J.B. Buckstone's 'Billy Taylor' (1830).

p.25, line 42, 'anything . . . to continentalise our English Sunday . . .' With the decline in strict Sunday observance in the late 19th century, efforts were made by the

National Sunday League to provide 'rational recreation' for working people on their day of leisure, for instance by encouraging provincial museums and art galleries to open on Sundays. It was not until 1896, however, that Parliament allowed Central London's museums and galleries to admit the public on Sunday afternoons. (See Pamela Horn, *Pleasures and Pastimes in Victorian Britain*, p.225.)

p.26, line 8, 'dropped in the Oak . . .' Now the Sussex Oak, Church Street, Horsham.

p.26, lines 30–1, 'our carriage, which was a saloon carriage . . .' Saloon carriages contained several rows of seats along a central aisle (as in most modern trains); they were an American innovation, and had slowly begun to replace the smaller compartments which mimicked stagecoach-style accommodation.

p.26, lines 34–5, 'We draw up at our door . . .' The Peerlesses had recently moved into a new red-brick maisonette, 12 St James's Avenue, Brighton, on the slum-clearance site of Little St James's Street about half a mile from the Middle Street timber-yard. Little St James's Street was the first of Brighton's slum areas to be demolished, in 1889, under the Housing of the Working Classes Acts. (See E.W. Gilbert, *Brighton: Old Ocean's Bauble*, p.157.)

p.26, line 35, 'Lily waiting to receive us . . .' Lilian Emily Peerless (1877–1958) was HHP's youngest sister.

p.26, lines 36–8, 'a terrific explosion . . . at a Foresters' Fête . . .' 'An explosion of fireworks occurred last night at a fête in Brighton, in connexion with the Foresters' meeting, and 16 persons were seriously injured. . . . Three mortars were on the ground, and two of them had been used; when the operators tried the third, which weighed one hundredweight, it burst. The pieces flew among the crowd, and the greatest consternation was created.' (*The Times*, 6 August 1895.)

1896

p.27, lines 15–16, 'our train runs right through the streets like a tram . . .' 'This was the only place in Britain where one could come across a main line train creeping along streets crowded with cars and pedestrians, a scene that disappeared in the late 1980s.' (John Hadrill, *Rails to the Sea*, p.63.)

p.27, line 17, 'a magnificent steamer named the Ibex *. . .'* Another diarist who was impressed by the *Ibex* was Beatrix Potter (1866–1943). 'The Jersey packet boats are fine vessels,' she noted on 9 April 1895. 'The *Ibex* very large, others called *Lynx* and *Antelope*.' (Leslie Winder, ed., *The Journals of Beatrix Potter, 1881–1897*; London: Penguin, 1989, p.374.)

p.29, line 6, 'Tobacco is free . . .' i.e. duty-free.

p.29, lines 21–2, 'some more of Mrs Langtry's cousins . . .' The actress Lily Langtry (1853–1925), one of the most celebrated beauties of her day and mistress of the future Edward VII, was the daughter of the dean of Jersey.

p.30, line 36, 'King of the Islands . . .' Philippe Pinel (1820–96) had taken up residence in a hut on La Maître Ile in 1848, and had claimed his title in 1863. He prided himself on having only non-essential possessions, including three Holy Bibles. (See F.L.M. Corbet, *A Biographical Dictionary of Jersey*, vol. 2; Jersey: Société Jersiaise, 1998.)

p.33, lines 2–3, 'the washerwomen using so much Reckitt's Blue . . .' Blueing agents such as Reckitt's were designed to improve the appearance of fabrics which had become yellow through over-washing with soap.

p.33, lines 29–30, 'the "Old Hundredth" was the only sacred tune they had . . .' A setting of the 100th Psalm. Strict sabbatarians objected to the playing of anything but sacred music on a Sunday.

1897

p.35, lines 5–6, 'what a prominent part the bicycle plays in modern life . . .' The cycling craze—sparked off by the invention of the chain-driven bicycle and the pneumatic tyre—reached its peak in the mid-1890s. The words of Lord Balfour of Burleigh echo HHP's opinion to a remarkable degree: 'There has not been a more civilizing invention in the memory of the present generation,' he wrote—'open to all classes, enjoyed by both sexes and by all ages.' (See J.A.R. Pimlott, *The Englishman's Holiday: A Social History*, p.166.) However, the ascendancy of the motor-car had become inevitable in 1896 with the repeal of the Road Locomotion Act, which had stipulated that any form of mechanical road vehicle must be accompanied by three attendants, and could not be driven faster than 4 mph.

p.35, lines 10–11, 'through Horsham, and at the Dog and Bacon . . .' This pub had once been run by another diarist, Henry Michell, who sold it because (as he wrote) 'the decrease of trade consequent on the completion of the London & Brighton Railway greatly diminished the business prospects for the future.' (See Kenneth Neale, ed., *Victorian Horsham: The Diary of Henry Michell 1809–1874*; Chichester: Phillimore, 1975, p.42.)

p.36, line 39, 'We row along to Boulter's Lock . . .' The lock was commemorated in this year, 1897, by Edward John Gregory, whose painting 'Boulter's Lock, Sunday afternoon' is now in the Walker Art Gallery, Liverpool. The art historian E.D.H. Johnson has described it as 'one of the most animated of all scenes of Londoners in a holiday mood. . . . In this period when boating excursions along the Thames were all the rage, it has been said that the traffic through Boulter's Lock on a fine Sunday might exceed 800 pleasure craft, and as many as seventy steam launches.' (*Paintings of the British Social Scene from Hogarth to Sickert*; London: Weidenfeld & Nicolson, 1986, p.210.)

p.37, line 26, 'bang went saxpence . . .' From *Punch*, 1868, volume 44, p.235.

p.38, line 2, 'the arrival of the King of Siam . . .' King Chulalongkorn (1853–1910)—who is generally credited with bringing his country into the modern world—was beginning a two-month tour of Britain. He was the son of King Mongkut, immortalised in the film *The King and I*, which was based on Anna Leonowens's book *The English Governess at the Siamese Court*. King Chulalongkorn remained a close friend of Anna Leonowens's son Louis who, like HHP, was a timber-merchant.

p.38, line 9, 'a Joe Millery kind of individual . . .' Joseph Miller (1684–1738) was an actor whose reputation as a humorist was enhanced after his death by an apocryphal publication entitled *Joe Miller's Jests*.

p.38, lines 17–18, 'Taplow Court, Mr Grenfell's residence . . .' William Grenfell (later Lord Desborough) lived at Taplow Court with his wife Ettie, one of the great hostesses of the era.

p.38, lines 41–2, 'find a chemist's shop to buy some Goldbeater's skin . . .' 'A prepared animal membrane . . . sometimes used to cover wounds' (*OED*).

p.39, lines 24–5, 'to . . . Sir Henry Harben's, to see a cricket match . . .' Henry Harben (1823–1911) had made his fortune by building up the Prudential Mutual

Assurance Association into a huge concern. A great cricket enthusiast, the ground he designed at Warnham Lodge was said to be one of the finest in the county.

1898

p.40, lines 2–3, 'Baby is between seven and eight months old . . .' Reginald Leslie Peerless had been born at 12 St James's Avenue, Brighton, on 5 December 1897.

p.40, lines 5–6, 'Tom, Burt and I should go to Norwich . . .' Burt Dale Garrett (1866–1947), like Tom, was an older brother of Millie's.

p.40, line 26, 'ride off to Mannering's shop . . .' Walter Mannering was married to HHP's sister Emma Cecilia ('Cis'). After running a men's outfitters on West Street, Brighton, he moved to Norwich, and became a rep for the trade journal *Drapers' Record*.

p.45, line 3, 'a large circular bicycle-riding railway . . .' Also known as the Velocipede, this was a fairground ride consisting of half a dozen bicycles attached to a circular track; its designer, Frederick Savage, had been born in Norfolk, the son of a petty criminal who was later transported to Tasmania. (See Adam Hart-Davis, *What the Victorians Did for Us*, p.114.)

p.46, line 19, 'Then we tried ringing the bull . . .' 'Of all English pub games, ringing the bull probably has the longest history of continuous play in this country' (Timothy Finn, *Pub Games of England*; Cambridge: Oleander Press, 1981, pp.54–6). In the original game a bull's nose-ring—attached to the ceiling by a halter—was swung towards a bull's horn mounted on the wall several feet away.

p.47, lines 7–8, 'In the cloisters at Trinity is a most curious echo . . .' 'The cloister with the echo is almost certainly the north side of Nevile's Court in Trinity. The door with the knocker is at the east end and is the entrance to the Parlour Passage, and the west end meets the cloister that runs under the Wren Library. To this day, tourist guides tell the story that Newton used this cloister to measure the speed of sound, and clap or stamp their feet to show the effect (presumably to the annoyance of the residents).' (Information supplied by Jonathan Smith, Manuscript Cataloguer, Trinity College Library.)

p.47, lines 31–2, 'he once rode . . . 135 miles in one day . . .' This is far in excess of the figures given by R.C.K. Ensor (*England 1870–1914*, p.166): 'The extreme limit for a day's visit by horseback was about fifteen miles [i.e. a total of thirty miles, there and back]; the usual one, about six. The bicycle doubled each of these.'

p.48, lines 21–2, 'I used to go to school with you at Pyemont's . . .' George William Pyemont's Academy was at 21 Middle Street, Brighton, just a few doors away from HHP's timber-yard (no. 47) and his birthplace (no. 33; see Introduction). A card pasted into the diary identifies HHP's former schoolmate as Thomas C. Jones, Family Baker, of South Street, Dorking ('Cyclists & parties catered for').

1899

p.50, lines 24–5, 'In Sackville Street is a high monument to Nelson . . .' The monument was blown up by the IRA in 1966, on the fiftieth anniversary of the Easter Rising; Nelson's head is now in Dublin's Civic Museum.

p.52, line 23, 'Our stopping place, Golding's . . .' 18 Patrick's Place, Cork.

p.52, lines 25–6, 'we . . . take train to Queenstown . . .' The Cove of Cork had been renamed Queenstown to commemorate the visit of Queen Victoria in 1849; in 1922 it took on the Irish name of Cóbh.

p.53, line 28, 'A man's a fool . . .' See Calderon's *Adventures of Five Hours* (v.3.483, trans. S. Tuke: 'He is a fool who thinks by force or skill/To turn the current of a woman's will'), and the anonymous inscription on a pillar in Canterbury, as reported by the *London Examiner* of 31 May 1829 ('Where is the man who has the power and skill/To stem the torrent of a woman's will?/For if she will, she will, you may depend on't;/And if she won't, she won't; so there's an end on't').

p.54, lines 8–9, 'the lighted candles . . . seem distasteful to me . . .' HHP's distaste for high church ritual and its trappings is a recurring theme in the diaries. His own church—St Mary's, on St James's Street—seems to have been austere even by Anglican standards. It left a lasting impression on the sculptor Eric Gill, who visited it in the 1890s and described it as 'arid, bare, and gaunt. . . . It was distasteful, but impressive.' (See his *Autobiography*; London: Jonathan Cape, 1940, pp.67–8.)

p.54, lines 25–6, 'where . . . Lord Frederick Cavendish and Mr Burke were cruelly murdered . . .' Lord Frederick Cavendish, Chief Secretary to the Viceroy of Ireland, and his deputy Thomas Burke had been murdered by extremist Fenians on 6 May 1882. The British government responded by bringing in a new Coercion Act.

p.54, line 37, 'Tom goes to the post office . . .' The Sackville Street Post Office was later to become famous as the centre of the Easter Rising of 1916, when it was seized by Irish Republicans. It was destroyed during the ensuing fighting.

p.54, line 38, 'a fishing-rod for Sidney . . .' Tom and Fanny Garrett's son Sidney Colston Garrett had been born on 13 November 1889.

p.55, line 27, 'his views on privileged railway cabs . . .' 'The privilege' was the name given to the railway companies' right to control which cabs might ply for hire from the railway stations; since the stations were private property, cab proprietors had to pay a weekly fee for this privilege.

1900

p.57, line 24, 'the terrible catastrophe at Hoboken . . .' The fire had broken out the previous Saturday afternoon, killing an estimated 200 people. According to *The Times*, 'Saturday was visiting day on the vessels and the docks were crowded with men, women and children anxious to see the officers and crews.' When the fire was at its height, 'the spectacle was magnificent and hundreds of thousands of spectators from New York gathered to watch.'

p.58, lines 7–8, 'by Miss Braddon the novelist's house . . .' The prolific 'sensation' novelist Mary Braddon (1837–1915) had a house at Annesley Bank, though she spent most of her time at her home in Richmond, Surrey.

p.59, lines 2–3, 'Oh come out in the garden . . .' cf. the Song of Solomon 2:12 and 3:16.

p.60, line 13, 'Many gypsies are to be met here . . .' The gypsy settlement near Fordingbridge was at Godshill; for a list of other settlements, see H.E.J. Gibbins, *Gypsies of the New Forest and Other Tales*; Bournemouth: W. Mate, 1909.

p.60, lines 27–8, 'an old native called . . . "Brusher Mills" . . .' Harry Mills (1840–1905) was the New Forest's last professional viper-catcher; according to his gravestone in Brockenhurst churchyard, 'His pursuit and the primitive way in which he lived caused him to be an object of interest to many.' The Railway Inn, Brockenhurst, was renamed the Snakecatcher after him. (See David Stagg, *Snake Catchers of the New Forest*, 2nd edn; Ashhurst: New Forest Association, 1989.)

p.60, lines 35–6, 'like Captain Cuttle's watch . . .' See *Dombey and Son*, Chapter 48.

1901

p.61, line 6, 'the ozonic air . . .' Cleansing and curative powers were ascribed to the toxic gas ozone, which was wrongly believed to be what gives the seaside its distinctive smell. However, the Peerless and Garrett families are themselves a testament to the health benefits of living by the sea, as the family tree on p.xv shows. If one discounts the six who died in childhood and the three who were killed in the Great War, one is left with 42 people, of whom 15 lived into their 80s, and five into their 90s.

p.61, lines 11–12, 'we fall to talking of the fire . . .' Captain Crouch was a fireman, whose heroism at the Royal Sea View Hotel on Bath Place was reported by the *Sussex Coast Mercury* of 25 May 1901: 'On Captain Crouch asking whether anyone was still in the building, he was informed that two visitors were still in their room. He at once went up the fire escape, and entering the building found the staircase alight. . . . Groping his way to the bedroom he brought out Mr and Mrs Roscher. The former . . . got down the escape. The lady could not face this ordeal, whereupon Captain Crouch, muffling his mouth and instructing the lady to do the same, got her on his back and succeeded in getting her to the ground floor.'

p.62, line 5, 'mixed bathing is quite decent and moral . . .' It was only in July 1901 that mixed bathing (from bathing-machines only) had been sanctioned in Brighton, after resorts such as Paignton had introduced it in the late 1890s.

p.62, line 37, 'Burt and Maude's twins are still very ill . . .' Walter and Edgar Thomas Garrett had been born earlier in the year. Although Walter subsequently recovered, Edgar died at the age of six months.

p.62, line 38, 'Empress Frederick is dead . . .' The eldest child of Victoria and Albert, and the mother of Kaiser Wilhelm II, had died at Friedrichshof on 5 August.

p.63, lines 39–40, 'Vanderbilt's . . . supposed to be the most costly yacht in the world . . .' William Kissam Vanderbilt (1849–1920), grandson of the multi-millionaire Cornelius Vanderbilt, used his inherited wealth to acquire a series of yachts. It was on one of these, in 1893, that he quarrelled so bitterly with his wife Alva (who had given her name to his first yacht) that the couple sued for divorce.

p.65, line 40, 'toasting to "our next holiday" . . .' The following August HHP went on holiday to Lyndhurst with Millie and the children (Cuthbert, Reginald and baby Gladys, who was born on 12 December 1901) and their neighbours Mr and Mrs Arty Lindo. Unfortunately the diary for 1902 is missing.

1903

p.66, line 9, 'our "Jehu" essays to pass . . .' See II. Kings 9:20, 'The driving is like the driving of Jehu the son of Nimshi; for he driveth furiously.'

p.70, line 8, 'God made the country . . .' HHP is slightly misquoting William Cowper.

p.70, line 13, 'the Lucania*, an immense steamer . . .'* The *Lucania* was a Cunard liner which, with its sister ship the *Campania*, had held the Atlantic 'Blue Riband' until surpassed by the German steamer *Kaiser Wilhelm der Grosse* in 1897.

1904

p.75, lines 3–4, 'his dusky Highness the Alake of——. . .' The *Weekly Scotsman* of 25 June 1904 carried the headline: 'The Alake of Abeokuta in Scotland: A Gross Insult at Aberdeen.' 'The Alake during his visit to Marischal College on Friday was grossly insulted. . . . One impertinent young man deprived the Alake of his headgear, substituting his own ordinary straw hat which, judging by its size, had hitherto covered but a very tiny brain. . . . This gave great offence to the chief, who comes from a race distinguished for its outstanding courtesy. The Alake gave pretty free expression to his feelings of resentment.'

Fortunately the Alake was better treated in Edinburgh; on Saturday evening he was welcomed by a crowd of about two thousand, and on the following day (when HHP saw him) he was taken to ceremonies at St Giles Cathedral and the Tolbooth Church.

p.76, line 14, 'At Loch Katrine we embark on a small steamer . . .' For a slightlier earlier description of a similar excursion, see H. and K. Kelsall, eds, *Diary of a Victorian Miss on Holiday*; Sheffield: Hallamshire Press, 1992, p.125.

p.79, lines 10–11, 'Millie is much taken with the electric staircase . . .' The electric escalator had been invented in the United States at the turn of the century, but it was not until 1911 that such a device was made generally available to the British public: at the underground station at (by coincidence) Earls Court.

p.79, lines 11–12, 'the airship in full swing . . .' For Hiram Maxim's captive airships, see the photographic section in the centre of this voume.

p.79, lines 20–1, 'a demonstration marching into park . . .' This was one of several demonstrations this year against the Licensing Bill, by supporters of the National Temperance League.

p.79, lines 26–7, 'Baby . . . with Harriett . . .' Harriett Tidy was a servant of the Peerless family.

p.80 lines 1–2, 'Mr W.C. Bartlett, his son Mr E.C. Bartlett . . .' The Bartletts lived at 21 Stanford Avenue. William Bartlett was a builder, like many of HHP's travelling companions; his son Ewart was a solicitor.

1905

p.81, line 16, 'the Customs take off their seal and they can sell them . . .' Excise Duty on playing cards had first been imposed during the reign of Queen Anne, and had later been fixed at threepence a pack. According to *Ham's Customs Year Book*, 1905, 'After payment of duty playing cards are not to be delivered out of the custody of the Customs until each pack shall have been enclosed by an Officer of I[nland] R[evenue] in a wrapper provided by the IR and fastened in such a manner that it cannot be opened without the package being destroyed.' (Information supplied by Eleanor Downes, HM Customs and Excise National Museum.)

p.83, lines 16–17, 'a-thinking of the girl I left behind me . . .' HHP is quoting from the 18th-century air 'Brighton Camp'.

p.83, line 18, 'perhaps she is handling Wilfred David now . . .' The Peerlesses' fourth child had been born on 12 December 1904.

p.86, lines 18–19, 'Mr G. . . . was shut in the saloon a prisoner . . .' Sailing from Naples in December 1902, the diarist Violet Elwell recorded a similar incident: 'Just as the stewards were beginning to get tea a fire alarm went off . . . and the great watertight iron doors were shut over the usual doors of the saloon. The passengers . . . in the saloon . . . were determined not to be done out of their tea so they began to get it for themselves. The pantry turned into a scene of confusion. . . . The stewards looked rather amused when they came back, whilst all those passengers who had been shut out by the watertight doors, were in a state of high indignation because we had been enjoying ourselves while they were standing outside waiting.' (From 'Violet's diary', unpublished manuscript edited by Ruth Longford; quoted by permission.)

p.86, line 33, 'There are eight boats, laden with . . . clouds . . .' A cloud was a woman's loose-knitted woollen scarf.

p.91, line 36, 'To Clarence Square and supper . . .' Mr and Mrs Garrett had recently moved to Clarence Square from Queen Square, Brighton.

1906

p.92, lines 5–6, 'Reggie we had sent to Mrs Thompsett . . .' Onslow Thompsett (a carpenter) and his wife Harriet Rebecca lived at 2 Keymer Park, Keymer.

p.92, line 6, 'Cuthbert we had arranged should stay at Mrs Peerless' . . .' Mrs Peerless was HHP's stepmother Esther, whom David John Peerless had married after the death of his first wife. In 1906 Esther Peerless was living as a widow at 43 Portland Street, Brighton.

p.92, lines 8–9, 'We had all our tickets . . . through the Polytechnic . . .' The Polytechnic Enterprise of Quintin Hogg (1845–1903) was established initially to give a technical education to young men and women from the lower-middle classes. Later it organised foreign tours for Polytechnic members, soon extending these facilities to the general public.

p.92, line 24, 'when thou thinkest thou standest . . .' See I Corinthians 10:12. For other Biblical references in this volume of the diary, see 2 June ('wisdom is justified of her children', Matthew 11:19) and 9 June ('he fleeth also as a shadow', Job 14:2).

p.93, lines 25–6, 'It's Mr Fellingham, isn't it? . . .' William Fellingham (then in his late 20s) worked as a sanitary engineer in Brighton.

p.95, line 1, 'Alaska award . . .' The boundary dispute between Alaska and Canada, following the discovery of gold in the Klondike, had been settled in favour of US claims in 1903.

p.95, lines 39–40, 'partaking of . . . diplomacy pudding . . .' A dessert consisting of glacé fruits with custard on a sponge base, supposedly invented by the French statesman Talleyrand. See the unpublished journal kept by members of the Warner family and their friends in France during the winter of 1860–61, describing 'those wonderful specimens of French cooking which quite justified to my mind the vague belief that a French cook can even turn an old pair of leather shoes to good account—the "pudding dipplomate", which as the waiter carried all round the table, he alternately varied by calling it "dipplomate pudding".' (Bodleian Library, MS Eng. Misc. D.720, f.9v.)

p.97, lines 1–2, 'one touch of Nature makes the whole world kin . . .' See *Troilus and Cressida*, III.iii.174.

p.99, lines 6–7, 'On the wall . . . we see an inscription . . .' cf. Ovid's *Heroides* (V, 149, 'Amor non est medicabilis herbis').

p.100, lines 29–30, 'The clerk of the weather having come to his senses . . .' See *The Golden Calf* by one of HHP's favourite authors, Miss Braddon: 'It was usually a brilliant day. The clerk of the weather appeared favourably disposed.'

p.101, line 14, 'from pitch-and-toss to manslaughter . . .' See Chapter 3 of *A Christmas Carol*: 'Gentlemen of the free-and-easy sort . . . express the wide range of their capacity for adventure by observing that they are good for anything from pitch-and-toss to manslaughter.'

p.106, lines 14–15, 'a horrible accident to the Plymouth Boat Express . . .' The accident took place on 1 July 1906, when the 'boat special' from Plymouth left the rails just after passing through Salisbury Station, killing 28 people.

1907

p.107, lines 8–9, 'Abbey's malthouse had been burnt out in the night . . .' The *Brighton Gazette* of 13 June 1907 described the fire as the worst in the town for 25 years: 'The scene was the building at the corner of Eastern Road and Sutherland Road, which belongs to Messrs Abbey & Sons, the well-known brewers, and is used by them as a maltings and store. The conflagration raged for over five hours, and when the flames were finally subdued, the building had been almost completely gutted. . . . Damage is estimated at £10,000. Happily the customers of the firm will suffer no inconvenience.'

p.107, line 13, 'Arrived at Woolston Floating Ferry . . .' The villages of Itchen and Woolston had been connected in 1836 by a double ferry known as the 'floating bridge'. Although the ferry was later replaced by a toll-bridge, a nearby street still bears the name Floating Bridge Road.

p.108, line 2, 'we walk to Bank . . .' i.e. Forest Bank.

p.109, line 3, 'we come to the Crown Inn . . .' Now the Crown Stirrup Inn.

p.109, lines 20–1, 'we have been over it on two or three former occasions . . .' In fact Beaulieu Abbey had not been formally opened to the public until 1906. Among other visitors to Beaulieu in 1907 was the Kaiser.

p.110, lines 4–5, 'at the bottom of Lyndhurst Street . . .' i.e. Lyndhurst High Street, where Holmfield (now divided into apartments) still stands.

p.112, line 16, 'I doubt if he ever did, though . . .' The diarist Violet Elwell had a similar encounter nearby on 26 September 1903. 'We saw a curious looking figure tearing down the hill from the village towards the road,' she wrote. 'It proved on closer view, to be a hunch-backed dwarf, who sat down by the roadside waiting for the coach to pass, and as soon as it approached began a series of somersaults; after which he collected himself together and, grinning, tore after the coach, trying to hang on behind. He seemed to be well known to the coachman and guard who exchanged jokes with him; he kept up with the coach for a marvellous distance, but at last dropped behind.'

Later the same day Violet Elwell went to the Fox and Hounds, where her lunch was 'extremely poor considering the price they charged for it. The potatoes were soggy, the meat pie was tasteless and the gravy just lapped in grease. I would have liked something sweet to take the greasy taste from my mouth, but a dessert was not included.' (From 'Violet's diary', unpublished manuscript edited by Ruth Longford; quoted by permission.)

1908

p.117, line 28, 'we notice Smedley's Hydro . . .' The Derbyshire mill-owner John

Smedley had become a fanatical advocate of hydrotherapy after contracting a fever in Switzerland. He is said to have designed his 'hydropathic establishment' on deliberately austere lines, so that if the cult of water-cures subsided, he could turn it into a mill (E.S. Turner, *Taking the Cure*, pp.185–9). However, Smedley's Hydro was still thriving in 1908, and it was in this year that an eight-car garage was built on the premises for the use of guests arriving by motor. John Smedley was also responsible for the construction of Riber Castle, where he spent his final years.

p.118, lines 21–2, 'commune with My Lady Nicotine . . .' The reference is to the title of a book by J.M. Barrie, first published in 1890.

p.118, lines 28–9, 'having toured . . . with Sims Reeves . . .' Sims Reeves (1818–1900) was the most celebrated English tenor of his day. One of his volumes of autobiography, *My Jubilee*, gives some light-hearted descriptions of the sort of tours Mr Davies would have accompanied him on.

p.118, lines 35–6, 'Mr Sweeney, something at Whitehall . . .' Possibly James Augustus Sweeney (1883–1945), who had entered the Indian Civil Service the previous year.

p.119, line 19, 'Through most beautiful gardens to the stately glass-house . . .' The conservatory (designed by Joseph Paxton, who went on to design the Crystal Palace) fell into disuse in the Great War, and in 1920 the 9th Duke gave orders for it to be destroyed. (See Deborah, Duchess of Devonshire, *The Garden at Chatsworth*; Derbyshire: Derbyshire Countryside Ltd, 1987, pp.18, 32.)

p.119, lines 23–4, 'The church contains a monument to Bess of Hardwick . . .' In fact the monument is to Bess of Hardwick's two sons. Edensor also contains the grave of Lord Frederick Cavendish (see p.54).

p.120, line 30, 'a petrifying well, a very quaint sight . . .' Matlock Bath had some of the most famous petrifying wells in the country. According to Andy Walker of Poole's Cavern, Buxton, 'The practice of petrifying objects in mineral springs was a popular part of many Victorian natural cave and spa attractions. Rainwater can react with calcium rocks, which dissolve to form calcium bicarbonate. As drips of water fall into a cave or appear at a spring, the carbon dioxide de-gasses from the solution, causing calcium carbonate to precipitate and form a crystal of pure calcite, making objects appear to have turned to stone.' These objects could be sold so profitably that, at some wells, lime from local quarries was introduced into the water to speed up the process.

p.120, line 38, 'I work . . . on the estate accounts . . .' Although HHP's father David John Peerless had died five years earlier, the administration of his estate continued to occupy HHP's attention long after the 1908 holiday; indeed, he was still referring to it when he drew up his last will some twenty years later.

p.120, line 42, '"The cheat," after the picture by —— . . .' HHP is probably referring to the painting by Ludwig Knaus (1829–1910), now at the Kunstmuseum in Düsseldorf.

p.121, line 3, 'Home they brought her warrior dead . . .' Based on Tennyson's 'The Princess' (introductory poem to Book vi, line 1). According to the hotel's brochure, 'A considerable feature is made of providing suitable and healthful amusement for visitors and patients. Entertainments (in-door and out-door) are regularly organised, according to season and circumstances, and include theatricals, *tableaux vivants*, concerts, musical sketches, charades, games, etc.'

p.121, line 21, 'under the spray needle shower . . .' A form of shower-bath with a very powerful fine spray. Among other treatments offered by the Matlock

House Hydro were the carbonic acid bath and hydro-electric bath (at a cost of 2*s* 6*d* per session) and the bran, gelatine, starch, and sulphur baths (1*s* 6*d* a session).

p.122, lines 1–2, 'Blessing she is: God made her so . . .' From 'My love' by the American poet James Russell Lowell (1819–1891).

p.123, lines 27–8, 'a caution to snakes . . .' This expression, deriving from HHP's description of the New Forest snakecatcher Brusher Mills, had evidently become a family joke (see p.60).

p.125, lines 4–5, 'up goes the curtain and the show begins . . .' The programme, pasted into the diary, shows that Millie performed 'The broken pitcher' and 'I know a bank'; HHP sang 'The anchor's weighed', and recited one of the soliloquys from *Hamlet.*

p.125, line 17, 'a kind of volcano has broken out . . .' Under the heading 'The Burning Cliffs of Lyme Regis' a contemporary guide-book described how 'the Cliff was riven asunder at mid-day on Wednesday, June 10th, one half falling into the sea and exposing huge masses of fire in the interior. The cleavage in the cliffs was nearly half-a-mile in length, and the flames emitted very strong fumes of sulphur' (*Munford's Bright and Bracing Seaton, Beer, & Neighbourhood*; Yeovil, 1908). Jo Draper of the Lyme Regis Museum, who provided this information, commented further: 'Lyme made much of this as a tourist attraction, and is said to have improved it with paraffin and newspapers.'

p.125, lines 19–20, 'Sir William Treloar . . . had quite a triumphal progress . . .' The carpet-manufacturer and philanthropist Sir William Purdie Treloar (1843–1923) was president of the National Sunday League (see pp. 271-2), and was serving as Lord Mayor of London when, in 1907, he returned to his Cornish birthplace. He described his visit as 'a regular royal progress. . . . [In] Helston, the people . . . went mad with delight as I danced the Furry dance through the hilly streets.' (W.P. Treloar, *A Lord Mayor's Diary*; London: John Murray, 1920, pp. viii, 132–140.)

p.126, line 24, 'We gaze at the Flip-Flap . . .' The flip-flap was a machine with passenger-cars at the end of two crane-like arms, about 80 yards long, which swung up and down. (See D.C. Somervell, *100 Years in Pictures*; London: Odhams, 1950.) 'The "Entente Cordiale" with France was cemented by an Anglo-French Exhibition at the White City, London, in 1908. Among the diversions provided for the patrons was the giant flip-flap. Over eight million people attended the exhibition, which, unlike most international exhibitions, finished up with a small financial profit.'

1909

p.127, line 8, 'news came of a great strike in Sweden . . .' The Great Strike of 1909 has been described as the most dramatic event in Sweden's labour history. A dock strike the previous year had spread to other industries, and between July and September 1909 Swedish industry came to a virtual standstill.

p.133, line 8, 'the world forgetting, by the world forgot . . .' See Pope's 'Eloisa to Abelard'.

p.134, line 36, 'a musical doctor had committed suicide . . .' Dr Warwick Jordan was organist at St Stephen's, Lewisham, and treasurer of the Royal Society of Organists.

p.135, line 33, 'a violin recital by the brothers Hambourg . . .' The violinist Jan

Hambourg had founded the Hambourg Trio with his brothers Mark (piano) and Boris (cello) in 1905.

p.138, line 1, 'so much for Buckingham . . .' The quotation is from Colley Cibber's adaptation of *Richard III* (1700), in which it is preceded by the words 'Off with his head.'

p.138, line 8, 'a great shame that it is not a corridor train . . .' In corridor trains, the separate compartments in each carriage were connected by a corridor, which allowed access to the dining-car and lavatories.

1910

p.139, line 7, 'the portly form of Dean Hannah . . .' The Very Reverend John Julius Hannah (1843-1931) had been vicar of Brighton before becoming Dean of Chichester in 1902.

p.141, line 10, 'Writing to Arthur, Burt? . . .' Arthur Dale Garrett was Maude and Burt's second son.

p.142, lines 27–8, 'to the Royal Magnets . . . rather poor . . .' The reviewer in the *Barmouth and County Advertiser* was more charitable. '"Sir" Edward Pare is really too funny for words. . . . Mr Harry Bowden was in great form. . . . Mr Fred Augett has a very charming way. . . . Mr Charles Elstree gave unbounded pleasure. Mr Willie Woodward accompanied the various songs.'

p.143, line 15, 'The clergyman's name is Conolly or Connolloy . . .' Charles William Herbert Connolly (b. 1862) was rector of Exton between 1908 and 1931. The *Barmouth and County Advertiser* also had trouble with his name, giving it as 'Cormelly' in its list of guests staying at the town's guest-houses (in which Henry and Amelia Peerless are listed correctly).

p.143, lines 37–8, 'Fate cannot harm us . . .' cf. Sydney Smith's 'Fate cannot harm me, I have dined to-day.'

p.144, lines 7–8, 'a light play entitled Old Virginia *. . .'* The musical comedy by Kennedy Allen and Edwin Adeler had had its première at the Olympic Gardens, Rockferry, two years earlier.

p.145, line 20, 'a dirty dismal little station . . .' Curiously it was at Portmadoc Station, in August 1897, that A.C. Benson began his monumental diary, which was eventually to run to four million words and cover a period of nearly thirty years. (See Percy Lubbock, ed., *The Diary of Arthur C. Benson*; London: Hutchinson, 1926, p.27.)

p.145, line 34, 'some measure or debate in Parliament . . .' The main debate on 12 July 1910 was on the Parliamentary Franchise (Women) Bill, intended as a step on the way towards granting votes to women.

p.146, lines 8–9, 'a vehicle that was made specially for Mrs —— . . .' Possibly Mrs H.B. Robertson (see M.E. Sara, *The Life and Times of HRH Princess Beatrice*; London: Stanley Paul, 1945).

p.146, lines 37–8, 'I hope their dogged perseverance will be rewarded . . .' The Ward Lock guide to Barmouth, published ten years later, stated resignedly: 'A Welsh El-Dorado has not yet been found.' The mines were abandoned commercially, but small amounts of gold have continued to be extracted, and Queen Elizabeth II's wedding ring was made from Bont-ddu gold.

p.147, lines 1–2, 'an outdoor concert given by the Keith Prowse Entertainers . . .' A review of this concert in the *Barmouth and County Advertiser* praised the 'exquisite interpretation in Miss Christine Bywater, . . . the lively optimism in the songs of Miss Gaston Murray, . . . and the fine humour [of] Mr Ivimey and Mr Sterndale Bennett, while Mr Percy Tarling can produce songs and monologues both grave and gay.'

p.147, line 21, 'Two are modern structures . . .' The topmost bridge was only three years old when HHP saw it.

1911

p.152, lines 12–13, 'and behold, there [was] Sam . . .' Sam Garrett was a brother of Thomas Garrett senior, and a co-founder of the building firm of W. & T. Garrett. According to HHP's nephew Robert Peerless, he never became a director of the firm, but 'lived in Grenville Place, Brighton, in considerable comfort'.

p.154, lines 30–1, 'Lloyd George . . . with his Form IVs . . .' 'Form fours!' is a military command (see *OED*), and is used loosely here.

p.156, line 40, 'to see the husbands' boat . . .' These boats would generally arrive from the metropolis on Saturday mornings during the holiday season, so that husbands could join their families for the weekend.

p.159, line 9, 'to Cave's in High Street . . .' Austin Cave & Co. ran a chain of oriental restaurants in the county at the beginning of the 20th century.

1912

p.161, line 3, 'crowded with Saturday-night shoppers . . .' Before the introduction of austerity measures during the Great War, it was not uncommon for shops to stay open till late in the evening—sometimes as late as midnight on Fridays and Saturdays—so that people could go shopping on their way home from the music-halls and pubs. (See Pamela Horn, *Pleasures and Pastimes in Victorian Britain*, p.3.)

p.161, lines 7–8, 'Asquith's advice . . . "wait and see" . . .' In the spring of 1910, the prime minister H.H. Asquith had told the House of Commons to 'wait and see' whether he would persist with the People's Budget and the reform of the House of Lords. It became a celebrated catchphrase, still able to evoke laughter over a decade later. See Arnold Bennett's diary, 17 May 1924: 'He wanted me to introduce into the part of the Prime Minister Holyoke (. . . supposed to be a mixture of Asquith and Balfour with a touch of Rosebery) the words "Wait and see." I refused absolutely at once. Imagine the cheap roar which would follow such a despicable sally.' (Frank Swinnerton, ed., *Arnold Bennett: The Journals*; London: Penguin, 1971.)

p.161, lines 11–12, 'The vicar, a most unhealthy-looking villain . . .' Charles Fursden Rogers was Vicar of St Mary's between 1901 and 1916. According to his successor Father Keith Owen, 'He was considered very high church, and had a healthy disrespect for his bishop. One story is told by Dr Eric Rogers (no relation) about a high mass at which the bishop presided in choir. The bishop complained afterwards that during most of the service and the whole of the eucharistic prayer he had been unable to hear him. Father Rogers' reply seems characteristic: "Oh, that's all right, my Lord, I wasn't talking to *you*!"'

p.163, line 15, 'a topical allusion to the terrible Titanic *catastrophe . . .'* The White Star Liner SS *Titanic* had sunk the previous month, with the loss of over 1,500 lives.

p.164, line 41, 'where the cables of the Eastern Telegraph Company touch the shores . . .'

The cables from the beach were connected to the Americas, the Far East and Australia, and the little beach at Porthcurno has been called 'the communication gateway to the British Empire'. (See Adam Hart-Davis, *What the Victorians Did For Us*, p.102.)

p.165, lines 21–2, 'Burt and waterfalls in the Lake District . . .' See HHP's account of his holiday with Burt Garrett in 1910 (p.140), not actually in the Lake District but in Wales.

p.166, lines 6–7, 'a series of pictures of the Seven Ages of Man . . .' Millie may have been referring to the canvas by William Mulready (1786–1863), now in the Victoria & Albert Museum in London, or to Henry Alken's illustrations for the 1827 book *Shakespeare's Seven Ages.*

p.170, line 33, 'one being almost a small Tichborne . . .' One of the most absurd anomalies concerning the claim of a petty criminal named Arthur Orton to be the long-lost heir to the Tichborne baronetcy was the striking difference in physique between the two men. The real heir, Roger Tichborne, had been a 'slight, delicate, undersized youth,' according to Sir John Coleridge, who cross-examined the claimant in court; miraculously he had 'developed into an enormous mass of flesh'.

p.171, line 30, 'I was surprised to find the said cavern right under one of the houses . . .' 'I can imagine no more unlikely or unromantic place for a cavern,' Beatrix Potter wrote in her diary on 14 March 1893; and, like Millie, she was 'pretty much exhausted' by the time she reached it. (Leslie Winder, ed., *The Journals of Beatrix Potter, 1881–1897*; London: Penguin, 1989, p.315.)

1914

p.174, lines 6–7, 'Mr and Mrs Manby's at Charleston Firle . . .' Mr Manby, who leased Charleston Farmhouse (near Firle, East Sussex), was a fellow Brighton builder. Three years later the painter Vanessa Bell came upon the house—which during the Great War had fallen into disrepair—and set about turning it into a home for herself and other members of the Bloomsbury group. There are extensive references to it in the diaries of Virginia Woolf (edited by Anne Olivier Bell), Dora Carrington (edited by David Garnett), and Frances Partridge. (See also Quentin Bell and Virginia Nicholson, *Charleston: A Bloomsbury House and Garden*; London: Frances Lincoln, 1997. The photograph of Quentin Bell, Duncan Grant, Roger Fry and others, on p.19, was taken in the walled garden where HHP and his extended family had posed in 1913; see the photographic section at the centre of this volume.)

p.174, line 15, 'We packed our large black box . . .' At the front of the 1914 volume, HHP listed what he and Millie packed for their fortnight's holiday. Although two of the three pages are now obscured by hotel leaflets pasted on top of them, the list includes: '24 gents' handkerchiefs, 3 pairs ladies' stockings, 1 pair corsets, 1 velveteen dress (black), 1 lace front with lace sleeves & tapes, 1 ladies' satin coat, 1 pair long black silk gloves, 1 pair ladies' reindeer gloves, 6 ladies' handkerchiefs, 1 satin evening dress (black), 1 gilt net front and sleeves, 1 ladies' brown dress, 1 white gauze motor veil, 1 check duster, 1 ladies' white straw hat, 1 black feather ruffle, 1 Persian lamb stole, 1 black alpaca ladies' coat, 1 gents' straw hat.'

p.177, lines 9–10, 'a Holophanes shade or reflector . . .' Holophane was the name given to a prismatic form of glassware by its American inventor, Otis A. Mygatt. The Valley Private Hotel was particularly proud of its decor; its tariff (pasted into

HHP's diary) boasted that it was 'equipped throughout with electric light', and also drew attention to the 'Coffee-Room Doors, with curious Brass Fittings, brought from a Russian Palace during the Crimean War.'

p.179, lines 15–16, 'Mr Marten . . . found the picture in the attic . . .' HHP's story appears to be somewhat garbled. Although a Joseph Martin held a position at Overhall, near Ledbury, from 1795 to 1828, he was never vicar of Ledbury. However, it was during this period that Thomas Ballard's copy of Leonardo's 'Last Supper' was unveiled in Ledbury Church, where it can still be seen.

p.180, lines 36–7, 'a kind of Madame Rachel made beautiful and young for ever . . .' As well as being an actress, Elisa Rachel (née Elisa Félix, 1820 or 1821–58) promoted the art of 'enamelling' with various face-powders and creams, and endorsed a book on cosmetics entitled *Beautiful for Ever.* (See Richard Corson, *Fashions in Makeup*; London: Peter Owen, 1972, pp.338–342.)

p.182, lines 6–7, 'Mr Noaks is in the Civil Service in South Africa . . .' Benjamin Noaks (b.1866) had been appointed headmaster of Queenstown High School in 1898, and later became inspector of schools in the Orange River Colony and Orange Free State.

p.184, line 7, 'Annie Hatherell comes running up to meet us . . .' Annie Hatherell (née Smith) may have been a childhood friend of Millie's. Her husband Edwin (1864–1943) was a tenant farmer.

1915

p.187, line 19, 'a car outside Mr E.C. Baldwin's house . . .' Edmund Baldwin, a public auditor and accountant, lived a few doors away from the Garretts at 9 Windlesham Avenue.

p.187, lines 21–2, '"Matilda" . . . was now "in her stride" . . .' Thomas Garrett's car was a 12/16 hp Sunbeam tourer. Between 1910 and 1914 almost 5,000 were sold at a cost of £375 each. Production of the model ceased at the start of the Great War, but Rover took up the design to provide staff-cars for the military.

p.187, lines 26–7, 'copious notes referring to the portion from Guildford to Reading . . .' 'On arriving in Guildford High Street turn to left and <u>first</u> to right, then make for a road over river bridge by the side of the Dennis Motor Works, keep straight on, <u>not</u> to take road for Frimley, but to go to Ash and turn sharp to right <u>before</u> the Church. You then go over railway bridge through Ash Vale to Farnborough and Frimley, but take sharp turn to left after passing Church, then sharp to right by an Hotel and the York Town and Sandhurst road faces you. Take left hand turn at the latter place and first turning <u>after</u> College (6 months if you go through the grounds), but no sign post, you then pass right through Sandhurst village, turn sharp to right for Wokingham, on excellent road, through the latter and left to Reading, also good road.'

p.189, lines 5–6, 'Mrs Rose . . . was quite a grande dame *. . .'* Mary and Alfred Rose had become joint custodians of Shakespeare's Birthplace in 1900; after Alfred's retirement due to ill-health in 1910, Mary was appointed chief attendant. When Mary Rose died in 1921, the popular novelist Marie Corelli published a tribute in the *Stratford-upon-Avon Herald*: 'So she has gone—good Mrs Rose! Her pleasant face, her cheerful voice will no more charm and interest the thousand of visitors to the Birthplace, of whom, surely, there was not one who failed to be impressed by her devotion to the memory of the World's Poet.' (Information provided by

Robert Bearman, Senior Archivist of the Shakespeare Birthplace Trust.)

p.190, lines 27–8, 'since Lloyd George came into the limelight . . .' David Lloyd George had served as chancellor of the Exchequer from 1908 to 1915. He left this post to become minister of munitions, and had spent June 1915 touring the country's munitions factories.

p.191, line 20, 'a famous London to Brighton run . . .' The Emancipation Run of November 1896 celebrated the repeal of the Road Locomotion Act (see above) and the raising of the maximum speed limit from 4 to 14 mph. Since then the rally has become an annual event, with vintage cars attempting to complete the 53-mile route from Central London to the Metropole Hotel in Brighton.

p.192, line 20, 'Before the hills in order stood . . .' See *Hymns Ancient and Modern.*

p.192, lines 23–4, 'he has a notion that they will "skip like young rams" . . .' cf. Psalm 114.

p.193, line 6, 'the wonderful doings in 1911 . . .' The investiture of the future Edward VIII, on 13 July 1911, was the first to have been held in Wales.

p.193, line 34, 'it appears to lack one great essential, viz. *truth . . .'* The Rev. D.E. Jenkins had exposed the legend as a fabrication in his 1899 book *Bedd Gelert: Its Facts, Fairies, and Folk-Lore.* The story was unknown in the neighbourhood before 1798, and seems to have been imported from South Wales by the first landlord of the Royal Goat Hotel, David Prichard.

p.194, lines 10–11, 'as an old war-horse sniffs the battle . . .' cf. Job 39:19–25.

p.196, lines 36–7, 'off we do agen . . .' Cuthbert's baby-talk at Malvern (see p.18) had evidently acquired the status of a family joke.

p.203, lines 7–8, 'And now . . . goodbye . . .' On their return from Wales, HHP lent his diary to Tom Garrett, whose letter dated August 1915 is appended to the back of the manuscript volume:

> Harry wishes me to add a few words to the foregoing, which I endorse as a faithful account of our holiday; it is so complete that I can find nothing to add, and so true that I can discover nothing to correct, unless it be in the too-kindly references to your humble servant.
>
> I bristle with pride as I read the tributes paid to the gentle Matilda. She certainly did her part well, and although protesting somewhat 'heatedly' at some of the heavier 'collar-work', she never failed us and needed no tool or adjustment to her anatomy during the whole run, and as she was a great factor in our enjoyment it may be of interest to state here that she is a 1914 'Sunbeam' of 12/16 hp with four-seater body and four cylinders, her bore being 80 mm, and her stroke 150 mm (millimetres). It is impossible this year to buy a new car of this make as the Government have taken over the whole output of the factory for the length of the War, which speaks well of Matilda's design and the stuff of which she is made.
>
> I somewhat regret that a camera was not included in our holiday kit, as it would have saved Harry some trouble in the direction of picture postcards. We must remember to take one next time.
>
> I hope that we four, in the not too distant future, may again join forces in another motoring holiday; I do not wish for better company or for more amiable, helpful or considerate passengers: sentiments which Fanny fully endorses, and if from such a holiday might be eliminated the doubt and dismay of a terrible war, what a holiday it might be to be sure.
>
> Tom

1916

p.204, lines 11–12, 'Derby recruiting schemes . . .' Edward Stanley, 17th Earl of Derby (1865–1948), was under-secretary for war. The failure of his scheme (intended to persuade young men to join up voluntarily) led to the Conscription Bill of 1916.

p.204, lines 18–19, 'no treating in many areas . . .' 'Treating (the purchase of a drink for another person) was prohibited, it being held that much drunkenness among soldiers was caused by the generosity of misguided patriots. The application of this ban became general. A man might be prosecuted (and this did happen) for buying a drink for his own wife.' (Trevor Wilson, *The Myriad Faces of War*; Cambridge: Polity Press, 1986, p.153.)

p.204, lines 34–5, 'the lines advocated by the late Mr Willett . . .' William Willett (1856–1915), who with his father had designed stylish garden-city-type houses in South Hampstead and Regent's Park, is said to have conceived the idea of daylight saving in 1907, during an early-morning ride in Pett's Wood near Chislehurst, when he was struck by the number of houses with their blinds still shut. He wrote a pamphlet entitled 'The waste of daylight', but died before his scheme was introduced as a wartime economy.

p.205, line 25, 'our old friend Matilda . . .' The Garretts' Sunbeam motor-car (see above). By coincidence a manuscript diary for 1916, kept by Tom Garrett's nephew Arthur, begins with a description of him servicing a Sunbeam car, which was presumably Tom's.

p.205, line 28, 'Tom was anxious about an appeal . . .' William Henry Scrase was HHP's foreman at the timber-yard; Frederick Fritz Howell was Tom Garrett's clerk. The *Brighton Gazette* of 1 July 1916 reports that over forty similar cases were dealt with by the tribunal on the same day, with F.W.A. Cushman appearing for many of the defendants.

p.206, line 8, 'a firm named Woolworth . . .' Frank Winfield Woolworth's chain of five- and ten-cent stores had already spread right across America, but the first UK store had not opened (in Liverpool) until 1909.

p.206, line 32, '"R/D" or "No a/c" . . .' 'Refer to drawer'/'No account.'

p.206, line 38, 'pleased with the favourable war news . . .' The *Observer*'s headline described the most disastrous day in British military history as 'A GREAT BEGINNING' and 'A TURNING POINT OF THE WAR' (while going on to admit that 'at the moment of writing our knowledge of details is almost as scant as may be'). Even Siegfried Sassoon, who witnessed the opening of the Somme offensive, recorded in his diary on 2 July 1916: 'Everywhere the news seems good. I only hope it will last.' (Rupert Hart-Davis, ed., *Siegfried Sassoon Diaries 1915–1918*; London: Faber & Faber, 1983, p.85.)

p.210, lines 9–10, 'we find Gunn senior and pay his account . . .' The bill, pasted into the diary, came to 16 shillings—15 shillings for towing the car, and a shilling for repairing the chains.

*p.214, line 24, 'saved us 1*s *6*d *a day each . . .'* It was common practice for hotels to charge motorists at a higher tariff than other travellers.

p.215, lines 11–12, 'the People's Refreshment House Association Ltd . . .' According to a booklet pasted into the diary, the first principle of the association was 'that all temptation to press the sale of INTOXICANTS be removed, as regards the Managers, by giving them a fixed salary, instead of any share in the profit of the Alcoholic branch of the trade.' The booklet listed over a hundred participating houses, mainly in small village locations.

p.215, line 29, 'A wounded Canadian soldier of Strathcona's Horse . . .' Donald Smith, 1st Baron Strathcona (1820–1914), was a Canadian financier who spent the last thirty years of his life distributing the huge fortune he had amassed. His regiment of rough-riders, which became known as Strathcona's Horse, had been raised during the Boer War at his own expense.

p.217, lines 8–9, 'a bathing-pool called Sir Thomas Acland's Pit . . .' Otherwise known as 'Sir Thomas's bath', the shallow pool had been made by the 10th baronet to afford a safe bathing place for those who were not strong swimmers. (See W. and F. Coumbe's *Guide to Bude-Haven*, 1876.)

p.219, lines 36–7, 'I sit in lounge and read A Girl of the Limberlost *. . .'* Gene Stratton Porter's light romance had been published in 1909 and remained in print till the 1960s. A 1928 biography of the author was entitled *The Lady of the Limberlost.*

p.221, line 29, 'regimental crests on the side of these hills . . .' Five of the regimental badges, cut into the chalk hills, still survive from the Great War; another three were added later. Some of them are nearly 200 feet across. The badges are now preserved by the Fovant Badges Society.

p.222, line 20, 'the gentleman whom we took to be Lord Montagu . . .' John, 2nd Lord Montagu of Beaulieu (1866–1929), is best known as a pioneer of the motor-car, but was also an aviator and motor-boat enthusiast. In 1905 he and Lionel de Rothschild had become world motor-boat champions, although narrowly failing to break the world water-speed record (then standing at 33.8 mph).

p.222, lines 29–30, 'a very pleasant change . . .' In September 1916, Tom Garrett wrote to HHP from 14 Windlesham Avenue, Brighton:

My dear Harry,

I have perused your diary of our 1916 joint holiday with great interest and pleasure, and hereby endorse it a true and faithful account of all that befell us. I marvel at its wealth of detail which must have necessitated a good many thumbnail notes *en route*, or you have a prodigious memory.

You do not seem to have forgotten anything unless it be some of the minor worries consequent upon the defection of the errant Matilda, which you have been pleased to gloss over as much as you dared, for although we all had a real good holiday, it can truly be said that it would have been all the better if Matilda or rather her German-made ignition apparatus had not 'busted up' so completely.

I am consoled in one way, and that is in knowing that the defect was not caused by any neglect on my part; everyone agrees that a 'burnt out' armature is a most unusual occurrence.

In conclusion, I hope if we four are spared and this terrible War does not rob us of every shot in the locker that we may have yet another holiday together, either with Matilda or one of her peers or perhaps it may be a second-hand 'TANK' should the War be over, at any rate on something that will *go*.

Yours sincerely,

Thomas Garrett

P.S. 1: May we never have to repeat our 'weeping at the waters of Bude' or anywhere else.

P.S. 2: Remember that I am ever pining for thee my Harry as at Bude.

P.S. 3: Would that I had the Scriptures at my fingers' ends as hast thee, my friend, also the immortal Bard.

1917

p.223, lines 7–8, 'At every turn we run against some restriction . . .' HHP's words are echoed by A.J.P. Taylor in the opening paragraphs of his classic text *English History 1914–1945*: 'Until August 1914 a sensible, law-abiding Englishman could pass through life and hardly notice the existence of the state. . . . All this was changed by the impact of the Great War.'

p.227, lines 9–10, 'a caravan left by the French . . .' One of the wooden walls of the caravan is still clearly visible at the front of the inn; see also the photographic section at the centre of this volume.

p.230, lines 26–7, 'the donor of the outing pressed a big cigar on to Rennie . . .' Reginald's nickname probably derived from his early attempts to pronounce his own name.

p.230, line 33, 'Telegram from Maisie to say "Unto us a child is born" . . .' 'Maisie' was Sidney Garrett's wife Dorothy May, née Carden, who had just given birth to their son Rodney. According to family tradition she later took to drinking heavily, and on the outbreak of World War II, Sidney (by then aged almost fifty) joined the Army to get away from her.

p.231, lines 36–7, 'The widowed King still bravely holds his own . . .' The King Oak continued to be a landmark in the New Forest as late as the 1980s.

p.233, line 38, 'Well, we have had a pleasant jaunt . . .' 'Hope we have not had the last of the "jaunts" together,' Tom Garrett wrote to HHP on 12 June, enclosing a cheque for £7 11*s* 1*d* 'to balance the holiday costs'. HHP had kept a meticulous tally, itemising every outlay, from the sixpenny toll at Shoreham Bridge, to the cost of tea at Chichester (2*s* 8*d*) on the way home.

1918

p.234, lines 1–2, 'the loss of our dear son . . .' Cuthbert Peerless had died at the Peerless family home on 12 May 1918, after falling off his horse while on active service as a 2nd Lieutenant with the Royal Sussex Regiment. Burt and Maude Garrett's son Arthur had also been killed just four weeks earlier at Kemmel Hill, Ypres; while HHP's nephew Leonard (b.1894) had been killed the previous year on the Western Front. His body was never recovered.

p.235, lines 9–10, 'the amount of yellow kilk in the fields . . .' 'Kilk' is a Sussex dialect word for charlock; see Thomas Turner's *Diary of a Village Shopkeeper* (ed. D. Vaisey; London: Folio Society, 1998). John Vine, a Sussex landowner, told Turner on 17 July 1756 that 'the only way to eradicate the weed vulgarly called "kilk" out of the ground was by pulling it up, for was it once permitted to stand to seed . . . the seed would lie in the ground 50 years.'

p.236, line 14, 'Mr Attree rather palls on me . . .' Since the Peerlesses' previous visit in 1909, W.G. Attree had set up the Lynrock Mineral-Water Company, with its own bottling plant. He also ran a motor char-à-banc service between Myrtleberry and Lynmouth to take people to his tea-shop. (See John Travis, *Lynton and Lynmouth: Glimpses of the Past*; Derby: Breedon Books, 1997, pp.171–2.)

p.236, lines 24–5, 'this fire was the work of suffragettes . . .' Hollerday House had been burnt down during the night of 4 August 1913, and the *North Devon Journal* was quick to report the 'strong suspicion that the crime was the work of Suffragists'. However, no evidence to support this was ever found.

p.240, line 22, 'speculate on what escaped German prisoners found to eat . . .' This episode lends credence to the assessment of Tom Garrett's character which his niece, Mrs Marjorie Fox, gave in July 2001: 'He wasn't very even-tempered. He would get very worked up about things, and would even use swear-words. . . . He used to throw in the towel so quickly!'

1919

p.243, line 2, 'Letchworth, the Garden City . . .' Letchworth in Hertfordshire was England's first garden city, designed by Ebenezer Howard to provide an escape from the overcrowded and unhealthy conditions of the large towns, and at the same time to check the depopulation of the countryside. Having been inaugurated in 1899, work started on it in 1905.

p.243, line 15, 'the Bull is going to be all right . . .' According to a leaflet pasted into the diary at this point, the Bull Hotel was 'patronised by the Royal Family, nobility, & gentry', and 'much frequented by Americans'.

p.243, line 37, 'the long lists of Trinity men who have perished . . .' The design of the impressive permanent memorial to the 650 members of Trinity College who were killed in the Great War was not approved until May 1920, so HHP must have seen some kind of temporary memorial or bare list of names.

p.243, line 40, 'Here is a hospital parade . . .' 'The Newmarket Trade and Friendly Societies' annual church parade, held on Sunday last, established a new record as regarded [sic] the collections which, as usual, were for Addenbrooke's Hospital and the local nursing associations. The total sum collected on Saturday and Sunday was over £115.' (*Newmarket Journal*, 12 July 1919.)

p.244, lines 30–1, 'the judge drives up to the Assize Court . . .' The Assize Courts were part of the prison and castle complex which in 1919 still dominated the city.

p.247, line 25, 'this evening should be devoted to jazz music . . .' The jazz craze had begun to sweep the USA in 1916; the first recordings were made in 1917, by the Original Dixieland Jazz Band, who toured Europe the following year.

1920

p.255, line 27, 'one called Yellow English *. . .'* Dorota Flatau's novel had been published in 1918.

p.256, line 7, 'the Bean is a good reliable car . . .' 1920 was the year in which the Harper Bean Company attempted to emulate Ford by mass production of its 11.9 model, with plans to manufacture 50,000 a year. In fact the car was merely an update of a flawed pre-war model; production peaked in July 1920, with just 505 cars made, and the company was wound up shortly afterwards. Despite this, Henry and Amelia Peerless seem to have been satisfied customers, and Robert Peerless remembers them driving their two-seater Bean until the end of the 1920s.

p.256, line 13, 'read The Car *. . .'* This magazine, edited by the Hon. J.S. Montagu, was published under a variety of names between 1902 and 1928.

p.258, line 27, 'to baths for Aix douche *. . .'* This method for directing water at the body at intense pressure, for the purpose of forcing it through the pores, had been made popular at the spa resort of Aix-la-Chapelle. It was intended as a supplement to the imbibing of the waters.

p.260, line 1, 'we want to change the book Doggie . . .' *The Doggie Book*, by Cecil Aldin, had been published in 1914.

p.263, line 14, 'Letters—one from Jack Port . . .' Jack Port, who married Sam Garrett's daughter Celia, worked as a butcher in Ship Street, Brighton. HHP's nephew Robert Peerless later recalled: 'Jack Port was rather a mystery. I do not think his business was prosperous, but he did not seem to be short of money. He was always full of fun except when talking about money; then he was very serious.'

p.263, line 21, 'T.G., B.D.G., Uncle Sam, J.M.P., C.M.P. . .' i.e. Tom Garrett, Burt Dale Garrett, Sam Garrett, and HHP's brothers John Moon Peerless and Charles Matthews Peerless.

p.263, line 25, 'gaze at a monument to Sir Somebody . . .' Sir Bevil Grenville defeated the Parliamentary general Sir William Waller at the Battle of Lansdown, but was himself killed.

Epilogue

p.267, 'to the Extra-Mural Cemetery . . .' The Peerless family plot, which contains the graves of Henry and Amelia Peerless and their two eldest sons Cuthbert and Reginald, is officially described as being at 'Barasford Corner front ground next beyond Thomas Garrett East Side.'

Chronology

1866 *Henry Heathfield Peerless born at 33 Middle Street, Brighton, the seventh child of Emily (née Pockney) and timber merchant David John Peerless (4 December).*

1867 Disraeli's Reform Act doubles the number of voters in England and Wales, and becomes one of the factors leading to the ascendancy of the new middle class.

1869 The publication of R.D. Blackmore's *Lorna Doone: A Romance of Exmoor* popularises the appeal of the more remote and unspoilt parts of England's countryside.

Amelia Sarah Garrett born at 35 Grenville Place, Brighton, the third and youngest child of Harriett (née Dale) and builder Thomas Garrett (3 December).

1870 Forster's Elementary Education Act sets up a system of universal education for five- to twelve-year-olds.

1871 Bank holidays introduced in England and Wales.

1874 The Factory Act limits the working week to 56 hours.

Lawn tennis invented in England.

1875 Introduction of the first luxury Pullman railway cars on the London–Brighton line.

1878 Act of Parliament restricts mechanical road vehicles to a maximum speed of 4 mph.

1879 Dining-cars introduced on Britain's railways.

1881 The world's first railway carriage to be lit by electricity introduced on the London–Brighton line.

1882 England's first electric trams begin to run, at Leytonstone, Essex (4 March).

1883 The first public electric railway in the UK, designed by Magnus Volk, opens in Brighton (4 August).

The London, Brighton & South Coast Railway inaugurates its 'semi-fast' service, covering the distance from Brighton to London in 5 hours 24 minutes.

1884 Straw boaters come into general use for men's summer wear.

1885 Gottlieb Daimler patents the internal combustion engine; his first motor-car takes to the road later the same year.

J.K. Starley begins manufacturing his chain-driven safety bicycle.

1888 A Scottish surgeon, J.B. Dunlop, invents the pneumatic tyre, which leads directly to the cycling craze of the 1890s.

1889 Jerome K. Jerome publishes *Three Men in a Boat.*

In women's fashion, the bustle disappears, and day dresses become shorter and more practical.

1890 Opening of the world's first underground railway, in London.

1891 *Henry Peerless marries Amelia Garrett (Millie) at St Nicholas's Church, Brighton, and begins his first diary (20 July).*

Work begins on the Palace Pier, Brighton.

Arthur Conan Doyle starts publishing his Sherlock Holmes stories in the *Strand Magazine.*

1892 *Cuthbert Henry, the first child of Millie and Henry Peerless, born at 20 Hanover Crescent, Brighton (10 June).*
The Grossmith brothers publish *The Diary of a Nobody*, satirising middle-class fashions and foibles.
Corridor trains introduced on Britain's mainline railway system.
Rudolf Diesel patents his petrol engine.

1893 The traveller Thomas Perkins (1872–1952) embarks on his self-imposed task of travelling every mile of the British railway network—an ambition he finally realises in 1932.
Karl Benz manufactures a four-wheeled motor-car.

1894 British Post Office abandons regulations prohibiting the sending of any but official postcards; craze for sending picture postcards begins to sweep the country.

1895 Britain's first motor-car show takes place at Tunbridge Wells in Kent.
Motor-cars seen in Brighton for the first time.
National Trust founded to preserve places of historic or natural interest for the nation to enjoy.

1896 Alfred Harmsworth launches the first popular newspaper, the *Daily Mail.*
The 'Emancipation Day Run'—the first London to Brighton car rally—takes place in commemoration of the Light Locomotives on Highways Act, which raises the maximum speed limit to 14 mph (14 November).
Brighton's chain pier destroyed in a storm (4 December).
J.B. Dunlop sells the rights to his pneumatic tyres for £3 million.

1897 *Reginald Leslie, the second child of Millie and Henry Peerless, born at 12 St James's Avenue, Brighton (5 December).*
Royal Automobile Club founded in London.

1899 Opening of the Palace Pier, Brighton—probably the finest pleasure pier in the UK (20 May); like Blackpool Tower (opened in 1894), its main purpose was to attract day-trippers to the seaside.
The London, Brighton & South Coast Railway introduces its 'Brighton in an hour' service.

1901 Death of Queen Victoria, and accession of King Edward VII (22 January).
Mixed bathing introduced on Brighton's beaches.
First petrol-engined motor-bicycle in Britain.
Gladys Amelia, the third child of Millie and Henry Peerless, born at 12 St James's Avenue (12 December).

1903 Henry Ford founds his motor company.
First motorised taxis introduced in London.
Brighton inaugurates one of the first motor-bus services in the country on Christmas Eve (though horse-drawn buses continue to run in the town till December 1916).
The Motor Car Act requires registration of all vehicles. Introduction of driving licences, and imposition of maximum 20 mph speed limit.

1904 *Wilfred David, the fourth child of Millie and Henry Peerless, born at 12 St James's Avenue (12 December).*

1905 London's first regular motor-bus service begins to run.
Automobile Association founded in London.

1906 *Daily Mail* coins the word 'suffragette'.
Launching of HMS *Dreadnought*, the world's first modern battleship.

1908 Kenneth Grahame publishes *The Wind in the Willows*, with its vision of the English countryside under threat from motorised transport.

1910 Death of King Edward VII and accession of King George V (6 May).
Women's hats reach their largest proportions; they are secured by veils when worn at the seaside or for motoring. The narrow 'hobble' skirt appears.

1912 Sinking of SS *Titanic* (15 April).

1914 *On the outbreak of the Great War, Henry Peerless enlists as a special constable of the Brighton Borough Police.*
Cuthbert Peerless enlists in the Inns of Court OTC; Reginald Peerless attests in June, before joining the Royal Navy.

1918 *2nd Lieutenant Cuthbert Peerless, of the Royal Sussex Regiment, dies at 12 St James's Avenue, from injuries sustained after falling from a horse while on active service (12 May).*
Women (aged 30 and above) allowed to vote in a British election for the first time (14 December).

1919 Victory parades in Britain celebrate the ending of the Great War, following the Armistice of November 1918 (19 July).

1920 *Henry and Millie Peerless travel to Bath in search of a cure for Millie's arthritis; the diary of their trip proves to be the last.*
Britain's national railway network reaches its maximum extent, with 20,312 miles of track.

1921 Amalgamation of the British railway companies into four main companies, under the Railway Act.

1922 *Reginald Leslie Peerless marries Dorothy Olga Pavitt at St Augustine's Church, Brighton (29 April).*

1926 Manually controlled traffic lights introduced in Central London.

1929 First public telephone boxes introduced.

1930 *Henry Heathfield Peerless dies at 12 St James's Avenue, aged 63, of 'apoplexy, diabetes and increased blood pressure' (8 September).*

1938 *Amelia Sarah Peerless dies at 7 Wilbury Road, Hove, aged 68, following an operation for the relief of an intestinal obstruction (16 October).*

Index